LEADERSHIP & ETHICS

MILITARY SCIENCE AND LEADERSHIP   MSL 302

Edited by

William L. Bolden

Daniel C. Hamilton

Sheila I. Visconti

McGraw Hill Custom Publishing

Boston   Burr Ridge, IL   Dubuque, IA   Madison, WI   New York   San Francisco   St. Louis
Bangkok   Bogotá   Caracas   Lisbon   London   Madrid
Mexico City   Milan   New Delhi   Seoul   Singapore   Sydney   Taipei   Toronto

The McGraw·Hill Companies

LEADERSHIP & ETHICS
Military Science and Leadership
MSL 302

McGraw-Hill's Primis Custom Publishing consists of products that are produced from camera-ready copy. Peer review, class testing, and accuracy are primarily the responsibility of the author(s).

1 2 3 4 5 6 7 8 9 0 QPD QPD 0 9 8 7 6 5 4 3 2

ISBN 0-07-286789-2

Sponsoring Editor: Judy A. Wetherington
Production Editor: Carrie Braun
Cover Design: Fairfax Hutter
Printer/Binder: Quebecor World

CONTENTS

INTRODUCTION

OVERVIEW OF THE ARMY ROTC ADVANCED COURSE

The Army ROTC Advanced Course is comprised of four courses, Military Science and Leadership (MSL) 301, MSL 302, MSL 401, and MSL 402 and the National Advanced Leadership Camp. Although presented in a four-semester model, the courses and associated lessons also support both quarter and trimester systems due to the modular design of the program.

The ROTC Advanced Course is designed to teach all knowledge, skills, and attitudes essential for commissioning as a new second lieutenant. Its purpose is also to establish a sound foundation for a career as a commissioned Army officer. The content and methods of the Advanced Course assume no prior cadet experience or other military training. This approach is taken because the Advanced Course comprises the minimum curriculum that an individual must complete in order to be commissioned.

Advanced Course lessons are carefully sequenced, linked, and progressive in their treatment of key officer knowledge and competencies. Students are encouraged to integrate learning across modules and lessons to form broader perspectives, deeper insights, and more robust problem-solving abilities. This is accomplished in part through the use of case studies and simulations that require skills and knowledge learned in earlier lessons. The sequencing of lessons is designed to meet the immediate needs of cadets by addressing topics needed for success in the performance of cadet responsibilities, and at the NALC, essential topics are developed to facilitate entry into active military service during the MSL 402 term.

OVERVIEW OF MSL 302 COURSE: LEADERSHIP AND ETHICS

The MSL 302 course is designed to continue the development of cadets as leaders by presenting instruction in the three foundational areas of interpersonal communication, values and ethics, and leadership. The course opens with an introduction and overview of the summer training opportunities at the National Advanced Leadership Camp (NALC) and other available training programs. Next, cadets address the topic of interpersonal communication in a module spanning seven lessons. These lessons focus on general communication theory as well as written and spoken communication skills. The highlight of the communication module is the opportunity for cadets to present an information briefing and receive feedback from both the instructor and from fellow cadets. The next module addresses officership. It has cadets research and present briefings on the Army's branches. This module provides cadets the information needed to make career choices and to practice their communication skills. Next is a ten-lesson module that focuses on values, ethics, ethical decision making, consideration of others, and spiritual needs. The final thirteen-lesson leadership module contains a five-lesson examination of Army leadership doctrine in FM 22-100. This is followed by eight lessons that expand on key leadership concepts and provide feedback for cadet leadership self-development efforts.

COURSE STRUCTURE: A MODULAR APPROACH

This course is structured in modules and lessons. There are five modules containing 36 one-hour (50 minute) lessons as follows:

MODULE	TRACK
Module I	Personal Development (Lesson 1)
Module II	Communications (Lessons 2–8)
Module III	The Army Profession: Officership (Lessons 9–13)
Module IV	Values and Ethics (Lesson 14–23)
Module V	Leadership (Lessons 24–36)

In addition, Leadership Labs that provide practical experience are scheduled during each semester. Leadership Labs meet a minimum of 1 hour per week.

HOW TO USE THIS TEXT

This textbook is divided by sections/modules, and is organized according to the Cadet Command class schedule model. Scope statements for each module are found on the module title pages. Within each module is a series of lessons that support the module. Each lesson begins with a purpose statement and a list of topics covered by the lesson, followed by the learning objectives identified for that lesson. Readings for each lesson follow.

WHAT IS EXPERIENTIAL LEARNING?

Experiential learning simply means learning from an experience. When participants are provided the opportunity to "experience" their learning rather than being told what they are to learn, experiential learning is taking place. Experiential learning is rewarding, yet demanding, for both learners and teachers because the learning takes place during class as much as it does outside the classroom. Learning is both unstructured as well as structured. Experiential learning is founded on the belief that interaction is central to the learning process: cadet to faculty interaction, cadet-to-cadet interaction, either in pairs or groups, and cadet to instructional material. Helpful synonyms include: direct experience, discovery learning, experience-based learning, action learning, active learning, and participatory learning.

THE CADET COMMAND APPROACH TO ACADEMIC INSTRUCTION

The Military Science and Leadership program is designed to focus on the student learner (the cadet), rather than on the instructor or on the subject matter. Focusing on the cadet requires student-centered objectives and conscious attention to how cadets react to the instruction received. For effective instruction, students need feedback that reinforces learning while identifying and correcting errors. Students need the opportunity to try to work with what has been taught. Too often instruction is limited to the delivery of information, either through reading assignments, lectures, or slide presentations.

Typically, we think of successful experiential learning as consisting of five steps:

1. Readiness/openness to the experience
2. The experience itself
3. Reflection upon the experience
4. Analysis, theory or additional information to clarify the relationship between theory and actions, with an understanding of lessons learned regarding any needed changes
5. The opportunity to re-experience (practice in new situations/practical exercises)

STUDENT RESOURCES

a. *Cadet Textbook.* The text contains the readings that support the MSL 302 course: Leadership Ethics.
b. *Cadet CD-ROM.* A CD-ROM is included in each cadet textbook and contains additional reference materials, readings and multimedia that support the MSL program.
c. *Cadet Workbook.* Packaged with cadet text of readings, this workbook contains the worksheets that support the exercises woven throughout the course. In addition, the workbook contains checklists and lesson overview statements for use by the cadet when preparing for class.
d. *Blackboard* (Bb). The Blackboard course site, *http://rotc.blackboard.com,* contains Military Science and Leadership course materials.

MODULE I

Personal Development

The Personal Development module is comprised of one lesson designed to introduce you to the requirements for summer training opportunities following this term. Much of the preparation for the National Advanced Leadership Camp (NALC) and other summer training is based on physical fitness and tactical skills.

Summer Training Events

This is the first lesson of the second academic term in the MSL III year. This lesson introduces cadets to the National Advanced Leadership Camp (NALC) and other training opportunities available following this term.

The following topics are addressed in this lesson:

- National Advanced Leadership Camp (NALC);
- Cadet Troop Leader Training (CTLT); and
- Other training opportunities.

The following Terminal Learning Objective (TLO) is supported in whole or in part by this lesson:

- Plan, Execute and Assess Individual and Collective Training IAW Army Doctrine.

Following this lesson you will be able to:

- Describe the progressive NALC plan;
- Explain the criteria for NALC success;
- Assess personal readiness for NALC and CTLT success; and
- Develop a personal plan for success at NALC and CTLT.

NATIONAL ADVANCED LEADERSHIP CAMP AND OTHER SUMMER TRAINING OPPORTUNITIES

1 NATIONAL ADVANCED LEADERSHIP CAMP

The ROTC National Advanced Leadership Camp (often referred to as simply "NALC") is one of the most important training events for an Army ROTC cadet (and selected Army National Guard Officer Candidate School candidates). The 32-day camp incorporates a wide range of subjects designed to develop and to evaluate leadership ability. The challenges are rigorous and demanding, both mentally and physically. NALC tests intelligence, common sense, ingenuity and stamina. These challenges provide a new perspective on an individual's ability to perform exacting tasks and to make difficult decisions in demanding situations.

The camp places each cadet and officer candidate in a variety of leadership positions and requires the accomplishment of a wide range of military training missions, many of which simulate stressful combat situations. In each position, cadets are evaluated by platoon tactical officers and by noncommissioned officers. In addition to proving their leadership ability, cadets and officer candidates must meet established standards in physical fitness, weapons training, communication, combat patrols, and demonstrate their proficiency in many other military skills. Cadets and officer candidates must excel at camp to be considered competitive for a commission as an Army officer.

Over 4000 Army ROTC cadets and National Guard Officer Candidates from throughout the nation will attend the ROTC National Advanced Leadership Camp each year. The camp normally consists of 12 training cycles (regiments) with the first cycle beginning in June and the last cycle graduating in August.

Since 1993, the Fort Lewis ROTC National Advanced Leadership Camp has conducted Army National Guard Officer Candidate School Phase III training concurrently with ROTC NALC training. Approximately 300 candidates from units throughout the country make up an OCS regiment which undergoes 15 days of training using NALC sites and facilities. The ROTC committee cadre provides leadership position evaluations of the candidates using the same criteria as for ROTC cadet regiments. Each OCS regiment has its own National Guard tactical staff and is under the command and control of the Washington State National Guard Military Academy.

One special aspect of Advanced Camp is the Regimental Affiliation Program. Each cadet regiment is affiliated with an established and honored Army Regiment. The cadet battalions adopt the honors, lineage and heraldry of their respective active regiments. The purpose of the program is to infuse each cadet with regimental esprit de corps and pride.

1.1 PROGRAM OF INSTRUCTION

The structure of the training program is sequential and progressive, starting with individual training tasks and building to complex, collective training. The training program includes:

Individual Training

- Physical Training (APFT)
- Confidence Training (Conf Tng)
- Field Leader's Reaction Course (FLRC)
- Water Safety (WS)
- Basic Rifle Marksmanship (BRM)
- Land Navigation (Land Nav)
- Automatic Weapons (AW)
- Fire Support (Fire Spt)
- Hand Grenade (HG)
- Nuclear, Biological, and Chemical Skills (NBC)
- Individual Tactical Training (ITT)
- Branch Orientation

Collective Training

- Squad Situational Training Exercise (Squad STX)
- Patrolling Situational Training Exercise (Ptrl STX)

1.1.1 Field Leader's Reaction Course (FLRC)

The FLRC is designed to develop and evaluate leadership and to build teamwork early in the camp cycle. The FLRC poses a variety of novel problems to small groups of cadets. Leadership of each cadet group changes with each new problem. The appointed cadet leader is assessed on problem solving and leadership skills including: assessment of the problem, development of a plan, communication of the plan, and supervision of plan execution. Cadet leadership potential is assessed by committee evaluators. Cadets are provided the opportunity to get early feedback on their leadership strengths, weaknesses, styles and techniques.

1.1.2 Confidence Training

Confidence training builds individual, team and unit esprit through a series of individual and team competitions. It gives cadets the opportunity to evaluate their courage and resolve, and gives cadre the opportunity to evaluate the cadets' mental attitude under different levels of stress.

1.1.3 Basic Rifle Marksmanship

Future Army Leaders must know the characteristics of the basic Army rifle, how to fire it accurately, and how to employ it in combat. Rifle marksmanship training teaches cadets to engage and hit targets on the battlefield. Cadets are required to fire for record. Qualification is required for successful camp completion.

1.1.4 Automatic Weapons

Squad Automatic Weapon or M60 machine gun training teaches cadets the characteristics, functions and employment of the weapons. This training provides skills used in later tactical phases of camp.

1.1.5 Land Navigation

Land navigation training must be mastered early in the camp cycle for the cadets to be fully successful in the tactical training that follows. The land navigation evaluation consists of three portions totaling 100 points. The written examination is worth 30 percent. The day land navigation test is worth 50 percent. Night land navigation is worth 20 percent. Each cadet must earn 70 percent on each test to pass this event. A passing score in land navigation is required for successful camp completion.

1.1.6 Individual Tactical Training

ITT is the first block of instruction in tactics at NALC. It covers individual battlefield skills, combat movement techniques, and procedures necessary for subsequent tactical training at the squad and platoon level.

1.1.7 Fire Support

Fire Support teaches cadets the importance and lethality of artillery fire on the battlefield, employment of indirect fires, and gives them the opportunity to perform the duties of howitzer crewmen.

1.1.8 Hand Grenade

Basic understanding and use of hand grenades is an important facet of weapons and tactical training. Cadets learn to identify major types of grenades. They learn the grenades' characteristics and uses. Cadets also employ live grenades.

1.1.9 Nuclear, Biological, Chemical

NBC training provides basic soldier skills that cadets must master to meet pre-commissioning requirements. Cadets learn characteristics, maintenance and employment of NBC equipment. They also develop confidence in defensive equipment during mask confidence exercises.

1.1.10 Squad Situational Training Exercises

The Squad STX is a five-day, two-phase event. The first two days, the Squad training phase, are designed to train squad battle drills and collective tasks. The last three days, the Squad STX lane phase, are designed to evaluate leadership using tactical scenarios. Each cadet receives two formal evaluations of their performance as a squad leader during this phase. Squad operations build on and reinforce all previous instruction. Cadets use knowledge of land navigation, terrain association, weapons systems, and all individual training previously presented.

1.1.11 Patrolling Situational Training Exercises

The Patrolling STX is a three-day event that provides cadets practical experience leading soldiers at the section level. The first day is a training day on which cadets are taught the fundamentals of patrolling missions. The following two days are designed to evaluate leadership potential using tactical scenarios by giving cadets opportunities to use the training as patrol leaders and assistant patrol leaders. Patrolling STX builds on and reinforces all previous instruction, and teaches cadets the basics of air assault operations. This event culminates cadets' training at NALC.

1.2 NALC Evaluation

The Leadership Development Program (LDP) is a critical part of NALC, providing evaluations of leadership potential through a series of formal and informal assessments conducted throughout camp. Teams of evaluators assess cadet performance in leader and follower positions. As cadets perform as leaders or team members, evaluators assess performance and identify strong and weak areas of leadership behavior. At the same time, each cadet has the opportunity to evaluate his/her own performance. Each cadet also receives one-on-one counseling at the end of camp as the TACs review the Cadet Command Form 67-9 summary of each individual's camp performance, a key document in the accessions process.

Cadets are evaluated in the following areas:

1. Army Physical Fitness Test. The three events are pushups, sit-ups, and the 2-mile run, as specified in FM 21-20.
2. Land Navigation. The Land Navigation score consists of three components: a written examination worth 20 percent, a daylight practical exercise worth 50 percent, and a night practical exercise worth 30 percent. The cadets will take both practice and record tests of each practical exercise. The minimum requirement for passing is a score of 70 percent on the written test (14 of 20 points), the daylight practical test (5 of 8 stakes, 35 of 50 points), and the night practical test (3 of 5 stakes, 21 of 30 points). One retest is available for each exam.
3. Leadership Performance. Cadets are rated in individual leadership performance.

LEADERSHIP ASSESSMENT

- Field Leadership Reaction Course
- TAC Leader Assessments (3)
- Squad STX Leader Assessments (2)
- Patrol STX Platoon Leader or Assistant Platoon Leader Assessments (selective)
- Leader Dimension Summary
- Performance and Potential

1.3 Camp Completion Criteria

To successfully complete camp, cadets must:

1. Meet Height/Weight and Body Fat standards outlined in AR 600-9.
2. Pass the APFT with a minimum total score of 180 points and 60 points in each event. If the initial test is failed, a retest will be administered three days later. A passing score on the retest is awarded the minimum score of 180 regardless of the retest APFT score.
3. Pass Land Navigation by attaining a cumulative score of 70 percent, with a minimum of 70 percent on all tests (written and practical).

4. Receive a "GO" (23 of 40 target hits) for Basic Rifle Marksmanship.
5. Earn a minimum rating of "Satisfactory" on each of the 16 leadership dimensions (part V) and the area of Values at the end of camp on the final evaluation report (Cadet Command Form 67-9) and a minimum rating of satisfactory for performance and potential (part VI a).
6. Complete at least 90% percent of training.

Cadets who fail to meet the standards above will be referred to a Performance Board to determine whether they merit camp graduation credits.

Note: Information on NALC is from the 4th Region ROTC Web Site (*http://www.lewis.army.mil/4rotc/*) and Cadet Command Circular 145-02-2 for the 2002 NALC. Check the 4th Region web site and/or the Cadet Command Directorate of Training web site (*http://www.rotc.monroe.army.mil/training/index.html*) for the most current information and Cadet Command Circular 145-02-2.

2 CADET PROFESSIONAL DEVELOPMENT TRAINING (CPDT)

Cadet Professional Development Training (CPDT) consists of cadet training in Army schools and with Active Army and Reserve units. The CPDT Program supplements campus training with practical leader development experiences and selected skill identifier awarding courses. The program consists of two subprograms, Cadet Practical Field Training (CPFT) and Cadet Troop Leader Training (CTLT). More information on the CPDT program can be found in *Cadet Command Reg 145-3*, Chapter 3, and Cadet Command Pamphlet 145-9, *ROTC Cadet Troop Leader Training*. Check the Cadet Command Directorate of Training, Training Ops Division web site (*http://www.rotc.monroe.army.mil/training/Training.html*) for the most current information and Cadet Command Regulation 145-3 and Cadet Command Pamphlet 145-9.

2.1 CADET PRACTICAL FIELD TRAINING (CPFT)

The program includes training at Army Schools and special courses for Air Assault, Basic Airborne, Mountain Warfare, Northern Warfare, Cadet Survival Training at the United States Air Force

Academy, and University Officer Training Center in the United Kingdom. Generally, in a typical year, the total number of CPFT allocations equals approximately ten percent of the cadet population at large. Battalion commanders prepare, select and send to CPDT only those with the highest potential for completing the CPDT training and for being commissioned. All cadets must meet the eligibility criteria to be selected.

Battalion commanders establish and announce to cadets a set of selection criteria for CPFT opportunities. The selection criteria must include physical fitness and drill and ceremony proficiency appropriate for the particular CPFT course. A common cause of cadet attrition at Airborne School is failing a progression run at the end of either Ground Week or Tower Week. A common cause of cadet attrition at Air Assault schools is failing the "Tough One" (rope climb) at the end of the initial day obstacle course. Commanders must ensure cadets are properly prepared in order to achieve a 95 percent graduation rate.

Units select and prepare the best-qualified cadets for CPFT training (i.e., those most likely to fulfill their voluntary promise to attend and succeed). Cadets must meet the following prerequisites in order to attend CPDT.

1. Be a cadet (non-contracted or contracted) as defined in paragraph 2-15. Completion Cadets and newly commissioned 2LTs are not eligible. Foreign cadets participating in ROTC with a waiver are also not eligible.
2. Completed at least one of the following training experiences:
   - MSL I and MSL II on campus.
   - Basic Combat Training during prior active or reserve service.
   - Leader's Training Course.
   - National Advanced Leadership Camp.
3. If enrolled in the English-as-a-Second Language program, meet the standards for oral and written proficiency required for cadets to attend the National Advanced Leadership Camp.
4. Pass the APFT no more than 30 days before Air Assault training or no more than 60 days prior to other CPDT training. Generally, commanders take into consideration the fact that cadets with low APFT scores (e.g., less than 225) are not likely to do well at CPDT training and are more likely to be injured or drop out.
5. For Airborne training, demonstrate the ability to run 4.0 miles in a formation in the Basic Airborne Course standard uniform at a consistent 9-minute pace throughout. Note that the heat and humidity conditions at the Fort Benning Airborne School may be far more severe than those in which cadets normally train. A cadet who can run 4 miles at a 9-minute pace in cool or moderate spring time conditions, may not be able to perform at this level in the summer time heat and humidity of Fort Benning.

2.2 CADET TROOP LEADER TRAINING (CTLT)

CTLT provides select NALC graduates the opportunity to increase their leadership experience by assignments to platoon leader or like positions with active Army units or with government agencies. Usually, the CTLT program begins immediately after cadets successfully complete NALC. CTLT is conducted in cycles immediately following graduation of NALC. CTLT cycles normally begin on or about 10 July and terminate on or about 28 August. The CONUS (continental United States) CTLT tours with Active Component units are three weeks in duration. OCONUS (i.e., overseas) CTLT tours are four weeks in duration. Cadets in CTLT maintain the same status held while attending NALC in regard to travel, pay, medical benefits, and allowances.

Program objectives are to:

1. Increase each cadet's leadership experience by assigning cadet to a platoon leader or like position with specific responsibilities and opportunities to lead soldiers.
2. Familiarize cadets with the command, training, administration, and logistical functions of assigned units.
3. Expose cadets to the on-duty and off-duty environment of the junior officer.
4. Familiarize cadets with the Junior Officer Development System.

2.3 TRAINING OPPORTUNITIES

- Cadet Troop Leader Training (CTLT). Training is worldwide, with active component units serving as platoon leaders.

- Advanced Individual Academic Development (AIAD). Cadets train for 3 weeks as interns with the Army Corps of Engineers or other government agencies.
- Cadet Intern Program (CIP). This is an initiative of Assistant Secretary of the Army (Manpower and Reserve Affairs). It allows cadets to work with the Department of the Army (DA), the Secretariat, Office of the Chief of Army Reserves (OCAR), National Guard Bureau (NGB), Office of the Secretary of Defense (OSD), and other agencies for 3 weeks. Cadets receive an officer evaluation report at completion.
- Nurse Summer Training Program (NSTP). The NSTP is an optional 3-4 week elective for cadets pursuing nursing degrees. It provides at least 120 hours of clinical experience, which supplements on-campus instruction with clinical and leadership experience in a hospital environment.

MODULE II

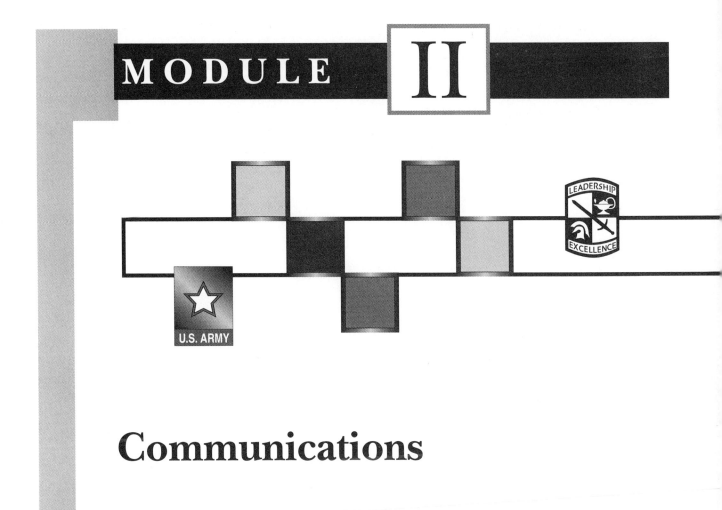

Communications

Although sometimes overlooked, communication skills are critical to leadership effectiveness. This seven-lesson Communications module introduces you to fundamental principles of effective written and oral communication. Another goal of this module is to sensitize you to the importance of nonverbal communication both for understanding others' communications and for accurately conveying your own intended message. The module culminates with selected cadet information briefings that are critiqued by both instructor and fellow cadets.

Models of Communication

This is the first of a series of lessons on communication. This lesson follows an introductory lesson on Summer Training Events, and precedes lessons on communication technology and practice sessions on how to deliver military briefings. The focus in this lesson is on a basic communication model, and techniques to create change through influence and proper communication.

The following topics are addressed in this lesson:

- Communication Theory and Models of Communication;
- Components of the communication model;
- Factors that influence the perception of a message;
- Communication flow within organizations;
- Communication techniques;
- Feedback; and
- Influencing with communication.

The following Terminal Learning Objective (TLO) is supported in whole or in part by this lesson:

- Apply communication theory.

Following this lesson you will be able to:

- Describe communication theory;
- Define effective communication techniques, including influencing behaviors;
- Recognize and practice effective communication techniques; and
- Analyze communications and recommend improvements.

Nonverbal Communications

This is the second in a series of lessons on communication. The previous lesson on communications focused on the communications model and the importance of feedback. This lesson stresses nonverbal communications and how it influences the communication message and its delivery.

The following topics are addressed in this lesson:

- Nonverbal communication;
- Significance of nonverbal cues;
- Use of nonverbal signals in effective communication; and
- Mannerisms to avoid when communicating.

The following Terminal Learning Objective (TLO) is supported in whole or in part by this lesson:

- Apply communication skills.

Following this lesson you will be able to:

- Recognize nonverbal signals;
- Describe nonverbal communications;
- Analyze and apply nonverbal communication signals; and
- Practice improvement of communications through the use of nonverbal signals.

THE NONVERBAL MESSAGE

by S. Tubbs and S. Moss

Nonverbal communication is going on all the time. In discussing the interpretation of nonverbal messages, we saw that a significant percentage of all social meaning is conveyed through nonverbal stimuli. We also saw that nonverbal channels convey primarily relational messages, messages about the emotional level of our communication, and that a nonverbal message can replace, reinforce, or contradict a verbal message. The source of most communication difficulties, double or contradictory messages, was considered in terms of double-bind situations and the kinesic slips common to daily experience. We suggested, however, that verbal and nonverbal responses qualify each other in so many ways that they are not totally separable.

THE VERBAL/NONVERBAL SPLIT IN MEANING

Nonverbal communication—indeed the entire communication process—must be viewed as a whole that is greater than the sum of its parts. Outside the laboratory we do not depend on isolated cues, or *hints.* In face-to-face communication, all cues, both verbal and nonverbal, are available to us. Although Mehrabian (1972) believed that as much as 93 percent of all social meaning in face-to-face communication is conveyed through nonverbal cues, recent surveys suggest that Birdwhistell's estimate (1970) of 65 percent is the more accurate. There are many times when we give greater credence to nonverbal cues. These include when we judge interpersonal style; when we respond to questions requiring interpretation; when we evaluate a person's genuine emotions, ideas, and attitudes from "inconsistent expressions"; and when we judge credibility and leadership qualities (Burgoon et al., 1996, p. 137).

As we've seen in Chapter 2, nonverbal cues also have greater influence when it comes to forming first impressions. In addition, we give greater weight to nonverbal over verbal cues when they are contradictory. Keep in mind, however, that for children, verbal cues have greater importance. Often children make their judgments in terms of what is said to them—literally—although to adults this often seems naive (Burgoon et al., 1996, pp. 136–142). The ability to interpret nonverbal cues seems to develop over a considerable period of time.

In a recent review of nonverbal research, Knapp and Hall (1996) conclude:

It appears some people rely more heavily on the verbal message, while others rely on the nonverbal.

We do not know all the conditions that affect channel preferences, but weighting of verbal, vocal, and visual cues probably changes in changing situations.

It has even been proposed that people have one of three preferences in how they make use of information from their senses:

Visual preference: People "see the world by constructing or remembering mental images."

Auditory preference: People "prize sound and can make decisions based on what they have heard or read."

Kinesthetic preference: People "handle the world through touch, taste, smell, or feelings. [For them] contact is communication." (Adapted from Madonik, 1990, p. 19)

It might be interesting to speculate about what your own preference is—and why.

NONVERBAL INFORMATION

We learn most about the meaning of nonverbal messages by studying them in relationship to verbal messages. Essentially, a nonverbal message functions in one of three ways: It replaces, reinforces, or contradicts a verbal message.

A nonverbal message that substitutes for a verbal one is often easy to interpret. Our culture provides us with gestures and expressions that are the equivalents of certain brief verbal messages: "Yes," "No," "Hello," "Goodbye," "I don't know," and so on. Likes and dislikes can also be expressed without words—smiling, clapping, smirking, frowning, and so on.

When a nonverbal message reinforces a verbal message, meaning is conveyed quickly and easily, and with increased comprehension. Sometimes a single cue such as a hand movement or a long pause gives special emphasis to one part of a message so that we are able to discern what the speaker feels is most important.

Nonverbal cues predominate by sheer number. In general, if as receivers we are caught between two discrepant messages, we are more inclined to believe the nonverbal message. One reason for this is that it is thought that nonverbal cues give information about our intentions and emotional responses. Thus, many businesspeople prefer face-to-face communication—whether it be meeting for lunch or in the formal setting of an office—to fax, mail, or telephone when solving problems or negotiating critical decisions. In negotiation, much is learned from "feeling your way," watching the other person's facial expression and gestures so that you can adapt your own responses. (In the future, tele-conferencing, which provides a wealth of nonverbal cues, will probably be used routinely.)

Another reason the nonverbal message seems to have greater impact is the popular belief that body movements, facial expressions, vocal qualities, and so on cannot be simulated with authenticity by the average person. Even children are quick to sense gestures or expressions that are not spontaneous.

Nonverbal channels convey primarily relational messages, messages about the feeling/emotional level of our communication, rather than the thoughts (best communicated by verbal communication); also, nonverbal messages are ambiguous for the most part, except perhaps for certain gestures (Ekman et al., 1984). A New Yorker who shot four teenagers on the subway claimed that he did so because their behavior was threatening; he acted, he said, in self-defense. Yet there was no consensus among the other passengers as to whether the injured youths were menacing. Incidents such as this have increased dramatically—particularly with the escalation of racial tensions in many of our cities.

We all have some sensitivity to nonverbal cues, or we would not be able to communicate with the ease we do. Still, there seem to be differences among people in how skilled they are in interpreting what they experience. Through tests such as the popular Profile of Nonverbal Sensitivity Test—the PONS—researchers have confirmed that some people do have greater sensitivities to nonverbal cues, but that this does not necessarily correlate with intelligence. Then too, we are not speaking about a single skill: just because you are especially perceptive in judging body movements and facial expressions doesn't mean that you are an astute judge of vocal cues. A recent sum-mary of the research (DePaulo and Friedman, 1998) notes that our nonverbal sensitivity does increase with age, that women tend to judge (nondeceptive) facial expressions more accurately than men, and that though there are those who have "special sensitivities" to certain people, "especially those with whom they have a special relationship. . . . they may have special insensitivities to such people as well" (p. 9).

THE DOUBLE BIND

Most of our problems in interpreting meaning arise when we receive a nonverbal message that contradicts a verbal message. Let us explore this subject briefly.

You are familiar with the word "bind" as used to describe a situation one cannot get out of. In 1956, the anthropologist Gregory Bateson and a group of his associates presented a theory of the **double bind** that revolutionized the study of schizophrenia. They proposed that schizophrenic communication—particularly within families—was characterized by the constant exchange of contradictory messages between two or more people, one of whom was designated the "victim."

The recurrent theme in the double bind is a sequence of three commands. The first says, "Do not do so and so, or I will punish you," or "If you do not do so and so, I will punish you." The second command contradicts the first and is often communicated nonverbally: "Posture, gesture, tone of voice, meaningful action, and the implications concealed in verbal comment may all be used to convey this more abstract message" (Bateson et al., 1956, p. 254). (Note the multiple channels through which these commands may be communicated.) The third negative command makes the victim's position completely untenable by forbidding him or her to leave this paradoxical situation. Laing (1969) has given us this summary of a chilling example taken from Bateson's work:

> A mother visits her son, who has just been recovering from a mental breakdown. As he goes towards her
>
> a. she opens her arms for him to embrace her, and/or
>
> b. to embrace him.
>
> c. as he gets nearer she freezes and stiffens,
>
> d. he stops irresolutely.

e. she says, "Don't you want to kiss your mummy?"—and as he still stands irresolutely

f. she says, "But, dear, you mustn't be afraid of your feelings." (p. 127)

Bateson's double-bind thesis explains a great deal about contradictory messages and the breakdown of interpersonal relationships that may result from them. Although the theory applies specifically to schizophrenic communication, it is relevant to more general studies such as ours because normal and so-called abnormal, or deviant, behavior exist along a continuum. Suppose, for example, that a supervisor always cautions her employees not to postpone discussing problem areas in their work. "Don't wait till it's too late to remedy the situation. I want you to come and tell me when you run into problems," she repeats. Yet as one of the assistant managers enters her office, she looks up annoyed and gives him an icy stare. Then, as the employee starts to back out of her office, the supervisor says, "Well, don't stand there looking so frightened. Tell me what's on your mind."

Within the normal range of experience, Birdwhistell (1970) uses the term **kinesic slips** for *contradictory verbal and nonverbal messages.* Imagine this conversation between a married couple who have just had a bitter quarrel. The wife asks the husband, "Honey, are you still angry?" "No," he replies, "it's all right." "But you *sound* as though you're still angry," she says. "I'm telling you *I'm not angry!*" he answers. The husband's words give one message, his voice another. He may not even be aware of the second. Which message is his wife likely to believe?

VERBAL/NONVERBAL INTERACTION

For purposes of analysis we speak of verbal and nonverbal messages as distinct, yet in daily life we are rarely able to separate their effects. For example, what we say is qualified, modified, by *how* we say it—tone of voice, facial expression, eye contact, and so on—as well as by the almost instantaneous verbal and nonverbal responses of others. And this interaction is ongoing. We depend on it and are continually modifying our responses.

In the remainder of this chapter, we shall see how through their nonverbal messages people give us many cues, or intimations, about their emotions, their intentions, their personalities, and even their social status. Thus, we shall look at several kinds of cues—spatial, temporal, visual, and vocal. In terms of our model, then, we are speaking about all nonverbal messages—both intentional and unintentional.

SPATIAL AND TEMPORAL CUES

by S. Tubbs and S. Moss

Only when we interact with people of other cultures or subcultures do we begin to realize that some of our most cherished ideas about what is appropriate conduct are **norms,** or *rules, whether stated or unstated, about behavior;* that is, they are relative, not absolute, values. Indirectly, our culture teaches us to communicate in many ways—through our voices, our gestures, and even our style of dressing. Yet each of us interprets and expresses these conventions somewhat differently.

Culture has an even more subtle and pervasive influence on nonverbal communication, however. Each culture continually provides its members with input about how the world is structured. (We saw this with respect to visual perception when we discussed the Müller-Lyer illusion in Chapter 2.) Slowly we develop preconceptions about the world. It is the cues derived from these preconceptions that we take most for granted and that imperceptibly set the limits for our style of communication. Our cues about space and time are among those most significantly influenced by culture and sometimes the source of many difficulties in intercultural communication.

SPACE

If you were to enter a restaurant with only one customer in it, chances are that you would not sit down right next to him or her. Edward Hall explains that though this behavior seems natural to an American, an Arab might have a very different notion of appropriate distance between strangers. Students of nonverbal communication are indebted to Hall for his cross-cultural studies of space.

Hall has given the special name of **proxemics** to the *study of space.* Social scientists make use of the Scale of Social Distance, an instrument that uses the term "distance" figuratively, to indicate degree of liking or preference. Hall (1959) goes a step further and speaks of measurable distances between people— 1 1/2 inches, 1 foot, 3 feet, and so on. In fact, he offers a four-part classification of distances between people. There is nothing arbitrary about this classification, as he explains:

> It is in the nature of animals, including man, to exhibit behavior which we call territoriality. In so doing, they use the senses to distinguish between one space or distance and another. The specific distance chosen depends on the transaction, the

relationship of the interacting individuals, how they feel, and what they are doing. (p. 128)

Hall describes human relationships in terms of four kinds of distance: intimate, personal, social, and public. Each distance zone is further differentiated by a close phase and a far phase within which different behaviors occur. Let us take a look at these four distances and Hall's findings about what they mean to most North Americans.

INTIMATE DISTANCE

At **intimate distance,** *eighteen inches or less,* the presence of another person "is unmistakable and may at times be overwhelming because of the greatly stepped-up sensory inputs" (Hall, 1959, p. 116). In its close phase (6 inches or less) intimate distance lends itself primarily to nonverbal communication. Any subject discussed is usually top secret. The far phase (6 to 18 inches) is often used for discussing confidential matters, with the voice usually kept to a whisper. Such close proximity is considered improper for public places, though dormitories seem to be exceptions to the rule. In general, Americans try hard to avoid close contact with one another on buses and other public vehicles.

PERSONAL DISTANCE

Hall (1959) compares **personal distance,** from *1 1/2 to 4 feet,* to "a small protective sphere or bubble that an organism maintains between itself and others" (p. 119). Topics discussed would still be personal. The close phase (1 1/2 to 2 1/2 feet) is still a distance reserved for very close relationships; the far phase (2 1/2 to 4 feet) is a comfortable distance for conversing with friends (see Table 6.1).

SOCIAL DISTANCE

Social distance, ranging from *4 to 12 feet,* is described as a psychological distance, "one at which the animal apparently begins to feel anxious when he exceeds its limits. We can think of it as a hidden band that contains the group." The close phase (4 to 7 feet) is suitable for business discussions and conversations at social gatherings.

For example, one study of plant managers suggests that supervisors can prove their control by periodically stepping forward when talking to subordinates. One supervisor succeeded in moving the listener across the room because when the supervisor edged closer, the subordinate took a step back to maintain a comfortable distance from him. The far phase (7 to 12 feet) is appropriate for meetings in a business office. People who are in the room but outside the 7-foot boundary can be ignored without being offended.

Those who violate the 7-foot boundary tend to be surprised if we do not acknowledge their presence, unless we are very busy. Humans have extended social distance by means of the telephone, radio, television, fax, computer (e-mail), as well as teleconferencing and other technologies.

PUBLIC DISTANCE

The largest of zones, **public distance**, denotes *12 feet or more of space,* and it exists only in human relationships. In fact, the public relationships and manners of Americans and Europeans are considerably different from those of other cultures. At the close phase (12 to 25 feet), a more formal style of language and a louder voice are required. At the far phase (25 feet or more), further accommodations to distance are usually made: Experienced public speakers exaggerate body movements, gestures, enunciation, and volume while reducing their rate of speech. Table 6.1 is a brief summary of how message content and vocal shift vary with distance between communicators.

Within a country as diverse as the United States, various subcultures develop their own proxemic norms. (A **subculture** is *a group having sufficient distinctive traits to distinguish it from other members of the same culture or society.*) One study (Albas, 1991) found that even for members of the same ethnic group, the comfortable distance they choose for interacting—in this case, during an interview—is negotiable. At the beginning of the interview, the distance was 12.3 inches, but by the end of the interview, it was 23.4 inches.

In research on intercultural communication, the distinction is often made between low-contact and high-contact cultures. One well-known study looked at the use of interpersonal distance by Venezuelans (high contact), North Americans (moderate contact), and Japanese (low contact). Researchers found that in speaking their own language, Venezuelans sit closest to each other, North Americans maintain an intermediate distance, and Japanese sit farthest from each other. When they use English rather than their native

language, people maintain interpersonal distances closer to North American norms, so it seems that when we speak a foreign language, we tend to approximate the distance norms of that culture (cited in Gudykunst and Kim, 1992, p. 178). And though there is a tendency to generalize about distance norms within Europe, it seems that people from northern European cultures—people from Sweden and Scotland, for example—require greater interpersonal distance than people from Mediterranean countries such as Italy and Greece.

Researchers are not saying that we calculate these differences while communicating. On the contrary, our sense of what distance is natural for a given interaction is so deeply ingrained in us by our culture that we automatically make spatial adjustments and interpret spatial cues. Latin Americans, Arabs, and the French, for example, stand so close to each other that if they exercise their own distance norms while conversing with an American, they arouse hostile or sexual feelings. If you want to test this concept in proxemics, the next time you converse with someone, keep inching toward him or her. See how close you can get before the other party starts backing away.

TERRITORY

Another influential approach to the relationship between space and human behavior is Altman's study (1975) of territory. He proposes that we can think about territory as being *made up of three categories: primary, public, and secondary.*

A **primary territory** is a space occupied by a person or group of people for a relatively long period of time and is important in their lives. It might be an apartment or a house or even an office within a larger office complex. It is usually in primary territory that we have the most privacy and that we set limits about the access and behavior of other people within it. These are our spaces and people who intrude upon them are aware—or may be made aware—that they are violating certain rules.

On the other hand, a **public territory** might be a beach, a park bench, a sidewalk. It is unprotected in the sense that many people have free access to it and usually the amount of time people spend in it is more limited.

A **secondary territory** falls somewhere between primary and public territories. It may be a private club, for example. It's been said that a sec-

Table 6.1   Social Distance Zones

DISTANCE	DESCRIPTION OF DISTANCE	VOCAL CHARACTERISTICS	MESSAGE CONTENT
0–6 inches	Intimate (close phase)	Soft whisper	Top secret
6–18 inches	Intimate (far phase)	Audible whisper	Very confidential
1 1/2–2 1/2 feet	Personal (close phase)	Soft voice	Personal subject matter
2 1/2–4 feet	Personal (far phase)	Slightly lowered voice	Personal subject matter
4–7 feet	Social (close phase)	Full voice	Nonpersonal information
7–12 feet	Social (far phase)	Full voice with slight over-loudness	Public information for others to hear
12–25 feet	Public (close phase)	Loud voice talking to a group	Public information for others to hear
25 feet or more	Public (far phase)	Loudest voice	Hailing, departures

Source: Table from *The Silent Language* by Edward T. Hall. Copyright ©1959, 1981 by Edward T. Hall. Reprinted by permission of Doubleday, a division of Random House, Inc.

ondary territory is semipublic; the rules for this space depend on the community that governs it, and not everyone has access to it (Bonnes and Secchiaroli, 1995, pp. 90–91).

There seem to be gender differences concerning territory, with males tending to "define their own territoriality through much larger spaces than females" (p. 90). In turn, there are studies of primary territory indicating that in houses people think of themselves as owning a particular room—it might be the study or the kitchen, for example.

Cross-cultural studies show that there are some marked differences between how national groups respond to others in public territories. For example, in a comparison of groups of German and French people at beaches:

> Germans show a much more striking sense of their own territory than the French. Much more frequently than the French, the Germans tend to define their own territorial space using signs (such as sand-castles) which have the precise function of indicating certain areas of the beach as "reserved." (p. 90)

PERSONAL SPACE

Yet another approach to space which centers on the body was developed by Sommer (1969). His concern is with **personal space**, *"an area with invisible boundaries surrounding a person's body into which intruders may not come"* (p. 26; italic added). The concept of personal space can be thought of as a person's portable territory, which each individual carries along wherever he or she may go. Sommer is careful to distinguish his use of personal space from Hall's use of the term "territory":

> The most important difference is that personal space is carried around while territory is relatively stationary. The animal or man will usually mark the boundaries of his territory so that they are visible to others, but the boundaries of his personal space are invisible. Personal space has the body at its center, while territory does not. (p. 248)

At least one investigator has suggested that personality variables such as need for affiliation influence the size of one's personal space (Rosenfeld, 1965). In his study of prison inmates

Issues in Communication

THE SPONTANEITY OF NONVERBAL CUES

Are many of the nonverbal cues you see in others spontaneous or are they controlled? And what about your own—for example, are your facial expressions and ways of moving your body different when you are alone? A further question that has been raised is: Do people *consciously* present themselves to others through their nonverbal cues—trying, in effect, to regulate and sometimes change the impressions they are making?

The issues are complex. Some scholars of communication, often citing research on the universality of human facial expressions, argue that the ability to regulate behaviors is infrequent and unusual:

If people are seen as deliberately regulating their behavior for self-presentational purposes only when they are totally focused on doing so, then the phenomenon is indeed the special domain of actors, con men, and ordinary people on job interviews and first dates. (Cited in DePaulo and Friedman, 1998, p. 15)

Scholars have also argues that:

Perhaps one of the most interesting aspects of nonverbal behavior is that it is only rarely totally unregulated. In social interactions, people more often exert some control over their nonverbal expressive behavior. This attempted control is not always conscious, and it is not always successful, but it is pervasive. . . .Self-presentation is inextricably linked to nonverbal expression [and] deliberate regulation of expressive behaviors for self-presentational purposes is essential to the smooth workings of social life. (DePaulo and Friedman, 1998, pp. 15, 17)

What do you think? Would controlling our nonverbal cues be insincere or necessary in most social interactions?

who had committed violent crimes, Kinzel (1969) observed that these men had a personal space, or "body buffer zone," twice as large as that of nonviolent prisoners. Members of the violent group felt threatened when a person came close to them, as if the person were an intruder who was "looming up" or "rushing in" at them.

Other research on personal space focuses on the relationship between spatial arrangements (architectural elements, interior design, seating, and so on) and human feelings and interaction. For instance, it is estimated that college students begin to identify a particular seat in the classroom as "their chair" by as early as the second class period. Although you probably would not ask another student to give up what you considered to be your chair if you arrived a little late, you might feel annoyed to see someone else sitting in it. This feeling is somewhat reminiscent of the belief that there is a home court advantage for basketball teams.

In the study halls of college libraries, students tend to protect privacy by sitting as far away from each other as possible. One way of communicating this need is by occupying a corner position. Or students sprawl out, resting their legs on a nearby chair. If they get up from the table, they may "reserve" the place by spreading out books and papers or leaving clothing draped over the chair

(Sommer, 1969, pp. 46–47). How far you go in defending your personal space will depend, of course, on both your personality and your communication style. If you sit too close to me in the library, I may get up and move. But reverse our roles and you glare at me and even spread out your notebooks and papers so that they take up a good part of the table.

Burgoon et al. (1996) explain that we are more confident when we are within own surroundings:

To allow yourself to be summoned voluntarily to someone else's home turf is a show of weakness. Inexperienced diplomats and politicians learn this only after having made too many concessions to adversaries or having lost the respect of allies. The recognized territorial advantage is the reason for insisting on a neutral locale for summit meetings and other serious talks. (p. 307)

ORIENTATION

Orientation—that is, *the angle of your body as you interact with another person,* may also reflect the nature of the relationship between the two of you. For example, some studies of British and North American seating patterns have shown that a 90-

degree-angle orientation facilitates conversation, face-to-face orientations tend toward competitive behaviors, and side-by-side orientations are more often regarded as showing cooperation (Hargie et al., 1987, p. 27).

TIME

When we study *how human beings communicate through their use of time,* we are concerned with **chronemics**. Have you ever received a phone call at three in the morning? You probably thought that it was a very important call, a wrong number, or a prank. How far in advance can a first date be arranged? Must it be several days ahead, or can one call 30 minutes before? In each case, timing leads to certain expectations that influence the face-to-face communication that subsequently occurs. Being very late for a job interview can have a disastrous effect, not just a dramatic one. Much of the verbal communication that ensues may be spent explaining away the nonverbal message that has already been conveyed.

Conceptions of what is "late" or "early" vary from culture to culture. Americans are "busy" people. We use our watches throughout the day. We like schedules and agendas. We value doing things "on time." It is sometimes jarring to see ourselves as others see us. Here, for example, is a Brazilian reaction to "Anglo-American" time:

> The rigid Anglo-Saxon attitude—"Time is money"—with an almost mystical cult of minutes and seconds on account of their practical, commercial value, is in sharp contrast to the Latin American attitude, a sort of "more-or-less" ("*mas o menos*") attitude. It is easy to understand why a Nordic was so shocked in Spain to know that a Spanish or Latin American guest in a hotel asked the desk to call him next morning not exactly at ten or ten-fifteen, as an Anglo-Saxon or an Anglo-American would have asked, but at ten or eleven. (Freyre, 1980)

Hall (1984) distinguishes between monochronic and polychronic conceptions of time. **Monochronic time** *is thought of as lineal and segmented.* In cultures with monochronic time, people like to do one thing at a time, and their preference is for precise scheduling.

Making appointments and deadlines is highly valued. In cultures with a **polychronic** conception of **time**, on the other hand, *many things are going on at once.* Nor is there great surprise when delays or interruptions occur. Indeed, they seem to be expected.

In illustrating these differences, Condon (1991) compares North Americans with Mexicans. North Americans, whose culture is monochronic, are seen—even by members of other monochronic cultures—as far too governed by schedules. Mexican culture, on the other hand, is polychronic: Mexicans often conduct many activities at the same time and tend to take interruptions in stride. When members of monochronic and polychronic cultures meet, the result can be misunderstanding:

> North Americans express special irritation when Mexicans seem to give them less than their undivided attention. When a young woman bank teller, awaiting her superior's approval for a check to be cashed, files her nails and talks on the phone with her boyfriend, or when one's taxi driver stops en route to pick up a friend who seems to be going in the same direction, North Americans interpret such behavior as showing a lack of respect and a lack of "professionalism," but the reason may lie more in the culturally different treatment of time. (p. 111)

Thus, explains Condon, "it is not so much that putting things off until *mañana* is valued, as some Mexican stereotypes would have it, but that human activities are not expected to proceed like clockwork" (p. 11).

It has been pointed out that for the American businessperson discussion is simply "a means to an end: the deal." Moreover, it's a sign of good faith to agree on major issues, assuming that details will be worked out later on. But like the Latin American, the Greek businessperson engages in what seems to us prolonged discussion and is excessively preoccupied with details. For the Greek, these concerns usually signify goodwill (Hall and Whyte, in Smith, 1966, p. 568; see also Storace, 1997).

Even for personal effectiveness with people of our own culture, we have to be aware of time as an aspect of communication.

VISUAL CUES

by S. Tubbs and S. Moss

The second category of nonverbal cues we will discuss is extremely broad, ranging from facial expressions and body movements to the clothing we wear and the objects we display. Let's begin with an anecdote.

At the end of the nineteenth century, a German horse named Hans was reported to know how to add. If you asked him to add 2 and 6, for example, he pawed the ground eight times. The curious thing was that Hans could do sums only in the presence of human beings. His mysterious talent was later explained rather simply: When he unwittingly reached the answer, he saw his audience relax, and he stopped pawing.

The people who came to see Hans perform would have been shocked to learn that they were, by their body movements, transmitting the correct answers visually. Yet they were probably leaning forward eagerly to take in every aspect of the spectacle before them, for we all know how much we gain by seeing a performer, a lecturer, or any person we are speaking to. In fact, members of discussion groups interact more frequently when seated facing each other rather than side by side. In other words, the greater our visibility, the greater our potential for communicating. And, the greater the number of channels the sender uses, the more information is received.

Visual cues add to the information transmitted through other channels and at times stand alone. Specific motions of the head, for example, give the equivalents of certain brief verbal messages such as yes and no, and these movements may vary from culture to culture. Even head orientation, the direction in which we turn our heads, communicates something. Mehrabian (1967) found that a person who gives more head orientation while speaking conveys more positive feeling. A study of how "warmth" and "coldness" are conveyed during an interview supports this conclusion: "Leaning toward the subject, smiling, and looking directly at him enabled the subject to judge the experimenter as warm. Conversely, looking away from the subject, leaning away from him, not smiling, and intermittently drumming the fingers on the table impressed the subject as coldness" (Reece and Whitman, 1962, p. 250).

Knapp's (1978) summary of research in Table 6.2 indicates which cues are usually associated with warm or cold people. Notice that the nonverbal cues described include facial expression, eye contact, and body movements. We shall be discussing each of these sources of information. Bear in mind, however, that when you look at another person, you get a total impression: We separate various cues here only to examine the kind of information that each conveys. These are nonverbal cues associated with North Americans; other cultures would be described by other lists.

A pioneering figure in research on nonverbal communication, Ray Birdwhistell, believes that the entire communication context must be observed in all its complexity and that it is productive to isolate individual variables only if they can be integrated into "the general communicative stream, including verbal behavior" (Weitz, 1979). It was Birdwhistell (1952) who introduced the term **kinesics** to refer to *the study of body movements in communication.* "Body movements" is used in a broad sense and refers also to movements of the head and face. Birdwhistell has estimated that there are over 700,000 possible physical signs that can be transmitted via body movement. The first group of visual cues we will be looking at has to do with facial expression.

FACIAL EXPRESSION

A blank face is a riddle, troubling and open to interpretation. Garbo's director in *Queen Christina* attributed the film's success to his direction in the last scene: "Think of nothing," he told the actress. The film closes as Garbo, her face expressionless, stands on board a ship and stares into the turbulent water. This ambiguous ending allowed each viewer his own interpretation.

Most members of this culture could not maintain a blank face for very long. (That's why staring contests usually produce laughter after a short time.) Indeed, the human face is so mobile that it can effortlessly register boredom, surprise, affection, and disapproval one after another in a few seconds. *We constantly read expressions from people's faces.* In fact, **facial cues** are the single most important source of nonverbal communication. Comments such as "If looks could kill" and "It was all over her face" bear witness to the significance we give to facial expression.

Table 6.2   Behaviors Rated as Warm and Cold

WARM BEHAVIORS	COLD BEHAVIORS
Looks into his eyes	Gives a cold stare
Touches his hand	Sneers
Moves toward him	Gives a fake yawn
Smiles frequently	Frowns
Works her eyes from his head to his toes	Moves away from him
Has a happy face	Looks at the ceiling
Smiles with mouth open	Picks her teeth
Grins	Shakes her head negatively
Sits directly facing him	Cleans her fingernails
Nods head affirmatively	Looks away
Puckers her lips	Pouts
Licks her lips	Chain smokes
Raises her eyebrows	Cracks her fingers
Has eyes wide open	Looks around the room
Uses expressive hand gestures while speaking	Picks her hands
Gives fast glances	Plays with her hair's split ends
Stretches	Smells her hair

Source: Adapted from *Nonverbal Communication in Human Interaction,* 2d ed., by Mark L. Knapp, copyright © 1978 by Holt, Rinehart and Winston, reproduced by permission of the publisher.

According to one study, we tend to describe faces in terms of a general evaluative dimension (good or bad, beautiful or ugly, kind or cruel, and so on) and a dynamism dimension (active or passive, inert or mobile, interesting or boring). And apparently some people are much more adept than others at interpreting facial cues.

We like a face or we don't; we think it's animated or relatively inert. These are general impressions. But what do we see that makes us judge someone to be sad or happy or frightened or angry? Isolating which facial cues specify particular emotions is more difficult than simply judging a face. In one early attempt (Harrison, in Campbell and Hepler, 1965) to decipher a facial code, subjects were shown simple illustrations (pictomorphs). A statistical analysis of the results led to the conclusions that half-raised eyebrows indicate worry; a single raised eyebrow, skepticism; half-closed eyes, boredom; closed eyes, sleep; an upcurved mouth,

happiness, and a down-curved mouth, unhappiness. The smile button with its brief suggestion of a face—pinpoints for eyes and a single upcurved line for the mouth—is enough to suggest to most people a happy face.

The study of facial cues as expressions of specific emotions has a long history. One of the most eminent scientists to examine this subject was Charles Darwin. Darwin tried to find out whether the facial behaviors associated with particular emotions are universal. One method he used was to ask subjects to identify specific emotions from still photographs of people's faces. In *The Expression of the Emotions in Man and Animals,* published in 1872, Darwin presented some of his conclusions and speculations about expressive behavior. He felt that most of a human being's expressive actions, like those of other animals, are instinctive, not learned behaviors. For example, "We may see children, only two or three years old, and even those born blind, blushing from shame" (Darwin, in Loewenberg, 1959, p. 398).

Darwin's argument about the facial expressions of blind children was given further support by several studies done more than half a century after his book was published. Ekman and Friesen (1971) asked members of a preliterate New Guinea culture to judge emotions from the facial expressions of Westerners. The subjects had had virtually no exposure to Western culture. Yet they made the same identifications that Westerners made, with one exception: They were not able to differentiate between fear and surprise. The researchers concluded that, at least in some respects, expressive facial behavior is constant across cultures. They acknowledged that cultural differences exist but argued that the differences are reflected "in the circumstances which elicit an emotion, in the action consequences of an emotion and in the display rules which govern the management of facial behavior in particular social settings" (p. 129).

According to anthropologist Melvin Konner (1987), smiling seems to be a human social display that is universal. For example, Eibl-Eibesfeldt's films from many remote parts of the world show smiling as a "consistent feature of greeting, often in combination with raising of the eyebrows" (p. 42). How our smiles are interpreted, however, will depend on many variables. Forgas (1987) found that the communicator's physical attractiveness can influence how cues of facial expression are interpreted: Smiles by unattractive subjects tend to be interpreted as reflecting submissiveness and lack of self-confidence; smiles by attractive subjects tend to be perceived as showing extraversion and self-confidence.

Research on more than 30 different cultures suggests that there is a high level of agreement in judging emotions from photographs of people's facial expressions. Most interesting, though, is the finding that there are cultural differences in the degree to which such expressions are recognized and also in how their intensity is rated.

In a recent study (Biehl et al., 1997), using Japanese and Caucasian Facial Expressions of Emotion (JACFEE), one of several tests for cultural differences, the subjects—from Hungary, Japan, Poland, Sumatra, the United States, and Vietnam—were asked to judge emotions from facial expressions in still photos. In general, judging expressions of happiness and surprise showed the highest level of

agreement, while judging fear was the lowest. But there were also several cross-national differences: In judging contempt, for example, Americans showed less agreement than subjects from other countries. Similarly, Vietnamese subjects found it more difficult to judge disgust, and Japanese subjects showed a lower level of agreement when judging fear.

Other experts on nonverbal communication, including Ray Birdwhistell and Weston La Barre, have challenged the view that facial cues are universal. They believe that the cues are culture specific. Today, there is a great deal of ongoing research and debate about the universality and functions of facial expressions in communicating (Kappas, 1997; Carroll and Russell, 1997). Earlier, Motley and Camden (1988) found that in interpersonal communication settings, spontaneous facial expressions of emotion are far more difficult to identify than the posed expressions traditionally used in formal studies. "If we depend upon facial expression alone," they say, "we can 'read a person like a book' only if the person intends to be read" (p. 19).

There is also a growing body of research about emotional contagion (Andersen and Guerrero, 1998) and how perceiving an emotional expression—a smile, for example—might cause us to mimic that expression and thereby experience that state of feeling. In other words, the implication is that we "catch" another person's emotions, through feedback from either the face or the body (Doherty, 1997). Generally, our accuracy in identifying emotions seems to increase with the number of cues we receive.

EYE MOVEMENTS

Proper street behavior among Americans permits passersby to look at each other until they are about eight feet apart. At this point, both parties cast their eyes downward so that they will not appear to be staring. The many other rules implicit in our culture about looking at others are a tacit admission that eye contact is perhaps the single most important facial cue we use in communicating. The *study of the role of eye contact in communications* is called **oculesics**.

Although the face has been called "the major nonverbal liar" (Ekman and Friesen, 1984), cues given in eye contact seem to reveal a good deal about personality. Apparently, we have greater control of the muscles in the lower part of our face than we do of the muscles around our eyes. (There are exceptions, of course. Machiavellian individuals and con artists are able to sustain good eye contact even when telling lies.) It has even been suggested that "the lower face may follow culturally transmitted display rules while the eyes may reveal the spontaneous or naked response" (Libby and Yaklevich, 1973, p. 203).

A broader study of eye movements began during the 1970s when a new form of therapy evolved that focused primarily on eye behaviors as clues to underlying problems. This approach, **neurolinguistic programming (NLP)**, is an attempt to change or "reprogram" patient behavior by discovering what patients are thinking. NLP therapists believe, for example, that eyes that move up and to the right indicate the individual is trying to envision an event that has never been seen; eyes that move up and to the left indicate the person is recalling an event that has been seen; eyes that are centered but glance to the right indicate the individual is trying to imagine a sound that has never been heard; eyes centered but glancing to the left indicate the person is recalling a sound that has been heard; eyes that move down and to the left indicate the person is carrying on an internal conversation; and eyes that move down and to the right indicate the sorting out of bodily sensations (Leo, 1983).

According to the theory that people have preferred channels by which they transmit and receive information: visual (sight-related), auditory (sound-related), or kinesthetic (data related to touch, taste, smell, or feelings), by observing a person's eye movements, we can track which kind of information is being processed:

> Notice that eyes looking upward or defocussed typically indicate people accessing a visual system, eyes moving side to side or down to the left are usually seen with people seeking and retrieving auditory data, and eyes traveling downward and to the right side most times are tending to indicate people going for kinesthetic information. (Madonik, 1990, p. 19)

At present, however, most of the research on eye movements has to do with eye contact. One study estimates that in group communication we spend 30 to 60 percent of our time in eye contact

with others (10 to 30 percent of the looks last only about a second). Several of the unstated rules about eye contact are:

a. A looker may invite interaction by staring at another person who is on the other side of a room. The target's studied return of the gaze is generally interpreted as acceptance of the invitation, while averting the eyes is a rejection of the looker's request.

b. There is more mutual eye contact between friends than others, and a looker's frank gaze is widely interpreted as positive regard.

c. Persons who seek eye contact while speaking are regarded not only as exceptionally well-disposed by their target, but also as more believable and earnest.

d. If the usual short, intermittent gazes during conversation are replaced by gazes of longer duration, the target interprets this as meaning that the task is less important than the personal relation between the two persons. (Argyle, 1985)

The second rule is corroborated by other researchers: Frequent eye contact does seem to be a sign of affection or interest. And personality will affect the degree of eye contact. For example, people who are high in their need to give help and comfort maintain eye contact to a much greater degree than do people who are rated low on this need (Libby and Yaklevich, 1973). Eye contact with friends can also help us to cope with stress. One study (Winstead et al., 1992) found that subjects who anticipated a stressful event perceived greater social support from interacting with a friend rather than a stranger. In this experiment, the event was delivering an extemporaneous speech. Researchers report the best nonverbal predictor of perceived social support and coping to be eye contact.

Even in public communication the frequency of eye contact affects the message sender. When an audience gives negative feedback (including poor eye contact), the speaker tends to lose fluency and to do poorly in presenting his or her message. In turn, audiences prefer speakers who give good eye contact.

Why is eye contact so rewarding to others? Perhaps it is because the eyes are considered such a valuable source of information. Hess (1965) found that Chinese jade dealers watch the eyes of their prospective customers for interest in a particular stone because the pupils enlarge with increased interest; similarly, magicians are able to tell what card a person is thinking about by studying his or her eyes. Hess's studies (1965; 1975) confirm that pupil size is indeed a sensitive index of interest.

There are several popular beliefs about what can be learned from watching someone's eyes. For example, two people who exchange knowing glances at a party seem able to communicate without words. Being able to look another person in the eye traditionally implies that you are being truthful and that your intentions are not to be questioned. Conversely, the person who averts his or her eyes is thought to be hiding something.

Norms governing eye movements and the interpretation of the implicit nonverbal message may be extremely clear in other cultures. For example, in the black township of Soweto in South Africa, a mother whose son had been killed in a violent confrontation with the police swore never again to avert her eyes or to bow her head in front of white people. In her culture, this was a major act of defiance.

BODY MOVEMENTS

If during a party you were asked to record and classify all the body movements of two people in conversation during a five-minute period, you would probably think this an impossible task. Nothing short of a film captures the rapid, often subtle changes of the body. Much of what we know about kinesics has come to us indirectly, from such disciplines as anthropology and psychiatry.

Do you think of yourself as a flirt—or do you know one? What are the nonverbal behaviors by which flirting is signaled? The classic work of Scheflen (1965) grew out of the patterns of nonverbal flirting, or "quasi-courtship," he noticed between males and females during psychotherapy. After studying films of a great many therapy sessions, he was able to classify some of the typical behaviors. Signs of **courtship readiness** included preening hair, pulling at stockings, adjusting the tie, and so on. **Positioning** was another source of cues about interpersonal attraction. For example, two people might face each other and lean forward eagerly. Sometimes they sat with the upper half of their torsos turned in an open position so that a third person might enter the conversation but with

their legs forming a circle and thus excluding the intruder. A third category, **actions of appeal**, included flirtatious glances and head cocking. Women signaled sexual invitation by crossing the legs, exposing the thigh, exhibiting the palm of the hand, and protruding the breast. Here is an example of these behaviors in context:

> At the beginning of the sequence . . . the therapist . . . turns to watch an attractive research technician walk across the room. The patient [female] begins to preen. . . . The therapist turns back to the patient and also preens, but he then disclaims courtship by an ostentatious look of boredom and a yawn. . . . Immediately afterward, the patient tells him she is interested in an attractive male aide. (p. 252)

A much later study of flirting between young men and women (Simpson et al., 1993) found that, though the sets of nonverbal behaviors were different for men and women, there was a clearcut pattern. Men who were flirting smiled and laughed more often, showed more flirtatious glances, and looked downward less frequently than men who were not flirting. In flirting women, body movements seemed to be more pronounced; women tended to cant their heads during conversation and to lean forward; of course, by leaning forward you maximize other cues from your face and head. Although earlier researchers have connected head canting with communicating submissiveness, this seems not to be the case here: women who canted their heads were actually rated not only as more engaging but slightly more dominant (p. 456). Future research may explain these discrepancies.

According to the findings of Ekman (1965b), cues from the head and face suggest what emotion is being experienced whereas the body gives off cues about how intense that emotion is. The hands, however, can give us the same information we receive from the head and face.

HAND GESTURES

Anthropologists distinguish humankind from other animals by their use of language and their superior manual dexterity. Flexible hands enable human beings to use tools and to draw on a wide range of gestures in communicating. As a mode of nonverbal communication, **hand gestures** *rank second in importance only to facial cues.*

On a recent television documentary series examining various American ethnic groups (Berger 1998), Nick Stellino, who is of Italian descent, described how family members used hand gestures when they talk to each other:

> Each family member adopted and honed his or her own singular flourish: Mr. Stellino himself liked to jab at the sky, while his father favored a to-and-fro motion with hands in front of chest, and his brother Mario adopted a dramatic shoulder-rolling arm movement. The gestures were like signatures, within which could be found clues to the speaker's personality. . . . Mr. Stellino embraces that old ethnic saw that Italians "speak with their hands" and shows us that in all those flying hands, there is a depth of feeling and a flair for individual expression that is to be envied, not mocked. (p. AR 25)

It is not only broad, expansive gestures that communicate mood. Less animated people often communicate inadvertently by means of their hands. The rather reserved husband of a lawyer we know repeatedly drums his fingers on a table or chair whenever his wife speaks about her practice. This behavior is the only sign of his impatience with her deep involvement in her profession.

In his analysis of foot, head, and hand movements of mental patients under treatment in hospitals, Ekman (1965a) was able to distinguish more than a hundred different hand acts. Coding them along with the other body movements, he discovered that from the time of the patient's admission to his or her discharge, hand movements corresponded with various stages of treatment.

Hand gestures sometimes substitute for verbal communication. Deaf-mutes use a system of hand signals so comprehensive that it literally replaces spoken language. The signals themselves are arbitrary. Many of our hand movements are culturally determined. Thus, the same gestures can convey different things to members of different cultures, and, over time, gestures change even within the same culture.

To an American, for example, making a circle with one's thumb and forefinger and extending the other fingers means "okay," but to a Brazilian it is an obscene sign of contempt. Apparently, American visitors and even statesmen unwittingly offend their Brazilian hosts with this gesture.

Desmond Morris and his colleagues in England (1979) have identified what they call twenty key gestures used in Europe. They are listed below.

1. The fingertips kiss
2. The fingers cross
3. The nose thumb
4. The hand purse
5. The cheek screw
6. The eyelid pull
7. The forearm jerk
8. The flat-hand flick
9. The ring
10. The vertical horn-sign
11. The horizontal horn-sign
12. The fig
13. The head toss
14. The chin flick
15. The cheek stroke
16. The thumb up
17. The teeth flick
18. The ear touch
19. The nose tap
20. The palm-back V-sign

Some of these, such as the nose thumb, the forearm jerk, the ring, and the palm-back V-sign, are quite familiar to us. Others, however, such as the cheek screw, the horizontal horn-sign, the chin flick, and the fig are almost completely unknown in the United States. They found that different meanings were assigned in different countries.

HAPTICS

The cues we receive from physical contact are especially revealing: Touch is one of our most important means of communicating nonverbally. **Haptics, the study of how we use touch to communicate,** has been receiving increasing attention among students of nonverbal behavior. Heslin and Alper (1983) indicate that in addition to conveying nurturance and caring, touch is also used to signify a professional relationship (being touched by a barber, for example); a social relationship (handshakes); friendship (for example, touching the upper arm); intimacy (hugs, for instance); and sexual arousal (for example, certain types of kisses). In each instance, touch is a bonding gesture.

Conversely, a limp handshake in our culture usually evokes negative feelings; Americans interpret it as a lack of interest or vitality. A moist hand is often considered a sign of anxiety, especially if the handshake precedes a potentially stressful situation such as an interview.

In discussing proxemics, we mentioned the distinction between low- and high-contact cultures. Hall identifies the United States and Northern European cultures as low-contact cultures, but a recent study (McDaniel and Andersen, 1998) of patterns of touch finds that there is a broad range of touching behaviors in most cultures. The exception is to be seen in Asian countries, especially in Northeast Asia. Like many others, the authors cite Confucianism as a possible influence on the "East Asian reluctance toward interpersonal touch" (p. 70). These findings confirm other recent work, suggesting that several other variables affect patterns of touching—among them the degree of familiarity between people; their status; and the communication context itself.

From summaries of research, we know that touch is essential for psychological and physical development in children and emotional well-being in adults. Being able to touch other human beings seems to be linked with high self-esteem and sociability.

We also use touch to influence others; in fact, touching increases self-disclosure and compliant behavior. The influence of touching on compliance has been demonstrated in several fascinating studies. For example, subjects touched lightly on the arm were more likely to sign a petition than those who were not touched (Willis and Hamm, 1980). Touch *avoidance* also turns out to be a good predictor of interpersonal distance, particularly when the other person is female—so in this instance, we see two nonverbal codes or messages interacting (Anderson and Sull, 1985).

Other work on touch (Jones and Yarbrough, 1985), conducted in naturalistic settings, found twelve different types of touches: *positive affect touches*, including support, appreciation, inclusion, sexual, and affectionate touches; *playful touches*, including those of playful affection and playful aggression; control touches, including touches of compliance, attention getting, and signaling a response; *ritualistic touches*, including touches for greeting and departure; *hybrid touches*, including greeting/affection and departure/affection touches. *Task-related touches* accompanying a verbal remark about someone's appearance (touching that per-

son's clothing or hair, for example) and instrumental ancillary touches (those not really necessary to perform a task—e.g., touching hands when passing the telephone to someone) as well as instrumental intrinsic touches (those that are part of a task).

Besides the need for touch to establish and develop our relationships with others, some touch appears to have unambiguous symbolic content or meaning. Further, the codes of interpersonal touch encompass a far broader "range of meanings and degrees than previous research would suggest" (p. 51); so we use touch to convey many different things, some far more ambiguous than others. Touch is also *involving;* it is a form of approach behavior. And finally, context is critical to the meanings touch conveys (p. 51)—verbal behaviors as well as nonverbal behaviors *and* situation all influence the kind of meaning we attribute to a given touch.

PHYSICAL APPEARANCE AND THE USE OF OBJECTS

In "Trial by Style" (1998), a recent magazine editorial on men's fashions, all the male models are dressed in expensive suits—the court stenographer with wire-rim glasses wears a pinstriped three-piece suit; the cross-examining attorney is in a three-button charcoal-gray pinstriped suit, complete with vest; and the attorney at the "judges conference" is dressed in herringbone. This spoof advises that "any man, regardless of his profession, can dress in the elegant style of the celluloid drama presented here. . . . Weigh all the evidence, and choose your style for fall" (p. 79).

Whether we intend to or not, we often project a personal style through how we dress. Clothes may not make the person, but dress, grooming, and general physical appearance are often the basis of first and relatively long-lasting impressions; even glasses affect the way the wearer is perceived by others.

Uniforms tell us a great deal about rank and status; many people believe that dress and personal grooming do too. In several studies, people received greater help or compliance with their requests (signing a petition, for example) when they were formally or neatly dressed than they did when their dress was casual or careless (Kleinke, 1986, pp. 77–78). One study of beards suggests that women find a bearded man more appealing, that he has "more status in the eyes of other men," and that his beard may even create more social distance between him and another unbearded male (Freedman, 1969, p. 38). The popularity of beards seems to be cyclical (Kleinke, 1986, p. 78).

The clothing we wear often communicates our compliance or noncompliance with traditional values. In general, people will tolerate a lot more deviation in dress if the person in question is rich or famous. Indeed, people often expect artists or performers to dress unconventionally. The athlete Florence Griffith Joyner ("Flojo") was known for her one-legged running suits and her long vivid fingernails.

Elegant, expensive clothing can sometimes prove a barrier to communication, however—especially in a country such as ours with its democratic values. For example, we don't expect a politician to show up wearing a three-piece suit when he makes a speech in a working-class neighborhood.

On a talk show with David Letterman, Dustin Hoffman complained that he was never given roles in which he had to dress formally. Once, just once, he joked—or was he joking?—he'd like to do a film in which he had to wear an Armani suit. Given current trends, Dustin Hoffman may have to find that part very soon, for there is a definite trend toward casual dress that has filtered down to the workplace.

The study of how we select and make use of physical objects in our nonverbal communication is referred to as **objectics.** Objectics is concerned with every kind of physical object from the clothing we wear to the food we serve to our dinner guests.

We communicate about ourselves by our choice of car, home, furniture, and many other things. For example, the novelist Sandra Cisneros created an uproar in a historic district of San Antonio when she painted her house purple (Rimer, 1998). At times, our choices suggest a desire to communicate status or power—for example, through a Rolex watch or expensive leather goods. A small pink triangle on an envelope conveys support for gay rights; wearing a red ribbon may draw attention to AIDS awareness; a nose ring may signal something about the wearer's unconventionality. In general, cosmetics, jewelry, and tattoos or decals—seen even on high-fashion models—often evoke strong responses from other people.

Whether we intend to communicate or not, the way we choose and display physical objects is taken by others as a source of information about us. It should go without saying that such information is not always accurate.

We have discussed a great many visual cues individually, but remember that as a communicator you are also taking in and interpreting cues about space and time as well as vocal cues, which we will look at in some detail.

VOCAL CUES

by S. Tubbs and S. Moss

A manager for the Bank of Montreal's Institute for Learning in Toronto who had worked in Canada for 25 years returned to her native country, England. Now she comes back to the Toronto office only six times a year. Most of her working time she is telecommuting:

> "I had to learn to read the body language in meetings by voice tone, and rely on colleagues to tell me if someone was reacting without speaking. Slowly I picked up these senses by ear instead of sight." It helped that her colleagues relayed assessments of body language in meetings. And it wasn't one-way traffic. [She] had to feed back to them her feelings as well. She developed a candor that most business meetings try to ignore. (*Communications News,* 1998, p. 87)

Communication can be verbal/vocal—that is, both verbal and vocal. The difference between the verbal and the vocal message is the difference between what is said and how it is said.

Take the sentence, "I hate you." Imagine these words being said to show anger or in a much different way to sound seductive. The simple sentence "I'm glad to meet you" can sound cold and insincere despite its verbal message. Or suppose you go to a friend's apartment and she opens the door and says, "Oh, it's you." It is the vocal cues, perhaps in combination with several visual cues, that tell you whether your friend is really pleased to see you, or indifferent, or even disappointed. Of course, if she simply groans when she opens the door, this is an example of nonverbal/vocal communication.

The study of vocal phenomena, **paralinguistics** or **paralanguage,** refers to *something beyond or in addition to language itself.* Paralanguage has two components: *voice qualities,* such as pitch, range, resonance, lip control, and articulation control; and *vocalizations,* or *noises without linguistic structure,* such as crying, laughing, and grunting (Trager, 1958).

Several distinct emotions can be accurately identified solely on the basis of vocal cues, but the more similar the emotions—admiration and affection, for example—the greater our difficulty in identifying them.

Much research on vocal characteristics and emotions parallels the studies of facial expressions. Mehrabian (1968) found that people are easily able to judge the degree of liking communicated vocally. One team of researchers identified four categories of emotion: positive feeling, dislike, sadness, and apprehension or fear. The results confirm that "voice sounds alone, independent of semantic components of vocal messages, carry important clues to the emotional state of a speaker" (Soskin and Kauffman, 1961, p. 78). People can detect aggressiveness from a tape recording of a speaker's message, though not from a written transcript, and can judge intensity of emotion from vocal characteristics. We cannot assume, though, that vocal cues are similar across cultures.

A common problem in interpreting vocal cues is misunderstanding sarcasm. This is especially true for children and people with poor listening and/or intellectual skills.

Vocal cues are sometimes the basis for our inferences about personality traits. If people increase the loudness, pitch, timbre, and rate of their speech, we think of them as more active and dynamic. If they use more intonation, higher speech rates, more volume, and greater fluency in their speech, we find them more persuasive.

It's interesting that judgments about status can be made quite rapidly (for example, after listening to a sample of a person's speech for only 10 or 15 seconds). Apparently, we can make such inferences with a high degree of accuracy.

Despite wide agreement about certain relationships between voice qualities and personality traits, no conclusive evidence supports such inferences. They seem to derive from vocal stereotypes. Even if our beliefs have no basis in fact, however, they have striking effects on our response to others; we act on what we believe to be true. Thus, when the talkies appeared, several stars of the silent films were ruined because the public expected their voices to sound consistent with their screen personalities. The great lover with the high-pitched voice was too great a disappointment.

VOLUME

One precondition of effective verbal communication is adequate volume. If your voice is so low that you can barely be heard, people rapidly become too tired or too embarrassed to ask you to repeat your last remark. In this case, it is you, the message sender, who becomes a source of interference for the receiver. In organizational communication, vocal intensity can reinforce or enhance a person's power base and convey a sense of confidence. For example, an employee who speaks loudly is more likely to enhance his or her expertise.

Appropriate sound level varies considerably from one culture to another. At social distance, Hall (1959) observes that "in overall loudness, the American voice . . . is below that of the Arab, the Spaniard, the South Asian Indian, and the Russian, and somewhat above that of the English upper class, the Southeast Asian, and the Japanese" (p. 121).

Most people link volume to certain personality traits: thus it is commonly thought that an aggressive person speaks in a louder voice than one who is reserved and shy. Volume, however, is not necessarily a function of personality. Our models in childhood also influence our volume level.

Feedback from the receiver is the best check on volume. If you are not getting through or if you're coming on too strong, adjust your voice accordingly.

QUALITY

Think of a violin, a viola, and a cello. Each is a stringed instrument but has a different size and shape. The same note played on each of these instruments will therefore have a different *resonance*—a distinctive quality of sound. Similarly, each of you has a distinctive voice quality because the resonance of your voice—which to a great extent determines its quality—is a function of the size and shape of your body as well as of your vocal cords.

There seems to be wide agreement in responses to vocal qualities. Judges could reliably distinguish voices described as shrill or harsh from those considered pleasant, or "resonant." In our culture, several voice qualities considered particularly unpleasant are *hypernasality* (talking through the nose), denasality (which sounds as though the speaker has a constant head cold), *hoarseness,* and *harshness* (or stridency). According to Pearson and associates (1994), differences in gender influence how vocal quality is interpreted. For example:

> A female speaker with a breathy voice is perceived as pretty, petite, feminine, highstrung, and shallow; a male speaker with a breathy voice is perceived as young and artistic. . . . Women with "throaty" voices are perceived as more masculine, lazier, less intelligent, less emotional, less attractive, more careless, less artistic, more naive, more neurotic, less interesting, more apathetic, and quieter. On the other hand, throatiness in men resulted in their being perceived as older, more mature, more sophisticated, and better adjusted.

Through practice and training, almost all of us can improve our vocal quality. One of the best media available for studying communication style is the videotape recorder, though even videotape loses some nuances of vocal inflection, eye contact, postural cues, and the like. The audiotape recorder is another valuable aid.

For discussion purposes, we have isolated three categories of nonverbal cues. People interpret messages on the basis of multiple nonverbal and verbal cues, and this is certainly the case with deception.

DECEPTION

by S. Tubbs and S. Moss

There are very few nonverbal behaviors that consistently differentiate liars from nonliars—for example, liars dilate their pupils more, shrug more often, hesitate and make more speech errors, and have a higher vocal pitch. As you try to judge whether a person is lying, you may be staring intently at her face; yet her facial expressions usually turn out to be far less revealing than other nonverbal cues, perhaps because we have greater control over our faces (Anolli and Ciceri, 1997).

The kinds of **leakage,** or *signals of deception,* that take place depend on whether the lie is spontaneous or rehearsed and whether we are concealing something emotional or factual. Deception cues are most likely to be given when the deceiver wants to hide a feeling experienced at that moment or feels strongly about the information being hidden. They also tend to occur when a person feels anxious, or guilty, or needs to think carefully while speaking.

One study found that deceivers delivering a prepared lie respond more quickly than truth tellers mainly because less thinking is necessary (Greene et al., 1985). When they are unprepared, however, deceivers generally take longer than both prepared deceivers and truth tellers. Those telling the truth generally maintain more eye contact than deceivers. Deceivers also show less body movement, probably in an attempt to avoid leakage cues. At the same time, they laugh and smile more often, presumably trying to keep their faces from displaying other expressions that may turn out to be leakage cues. It's especially interesting that these people continue to behave "deceptively" even when telling the truth. They probably fear that they will lose control if the situation in which they need to lie should recur (Greene et al., 1985). We must note here the great potential for intercultural misunderstandings when cultural conventions of little gesturing and infrequent eye contact may be interpreted as deception.

A recent study of naive and able liars (Anolli and Ciceri, 1997) emphasizes that lying is for the most part a vocal act, one that is very demanding. The researchers found that when people were lying their pitch was higher, they used more words, paused more, and showed greater eloquence and fluency in their speech. Liars were classified as good, tense, or overcontrolled. The study empha-

sizes that lying, a "strategic act," is intellectually demanding because the liar, who knows the truth, is trying to be more persuasive—and also to conceal the emotional arousal that is sometimes created by the act of lying (especially if the liar is unprepared). At times the control a liar must exert is transformed into overcontrol so that the voice becomes flat and deeper in tone.

Much deception research has focused on the nature of deception cues and on how information is leaked, but research by Buller and others looks at mutual influence in deception and the actual communication exchange between deceivers and detectors.

Do you think it would be easier to tell if your roommate was lying or if a total stranger was lying? And what about probing questions? By asking questions could you figure out whether someone was telling the truth? One study (Buller et al., 1991a) examines how effective probing is as a strategy for detection and whether knowing the source—that is, the deceiver—affects our ability to distinguish what is truthful. Buller found that as receivers we communicate whether we accept or suspect a message and we also communicate our suspicion nonverbally through our increased vigilance. When receivers were suspicious, they "spoke slower, were less fluent, and lacked clarity in their messages. When probing . . . [they showed] longer response latencies [delays] as the conversation progressed" (p. 18). In fact, they may have tried to conceal their suspicion by asking *fewer* probing questions—in effect, they themselves become less truthful. Deceivers, in turn, can judge our reactions to see how successful they have been and sometimes even modify their behavior to appear more truthful.

In another study (Buller et al., 1991b), people participating in a conversation "relied more on facial and head cues when judging deceit—head nodding, smiling, head shaking, and facial animation—while observers relied more on vocal behaviors—interruptions, talkovers, and response latencies" (p. 37).

Most deception studies have used college students as subjects. Over the last 25 years of research, Ekman and Sullivan observe, "people have not been very accurate in judging when someone is lying," with average accuracy estimated as rarely above 60 percent (1991, p. 913). One study of professional lie catchers looked at members of the U.S. Secret Service, federal polygraphers, judges, police, psychiatrists, a diverse group of working adults, and college students. Most groups did no better than college students. Secret Service people were the only ones who had greater than chance accuracy in detecting liars.

But what about the rest of us? Can we train ourselves to be more skilled in our judgments? Costanza (1992) has designed a training program to improve accuracy in interpreting both verbal and nonverbal cues. Although hearing a lecture on verbal and nonverbal cues did nothing to increase accuracy, practice in identifying relevant cues after viewing videotaped interactions—and then getting feedback about one's judgments—did improve decoding skills. This program emphasized several deception cues established as important from earlier studies; cues included greater speech disfluencies, greater delays in response, more pauses, briefer messages, and more hand gestures (p. 309).

This study also confirms other research that women are more skilled than men in interpreting both verbal and nonverbal cues. Costanza explains this as the result of socialization practices emphasizing "interpersonal skills in women" (p. 312). Although women had higher pretest accuracy scores, they were less confident than men that they had performed well. So, again, we see that greater sensitivity or competence is not always correlated with self-confidence.

The study of deception has much to teach us not only about individual nonverbal cues but about the interaction of verbal and nonverbal behavior. If at times we have spoken of verbal and nonverbal messages as if they could be separated, this has not been our intention. Face-to-face communication is a total experience. No matter what a person is trying to say, you can see his or her face, body movement, clothing, and so on, and you are responding, whether you are aware of it or not, to all these cues.

Using Technology to Communicate

This is the third in a series of seven lessons on communications. This lesson introduces you to basic concepts, principles and processes for working with communications technology.

The following topics are addressed in this lesson:

- Determining the audience and the message;
- Determining the most appropriate technology and mode of delivery for the message;
- The impact of technology on communication;
- Types of communications technologies and modes of delivery;
- Advantages and disadvantages of communication technologies; and
- Ways to determine the most appropriate technology for the message and the audience.

The following Terminal Learning Objective (TLO) is supported in whole or in part by this lesson:

- Understand the limitations of technology.

Following this lesson you will be able to:

- Describe commonly used communication technologies;
- Discriminate when and under what circumstances to use communication technologies; and
- Practice using a current communication technology.

E-MAIL POLICIES

by The ePolicy Institute

BAD E-MAIL IS BAD BUSINESS

- 27% of Fortune 500 companies have defended themselves against claims of sexual harassment stemming from inappropriate e-Mail and/or Internet use. Chevron was ordered to pay female employees $2.2 million to settle a sexual harassment lawsuit stemming from inappropriate e-Mail sent by male employees.
- If a former employee subpoenas company e-Mail in the course of a wrongful termination lawsuit, you could face an expensive back-up tape search. One Fortune 500 company was ordered to search more than 20,000 back-up tapes at a cost of $1,000 per tape. That's $20 million spent before the case went to trial.
- 50% of employees report receiving racist, sexist, pornographic, or otherwise inappropriate e-Mail at work.

CONFUSED ABOUT WHEN TO USE E-MAIL?

Avoid e-Mail When ...

1. A message is extremely important or confidential, and you cannot risk a breach of privacy. Never use e-Mail to communicate proprietary corporate information. With millions of hidden readers and dastardly hackers lurking in cyberspace, e-Mail simply is not secure.
2. You want to conduct negotiations or hold a give-and-take conversation. Whether you want to negotiate a price reduction with a supplier or persuade your supervisor to give you a pay raise, dialogues that call for back-and-forth discussion are best held on the phone or in person.
3. You need to conduct a lengthy interview with a long list of questions that call for detailed answers.
4. You want to deliver bad news or discuss an emotionally charged matter. Without the benefit of facial expressions, intonation, and body language, hurt feelings could ensue and flame wars could erupt if you deliver bad news electronically.

5. You seek an immediate response from someone who may not check e-Mail regularly or who has a tendency to procrastinate.
6. You run the risk of intimidating or turning off the reader with a written message.
7. You suspect your written message may be misunderstood or misconstrued.

Use e-Mail When....

1. You want to deliver a message quickly and the speed with which you receive your reply does not matter. e-Mail is a terrific way to send a quick message, but it is not necessarily the best route to a quick reply. Your reader is under no obligation to read or act upon your message in a timely fashion.
2. You want to communicate directly with the decision-maker, rather than fight your way past a gatekeeper. As long as you have the decision-maker's correct e-Mail address, chances are your message will be read by your intended reader. Few people have assistants screen their e-Mail. Bear in mind, however, senior executives are busy people. As such, they may be impatient with wordy or poorly constructed messages. Follow the organization's eWriting guidelines to ensure your e-Mail messages are powerful, persuasive documents that motivate readers to act.
3. You want to avoid the cost of long-distance phone calls and faxes, local or overnight delivery services, and/or snail mail.
4. You need to communicate with a colleague or a customer in a different time zone or country, and you don't want to get out of bed in the middle of the night to make a phone call. Thanks to e-Mail, both the sender and the receiver can conduct business during normal working hours.
5. You want to deliver the same message to multiple readers. Whether it is a memo intended for six readers or an electronic newsletter with 6,000 subscribers, e-Mail makes it easy to deliver news quickly, easily, and inexpensively.
6. You need to maintain a written record of your electronic conversation. Before saving a message, however, review the company's document retention and deletion policy or ask your supervisor for authorization to store the e-Mail.

7. You are on a tight deadline. If an assignment is due on the president's desk at 8:00 Monday morning, you can work all weekend, send the document Sunday night, and sleep soundly, knowing your material is sitting in the boss's mailbox, awaiting review. Be careful not to wait until the last minute, however. Electronic delays and e-Mail delivery problems sometimes occur. While the majority of messages are delivered without problems, there always is the possibility that your recipient's mail server will be down, keeping your message from getting through.

8. You want to communicate quickly and cost-effectively with coworkers. Why waste paper and time writing and distributing hard copies of memos when you can send internal e-Mail messages with a click of your mouse? Just remember that the organization's netiquette policy and cyberlanguage guidelines apply to internal e-Mail as well as external correspondence.

9. You need to stay in touch with the office and your customers when you are on the road. E-Mail can be accessed from anywhere, as long as you can log onto the Net. Electronic communication beats phone tag any time, particularly for weary travelers caught between flight schedules, time zones, and competing priorities.

HOW TO WRITE BUSINESS E-MAILS

by The ePolicy Institute

This article from a British training magazine is reproduced from a web site in the UK, so you will notice British spelling of some words.

Training employees to write electronic mail effectively could save readers time and effort and even reduce stress related illnesses. Gina Cuciniello explains.

Frequent business users of electronic mail face a tidal wave of written words. They feel increasingly swamped by the quantity of written text they are expected to read every day. This feeling comes as no surprise when you consider an estimated one billion messages will be sent worldwide by the year 2000. Technological developments, instead of making our lives easier, can cause increased workloads and even lead to stress, as managers are now required to wade through volumes of technological mail each day; this includes mail which directly concerns them, indirectly concerns them and mail that does not concern them at all.

Instead of welcoming the correspondence, managers are beginning to dread the news of incoming mail and fear the task of untangling messages that are often irrelevant, longwinded or just plainly trivial. One American multinational has even taken the extraordinary step of banning the use of internal mail and gone back to promoting face- to-face communication within the organisation.

So how can the business e-mail writer make the message more reader-friendly and appropriate? The main problem lies with how the writer currently views the very medium of electronic mail to convey his or her message. The tone, language and structure used often resembles that of a telephone call:

- grammatically incorrect
- cursory
- disorganised
- full of irrelevancies

STRIKING AN APPROPRIATE TONE

Writers of business e-mails often aim for a cheerful, informal tone, irrespective of who the reader is and how well he, or she, is known to the writer. The tone used needs to be more formal but at all times polite. There is no excuse for rudeness in the form of abruptness. The writer should never forget that his e-mail message or lotus note can be distributed and hard copies circulated and kept on file for years. They can be read at any time by numerous people at different levels in an organisation and reflect well, or indeed badly, on the writer and the company he or she is representing.

Many writers assume that readers of e-mails expect the first paragraph to consist of social pleasantries and not to supply this would constitute a social blunder. This idea is misplaced. An opening sentence along the lines of "It was good to talk the other day" is sufficient before getting down to the main point of the message. A busy manager would far prefer that the information is conveyed in a direct meaningful way and not have to plough through distracting sentences before getting to the crux of the matter.

STRUCTURE AND FLOW

In longer e-mails there is often evidence of unformulated thoughts and detailed working-outs of how conclusions have been reached. Disorganised ideas, long-winded and confusing sentences are rife, all implying that the writer has given little consideration to the poor reader trying to make sense of the information.

Of course, writing directly on to a computer screen has a major disadvantage: the speed with which it is possible to write a document does not encourage much thought to go into its very structure. But speed does not equate quality. If business communication today is about putting over ideas and information in a way that the intended meaning can be grasped quickly, then more time needs to go into planning the structure of the document. A well-structured e-mail will help the reader to understand the writer's ideas fully and follow the logic of the writer's argument.

The use of headings and bullet points will also make the text more digestible. Readers find information in large blocks of text difficult to take in, so breaking the text up with headings, bullets or numbered points will all help ease the task. Headings will guide the reader and prepare him for what is to follow, while the use of bullets make certain points jump out and become more memorable.

HOW CAN LAYOUT HELP THE E-MAIL READER?

One of the main advantages of using electronic communication is the plethora of visual aids that the average computer can supply. The use of colours, boxes, bold and italics can all help distinguish certain points in the text. They can create a visual impact and make the written message more attractive for the reader. Time spent thinking about the physical presentation will be time well spent.

However, the writer should bear in mind the possibility that documents may be transferred on to a hard copy form. Attention should always be given to the point at which one page ends and the next begins, or the recipient could be left with a document on their hands that has tables cut off and paragraphs broken up at inappropriate points.

A PAPERLESS OFFICE?

Electronic technology makes it easy for a writer to whisk off copies of documents at a touch of a button. Everyone is kept informed of new developments and therefore happy. However, readers may find themselves reading copies of correspondence that are not strictly relevant to them and become distracted and even irritated by the messages. Copy addressees need to be limited and lists should be amended each time a new document is circulated.

More thought needs to go on whether the document is relevant to each addressee before transmission. The writer could, in fact, be doing the reader a favour by not sending him a copy.

With the number of electronic mail messages being sent increasing at such a phenomenal rate the need for some form of company guidelines on the usage becomes more and more evident.

GUIDELINES FOR WRITING E-MAIL

- keep sentences brief, crisp and simple
- make good use of headings, bullets and numbered points
- keep social banter to a brief opening sentence
- use boxes, colours, italics and bold highlighting to draw attention to key points and create a visual impact
- always edit documents to make sure spelling is consistent and sentences are grammatically correct
- form ideas clearly into a planned structure before starting to write and check that only
- relevant parties are sent copies

INFORMATION LITERACY DEFINED

by Training Journal

Information literacy is a set of abilities requiring individuals to "recognize when information is needed and have the ability to locate, evaluate, and use effectively the needed information."[1] Information literacy also is increasingly important in the contemporary environment of rapid technological change and proliferating information resources. Because of the escalating complexity of this environment, individuals are faced with diverse, abundant information choices—in their academic studies, in the workplace, and in their personal lives. Information is available through libraries, community resources, special interest organizations, media, and the Internet—and increasingly, information comes to individuals in unfiltered formats, raising questions about its authenticity, validity, and reliability. In addition, information is available through multiple media, including graphical, aural, and textual, and these pose new challenges for individuals in evaluating and understanding it. The uncertain quality and expanding quantity of information pose large challenges for society. The sheer abundance of information will not in itself create a more informed citizenry without a complementary cluster of abilities necessary to use information effectively.

Information literacy forms the basis for lifelong learning. It is common to all disciplines, to all learning environments, and to all levels of education. It enables learners to master content and extend their investigations, become more self-directed, and assume greater control over their own learning. An information literate individual is able to:

- Determine the extent of information needed
- Access the needed information effectively and efficiently
- Evaluate information and its sources critically
- Incorporate selected information into one's knowledge base
- Use information effectively to accomplish a specific purpose
- Understand the economic, legal, and social issues surrounding the use of information, and access and use information ethically and legally

INFORMATION LITERACY AND INFORMATION TECHNOLOGY

Information literacy is related to information technology skills, but has broader implications for the individual, the educational system, and for society. Information technology skills enable an individual to use computers, software applications, databases, and other technologies to achieve a wide variety of academic, work-related, and personal goals. Information literate individuals necessarily develop some technology skills.

Information literacy, while showing significant overlap with information technology skills, is a distinct and broader area of competence. Increasingly, information technology skills are interwoven with, and support, information literacy. A 1999 report from the National Research Council promotes the concept of "fluency" with information technology and delineates several distinctions useful in understanding relationships among information literacy, computer literacy, and broader technological competence. The report notes that "computer literacy" is concerned with rote learning of specific hardware and software applications, while "fluency with technology" focuses on understanding the underlying concepts of technology and applying problem-solving and critical thinking to using technology. The report also discusses differences between information technology fluency and information literacy as it is understood in K–12 and higher education. Among these are information literacy's focus on content, communication, analysis, information searching, and evaluation; whereas information technology "fluency" focuses on a deep understanding of technology and graduated, increasingly skilled use of it.[2]

"Fluency" with information technology may require more intellectual abilities than the rote learning of software and hardware associated with "computer literacy," but the focus is still on the technology itself. Information literacy, on the other hand, is an intellectual framework for understanding, finding, evaluating, and using information—activities which may be accomplished in part by fluency with information technology, in part by sound investigative methods, but most important, through critical discernment and reasoning. Information literacy initiates, sustains, and extends lifelong learning through

abilities which may use technologies but are ultimately independent of them.

REFERENCES

1. American Library Association. *Presidential
Committee on Information Literacy. Final
Report.* (Chicago: American Library
Association, 1989.)
http://www.ala.org/acrl/nili/ilit1st.html

2. National Research Council. Commission on
Physical Sciences, Mathematics, and
Applications. Committee on Information
Technology Literacy, Computer Science and
Telecommunications Board. *Being Fluent with
Information Technology.* Publication.
(Washington, D.C.: National Academy Press,
1999) *http://www.nap.edu/catalog/6482.html*

Military Briefings

This is the fourth in a series of seven lessons on communications and the first in a series of three lessons on briefings. Excellent communication skills are one of the hallmarks of good leaders. This lesson provides you with briefing definitions, concepts, and characteristics of good briefings.

The following topics are addressed in this lesson:

- Types of briefings you may hear or be expected to deliver as an officer;
- Characteristics of good briefings;
- Parts of an information briefing;
- Practical techniques for developing a briefing thesis statement;
- Preparing an information briefing; and
- Critiquing a presentation.

The following Terminal Learning Objective (TLO) is supported in whole or in part by this lesson:

- Conduct a military briefing.

Following this lesson you will be able to:

- Identify the types of briefings;
- Identify the characteristics of effective briefings;
- Identify the components of an information briefing; and
- Write an information briefing thesis statement.

BRIEFING DIRECTIONS AND SUGGESTIONS

from FM 101-5, Appendix E

The Army is effective only if information and direction are clearly communicated. As you carry out your military duties, you may frequently brief for many purposes. This Appendix gives you tips and techniques you can use as you prepare and deliver briefings. First, it is important to determine the purpose of a briefing. The following chart provides some tips on determining a briefing's purpose and the audience's probable reaction.

PURPOSE	AUDIENCE REACTION
To Inform: "My purpose is to tell you about our unit's Standard Operating Procedures (SOP)."	Make the audience aware, knowledgeable, or better informed. An audience who had been unaware of the SOPs will be informed as a result of the briefing.
To Persuade: "My purpose is to gain a decision from the commanding officer by making a recommendation to her."	Persuade the audience to accept a recommendation, act on a recommendation, or arrive at a decision. A decision-making audience will receive the facts from the briefing and will be able to make an informed decision by affirming a recommendation.

Following are the four major steps used to prepare and deliver an *information* briefing:

STEP NUMBER	DESCRIPTION
1	Analyze the situation
2	Construct the briefing
3	Deliver the briefing
4	Follow-up

Each major step has a number of substeps. The substeps for Analyze the Situation are as follows:

Step 1—Analyze the Situation	
SUBSTEP NUMBER	**DESCRIPTION**
A	Determine the purpose of the briefing
B	Obtain information about the subject
C	Write detailed notes
D	Write a thesis statement
E	Determine the setting
F	Determine the audience
G	Determine the timing constraints
H	Determine the role of the briefer

STEP ONE—ANALYZE THE SITUATION.

Research requires that you analyze your purpose, your role, and the audience's role. Is your purpose to inform, persuade, or direct? The general purpose of the briefing will provide you with a tentative focus for a thesis statement. Additional research will help you tighten the thesis.

A. ***Determine the purpose of the briefing.*** Is it an information, decision, staff, or mission briefing?

B. ***Obtain information about the subject.*** Collect everything you can find about the subject. Use public and unit libraries. Record the information and coordinate your research with subject matter experts.

C. ***Write detailed notes.*** Ensure that your notes provide sufficient detail to clarify and answer the questions the briefing must address.

D. ***Write a thesis statement.*** Use the information you have gathered to develop the main idea of the briefing into a thesis statement. Your thesis should clearly communicate what the briefing is intended to accomplish. A thesis is a simple, declarative statement that captures the common thread, the meaning, and the intent of the briefing. The thesis sentence contains a topic and your attitude about the topic. Be sure the attitude is consistent with the information you gather and that it suits your purpose and audience.

E. ***Determine the setting.*** Location and room arrangement vary widely. When necessary, make a reconnaissance of the facilities to determine how to present the briefing. Is the intended setting a large auditorium, a small room, or something in between? Find out whether you need and can get equipment, such as microphones, lectern, projection equipment, and extension cords. Will the audience sit theater style, classroom style, or around a conference table? Who needs reserved seating? You will want to rehearse at least once in the actual setting with the equipment you will be using. On site practice helps overcome jitters and unexpected problems with the stage, equipment, and visual aids.

Making a checklist of all the needed items is often helpful.

F. ***Determine the audience.*** Before briefing a superior, ask one of his/her close subordinates about the boss' major concerns and policies. Ask about minor preferences of procedure and style—whether and how to use viewgraphs, slides, "read-aheads," and how much formality is required. Considering human behavior helps you anticipate audience reaction. Consider the perspectives of audience members, their varied backgrounds, and concerns. This is particularly important when a decision maker has advisors to whom he/she will turn before making a decision or accepting information or recommendations. Also consider audience demographics—age, experience, past assignments, and education level. Demographics alone will not provide the best audience analysis. In addition, you must consider audience "psychographics"—values, opinions, attitudes, beliefs, perceptions, and prejudices. This type of analysis gives you more confidence about the expected audience reaction to the briefing.

G. ***Determine the timing constraints.*** When must you brief? How much time is allotted for the actual briefing? Are there any conflicting events? Are there any deadlines for reserving the room, equipment, or other materials? Is there a need or interest in videotaping the briefing? Will there be a review or follow-up after the event? Will an open question and answer period follow the briefing? These are some of the considerations involved in determining the amount of time necessary.

H. ***Determine the role of the briefer.*** The boss may ask you to prepare a persuasive briefing that he/she will deliver. On the other hand, you may be on a briefing team—preparing or delivering part of the presentation, or you may be coaching subordinates who will deliver the briefing. Your boss may have you prepare a briefing, and ask you to attend in the role of a subject matter expert to answer questions or help with visual aids. Asking the question, "What's my role?" early in the process allows you to restrict and focus your preparations.

Once you have thoroughly analyzed the situation, you begin constructing the briefing. The substeps for the second major element of briefing preparation, Construct the Briefing, are as follows:

Step 2—Construct the Breifing	
SUBSTEP NUMBER	**DESCRIPTION**
A	Refine the thesis statement
B	Collect any additional material
C	Know the subject
D	Isolate the key points
E	Arrange the key points in a logical order
F	Provide supporting data
G	Establish the wording
H	Prepare visual aids
I	Rehearse

STEP TWO—CONSTRUCT THE BRIEFING.

The next step in the process of developing an effective briefing is to develop a good plan. This step determines whether you have an effective organization for the briefing.

A. ***Refine the thesis statement.*** Review and refine your thesis statement to ensure it clearly expresses the purpose of the briefing.

Look directly for relevance, focus, and support in the thesis statement and indirectly look at the information it comprises. Ask yourself the following questions:

- Is the thesis statement relevant to the purpose and the audience? Does it waste the audience's time?
- Is the thesis statement focused on the topic of the briefing—not too long (won't be read) or too short (won't get the job done)?
- Is there enough information/evidence to support the thesis statement? Are relevant views and questions accounted for?

A *weak* example thesis statement is, "To inform the brigade commander about our maintenance problems."

A *strong* example thesis statement is, "The battalion maintenance problems are largely the result of inexperienced motor sergeants."

B. ***Collect any additional material.*** Gather any additional material you need to prepare the briefing. Coordinate with other subject matter experts as necessary.

C. ***Know the subject.*** Thoroughly learn your subject. Learn the subject well enough to anticipate possible problem areas and formulate answers to cover those areas in advance.

D. ***Isolate the key points.*** Aristotle noted that we prefer our ideas in threes or at least in three parts. In writing or speaking, the three parts are the introduction, the body, and the conclusion. These three parts are present in most briefings. While some might consider a conclusion redundant in a short briefing, not bringing the audience back to the thesis may result in the audience losing the idea. If the audience loses the idea, you won't communicate the message.

Divide the information into precise groups and focus on each group, one at a time, in the best order to support the thesis statement. For each major group, write a simple, declarative statement consistent with the information in that group and supportive of the thesis. You are developing a "subordinate thesis statement" for each major part.

Test and modify each trial subordinate thesis statement until it accurately represents the information in that group. Check each statement for efficiency and focus. If you find two or more ideas in one statement, break it into two statements. Eventually you will have a sentence for the thesis statement and one for each major part.

E. ***Arrange the key points in a logical order.*** List the supporting ideas in different sequences to determine what is most effective. Sometimes the topic or situation will suggest a sequence that the audience will be most receptive to or expects from you. You have choices in the manner of presentation. Following are a few possibilities:

- *Chronological order.* Describing events in time sequence.
- *Spatial arrangement.* Top to bottom, left to right.
- *Cause and effect.* Demonstrating results or origins.
- *By importance.* Open with strength or finish with climax.
- *General to specific or specific to general.*
- *Bad news first, then good; or good news first, then concession.*
- *Compare and contrast,* similarities and differences.
- *Problem and solution.*

Your audience should dictate your choice. When you have finished sequencing the major parts, check for consistency between the thesis statement and the purpose, the thesis and the audience, and the thesis and the major parts.

F. ***Provide supporting data.*** Now formulate and sort the minor parts as supporting data for the major parts of your outline. How much foundation you develop often depends upon the audience expectations. Somewhere along the path from major to minor part, you must establish a credibility point at which your audience will consider your ideas as evidence, not just opinion. Evidence is what the audience believes without the need for further analysis or support. Analysis should end only when the audience accepts your information as evidence in support of your thesis. If you

modify, move, or delete a part, retest the whole to ensure it still holds together.

G. ***Establish the wording.*** Prepare a draft briefing from your outline.

Introduction. The essential elements for an introduction include an attention-getting step, a plan for setting the stage, a thesis statement, and the major parts. You may still be unsure how to state the thesis in its most accurate and efficient form. You can finalize the thesis after you rehearse. You don't have to polish the outline, but the more information you include, the easier you will find it to rehearse because you will already have your thoughts on paper.

Body. Prepare a draft by using a tape recorder or by quickly writing out the briefing. Follow your outline to ensure you capture the important points of your briefing. Don't worry about the PERFECT word or sentence, but work on capturing the ideas. When you play back the recorder or read over the draft, you can correct word choice and sentence structure.

As ideas develop and words begin to flow, it can be easy to lose sight of the direction or the details and connections you need to make. Use the outline to keep you on course. Be flexible. A previously overlooked but relevant idea may challenge your plan. Refer to the outline and accommodate the omission. If your draft seems to consistently be going in another direction, stop drafting and refer to the outline. Spend some time getting the outline right.

Listeners, like readers, want concrete examples. They want believable assertions and assumptions. They want specific cases presented in clear, memorable language. In addition to hearing you, they want to see what you mean, have a feel for your point of view, agree with your good taste, and believe you. Therefore, use active voice verbs, precise nouns, vivid adjectives and adverbs, and just enough well-chosen illustrations to help the audience understand and remember.

Use definitions when you expect the audience to ask, "What do you mean by that?" You would rather have control of the briefing than deal with interruptions, so why not anticipate?

Examples are critical to credibility. When explained and believed, they are the foundation of evidence. Examples and illustrations are verbal pictures that hold an audience's interest. They may be factual or imaginary, but factual are always better. Some examples involve comparison and contrast—bridges between the known and the unknown. Showing a new idea's similarity to something already known often clarifies the new idea. Our comparisons, factual or imaginary, often occur as analogies.

Quotations can add variety and authority to your own words. Quotations of respected persons are often most effective to open or close speeches, but you can find suitable occasions almost anywhere. Supporting quotations ought to come from sources the audience will recognize and accept.

Statistics frequently define or verify observations. Used wisely, they can save an otherwise vague or unpopular, but valid idea. Used unwisely, they can confuse the audience or embarrass the speaker. If you use numbers, be sure to—

- Verify not just the math, but also the assumptions and the sources.
- Use only as much precision or complexity as your purpose requires.
- Explain the numbers in terms the audience will understand.
- When appropriate, depict your numbers graphically. Some people must visualize numbers to understand them.

Stating facts a second time can firmly plant ideas in the listeners' minds and are critical when you have points you want the audience to remember.

Plan the transitions carefully. Add the appropriate transitions between the major parts. Some phrases to consider as effective transitions include:

- Let me illustrate this point …
- Most importantly, we must consider …
- In the meantime, we will continue to …
- Despite those disadvantages, option three is best because …
- Now let me summarize our findings by …

Conclusion. A reader can look back in a document to refresh his/her memory, but the briefing audience has to rely on the speaker to bring him/her back to the main point. Reiterating the thesis statement and the major parts in the conclusion will leave this information fresh in the audience's mind.

H. ***Prepare visual aids.*** Using visual aids is not a requirement. However, they can help simplify complex ideas and statistics. Research studies show we retain only about 10% of what we read and 20% of what we hear. Yet when sight and sound are combined, we retain facts up to 55% longer. That is why your briefings will improve with visual support. Study your outline to determine where you need visuals to simplify or explain. When you have identified the locations, sketch the words and the layout. Next, draft, rehearse, critique, condense, and revise. As you draft each visual, keep the following in mind:

- Is it relevant? Is it necessary? Is it appropriate to the purpose and audience?
- Does it communicate one idea?
- Does it have balance and visual appeal, without becoming a distraction?
- Does the entire visual flow with parallelism, connecting words, and transitions?

Maintain consistency in type style, size, format, and borders. When generating visuals via computer, select the simplest typefaces. Use boldface type for headers. To show emphasis or contrast, use a second typeface or color.

If you need line drawings or photographs, try using cutaways or close-ups. Your audience will recognize them quicker than overall views.

Take advantage of white space to help your reader skim the visual.

Some studies have reported that using color can increase an audience's willingness to read up to 80% and accelerate recall by almost the same amount. The correct colors in a presentation help you convey the message you want. Colors and some of their uses are as follows:

- Red stimulates and is a good color to signal danger or caution.
- Blue cools, and the mind perceives it as a receding color.

- Green refreshes and makes a good background color.
- Orange activates. It has high attention value without the aggressive potential of red.
- Yellow is the subtlest highlighter and can signal caution.
- Violet subdues. Be careful—it can suggest sleepiness.
- Gray can suggest good taste and conservatism.

Pale blue, yellow, or green backgrounds are usually easier on the audience's eyes than a clear or white background.

Remember that the purpose of your visuals is to simplify information, illustrate parts and relationships, and support (not distract from) your briefing.

I. **Rehearse.** Practice the briefing. This is the step where you validate your briefing style by focusing on coherence, efficiency, tone, voice, and body language.

Develop your delivery method. Use a manuscript or note cards. You can write your briefing word for word before you practice and deliver it. The major drawback to this approach is lack of spontaneity. A better approach may be to follow your outline and make a tape or video recording to help you identify problem areas. You can also practice in front of a mirror. If you need to, transcribe the tape and polish the words and phrases as you proceed. However, you should still distill the written speech to a series of note cards with words or phrases to use as a memory jogger.

Deliver multiple practice briefings. The first run-through should not be your last one. Several rehearsals before the actual speaking occasion will help you iron out potential problems and boost your confidence.

Rehearsal allows you to hear how your words sound and how the presentation looks. Rehearsal also reduces anxiety for you and confusion and frustration for the audience. If you have developed poor preparation and delivery habits, rehearsal will allow you to pinpoint and correct the problems.

The best critique will come from discerning listeners. Get listeners who have experience and provide them with enough background to clarify your purpose and intended audience. Have them use an evaluation form as feedback. Deliver your presentation using all your props and visual aids. Speak in a conversational style. Listeners should comment on flawed or missing substance or organization, as well as the way you look, sound, and move.

Resist the temptation to memorize everything. Memorized opening and closing statements can help, but an entirely memorized speech will almost always sound stilted. If your memory lapses, your briefing will suffer. Instead, rehearse until you are comfortable with your language. You'll speak the right words without vocalizing the pauses (such as *uh, ah, umm,* etc.).

Following each rehearsal ask yourself the following questions:
- Were you comfortable with the words you chose?
- Was your voice natural?
- Did you enunciate each word clearly?
- Did you speak too fast, too slow, or at the right pace?
- Did you pause at the right place to reinforce your speech?
- Did your gestures reinforce your speech?
- Did you look at your audience?
- Was your posture appropriate to the setting?
- Did you control your nervousness?
- Did you hide behind the podium?
- Did you use your visual aids appropriately?

Once you have completed your briefing preparations, the third step is to deliver your briefing at the designated time and location. The sub-steps for the next major element of briefing preparation, Deliver the Briefing, are as follows on the next page:

Step 3—Deliver the Briefing	
SUBSTEP NUMBER	DESCRIPTION
A	Ensure audience understands the subject
B	Stay relaxed and focused
C	Enunciate clearly
D	Be concise
E	Use natural gestures and movements
F	Avoid distracting mannerisms
G	Use visuals appropriately
H	Answer questions

STEP THREE—DELIVER THE BRIEFING.

The next step in the briefing process is to deliver the briefing. The success of your briefing delivery depends on the quality of your briefing preparation.

A. ***Ensure audience understands the subject.*** Maintain eye contact with the audience. Watch their facial expressions and body language to determine whether you need to add examples or additional explanation as you proceed.

B. ***Stay relaxed and focused.*** Stage fright is common. Even long time performers and speakers have it. Exercising, breathing deeply, yawning, singing, and sipping water are ways that many speakers control their jitters.

Before beginning your briefing, sit with your feet flat on the floor—don't cross your legs. Crossing your legs is a sure way for one leg to go to sleep. When you stand up and start walking to the podium, you may stumble because one leg is asleep. Wiggle your toes just before you stand up to approach the podium. This will help get the blood flowing and prevent a lurching walk to the podium.

Make and keep eye contact with your audience. Remember, you are speaking to a group of individuals, not a blur of faces. Good speakers seek out individuals in the audience and focus their remarks to the individual. Identify friendly faces in different sections of the audience and talk to them one after the other.

C. ***Enunciate clearly.*** Keep your voice primarily in the natural range because it's easier to hear and comprehend. Avoid speaking in a lower than normal register for long periods because you could damage your vocal cords. Talk occasionally in a higher pitch to emphasize major points. When you don't have a microphone, a higher pitch will carry your voice farther. Always prepare your throat properly. Drink water, preferably with some lemon juice in it, to clear your vocal cords.

Listeners think many times faster than anyone talks. Fortunately, the goal is not to keep up with them, but to communicate and support a thesis statement. Typically, a speaking rate of 125–150 words per minute is adequate—and the larger the audience, the slower you want to speak. Audience noise and the slightly longer traveling time of your voice will swallow up a too rapidly spoken sentence. You want to develop a voice that is agile and flexible, yet not erratic in rate.

Speak clearly and distinctly. Take the time to use each new word in casual conversation until you master the enunciation of each without dropping syllables and slurring sounds.

Consider the age of your audience. You can irritate an audience older than you by frequently including youthful phrases like "you know." Your actions may even tempt some of the audience to say, "No, I don't know."

On the other hand, use nostalgia with caution whenever you speak to a younger audience. If you're not careful, you will quickly cast yourself as out of touch with current thought.

D. **Be concise.** Using the right words to accurately convey your message is important. The audience can quickly become lost if you use jargon or needlessly complex words and sentences.

Long and difficult words and phrases in a speech quickly alienate the audience. Difficult words and phrases, especially if mispronounced, focus the audience's attention on your delivery style and not on what you have to say. If you must use a difficult-to-pronounce word or phrase, practice it until it becomes natural. Where appropriate, use it in everyday conversation until it becomes natural to you. Then when you use it in your speech, it will sound natural. Also, clarify any new words or phrases that are not common to your audience.

E. *Use natural gestures and movements.* All gestures should appear natural and well-timed, and they should help the audience focus on what ought to be your primary signal—words. Keep your hand gestures above your waist. You want your audience to look at your face most of the time. If you inhibit your impulse to gesture, you may become tense and distract the audience.

Plan your body language, especially for the introduction. The first thirty seconds or so of your presentation become a lingering snapshot for the audience. Unfortunately, the first thirty seconds are also difficult because you have not yet settled down and the audience isn't wholly attentive yet.

Look at your audience when using a pointer. When using chalk, pens, and markers, don't talk to the board. Doing this muffles your voice and distracts from what you intend to communicate. Make your comments to the audience, add your markings to the board, and return to your audience. Practice this until it becomes natural.

If you conduct a briefing while seated at a conference table, maintain good posture either by keeping your spine against the back of the chair or by sitting forward in the chair and leaning slightly into the table.

When practical, move comfortably and naturally away from the lectern for a time. Then return. If you rehearse these movements, you won't be away from your notes when you need

them. You'll also prevent aimless wandering that may increase your stage fright and tires and exasperates your audience. Eliminate "happy feet," the nervousness that manifests itself in aimless pacing, swaying, and shifting. When you make planned movements, stop completely at each destination, and then speak for a while before moving again. Are you a podium rocker? The easiest solution to this problem is to eliminate the podium. However, if you need it to support your notes or props, take one step away from the podium while keeping your weight on both feet.

F. *Avoid distracting mannerisms.* Keep gestures meaningful and moderate. When using pointers, chalk, pens, and markers, put them down when not in use so you won't drop them or play with them. Rings and other jewelry can also become unconscious distracters. For informal settings, placing a hand in a pocket or putting it on one hip for a brief time could communicate an intended tone. Note the emphasis on *brief*. Any stance or position you hold too long becomes monotonous at the least, and distracting at the worst. Remove coins or keys from your pockets before you begin to resist the temptation to jingle them.

G. *Use visuals appropriately.* Allow time for an audience to look at or read the visuals before you speak. Many people experience frustration whenever they need to read and listen at the same time. Allowing silent pauses will permit your audience to absorb both the visuals and your words. The following five-step approach will help you use visuals appropriately during your briefing:
- Introduce the visual orally.
- Reveal the visual and allow time for the audience to absorb its meaning and relevance.
- Discuss how the visual supports and simplifies your idea, keeping it in sight only as long as it supports your remarks.
- Remain close to the visual during your explanation. Don't confuse the audience with competing focal points.
- Remove the visual from sight when you have finished using it.

In general, it is better to provide the audience with a copy of your visuals (if appropriate) *after,* rather than before or during your briefing. Otherwise, your audience will look through the packets during your presentation and may miss your message.

H. **Answer questions.** Develop a method of answering questions. Establish eye contact with both the questioner and the audience. Turn non-questions into questions that help achieve the objective. If someone says, "I don't think we need all this new equipment." Simply convert the remark into a question. I believe I hear you asking, "What are the benefits from purchasing this equipment?" In general, effective answers include one or more of the following:

- Your own professional and personal experience
- Quotations from experts
- Facts and comparisons
- Simplifications and examples
- Bridging responses that get back to the objective

Other tips on handling questions from the audience include the following:

- *Listen carefully to the question and repeat it aloud.* Ensure you correctly understand the question and that your audience knows the question to which you are responding.
- *Look directly at the person asking the question and answer directly.* Give simple answers to simple questions. If the question demands a lengthy reply, agree to discuss it later with anyone interested.
- *Refer to your speech.* Whenever possible, tie your answer to a point in your speech. These questions are a way to reinforce and clarify your presentation.
- *Anticipate questions.* Prepare supporting material for three or four areas in which you anticipate questions.

- *Be friendly; always keep your temper.* A cool presentation creates an atmosphere of confidence. When a hostile questioner responds, act as if he or she were a friend. Don't put down your questioner with sarcasm, as you will immediately create an atmosphere of sympathy for the questioner.
- *Always tell the truth.* If you try to bend the truth, someone will almost always catch you. Always play it straight, even when your position is momentarily weak.
- *Treat two questions from the same person as two separate questions.*
- *Don't place your hands on your hips or point at the audience.* These are scolding poses and give the appearance that you are preaching.
- *Keep things moving.* Keep your answers short and to the point, especially when many members of the audience are participating.
- *Conclude smartly.* Be prepared with some appropriate closing remarks. Conclude with a summary statement that wraps up the essential message you want your audience to remember.

Be flexible. Your listeners will react, ask questions, misunderstand, and disagree. So be prepared to handle any distraction—respond, dispel confusion, support your thesis, and proceed without obvious frustration. *And when you don't know the answer, say so!* However, tell the questioner you will get the answer and get back to him/her by a specified time. *Then do it!*

After you have delivered your briefing, the fourth and final step is to follow-up the briefing, particularly if decisions are made as a result of the briefing. The substeps for the next major element of briefing preparation, Follow-Up the Briefing, are as follows:

Step 4—Follow-Up the Briefing	
SUBSTEP NUMBER	**DESCRIPTION**
A	Prepare a Memorandum for Record (MFR)
B	Distribute the MFR

A. ***Prepare a Memorandum for Record (MFR).***
Prepare a MFR to record the subject, date,
time, and place of the briefing and ranks,
names, and positions of those present. Include
a concise record of the briefing's content. Also
record recommendations (if any) and their
approval, disapproval, or approval with modification, as well as additional directed actions. If
you have any doubt about a decision-maker's
intent, submit the MFR to him/her for
approval prior to preparing it in final form.

B. ***Distribute the MFR.*** Distribute the MFR to
staff or other agencies that must act on the
decisions or instructions or whose plans or
operations may be influenced.

Prepare a Briefing

This is the fifth in a series of seven lessons on communications and the second in a series of three lessons on briefings. This lesson requires you to practice preparation of an information briefing, while the following lesson requires them to deliver the briefing they prepared.

The following topics are addressed in this lesson:

- Major and minor points in an information briefing;
- Introduction, body and conclusion for an information briefing; and
- Preparing an information briefing.

The following Terminal Learning Objective (TLO) is supported in whole or in part by this lesson:

- Use standard Army briefing formats.

Following this lesson you will be able to:

- Identify the major and minor points for an information briefing;
- Develop an outline for an information briefing; and
- Develop an information briefing, including introduction, body, and conclusion.

Deliver a Briefing

This is the sixth in a series of seven lessons on communications, and the last in a series of three lessons on briefings. This lesson requires you to deliver an information briefing that you prepared in the previous two lessons.

The following topics are addressed in this lesson:

- Developing audiovisual aids for a briefing;
- Delivering an information briefing;
- Presentation techniques; and
    - Nonverbal communication
    - Body language (posture, facial, and vocal cues)
    - Dress cues
    - Mannerisms to avoid when communicating
    - Visual Aids
- Military bearing.

The following Terminal Learning Objective (TLO) is supported in whole or in part by this lesson:

- Conduct a Military Briefing.

Following this lesson you will be able to:

- Develop audiovisual aids for an information briefing;
- Demonstrate military bearing during briefing presentation; and
- Deliver an information briefing.

Military Writing

This is the last in a series of seven lessons on communications and the first on effective writing skills. The importance of good communications cannot be overstated, as good communication skills are a necessary component of good leadership. *Failure to communicate effectively while solving problems and while executing plans is one of the greatest obstacles to success in training and in battle. A leader's communication skills either help or hinder him/her in the use of all his/her other skills.*

The following topics are addressed in this lesson:

- Active versus passive voice;
- Common writing errors;
- Organizing ideas for written communication; and
- The Army writing style.

The following Terminal Learning Objective (TLO) is supported in whole or in part by this lesson:

- Write in the Army style.

Following this lesson you will be able to:

- Differentiate between active and passive voice and use active voice in writing;
- Identify and correct the most common writing errors; and
- Organize ideas for effective writing.

MODULE III

The Army Profession: Officership

This Officership module provides you an opportunity to conduct research in order to learn more information about the branches of the Army and its components. This valuable information will aid you in making an important career decision regarding which branch you request for your initial assignment. Following your research, you are to develop and deliver a briefing to your classmates about the assigned branch. While providing valuable information to your fellow cadets, practicing delivery of a brief also reinforces the communications concepts and techniques you learned in the previous module.

LESSON NINE

Overview of Army Branches Briefings

This is the first of a series of five lessons on the U. S. Army branches. This lesson follows and builds on lessons involving delivering briefings and writing in the Army style. The lesson also anticipates a series of lessons that focus on FM 22-100.

The following topics are addressed in this lesson:

- Army branches;
- Sources of information on Army branches;
- Developing an information briefing; and
- Delivering an information briefing.

The following Terminal Learning Objective (TLO) is supported in whole or in part by this lesson:

- Apply U.S. Army branch information to career decisions.

Following this lesson you will be able to:

- Plan a briefing of an Army Branch; and
- Research an Army Branch.

ARMY BRANCHES

A "Branch" is a grouping of officers that comprises an arm or service of the Army in which, as a minimum, officers are commissioned, assigned, developed and promoted through their company grade years. Officers are accessed into a single basic branch and will hold that branch designation, which is later augmented between the 5th and 6th years of service with a functional area. An accession branch admits officers upon commissioning; a nonaccession branch admits experienced officers from the accession branches. With the exception of Special Forces, all other branches are accession branches. Special Forces recruits officers with a minimum of 3 years experience. (See DA PAM 600-3, chapter 15 for further discussion.) Officers will serve their first 8 to 12 years developing the leadership and tactical skills associated with their branch. They will continue to wear their branch insignia throughout their military service. All career branches are in the Operations Career Field.

Assignments. Through company grade years, most officers will serve predominately in positions from within their basic branch. Some officers will serve in functional area or branch/functional area generalist positions (not related to a specific branch or functional area) after they are branch qualified as captains. Following Career Field designation, officers will be assigned to positions within their Career Field (basic branch or FA) or to generalist positions. This type of assignment pattern promotes assignment stability and development within a branch or functional area.

The following is a list of the branches DA PAM 600-3 *Commissioned Officer Development and Career Management* (Chapters 8 - 50):

BRANCH	REFERENCE
	COMBAT ARMS
Infantry (IN)	DA PAM 600-3 *Commissioned Officer Development and Career Management* Chapter 10
Armor (AR)	DA PAM 600-3 *Commissioned Officer Development and Career Management* Chapter 11 and DA PAM 600-3-12
Field Artillery (FA)	DA PAM 600-3 *Commissioned Officer Development and Career Management* Chapter 12 and DA PAM 600-3-13
Air Defense Artillery(ADA)	DA PAM 600-3 *Commissioned Officer Development and Career Management* Chapter 13 and DA PAM 600-3-14
Aviation (AV)	DA PAM 600-3 *Commissioned Officer Development and Career Management* Chapter 14 and DA PAM 600-3-15
Special Forces (SF)	(minimum of 3 years service) DA PAM 600-3 *Commissioned Officer Development and Career Management* Chapter 15
Corps of Engineers (EN)	DA PAM 600-3 *Commissioned Officer Development and Career Management* Chapter 16 and DA PAM 600-3-21
	COMBAT SUPPORT
Signal Corps (SC)	DA PAM 600-3 *Commissioned Officer Development and Career Management* Chapter 17
Military Police (MP)	DA PAM 600-3 *Commissioned Officer Development and Career Management* Chapter 18 and DA PAM 600-3-31
Military Intelligence (MI)	DA PAM 600-3 *Commissioned Officer Development and Career Management* Chapter 19 and DA PAM 600-3-35
Civil Affairs (CA) (RC Only)	DA PAM 600-3 *Commissioned Officer Development and Career Management* Chapter 20
Chemical (CM)	DA PAM 600-3 *Commissioned Officer Development and Career Management* Chapter 23 and DA PAM 600-3-74

BRANCH	REFERENCE
COMBAT SERVICE SUPPORT	
Adjutant General's Corps (AG)	DA PAM 600-3 *Commissioned Officer Development and Career Management* Chapter 21 and DA PAM 600-3-42
Finance Corps (FI)	DA PAM 600-3 *Commissioned Officer Development and Career Management* Chapter 22
Transportation Corps (TC)	DA PAM 600-3 *Commissioned Officer Development and Career Management* Chapter 24
Ordnance Corps (OD)	DA PAM 600-3 *Commissioned Officer Development and Career Management* Chapter 25
Quartermaster Corps (QM)	DA PAM 600-3 *Commissioned Officer Development and Career Management* Chapter 26 and DA PAM 600-3-92
SPECIAL BRANCHES	
JAG Corps (JA)	DA PAM 600-3 *Commissioned Officer Development and Career Management* Chapter 48
Chaplain (CH)	DA PAM 600-3 *Commissioned Officer Development and Career Management* Chapter 49
Medical Corps (MC) ■ **Dental Corps (DC)** ■ **Veterinary Corps (VC)** ■ **Medical Specialist Corps (AMSC)** ■ **Nurse Corps (AN)** ■ **Medical Service Corps (MS)**	DA PAM 600-3 *Commissioned Officer Development and Career Management* Chapter 50 and DA PAM 600-4 *AMEDD Officer Development and Career Management*

FUNCTIONAL AREAS (FOR INFORMATION ONLY)

a. Definition. A functional area is a grouping of officers by technical specialty or skill, which usually requires significant education, training and experience. An officer receives his or her functional area between the 5th and 6th years of service. Individual preference, academic background, manner of performance, training and experience, and needs of the Army are all considered during the designation process.

b. Assignments. Depending on FA educational requirements, professional timelines of the individual officer and individual preference, officers may serve in a functional area assignment during their company grade years after they have completed branch qualification longer serve in their basic branch. FA 90 positions are filled by officers from Transportation Corps (Br 88), Ordnance Corps (Br 91), Quartermaster Corps (Br 92), Aviation (AOC 15D) and Medical Service Corps (MFA 67A), all of who remain affiliated with their branch. FA 39, FA 51 and FA 90 are the only functional areas that afford command opportunity. (See their respective chapters for further discussion.)

c. Officer functional areas and codes (by Career Field).

(1) *Operations Career Field.*
  (a) Psychological Operations/Civil Affairs (39) (DA PAM 600-3, Chap. 27)
  (b) Multifunctional Logistician Program (90) (DA PAM 600-3, Chap. 28)

(2) *Institutional Support Career Field.*
  (a) Human Resource Management (43) (DA PAM 600-3, Chap. 30)
  (b) Comptroller (45) (DA PAM 600-3, Chap. 31)
  (c) Academy Professor, United States Military Academy (47) (DA PAM 600-3, Chap. 32)

(d) Operations Research/Systems Analysis (49) (DA PAM 600-3, Chap. 33)

(e) Force Management (50) (DA PAM 600-3, Chap. 34)

(f) Nuclear Research and Operations (52) (DA PAM 600-3, Chap. 35)

(g) Strategic Plans and Policy (59) (DA PAM 600-3, Chap. 36)

(3) *Information Operations Career Field.*

(a) Information Systems Engineering (24) (DA PAM 600-3, Chap. 38)

(b) Information Operations (30) (DA PAM 600-3, Chap. 39)

(c) Strategic Intelligence (34) (DA PAM 600-3, Chap. 40)

(d) Space Operations (40) (DA PAM 600-3, Chap. 41)

(e) Public Affairs (46) (DA PAM 600-3, Chap. 42)

(f) Information Systems Management (53) (DA PAM 600-3, Chap. 43)

(g) Simulations Operations (57) (DA PAM 600-3, Chap. 44)

(4) *Operational Support Career Field.*

(a) Foreign Area Officer (48) (DA PAM 600-3, Chap. 46)

(b) Army Acquisition Corps (51) (DA PAM 600-3, Chap. 47)

EFFECTIVE SPEAKING

You, the speaker, have the task of clearly communicating your message to your audience so that they understand your intention(s). There is an old saying that illustrates some of the difficulties:

You have told me that you understand what I said.

But I'm not sure that you heard what I said, because I'm not sure what I said.

Every message you send will pass through noise filters before it reaches the intended audience. Your audience will receive the "perceived message" and act accordingly. However, you will never know whether your audience received it as you intended until they give you feedback. Remember feedback always passes through noise filters before it reaches you. Considering the communication process (see fig 9.1 below), it's amazing that we communicate as well as we do.

Effective speaking, like effective writing, *requires you to use the same systematic approach and attention to detail whenever you prepare for a speaking engagement.* Like writing, you begin your speech preparation by using **critical reasoning** and **creative thinking** skills to **research** your topic. As you conduct your research you begin to develop a

plan on what you are going to say and how you will say it. Then you **draft** or **run through** your speech to ensure you include what you need to say.[1] Next, you revise and **rehearse** your speech to ensure you clearly communicate your message. Finally, you conduct **dress rehearsals (proofing)** to prepare yourself emotionally to speak before your audience.

RESEARCH

The first step in preparing to speak which is also the first step in writing is research. The research process you use in writing will also apply to preparing a speech. However, in developing a speech you need to consider additional factors. Begin by identifying the central issue of your speech (see fig 9.2). Next focus your attention on the requirement, clarify your role, identify the audience, determine the setting, and consider issues of timing.

WHAT IS THE ISSUE?

Every speaking event revolves around some issue. It could be safe driving, prevention of sexual harassment, registering voters, esprit de corps, etc. The issue provides the subject of the speech. Circling the issue are the requirements for the speaker, the speaker's role, the audience, the setting for the speech, and the factors affecting timing.

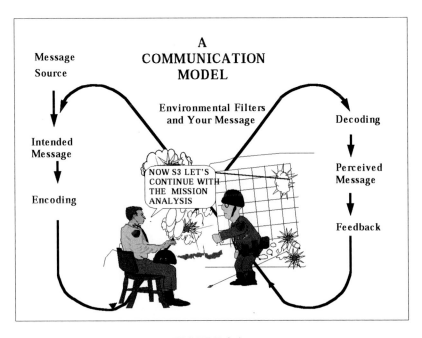

FIGURE 9.1

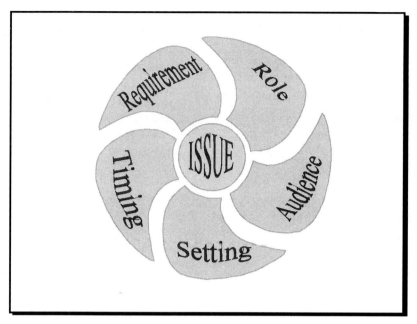

FIGURE 9.2

a. Requirement? It is very important that you understand the actual requirement, not what you think it is, before beginning to develop the speech. You have probably sat in a briefing or maybe even delivered a briefing where the boss said, "This is not what I asked for." For example, your commander assigns you the task of briefing junior officers on the benefits of effective presentations. The focus of this speech would be the benefits for the speaker and the audience. However, if you focus on the process of preparing a briefing instead of the benefits of effective presentations, you fail to fulfill the assigned requirement.

b. Role? Think for a moment about your role as a speaker. Why is it important to know what your role is? You should know if you are flying solo on this one, part of a team, or the subject matter expert. This knowledge will help focus your attention on *your* role.

c. Audience? Your first step is to determine the requirement and the audience. This information is easy to overlook as you begin preparing the speech. For example, you can prepare a very moving speech, but if it does not fit the needs of your audience, then you have failed to address what is important—their needs.

Audience analysis is critical when beginning your research. It helps you anticipate the audience's reaction and to prepare yourself to respond effectively to their feedback. The word AUDIENCE can serve as an acronym to help you identify the categories your analysis needs to consider.

- **A** analysis—Who is the audience? Who will be there? How many will be there?
- **U** nderstanding—What is it they know? What is it they need to know?
- **D** emographics—What is their age, gender education, social background, ethnic background, etc.?
- **I** nterest—Why is the audience there? Who asked them to be there?
- **E** nvironment—What can distract the audience? Where will I stand? Can they see and hear me?
- **N** eeds—What does the audience need? What are my needs?
- **C** ustomized—What specific need(s) should I address?
- **E** xpectations—What should I expect to accomplish? What do they expect from me?

d. Setting? As an instructor, you would not develop a lesson plan around viewgraph transparencies if your classroom did not have an overhead projector. Also you could not develop an effective computer aided presentation for a large audience if your equipment was only adequate for an audience of 1 to 15 members. The same is true for a speech or briefing. The size and dimensions of the room where the speech will take place are critical. Find out, for example, if you will need a sound system, lectern, projection equipment, and extension cords. What are the seating arrangements for the audience? How will this affect your delivery? Take the time to check out the location for your briefing. Knowledge of these details will help you plan for and deliver your presentation.

e. Timing? This may not seem like a very important point, but you don't want to design a 40-minute briefing for a 20-minute timeframe. Identify how much time you have to speak. Find out what else is occurring that may affect your presentation. How do these factors conflict with or support your speech? Whenever you use any special materials or equipment, you must consider how much time you need to set up and operate. Timing concerns affect the length of your speech, the resources you may want to use, and what you have to say.

In summary, speech development requires that your research starts with an issue important to your audience. Revolving around the issue are "five Ws" that you must consider.

- What is my requirement?
- What is my role?
- Who is my audience?
- What is the setting?
- What is the timing?

PLAN

Coincidentally, the second step for writing and speaking is planning. Here we will only concentrate on what's unique to speaking.

a. Beginning with the introduction, what's different about speaking than writing? The introduction is your "show time." If you have ever given a speech or taught a class, you know how important it is to get off to a strong start. There are two goals you must achieve during the introduction. First, you must gain the audience's attention. Second, you must establish credibility with the audience. Introductions are important. An introduction should smoothly lead the audience from your opening remarks into the body of the speech. In far too many speeches the introduction fails to accomplish this purpose. Remember the introduction sets the stage for everything that follows.

b. Effective writing includes forming the major and minor parts. Basically, you do the same thing for speaking. However, there are four unique differences:

(1) Plan your verbal supports. Use active verbs, precise nouns, vivid adjectives and adverbs along with well-chosen illustrations to help your audience understand and remember the speech.

(2) Design your verbal supports. If you use visual supports to reinforce your speech, you must keep in mind the following considerations:
- *Are they necessary and appropriate?*
- *Does each visual aid focus on only one idea?*
- *Does each visual aid have balance and visual appeal?*
- *Does each visual aid have coherency?*

(3) Add the transitions. Transitional words and phrases such as the following help your audience follow your argument.
- *Let me illustrate this point . . .*
- *Most importantly, we must consider . . .*
- *In the meantime, we will continue to deadline . . .*
- *In spite of these disadvantages, there are many advantages we must consider . . .*

(4) Plan the setting. Identify the equipment you need and how to arrange it.
- *Podium.*

- *Microphone and cables.*
- *Projector and extra projector bulbs.*
- *Props, displays, and handouts.*

c. Some other differences between speaking and writing include:

(1) Keep the listener in mind. You are conveying a message, not a report.

(2) Organize the speech or briefing to take the listener in one direction.

(3) Organize the speech to help the listener grasp your thoughts the first time heard.

DRAFT THE SPEECH (THE RUN THROUGH)

Whether you work from an outline or a manuscript, you must *rehearse.* This is the only way to achieve a delivery that has spontaneity, personality, and authority.

We recommend that you conduct several rehearsals after you complete the outline or manuscript and before the actual speaking occasion. Use the available resources when you rehearse. These include speaking in front of a mirror, using a tape recorder, or, better yet, a video recorder. Probably the most effective resource available is a discerning listener who will provide you appropriate and accurate feedback.

You need to pay attention during each rehearsal to the words and tone you use. Practice your gestures, voice quality, dress, and using your visual aids.

Keep your voice natural, but change pitch to emphasize important points.

Pronounce your words correctly. How you pronounce words can enhance or detract from what you are trying to say. Have someone you trust listen to your rehearsal. Ask them to identify any mispronunciations and give you honest feedback. Then practice pronouncing the words that give you difficulty. Use these words in sentences until you are pronouncing them correctly.

Enunciate your words clearly. Speak clearly and distinctly. Take the time to use each new word in casual conversation until you master the enunciation of each. With time and practice you will cease dropping syllables and slurring sounds in both casual and formal speaking situations.

REVISE

Following each rehearsal, take the time to review your speech and revise as necessary. Use the speech evaluation form to assist you with revising. Also, ask yourself the following questions:

- Were you comfortable with the words you chose? Don't use long words when one or two syllable words will do the job.
- Was your voice natural? Vocal variety is a feature of your ordinary conversations; use this variety in your speeches.
- Did you enunciate each word clearly? Do practice enunciating unfamiliar words until you are comfortable using them. Do not drop syllables and slur your words.
- Did you speak too fast, too slow, or at the right pace? Pace your delivery to your audience and material. Use a faster tempo when the material is familiar to your audience, and a slower tempo when it is new.
- Did you pause at the right places to reinforce your speech? Do pause at the end of a thought. Do not pause in the middle of a thought.
- Did your gestures reinforce your speech? Do use gestures that clarify or reinforce your ideas. Do use gestures appropriate to the audience and occasion.
- Did you look at your audience? Look your audience in the eye. Let your eyes move from person to person. Do not look over the audience's heads.
- Was your posture appropriate to the setting? Do not be informal in a formal setting. Do not be formal in an informal setting.
- Did you control your nervousness? Don't tell your audience you are nervous. Do visualize keeping your hands at your sides between gestures.
- Did you hide behind the podium? Don't hold on to the podium. Do step away from the podium while speaking.
- Did you use your visual aids appropriately? Don't read your visual aids to your audience. Do face your audience, not your visual aids, when speaking.

DRESS REHEARSAL (PROOFING)

Dress rehearsals are very important. This is as close to the real thing as you're going to get. Dress rehearsals should approximate the actual speaking situation.

Wear the clothes you'll wear during the speech. Practice your speech, whenever possible, using the equipment in the setting where you will deliver the final speech.

EVALUATION

Take a few minutes after the actual speech or briefing to evaluate what you did, how you spoke, and what happened. Record the questions and answers that followed your presentation. Write down the lessons you learned about yourself as a speaker and your audience. Be specific.

Take advantage of every opportunity to deliver speeches. Keep practicing. Keep reviewing. Always evaluate your speech, your delivery, yourself as a public speaker, and your audience.

MILITARY BRIEFING GUIDES

Following are some suggested approaches to briefings. You must determine the specific format of each briefing according to the purpose and the audience. Some briefings fit neatly into traditional formats; others do not.

We've prepared this guide to assist in preparing a briefing. These guides do not deal with mission briefings, situation briefings, command and staff briefings, or any other derivatives of the five-paragraph field order.

Ask yourself as you create a briefing, "Is this briefing to *inform* (describe facts) or *to request a decision?*"

Based on the purpose and audience, you decide how much information to include, what interpretation of facts to explain, and how to defend the recommendation.

By recognizing these different activities, you can analyze your own thinking process as you prepare each briefing. Keeping them separate in your mind will help you remember that just presenting facts is not the same as interpreting those facts. Further, correctly interpreting the problem is not the same as justifying your recommendation.

GENERIC ELEMENTS FOR ALL BRIEFINGS

a. Introduction.
   (1) Early on, if not in the first sentence, summarize the bottom line and the major parts of the briefing.
   (2) Announce the classification of your briefing. Observe security procedures when showing classified visual aids. (Skip this step for unclassified briefings.)
   (3) Open with a brief thought that is relevant to the briefing and gains the attention of the audience. (Your name and the purpose of the briefing do not accomplish this.)
   (4) Introduce yourself to the senior officer and the audience. If you employ visual aids, ensure they show the title of the briefing or summarize the bottom line and major parts or include background that doesn't delay the bottom line and major parts.

b. Development.
   (1) Cover the necessary background material. Follow an organizational plan that corresponds to your major parts and includes enough detail (not too much, not too little) to satisfy your audience. Stick to the subject.
   (2) Show how and where you got your information. If you use visual aids ensure they summarize each major part and, if appropriate, the minor parts.

c. Conclusion.
   (1) Repeat your bottom line and major parts. Conclude with a sentence that clearly shows the audience you've finished.
   (2) Ask for questions and comments.

INFORMATION BRIEF

Information briefings all include an introduction, body, and a closing. The *introduction* contains the bottom line and the major parts summed up in a few short sentences. The *body* includes the discussion of the items, actions and analysis. These help your audience to understand the information you present. The *conclusion* draws together the briefing by recapping the main ideas, making a final statement and asking for questions.

9.3

FORMAT FOR AN INFORMATION BRIEFING*

1. Introduction.
Greeting.
   Address the person(s) being briefed. Identify yourself and your organization.
   "Good morning, General Smith. I'm Captain Jones, the S3 of the 1st Bn 28th Artillery."
Type and Classification of Briefing.
   "This is a SECRET information briefing."
   "This is an UNCLASSIFIED decision briefing."
Purpose and Scope.
   Give the big picture first.
   Explain the purpose and scope of your briefing.
   "The purpose of this briefing is to bring you up to date on our battalion's General Defense Plan."
   "I will cover the battalion's action during the first 72 hours of a general alert."
Outline or Procedure.
   Briefly summarize the key points and your general approach.
   Explain any special procedures (demonstrations, displays, or tours). "During my briefing, I'll discuss the six phases
   of our plan. I'll refer to maps of our sector, and then my assistant will bring out a sand table to show you the
   expected flow of battle."
2. Body.
   Arrange the main ideas in a logical sequence.
   Use visual aids correctly to emphasize your main ideas.
Plan effective transitions from one main point to the next.
   Be prepared to answer questions at any time.
3. Closing.
   Ask for questions.
   Briefly recap your main ideas and make a concluding statement.
   Announce the next speaker.

*Department of the Army, Field Manual 101-5, *Staff Organization and Operations* (Washington, DC, 31 May 1997), E-5.

We have reproduced as figure 9.3 the format for an Information Briefing found in FM 101-5, page E-5.

DECISION BRIEF

Decision briefings, like an information briefing, include an introduction, body, and a closing. The *introduction* contains the bottom line and the major parts summed up in a few short sentences. The *body* includes the discussion of the evaluation criteria, proposed courses of action, and analysis. These help your audience to understand the proposed courses of action you present. The *conclusion* draws together the briefing by asking for and answering any questions, by showing how the courses of action rate against the evaluation criteria, restating the recommendation so that it only needs approval/disapproval, and requesting a decision.

We have reproduced as figure 9.4 the format for a Decision Briefing found in FM 101-5, page E-6.

9.4

FORMAT FOR A DECISION BRIEFING*

1. **Introduction.**
   Military Greeting.
   Statement of the type, classification, and purpose of the briefing.
   A brief statement of the problem to be resolved.
2. **Body.**
   Key facts bearing upon the problem.
   Pertinent facts that might influence the decision.
   An objective presentation of both positive and negative facts.
   Necessary assumptions made to bridge any gaps in factual data.
   Courses of Action.
   A discussion of the various options that can solve the problem.
   Analysis.
   The criteria by which you will evaluate how to solve the problem (screening and evaluation).
   A discussion of each course of action's relative advantages and disadvantages.
3. **Comparison.**
   Describe why the selected solution is best.
4. **Questions.**
5. **Restatement of the Recommendations** so that it only needs approval/disapproval.
6. **Request a decision.**

*Department of the Army, Field Manual 101-5, *Staff Organization and Operations* (Washington, DC, 31 May 1997), E-6.

SPEAKING TIPS

HANDLING NERVOUSNESS

When it comes to standing up and giving a speech, most people are nervous. It does not matter whether the speech is before a group of friends, strangers, unit members, senior leaders, or even family members—everyone gets nervous. Actors are nervous before the play begins, politicians are nervous before campaign speeches, and most ministers and priests express nervousness before delivering the weekly sermon. It is little wonder then that the average person is very nervous when called on to give a speech. Surveys indicate that 75 percent of experienced speakers encounter nervousness and stage fright before any speech. Other surveys indicate that the fear of public speaking rates higher than the fear of death or disease. It appears that nervousness or "stage fright" is perfectly normal at the beginning of a speech. In fact, it is desirable. To be nervous at the start of a speech heightens your awareness. The question is not how to remove nervousness, but how to make your nervousness work for you rather than against you. The following tips can help you use your nervousness to work for you.

a. Don't fight it. Nervousness can be like a rip tide at the beach. The more you fight it, the more it will wear you down until it finally drags you far out to sea. However, rip tides are easy to conquer. You do this by swimming across the tide instead of against it. Shortly you will be out of it and free to swim to the beach. Nervousness is the same way. Accept that nervousness is a positive experience that will heighten your senses.

b. Take a brisk walk. A brisk 5-minute walk shortly before standing up to speak gets your whole body loosened up while burning off excess nervousness.

c. Memorize your introduction. Spend time crafting your introduction so your audience clearly understands where you are going with your speech. Practice the introduction over and over so you can look at your audience and not at your notes. This will help your audience to feel that you are in control, and they will listen to what you have to say.

d. Sit with your feet flat on the floor—don't cross your legs. Crossing your legs is a sure way for one leg to go to sleep. When you stand up and start walking to the podium, you may stumble because one leg is asleep. We suggest that you wiggle your toes just before you stand up to approach the podium. This will help get the blood flowing and prevent the lurching walk to the podium.

e. Let your body relax as you wait for your introduction. This is the time to drain the tension out of your body. Relax your shoulders and let your arms dangle. Look over the audience for friendly faces you can focus on when you stand to speak.

f. Concentrate on communicating with your audience. They have come to hear you. Concentrate on what you have to tell them, not on your nervousness.

g. Breathe properly. Take a couple of breaths, exhaling slowly and deliberately before you stand up to speak. In the course of your speech don't forget to breathe. Breathing properly can help you relax and lessen your state of anxiety.

h. Tell yourself "Let's go!" You are telling yourself that it is time for your whole body to concentrate on communicating to your audience what you have spent time preparing.

i. Make and keep eye contact with your audience. Remember, you are speaking to a group of individuals, not a blur of faces. Good speakers seek out individuals in the audience and focus their remarks to the individual. Identify friendly faces in different sections of the audience and talk to them one after the other.

j. Your audience wants you to succeed. You're going to stumble as you speak. This happens to all speakers at one time or another. Take time to look at your audience. You will see and feel encouragement and acceptance from them. Just talk to the audience and they will listen to you.

WORD CHOICE AND ENUNCIATION

Long and difficult words and phrases in a speech quickly alienate the audience. Difficult words and phrases, especially mispronounced, focuses the audience's attention on your delivery style and not on what you have to say. If you must use a difficult-to-pronounce word or phrase, practice it until it becomes natural. Where appropriate, use it in everyday conversation until it becomes natural to you. Then when you use it in your speech it will sound natural. Also, clarify any new words or phrases that are not very common to your audience.

1. *Consider the age of your audience.* You can frequently irritate an audience older than you

by frequently including youthful phrases like "you know." Your actions may even tempt some of the audience to say, "No, I don't know."

2. ***On the other hand, use nostalgia with caution whenever you speak to a younger audience.*** If you're not careful, you will quickly cast yourself as out of touch with current thought.

3. ***Remember, your audience's focus is not you but their problems.*** Therefore, begin by focusing on their needs, then your words will find acceptance.

   - Apply your knowledge to address your audience's problems.
   - Draw on your own experience as it relates to your audience.
   - Dress according to your audience's expectations (e.g., formal, be formal; informal, be informal).

4. ***Don't patronize your audience, but do select your words that address their needs.*** Your audience is your partner. They will apply their own experiences to understand your words. For example, how would you describe the Grand Canyon to an engineer who had never seen it before, or tank operations to a group of women who had no understanding of the military? Your task is to make your topic understandable to your audience's experiences. An effective way is to tailor your words to your audience's understanding. You accomplish this by analyzing your audience to identify their experiences, values, interests, and any taboos that may affect your speech.

GESTURES

Gestures reflect the speaker's individual personality. What gestures are comfortable and right for you may not be right for another. The following rules apply to anyone who wants to become an influential, effective speaker.

1. ***Respond naturally to what you think, feel, and see.*** All gestures should appear natural and well timed, and they should help the audience focus on your primary message. If you inhibit your impulse to gesture, you will probably become tense which may distract the audience.

2. ***Let the content motivate your gestures.*** When you speak you must focus on communicating—not thinking about your hands.

3. ***Suit the action to the word and the occasion.*** Every gesture you make should be purposeful and reflective of your words, so the audience will note the effect and not the gesture itself. Don't overdue gesturing. This will detract from your message. Consider the age of your audience. Young audiences usually respond to speakers using vigorous gestures; on the other hand, older audiences or more conservative groups may feel threatened by vigorous gestures.

4. ***Be convincing with your gestures.*** Effective gestures are vigorous enough to be convincing, yet slow enough to be clearly visible without overpowering.

5. ***Make your gestures smooth and well timed.*** Every gesture has three parts: (1) the approach when your body begins to move in anticipation of the gesture, (2) the gesture itself, and (3) the return when your body moves back to a balanced posture. You must practice gesturing during rehearsals, but don't try to memorize every move. This will make your gestures stilted and ineffective.

6. ***Make natural, spontaneous gesturing a habit.*** Begin by looking at what you do, if anything, when you speak. A good way to do this is to videotape your rehearsals. The video camera is both truthful and unforgiving. It will capture your bad habits that you can then work at eliminating.

7. ***Use pointer, chalk, pens, and markers to reinforce.*** Look at your audience when using a pointer. When using chalk, pens, and markers, don't talk to the board. Doing this muffles your voice and distracts from what you intend to communicate. Make your comments to the audience, add your markings to the board, and return to your audience. Practice this until it becomes natural.

MOVEMENT

1. ***Oral animation keeps an audience alert and helps them focus on the right things at the right time.*** Physical animation does the same thing. In a process called "blocking," actors and singers carefully plan in advance—even

diagram—each movement from place to place. During rehearsal, they mark off the stage with pieces of tape.

Although military briefings and speeches certainly aren't performances on that level, we encourage you to plan and perhaps even block movements during rehearsal so you'll move confidently and naturally during your presentation.

When you speak from a large stage, plan some movement so people on both sides of the auditorium can see you "up close." In a smaller, more intimate setting, body movement is still important.

When practical, move comfortably and naturally away from the lectern for a time. Then return. By planning these movements, you won't be away from the notes when you need them. Even better, you'll prevent aimless wandering that often increases your stage fright and tires and exasperates your audience.

Small movements also demand attention. Eliminate "happy feet"—the nervousness that manifests itself in aimless pacing, swaying, and shifting—this can tire and exasperate the audience too. When you make planned movements, stop completely at each destination, and then speak awhile before moving again.

2. *Lecterns likewise demand your attention.* They are useful tools with only one purpose—they hold up your script. Sometimes they hold up the speaker, too. Lecterns have other built-in difficulties for speakers. When you stand behind some lecterns, all the audience can see of you is your head bobbing around like one of those ducks at a shooting gallery. Others have lights designed to illuminate your notes. Incidentally, have you ever considered what effect this has on you and your audience? To your audience you may appear in a most unflattering posture—a bobbing Frankenstein head.

"Lectern rockers" are speakers who rely on the lectern. You can imagine what you look like standing behind the lectern and holding it so tight that it begins to rock back and forth. I suspect your audience is holding its breath waiting to see if you fall into the front row.

The best speakers may stand behind the lectern for a few seconds to compose their thoughts before they move into the light.

Practice stepping away from the lectern and speaking directly to your audience. Your eye contact with the audience will improve and you will convey more confidence in your abilities as a speaker.

USING OVERHEAD TRANSPARENCIES

1. *Practice giving your presentation using your visual aids* to find out how well they project and to check for spelling errors. Have a friend sit and watch your presentation and make notes on any problems and improvements needed to your visual aids. Practice using your overhead transparencies so you will be comfortable with handling them correctly.

2. *Stand off to one side of the overhead projector while you face the audience.* Too many people stand between the overhead projector and the screen causing a shadow of the presenter's body. Standing to one side will allow the audience to see you, the presenter, and will prevent you from blocking their view of the visual aid.

3. *Do not face the "projected" image on the screen.* Face your audience and not the screen. Many presenters face the screen and end up talking to it.

4. *Right-handed speakers need to place the overhead projector to their right, and left-handed speakers need to place the overhead projector to their left.* This will make it easier for you to face your audience and write if you need to. In either case, you want to stand in the center of the speaking area.

5. *Place your overhead projector on a table low enough so it does not block you or the screen.* Have a small table next to the overhead projector so you can stack your viewgraphs before and after you use them.

6. *Tape the power cord to the floor to protect you or someone else from tripping.* As the presenter, tripping over the cord and falling, although humorous, is one gesture you would prefer to avoid.

7. *Store your overhead transparencies in a sturdy container so they will stay clean and protected.* Label the box and include a "clean" copy of your handouts. This will make it easier for you the next time you give this presentation.

THE FLIP CHART—OLD, BUT RELIABLE

Most of the presentations you will deliver are before small groups of 35 people or less; the flip chart is the perfect size for informal settings and training seminars.

There are several advantages of using a flip chart. Here are just a few:

- Flip charts do not need electricity.
- Flip charts are economical.
- You can easily add color to flip charts with inexpensive markers.
- Flip charts allow spontaneity.

Although flip charts are not today's state of the art media, they are reliable and don't require any special skill to use them. The following tips will help you use them effectively.

- Design your charts on paper before drawing them on the flip chart.
- Write in pencil before using flip chart markers.
- Follow the 7x7 rule: no more than 7 words on each line and no more than 7 lines to a sheet.
- Use flip chart markers, not regular magic markers. (Flip chart markers will not "bleed" through the paper.)
- Avoid using the colors yellow, pink, or orange, as they are hard to see.
- Avoid using too many colors per page. Recommend one dark color and one accent color.
- Keep a blank sheet of paper between each page to prevent material from other sheets "peeking through."
- Print neatly and legibly.
- Give yourself plenty of time to prepare your charts so you can review and make any needed changes or corrections.

TIPS ON HANDLING QUESTIONS FROM THE AUDIENCE

1. *Listen carefully to the question and repeat it aloud.* Ensure you correctly understand the question and that your audience knows the question to which you are responding.
2. *Look directly at the person asking the question and answer directly.* Give simple answers to simple questions. If the question demands a lengthy reply, agree to discuss it later with anyone interested.
3. *Refer to your speech.* Whenever possible, tie your answer to a point in your speech. These questions are a way to reinforce and clarify your presentation.
4. *Anticipate questions.* Prepare supporting material in three or four areas in which you anticipate questions.
5. *Be friendly; always keep your temper.* A cool presentation creates an atmosphere of confidence. When a hostile questioner responds, act as if he or she were a friend. Don't put down your questioner with sarcasm, as you will immediately create an atmosphere of sympathy for the questioner.
6. *Always tell the truth.* If you try to bend the truth, someone will almost always catch you. Always play it straight, even when your position is momentarily weak.
7. *Treat two questions from the same person as two separate questions.*
8. *Don't place your hands on your hips or point at the audience.* These are scolding poses and give the appearance that you are preaching.
9. *Keep things moving.* Keep your answers short and to the point, especially when many members of the audience are participating.
10. *Conclude smartly.* Be prepared with some appropriate closing remarks. Conclude with a summary statement that wraps up the essential message you want your audience to remember.

OTHER SPEAKING OCCASIONS

Frequently, you'll address audiences on occasions that are not briefings. You may introduce speakers, present awards, speak to the press, or speak as an instructor. Here are some general guidelines to help you through each situation.

Introducing Speakers

Your job is to prepare the audience. *Be brief and to the point.* Avoid telling a story about yourself or promoting your own philosophy. Set the stage by introducing the speaker by name (pronounced correctly—personally check with the individual beforehand). Then announce the topic, its importance, and the speaker's qualifications to talk on the subject.

In military settings, it's common to enumerate a speaker's past jobs. Be creative with those stuffy laundry lists. Tell a story about one of the jobs that has some bearing on the speaker's topic.

Where do you get such tidbits? They're rarely in the provided biography sheets. Your best bet is to talk to the speaker or a colleague.

When telling any story, though, keep in mind your goal—to smooth the speaker's entrance. An irrelevant or embarrassing story won't do that.

Here are two other things to avoid. First, don't delay your announcement of the speaker's name unless surprise is really important. Second, don't steal the speaker's thunder by summarizing the speech's major parts or telling the speaker's favorite joke.

Following the speech, it's often appropriate for you as the one making introductions to express appreciation for the audience. Be sincere and brief.

Making An Announcement

Announcements should be simple presentations. You may use humor or visuals to help listeners remember, but keep the message brief. In *How to Speak Like a Pro*, Leon Fletcher suggests a basic outline that may be helpful in your next announcement.

    Introduction
        —Attention-getter
        —Preview
    Discussion [Development]
        —Name of event
        —Date and day
        —Time
        —Location
        —Cost
        —Special features
        —Importance
    Other necessary details
    Conclusion
        —Recap
        —Memorable statement

Presenting Awards

The award ceremony honors someone in the presence of friends and colleagues. Your role is to keep the focus where it belongs—on the recipient. After a brief attention step, explain why the award exists and name some previous winners. Then praise the new winner in credible terms and invite him or her to speak.

Resist using this occasion for unrelated ideas of your own. Let the recipient have the spotlight.

Receiving Awards

We often joke about the long-winded acceptance speech, but almost never hear one. Unless you're the famous exception, take time to fully thank the person who presents the award and those who have helped you earn it. Relate some personal experience or plan for the future that helps people share in your happiness.

Avoid the extreme *"I-don't-deserve-this"* approach that leaves an audience ill at ease. They need some reassurance from you that the ceremony has been worth their trouble. Enjoy for them your moment in the limelight.

Impromptu Speaking

Effective ad-libbing comes naturally for only a few people. The rest of us need much trial and error to overcome anxiety, think quickly on our feet, clearly express ourselves, and then know when to stop.

Normally, you'll speak impromptu only on topics you know something about: for example, in a meeting when the boss asks a question in your area of expertise. To answer effectively, listen carefully so that you'll understand both the question and the questioner.

If the situation allows, plan your answer by writing a short list of phrases responding to the question. Draft your answer mentally and revise the list as appropriate. Plan mentally a thesis statement and two to three major points, and deliver your answer with the thesis statement up front.

If you have to answer immediately, but don't yet know exactly what to say, repeat the question aloud in your own words. That will confirm whether you understand the question and allow some time to mentally research an answer.

Always close your impromptu remarks with a return to your controlling idea, remembering not to leave a "so what" in the mind of your audience. Then stop talking. Don't ramble on with more and more details just because everyone is listening.

Speaking to the Media

All of us (Army, Air Force, Marine, and Naval officers; NCOs; enlisteds; or DOD civilians) are always ambassadors for the military. Our speech and our actions reflect on the military. This is especially true whenever we talk with the media. We must remember that as ambassadors we represent our service to the media and the civilian community. We have provided the following guidelines to assist you whenever you comment to the media on the military.

When approached by the media to comment as a spokesperson for your service on any subject, your first question should be, "Have you coordinated this request with the public affairs officer (PAO)?" Even the most innocent-appearing request can backfire, causing you and the military embarrassment. Regardless of the reporter's answer, always solicit and follow your PAO's advice before proceeding with an interview.

Ask the reporter to define the topic clearly. Ask whether the interview will be "live" or taped in a studio, your office, or elsewhere. Then ask your PAO to help you prepare, which may include rehearsing with potential questions. The PAO can play the reporter's part and assist you on ways to respond most effectively.

During your consultation with the PAO, you can plan how to deal with difficult questions. "No comment" is never appropriate. When information is sensitive, classified, or you just don't know the answer, say that. Most reporters appreciate and deserve that kind of honesty. If a question goes beyond the agreed topic, say that—and terminate the interview when a reporter persists.

Most reporters enter an interview with specific goals in mind. You should, too. Here's your chance to tell the military story accurately and forcefully. If necessary, write out and study the points so you'll clearly implant them when the opportunity occurs.

Speaking as an Instructor

During your military career, you'll often teach by focusing and shaping complex ideas and skills for your peers and subordinates. Teaching needs more preparation than just briefing or lecturing. Your students will have to demonstrate understanding; they will question you more frequently and deeply. The following tips will help you prepare yourself to teach.

- Be in control, yet demonstrate willingness for give-and-take.
- With an enthusiastic, conversational style, communicate your personal interest in the subject and in each student individually.
- Use examples that relate to your students' lives here and now.
- Maintain your credibility; know your subject.

Branches II–V

Lessons ten through thirteen are designed for you to research your career choices leading to more informed decisions. Since each of the branches is presented, you will acquire the basis for comparing branches while at the same time practicing briefing skills.

The following topics are addressed in these lessons:

- Army branches;
- Sources of information on Army branches;
- Developing an information briefing; and
- Delivering an information briefing.

The following Terminal Learning Objective (TLO) is supported in whole or in part by these lessons:

- Apply U.S. Army branch information to career decisions.

Following these lessons you will be able to:

- Deliver a briefing on an Army branch;
- Describe the key characteristics of Army branches; and
- Make a career choice.

MODULE IV

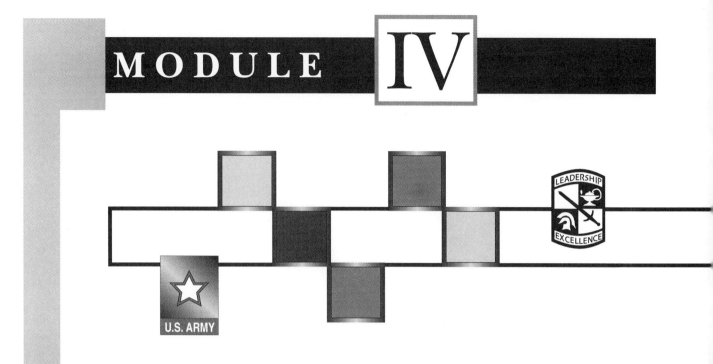

Values and Ethics

This module complements officership, leadership, and problem solving lessons addressed earlier in this academic year. The primary objectives of values and ethics instruction are to convey to you an understanding of the relationship between the fundamental values of our nation and those of the Army; to facilitate the internalization of Army values; to produce an awareness of the moral leadership responsibilities of officers; increase your understanding of the Army's consideration of others policies and expectations; and to improve your ability to recognize and resolve ethical problems. This module focuses on developing your knowledge and understanding of what it means to be a professional military officer. The module also highlights the critical role ethics plays in the daily exercise of command and leadership.

National and Army Values

This is the first of ten lessons that focus on values, ethics, ethical decision-making, consideration of others, and spiritual needs. This lesson focuses on the Army's seven values: 1) Loyalty; 2) Duty; 3) Respect; 4) Selfless-Service; 5) Honor; 6) Integrity; and 7) Personal Courage. The lesson provides a hands-on exercise to help you recognize the source of the Army's values

The following topics are addressed in this lesson:

- National values and their implications for officers;
- Sources of national values;
- Army values and the linkage to national values;
- Importance of living Army values;
- Values-based organizations; and
- How Army values can be internalized by cadets.

The following Terminal Learning Objective (TLO) is supported in whole or in part by this lesson:

- Understand and Live Army Values.

Following this lesson you will be able to:

- Describe the source of National Values;
- Identify and define Army values;
- Relate Army values to national values; and
- Recognize the importance of a values-based organization.

Moral Leadership

This is the second in a series of two lessons on Army Values. You will examine how an understanding of Army values helps define an effective climate of moral leadership.

The following topics are addressed in this lesson:

- Army values;
- Moral leadership;
- Identification of legal and moral issues in a situation; and
- Application of values in leadership for the resolution of legal and moral decisions.

The following Terminal Learning Objective (TLO) is supported in whole or in part by this lesson:

- Identify National and Army values and obligations.

Following this lesson you will be able to:
- Explain how national, Army, and individual values help influence the professional obligations of a US Army officer;
- Identify factors that may affect one's ability to solve moral dilemmas; and
- Analyze the merits of Army values during moral dilemma problem solving.

DECISION IN KOREA

by Henry J. Meihafer

On Saturday, June 24, 1950, things were quiet in the nation's capital. President Truman, in fact, had gone home to Missouri for the weekend. On that same day in South Korea, members of the American mission, both military and civilian, were relaxing in the sun; in the afternoon some even went by rail to a tiny beach resort a few of them were building into a vacation spa.

Later that day in Japan, the officers' club in Kokura held a costume party. The commander of the U.S. 24th Infantry Division, Major General William F. Dean, came as a Korean elder, or *yang-ban;* his wife, Mildred, was dressed as a proper Korean lady. Everyone enjoyed seeing their hardworking boss in a playful mood. Dean himself, however, thought he looked a bit ridiculous in his long white robe and black stovepipe hat, souvenirs from his time as deputy commander of Korean occupation forces. Still, it was all in fun.

Bill Dean, six feet tall, 210 pounds, a self-proclaimed physical fitness nut with a bristling crew cut, was a month shy of his fifty-first birthday. He was known as a bluff, no-nonsense, "can-do" career soldier, an ROTC graduate who had little use for hypocrisy or showmanship. In the years preceding World War II, he had climbed slowly but steadily up the military career ladder. He had then performed with distinction during the war itself, and in the war's final stages he had commanded the U.S. 44th Infantry Division during tough fighting in southern Germany.

Now, in his present peacetime assignment, he was doing his best to bring the U.S. 24th Infantry "Taro Leaf" Division up to speed. It wasn't easy. In Japan's comfortable, relaxed atmosphere, it was almost impossible to keep men charged up. Moreover, peacetime economies, reflecting general U.S. complacency, forced him to operate at greatly reduced strength and with inferior equipment. His infantry regiments, for example, had but two battalions instead of three. Similarly, everything else was at two-thirds capacity or less. Still, Bill Dean did his best with what he had. His men trained hard, and even had he known what lay just ahead, there wasn't much he could have done differently.

On Sunday morning, June 25, after attending church, General Dean headed for the post office near his division headquarters building. Maybe there'd be some mail waiting for him, possibly a letter from his son, Bill, or his daughter, June. Bill was taking the West Point entrance examinations; June was en route to Puerto Rico with her husband, an army captain.

A duty officer, looking rather excited and waving a message, caught up with him. North Korean forces were reported to have crossed the 38th Parallel—it might be a full-scale invasion! A thought flashed across Dean's mind: Was this the beginning of World War III?

For a time, as information trickled in, it looked as though the South Korean army, said to be counterattacking, might have the situation contained. Dean asked MacArthur's headquarters about the South Korean officers now training with the 24th Division in Japan. Should they return home at once? No, he was told, have them complete their training; also, prepare to receive another group in July. Evidently higher-ups expected this to be a short war.

Within days, they learned that initial reports had been wrong. The South Korean army, after a brave initial resistance, was now being overwhelmed. Dispirited South Korean soldiers were straggling into Seoul, and American civilians were being evacuated.

At the United Nations, upon orders from President Harry Truman, U.S. Ambassador Warren Austin recommended to the Security Council that "Members of the United Nations furnish such assistance to the Republic of Korea as may be necessary to repel the armed attack and to restore international peace and security in the area." The motion was carried; fortunately the Soviet Union's representative, Jacob Malik, did not attend the meeting. If he had, he might well have exercised his right to veto.

President Truman made the crucial decision to commit U.S. forces. Within hours, American planes were flying support missions. A serious Bill Dean, summoned to a hastily called meeting in Tokyo, started out by sedan but was halted en route. Orders had been changed: He was now to go back to Kokura and await teletyped instructions.

The message came in around midnight. Dean read that his 24th Division had been selected to provide the first American combat troops for Korea. One battalion should head there as soon as possible. Dean himself was also to go, and once there, he'd assume two jobs—as overall U.S. ground commander and as commander of his own 24th Division.

Bill Dean, a skilled professional, was well aware that his division was in no way prepared for combat. Nevertheless, the 24th was probably as good or better than anything else MacArthur had available. Dean called Colonel Richard Stephens, commander of the 21st Infantry Regiment, and told him to put together a battalion task force and select someone to lead it. Stephens, in turn, called on thirty-four year-old Lieutenant Colonel Brad Smith.

Military air transport was limited, so initially Smith's force would consist of just two rifle companies and one artillery battery. They'd go at once by air and report to Brigadier General John Church, who was already on the ground with a small detachment. The remainder of the division would follow as soon as possible by surface transportation.

At 3 A.M. on July 1, Smith's group, mounted in trucks, rode the seventy-five miles from Camp Wood to the air base at Itazuke. General Dean was there to meet them. As transport planes warmed up, Dean told Smith, "When you get to Pusan, head for Taejon. We want to stop the North Koreans as far from Pusan as we can. Block the main road as far north as possible. Contact General Church. If you can't locate him, go to Taejon and beyond if you can. Sorry I can't give you more information. That's all I've got. Good luck to you, and God bless you and your men."

Smith and his group landed in Korea and headed north. Next day, more of Dean's 24th Division began to arrive. As each contingent made its way through Pusan, people lined the streets, laughing, waving, and cheering them on. A band played and the mood was festive; flags, banners, and streamers were everywhere. The prevailing attitude seemed to be that the Americans had landed and would soon have the situation well in hand.

Dean himself started out on July 2, aboard a four-engine C-54, which also carried a jeep and several members of his staff. Once over Pusan, however, they learned the mud airstrip had been torn up so badly that no more big planes could land. Back in Japan, they transferred to a smaller C-45 and started out again. This time they landed successfully at Pusan and, after a brief stop, took off for Taejon so Dean could assume command. It was nearly dark when they arrived over Taejon, and the pilot, after seeing the small unlighted field, just shook his head. Back they went to Itazuke Air Base

in Japan. After a quick meal and about three hours' sleep, they again took off.

This time they found their destination socked in. Fog covered the whole area, and they couldn't even see Taejon. "But I was desperate," Dean later wrote, "so we finally flew out over the Yellow Sea, bored down through the fog bank, then came back east, following the Kum River line and dodging mountains under the high fog, and eventually landed. I never thought I'd have so much trouble in getting to a war!"

Task Force Smith, meanwhile, had moved north and taken up positions near Osan. Many people at this point, both in Korea and in the States, felt a mere American show of force would be enough to turn the tide. Surely the North Koreans, once they learned America had joined the fight, would stop their aggression and head home.

Dean, beginning to operate from his headquarters in Taejon, next sent elements of his newly arrived 34th Infantry Regiment to blocking positions near Pyongtaek, a few miles south of Smith's men at Osan.

On the morning of July 5, at Osan, Brad Smith spotted a Korean tank column heading his way. Recoilless-rifle and rocket-launcher "bazooka" teams coolly held their fire. Then, as the lead tank closed to within range, Smith gave the word to open up. Several direct hits were made, but to the Americans' horror, the rounds bounced harmlessly off the thick armor plate of the Soviet-made T 34s. When the tanks came abreast of Smith's position, they began firing their cannons and machine guns, thereby inflicting the first American casualties of the war. The tanks, seemingly undamaged, then kept moving south.

An hour later, more tanks arrived, this time accompanied by a long truck convoy carrying North Korean infantry. Smith's men opened up with everything they had: Mortar shells landed among the trucks; machine-gun bullets raked the column; trucks burst into flames; men were blown into the air. However, as other troops arrived on the scene—a full two regiments, as it turned out—Smith saw hundreds of men maneuvering so as to surround and cut off the Americans.

Reluctantly, Brad Smith gave the order to withdraw. Within moments the situation became chaotic. Abandoning the position, men fled in confusion.

The first tanks, meanwhile, had continued to advance and, a mile farther on, had overrun the supporting artillery battery. Adding to the problem, tank treads had torn up the signal wire that had been laid, effectively cutting off U.S. communications.

Bill Dean knew something bad had happened, but there was no way of telling *how* bad. Even though it was dark by this time, he started forward by jeep. At Pyongtaek, finding there was no word from Smith, he realized that the first American contact with the enemy had resulted in disaster.

Next day the 34th Infantry's position at Pyongtaek, which Dean had considered crucial, was also abandoned. The situation was deteriorating rapidly, and to Dean's mind some of the Pyongtaek problem had been caused by poor leadership.

On July 7, Dean gave command of the 34th Infantry to an old friend, Colonel Bob Martin. He and Martin had been together in Europe, and as soon as he'd received orders to go to Korea, he'd asked for Martin by name. GHQ, in turn, had released Martin from his staff assignment and made him available to the 24th Division. With the capable Bob Martin on board, Bill Dean felt he could breathe a little more easily. The two understood each other, liked each other, and when they'd been together in combat previously, it had been almost as though Martin could read Dean's mind and anticipate what he wanted. Under Martin, the 34th Infantry took up position near the town of Chonan.

Next day, the Eighth Army's new commander, stocky, pugnacious Walton Walker, arrived on the scene. That was good news; now Dean, relieved of the overall responsibility, could concentrate on his own 24th Division. Meanwhile, another report had been received. Intense fighting was under way near Chonan; Colonel Martin had gone forward to take personal charge of the situation. Walker and Dean went to see for themselves. South of Chonan, they watched the action from a hillside observation post. It appeared the Americans were falling back. Just then a breathless, sweating officer arrived with heartbreaking news.

Scrappy Bob Martin had been caught in Chonan as enemy troops and tanks entered the town. Rather than retreating, he had obtained a rocket launcher and posted himself in a house on the main street. An enemy tank had driven up; Martin, aiming the rocket launcher, had prepared to fire. As he did so, the tank's cannon had blasted away pointblank, cutting Martin in half.

For Bill Dean, it was a wrenching moment, both personally and professionally. Still, with the situation worsening, he had little time to mourn the loss of his friend. Other troops were arriving and new missions had to be assigned. Trying to stem the enemy advance, Dean ordered Colonel Richard Stephens to deploy his 21st Infantry Regiment in a blocking position near Chochiwon.

The last of the 24th Division regiments to arrive in Korea was the 19th, the "Rock of Chickamauga." In a way, they had a special place in Dean's heart. In the mid-1930s, as a young captain, he'd served with the "Chicks" in Hawaii. Now, still hoping to establish a firm line, he told his old regiment to set up and dig in along the Kum River.

By this time, the main 24th Division headquarters was back at Yongdong. Dean himself, however, with a small group, remained at Taejon in the schoolhouse serving as the 34th Infantry's command post. Some might have argued that Taejon was no place for a division commander. Later, Dean himself wondered if it was a mistake. At the time, though, he felt his big problem was communication. If he'd been in touch, perhaps the position at Pyongtaek would not have been given up so readily. He'd always been a hands-on kind of leader, one who felt that only by being up front, close to the action, could you make timely decisions in a fast-moving situation. For now, Dean and his aide, Lieutenant Arthur Clark, threw their sleeping bags on the schoolhouse floor and tried to catch a bit of rest. Dean felt confident that General Pearson Menoher, his capable assistant division commander, could run things back at Yongdong.

By 6:30 next morning, July 20, Dean was awake and hearing sporadic gunfire. Clark told him enemy tanks had already been sighted entering Taejon. As Dean later wrote: "There was only one difference between this report and many previous ones like it—this time there were no immediate decisions to be made, for the moment no general officer's work to be done." What should he do, then? Well, he wasn't about to turn tail and run; that surely wouldn't do the soldiers' morale much good. Moreover, if there *were* tanks in the town, maybe he could take a personal hand and hunt one down.

The Americans heard that a lone tank was parked at an intersection in the town's business area. Dean and his small group, along with a soldier carrying a bazooka, headed in that direction. Soon they came under rifle fire from snipers accompanying the tank. They returned the fire, probably knocking out one or more snipers, and kept going. Dean and the soldier with the bazooka went through one of the buildings on the main street and came out onto a rear courtyard. After circling, they entered the building closest to the tank. To get upstairs from the courtyard, Dean and the soldier chinned themselves on a window ledge, then climbed inside. Cautiously, Dean looked out a window, directly into the muzzle of a tank cannon no more than a dozen feet away.

Motioning to the bazooka man, Dean pointed to a spot at the base of the cannon where the turret joined the tank's main body. The bazooka fired, and screams could be heard coming from inside the tank. "Hit them again!" Dean yelled. Again the bazooka fired, the screaming stopped, and the street grew quiet.

By this time it was evident that Taejon could not be held Enemy soldiers were throughout the town; to the south, other North Koreans were already starting to block the exit roads. Dean returned to the schoolhouse and gave orders for the 34th Infantry to start withdrawing. Even so, he knew they'd have to fight their way out.

A terse message was sent to headquarters: "Enemy roadblock eastern exit Taejon. Send armor immediately. Dean." With grim humor, he later said that if he'd known this would be his last official communication, he'd have tried to say something more memorable and dramatic.

A group of vehicles was organized into a rough convoy. Outside town, they ran into the tail of a previous column that had been ambushed. Trucks were on fire; streets were blocked; rifle fire poured from the buildings on both sides. Dean's jeep, and the escort vehicle following it, turned onto a secondary road, bypassing the stalled trucks. Soon they came upon wounded men on foot; they piled as many as possible into the two jeeps. Unhappily, they soon hit yet another roadblock. As machine gun fire swept the road, everyone dove into a ditch and tried to crawl to safety.

After dark, and on foot, the little group—more than a dozen strong by this time—began working their way south along a ridge. It was slow going, especially since one of the men was badly wounded. Dean, ignoring his general's "dignity" and forgetting his fifty-one-year-old legs, tried to carry the wounded man by himself. He was soon too exhausted to maintain the solo effort, but continued to take his turn of a two-man carry. Finally the group halted, and in the darkness, weary men slumped to the ground. The man they were carrying, delirious, had drunk all available water and was calling for more.

Around midnight, Dean thought he heard water running just off the ridge to one side. He started in that direction, and before he knew it, he was stumbling headlong down a steep slope and couldn't stop. He tripped, fell, and lay unconscious.

The Americans, now led by Lieutenant Clark, started out again, and in the darkness didn't realize the general was missing. When they did, they turned back and waited, hoping he'd return. Finally, after several hours, they decided it was no use and went on.

When Dean finally came to, he had no idea how long he'd been knocked out. There was a deep gash in his head, and when he tried to raise himself onto his hands and knees, he realized he had a broken shoulder. Bit by bit, he began crawling up the tricky slope that had been his undoing, but before long he passed out again. When he came to this time, it was just beginning to get light. A North Korean patrol was moving along the ridge, just a few feet away. How they missed him he'd never know.

Walking, staggering, sometimes crawling on all fours, he tried working his way south. He was thirsty, hungry, and suffering constant pain, which often made him semi-delirious. Over and over he kept telling himself he must never, under any circumstances, allow himself to be captured. With a general officer as prisoner, the Communists would have a field day, might even try to convince the world Dean had "seen the light" and gone over willingly.

Some time later, he saw another American lurching along. "Who are you?" Dean said. "What outfit are you from?"

"I'm Lieutenant Tabor—Stanley Tabor—from the 19th Infantry. Who are you?"

"Well," said Dean, "I'm the S.O.B. who's the cause of all this trouble." With Tabor's help, Dean kept going, slowly and painfully. Frequently he told Tabor to go on ahead and save himself, but Tabor always refused, saying two together had a better chance. About three days later, they met two Korean civilians who spoke a little English; they gave the Americans food and led them to a hut where they could rest. Thankfully, the two took off their boots, relaxed, and were soon asleep.

Suddenly a rifle shot rang out in the night air. They had been betrayed! Dean and labor, instantly awake, heard a voice call out in surprisingly good English: "Come out, Americans! Come out! We will not kill you. We are members of the People's Army. We will not kill you."

"Come on," said Dean. "Get your boots on in a hurry. I'm not going to surrender, Tabor. There'll be no surrender for me."

"That's the way I feel too," said Tabor. The two Americans slipped out a back door and began crawling away through thick weeds that offered some concealment. As shots were fired in their general direction, they reversed their course, going back through the village, then through a series of rice paddies. With Dean leading the way, they crawled snakelike through shallow paddy water. At the end of each paddy section, they inched their way carefully over low intervening dikes.

After traversing one of the fields, Dean looked back and called softly for Tabor. There was no reply. Somehow the two had become separated in the darkness. Bill Dean would not see another American for the next three years. (The gallant Tabor, who had refused to abandon Dean and go on alone, was eventually captured. He later died in prison camp.)

Dean, mostly hiding by day and traveling at night, somehow managed to avoid the enemy for a total of thirty-five days. It was a remarkable display of courage and willpower. At times he was given food by friendly Koreans; more often they ignored him; and more often yet, people gave the alarm, called out the home guard, and tried to seize him. Each time, he managed to escape. As the days went by, however, his injuries, plus the lack of food, made him increasingly weak.

On the thirty-fifth day, he met two men who offered to guide him to a place where he could be sheltered and fed. It was a trap. As they neared a village, Dean was surrounded by about fifteen men. He tried to pull his pistol, but as he did so, one of the men grabbed his arm and wrestled him to the ground.

"This is it," thought Dean, still determined not to be taken alive. "Shoot! Shoot, you sons of bitches! Shoot!" Instead, his arms were twisted and tied behind his back. He tried to run, hoping they would kill him, but in his condition, he was able only to stumble a short distance. Someone shoved him from behind and he fell on his face in the dust. Everyone

laughed. By this time his shoulder hurt unmercifully. The greatest pain, however, came from knowing that, despite his best efforts, he was now a prisoner.

For the next several weeks, and as his identity became known, Dean was moved from place to place and subjected to a series of interrogations. He refused to cooperate, steadfastly refusing to sign anything or to go on the radio, even to tell his family he was safe.

Over and over, he was asked why he had come to Korea, and each time he would infuriate his questioner by saying he had come so as to help South Korea repel the illegal aggressors from the north. Mostly, though, he thought the questions were rather stupid, as when the interrogators asked about the South Korean army's defense plans, which by this time were hardly relevant. On matters of any significance, such as infantry tactics or organization, or the defense plans for Japan, he simply refused to answer.

If he'd only cooperate, one officer told him, by admitting the merits of communism and the evils of American policy, they would then leave him alone. Finally the officer gave up, saying: "General, you're a brave man, but you're very ignorant politically!"

He was passed from one captor to another, always closely guarded, at first retracing his way through Taejon and Osan, then continuing farther north, through Seoul and on into North Korea, passing through the capital city of Pyongyang. So far the treatment had been crude and uncomfortable, with little consideration for health or living conditions. However, there had been no outright cruelty. Then, a few weeks later, when he was given over to an unpleasant North Korean colonel named Kim, things changed dramatically.

At first Kim was rather friendly, even kind, and seemingly interested in Dean's welfare as he produced documents for the prisoner to sign. They were all of a type: a request for the misguided Americans to stop fighting; a letter thanking the North Koreans for their kind treatment of prisoners; another letter blaming the South Koreans, especially the "no-good crook" Syngman Rhee, for starting the war. When Dean refused to comply, the mood changed abruptly.

"These statements," said Kim, "are my minimum requests. If you sign these, you won't be tortured." As Dean stood firm, Kim grew increasingly hostile. In session after session, the questioning continued for hours on end even when Kim paused,

Dean usually was unable to rest. Often he would be awakened in the middle of the night and taken to an interrogation room, where Kim insulted him, threatened him, and told him that he'd never yet failed to get what he wanted from a prisoner, even "ones tougher than you."

After the American landing at Inchon, of which Dean was unaware, Kim and his henchmen grew even worse. Once, for example, Dean was made to sit in a straight chair and face three different questioners, Kim plus Lieutenant Colonels Choi and Hong. They took turns, spelling each other when one grew tired. The first questioner was Choi, who asked for military information that Dean didn't have and wouldn't have given if he did have.

How many airfields were in Japan? How did planes home in on a target? Was the United States going to use the atomic bomb? When Dean protested, saying that under the Geneva Convention he could be asked only his name, rank, and serial number, he was told the Convention didn't apply. Dean, they said, was a war criminal, and therefore considered a special case.

This particular session had started around nine in the morning, being interrupted only for food and for frequent dashes to the latrine because of Dean's dysentery. On and on it went, even as day turned into night. In the early-morning hours, Kim became aware that Dean's teeth were chattering.

"What are you shivering for, making your teeth go that way? Are you cold?"

"Yes, I'm a little chilly."

"This isn't cold," said Kim. "Take off your coat. Take off your shirt. Take off your trousers and your undershirt. I'll show you what it means to be cold."

Although the room temperature was near freezing, Dean was made to strip to his undershorts. At one point, the frustrated Colonel Kim threatened to have Dean's tongue cut out, to which Dean replied: "Go ahead and cut it out. Then you won't be able to make me talk." That was the end of that particular threat.

Finally Kim called a temporary halt, after using the last hour to harangue his prisoner, telling Dean that since he wouldn't cooperate, he was a dog and a robber, and would therefore be treated like a dog. "No more washing. You can't wash, you dog! You can have one blanket and sleep over there in a corner on the floor. . . . You want to remember that it's getting colder. If you fail to cooperate, we not only

won't give you any clothes, we'll keep you outdoors."

Dean was allowed to sleep on the floor for a few hours; then the ordeal started again, with the three interrogators, Kim, Hong, and Choi, taking turns. Dean, forced to stay awake and respond, answered mechanically and unemotionally. Once, however, he lost his composure when Kim started to rant about American planes killing innocent people.

"Listen," said Dean, "I've seen atrocities committed by your troops worse than anything you've mentioned! At Chochiwon, I saw men murdered in cold blood while they had their hands tied behind them. And I talked to a lieutenant who saw your men drive prisoners ahead of them, to try to get others to surrender—then shoot them when we opened fire to repel an attack."

Kim became so angry that he yelled: "Close your eyes! I'm going to spit in your face!"

"Go ahead and spit," said Dean. "You've been spitting in my eyes for the last half-hour!"

"All right," said Kim. "This is the end. We're going to torture you." He then went on to describe certain ghastly measures, including the driving of bamboo splinters under the fingernails and then setting fire to them. Another possibility was to force water into the body through the rectum, causing, in Kim's words, "everything in you, everything, to come out through your mouth. It's very sickening."

Dean said: "That sounds good to me. The shape I'm in, you won't have to use much pressure. I think that'll kill me quickly. That sounds all right."

After more of this, Kim said Dean would be taken to the torture building early the next morning. "Under torture," said Kim, "you will probably die, but not before you've given us the information we want." He then asked Dean if he wanted to write a last message.

At first Dean declined the offer; then he changed his mind. "Okay," he said, "I'll write a last letter to my family." They gave him a pencil and paper, and he proceeded to write:

> Dear Mildred, June, and Bill, I was physically captured on 25 August and have been a prisoner of war ever since. I did not surrender but was physically overpowered. Before I was captured I wandered in the hills for 35 days without food. As a result I am terribly ill and do not think I will live much longer. Therefore this is my last

letter. June, do not delay in making your mother a grandmother. Bill, remember that integrity is the most important thing of all. Let that always be your aim. Mildred, remember that for 24 years you have made me very, very happy.

That was all. Kim, reading the message, was puzzled. Why did Dean say he was ill? Why not say he was about to be executed? Didn't Dean realize they could now kill him without being blamed?

"You dumb bastard!" said Dean, who explained, as to an idiot, that he'd written it not for Kim, but for his own family, and he wanted them to receive it. If he'd said he was about to be killed, obviously the letter would never be sent. Kim stomped out, after promising to see Dean in the morning at the torture chamber.

Dean now realized they intended to torture him until he was dead. Was this willingness to let prisoners die, or to kill them outright, part of a pattern? Unfortunately it was. Up to this point, the enemy, realizing the value of an important POW as a possible bargaining chip, had made an effort to keep their high-ranking prisoner alive. For other POWs, however, there were no such compunctions, either then or later.

By the time truce talks began, for example, the South Koreans carried over 88,000 men missing in action and the United States more than 11,500. The Communists, however, who had earlier claimed via news releases and radio broadcasts to have taken more than 65,000 prisoners, said they held only 7,142 South Koreans and 3,198 Americans. Obviously the vast majority of those captured died while in enemy hands.

As Dean was being threatened with torture and death, it would only have added to his pain had he known what was taking place only a few miles away, where eighty-seven civilian noncombatants were being herded into line and told to start walking.

Had Dean known of them, he would have protested strongly on their behalf, though it would have done little good. The little band included a Salvation Army official, many Roman Catholic nuns and priests, and six Methodist missionaries, both men and women. Presently they fell in behind a long line of about 700 haggard American POWs, many of whom, with bleeding feet, were near collapse. It was

the beginning of a ghastly journey of death, one which would rival in cruelty the infamous Bataan Death March of World War II.

After stumbling along for hours through bitter cold, they were lined up in front of a North Korean major. The major—they thought of him as the Tiger—told them they would have to march in military column to a city a hundred miles away. They must first abandon all their belongings, even the walking sticks used by some of the elderly.

Was the major insane? One of the nuns, Mother Thérèse, was being carried in an improvised stretcher. Eighty-two-year-old Father Villemot and seventy-six-year-old Mother Beatrix could walk only with help. Then there was blind Sister Marie-Madeleine, whom Sister Bernadette had to lead by the hand.

Commissioner Herbert Lord of the Salvation Army tried to protest: "They will die if they have to march!"

"Then let them march till they die. That is a military order!"

On they went. That night, sleeping in an open field, they huddled together for warmth. Next day, in the snow, they started out again, and before long people were collapsing by the wayside, too exhausted to continue. The major stopped the column and screamed: "I order you not to allow anyone to drop out. If you do, I will punish you with the extreme penalty of military discipline. Even the dead must be carried!"

The march resumed, but before long, people again began to fall out. "Who is responsible for my orders not being obeyed?" asked the major. Irrationally, he now threatened to shoot them all.

During their captivity, the Tiger's victims would see many splendid examples of self-sacrifice, some of which are long forgotten. However, the magnificent act of moral courage that now took place was one they would always remember.

From the column, a young officer, Lieutenant Cordus Thornton, stepped forward and said that if anyone was responsible, he was.

"Why did you let those five men drop out?"

"Because they were dying, sir."

"Why didn't you obey my orders?" Because, said Thornton, to force anyone to carry the dead would have meant condemning those people to die as well.

Very well, if Thornton was accepting responsibility for all, the major would act accordingly. One of the guards, taking a small towel, bandaged Thornton's eyes. Then the major stepped behind the young lieutenant, pulled up the flap of Thornton's pile cap, cocked his pistol, and pulled the trigger.

Those nearby felt they had witnessed the death of a martyr. Two of the soldiers then carried Thornton's body to the side. An American sergeant, using a stick, started to dig a grave. "Won't anyone help me?" he asked.

Other volunteers, joining in, began scratching at the ground with sticks or even with their bare hands. Eventually they clawed out a shallow grave, and in it they laid the heroic lieutenant's body.

The march continued, but the horrors had not yet ended. Mother Beatrix, too tired to go on, collapsed by the roadside. Mother Eugénie pleaded with the guards for compassion, saying Beatrix, seventy-six years old, had for fifty years been caring for Korea's poor and orphans.

It was no use. "Go on, my sister, go," said Beatrix. The guards pushed Eugénie down the road. She heard a shot, and looking back, saw a tiny body being shoved down a steep slope, rolling over and over, and finally coming to rest at the bottom of a ravine.

Before the long trek was over, the prisoners would plod a hundred miles over rugged terrain, and nearly a hundred bodies would be left behind in the snow and cold.

Bill Dean, like the heroic Lieutenant Thornton, was faced with a decision. The easier choice, cooperating with the enemy, he dismissed at once. Up to now, he had given them nothing of value. Under torture, however, while he might very well die, he might also reveal something they could use. He was, for example, intimately familiar with the defense plans for Japan.

He could not take the chance of revealing valuable information, and as he saw it, there was only one way to choose the "harder right": He must take his own life. If possible, of course, he wanted to go down fighting. If he could seize a weapon, perhaps he could take someone with him, preferably the sadistic Colonel Kim. In any case, he'd save the last bullet for himself.

In Dean's room was a Western-style padded chair, which Dean himself was forbidden to use.

Although a light was always on, the ever-present guard would sometimes slump into that chair and doze off. Previously, there also had been a cot in the room, but on Kim's orders, it had been taken away and was now next door, in the room where the guards stayed.

This had to be the night. Peeking through a crack into the guards' room, Dean saw a submachine gun leaning against the wall. Perhaps, when the guard in his room fell asleep, and the men next door went to eat, he could slip in and grab that weapon. He would then point it out the window and fire a burst toward the building where Kim slept. Kim would come running out, and Dean, after shooting Kim, would then stick the barrel in his own mouth and pull the trigger.

Soon after dark, just as he'd hoped, his guard eased into the chair and closed his eyes. A bit later, the men next door all left to eat. It was now or never. Slowly, Bill Dean began to crawl along the floor, out of his room and into the next one. He found the weapon, lifted it, and pulled back on the bolt. It wouldn't budge. Again and again, he tried forcing it, and in doing so he must have made a noise.

The room wasn't empty. Someone was sleeping on the cot—it was Colonel Hong. Hong, a brave man, rushed at Dean, right in the face of the submachine gun. Hong grabbed Dean, who was still trying vainly to work the bolt. Meanwhile, his own guard, who had come awake, dashed in and jumped Dean from the rear. Soon there were Koreans all over him. It didn't take much to overpower the weakened American.

"You were trying to escape, weren't you?"

"No, in my condition I don't think I could have. I wanted to kill Colonel Kim, and then I was going to kill myself."

Next morning, Bill Dean was criticized for his actions. Nevertheless, something seemed to have changed. He never again saw the vicious Colonel Kim. Perhaps the suicide attempt had caused Kim to lose face. If so, thought Dean, that was more than fine by him. In any case, Colonel Choi gave orders that Dean be given new clothes, that his cot be returned, and that a doctor come and try to restore him to good health.

A few days later, Dean was again moved to a new location. The last person who talked to him was Lee, an interpreter who'd been present at all the interrogations. Lee whispered: "Good-bye, General.

Don't give up hope or try to kill yourself. You must live, and everything will be fine again, and you will see your family once more."

Lee was right. Many more months were to pass, none of them pleasant, but General Bill Dean, through courage and fortitude, did manage to survive and to come home with head held high.

Dean never felt he himself had done anything special; he was truly surprised when a grateful nation rewarded him with the Congressional Medal of Honor. If he'd had his way, he'd probably have given his medal to someone else, perhaps to some-one such as Lieutenant Stanley Tabor, who had refused to leave his companion and go on alone, or to Lieutenant Cordus Thornton, a man Dean never met, but who he knew had given his life so that others on the terrible journey of death might live.

Unfortunately neither Tabor nor Thornton managed to survive America's "forgotten war" in Korea. Both men, however, along with the indomitable General Bill Dean, the highest-ranking American POW of the twentieth century, surely deserve to be remembered and appreciated by a grateful nation.

COMPETENCE AND CHARACTER: SCHWARZKOPF'S MESSAGE TO THE CORPS

By Lieutenant General Dave R. Palmer '56
(Retired)
Assembly Magazine, May 1992
(Extract From Article)

General H. Norman Schwarzkopf, Class of 1956, returned to his Alma Mater on 15 May 1991 to speak to the Corps of Cadets. It was a rare event, for not since Dwight D. Eisenhower returned from Europe in 1945 had America or West Point been able to welcome home a victorious war hero. Excitement and anticipation could hardly have been higher. At that moment, with images of his stunning success in DESERT STORM fresh in everyone's mind, Schwarzkopf was arguably the most popular person in America. George Bush was due to arrive at West Point just two weeks later—but even a Presidential visit was quite over-shadowed by the triumphant general's return.

The day was as beautiful as they come in the Hudson Valley. A brilliant umbrella of blue sky enriched the deep green of the Plain, still fringed by splotches of spring color. A large crowd turned out, hoping for a glimpse of the famous visitor. The helicopter was right on time; spectators were not disappointed as Schwarzkopf arrived wearing his trademark desert camouflage uniform. Everything seemed to be on track.

Relaxing for a moment before starting a scheduled press conference, sipping a glass of iced tea in the garden behind the Superintendent's quarters, our guest gave me the first indication that we might have a problem. He had a speech ready, he said, but for some reason he just didn't feel comfortable with it. "What would you like me to talk about?" he asked. Now it was my turn to be uncomfortable. The address was set to start in just three hours, and in that time we had the press conference, a brigade review in his honor and dinner with the Corps in Washington Hall. No time to start over.

"Well, any topic would be fine," I responded tentatively. "Stories from DESERT STORM, your summary of the entire deployment and employment, international problems remaining, things like that." I added that many cadets had followed the fighting closely through a situation room the Commandant had set up and that a group of commanders from the desert, from platoon through division level, had recently spent several days in seminars with the cadets. He was not visibly encouraged by my suggestions.

Sitting backstage in Eisenhower Hall, due to go on in about ten minutes, he confided that he still was perplexed, that he did not have a good idea for a new approach if he abandoned the prepared remarks. "Really, anything you talk about will be suitable," I ventured. "You are a national hero, and a valuable message is conveyed just by your being here." He looked at me ruefully, the way classmates can. Still unsatisfied.

"There simply isn't a more respected leader in the nation right now than you," I tried again. "Remember, the Academy's very reason for being revolves around leadership. Our purpose is to produce leaders of character. So any topic you are comfortable with will fit the purpose squarely."

His face lit up. "That's it!" Three minutes to go. The technician had fitted him with a wireless microphone. In that short time, in that small holding room, he put his thoughts together. "Now I know why the original talk wasn't right," he said. "There is only one topic for me at this time at this place." Following the introduction, he strode out onto the stage, which was vast and empty except for a huge American flag hung as a backdrop, reminiscent of the famous scene from the movie *Patton*. I took my seat, probably the most curious person in the packed theater.

Still in desert camouflage battle dress, he paced the stage, as one reporter said, "like a lion." He had no script, no notes whatsoever. His address that night was totally unrehearsed. He delivered it in a straightforward fashion, the way he might have talked to soldiers in the field or in some other informal setting. It did not have the rhetorical flourishes or the practiced eloquence of MacArthur's 1962 "Duty, Honor, Country" speech. Nor was it intended to be anything more than what it was: the right-from-the-heart sentiments of an old soldier about to hang up his uniform after 35 years of service, speaking to 4400 young men and women who were preparing for leadership in the 21st Century. Personal. From him to them. It had force and a simple majesty. It moved those who heard it. For the rest of their lives, those cadets will remember the night General H. Norman Schwarzkopf talked to them about competence and character.

(Schwarzkopf opened with a story of an event occurring when he was on the Academy's faculty in 1967, then got right to the substance of his remarks.)

"What do you say to the leaders of the 21st Century? That's what you are, America's leaders of the 21st Century. I'm in the twilight of a mediocre career, and in three short months I'm gone—because that's the Army way. And that's the right way; we can't have the top plugged up and block the upward movement of many, many outstanding leaders. So what does an old warhorse, in his last three months in the Army, say to the leaders of the 21st Century?

I think that some of the lessons I have learned in 35 years in the Army are applicable to you who—this year or next year or the year after or the year after—are going to be leading this great Army of ours. And I thought I'd talk about them just a little bit.

First of all, let me talk about the environment when we graduated in 1956. There weren't going to be any more wars. [President Eisenhower] had adopted a military strategy of massive retaliation. Simply stated, we told the world that anyone who dared attack the vital interests of the United States would be faced with nuclear destruction. Many in that day were espousing that there was absolutely no need for an Army. "We ought to get rid of it, expand the size of our Air Force—ground battles will never be fought again." I've been to war four times since then. And I've been to war in places where, in 1956, no one—absolutely no one—would have ever predicted. When I was a cadet, there was something going on over in a place called Dien Bien Phu. I don't really remember very well what it was because I wasn't interested in that. After all, who cared about a tiny little place way over in Southeast Asia. When Dien Bien Phu fell, it didn't even impress us. A couple of Social Science instructors tried to get us interested, but we didn't pay any attention to them. And certainly, certainly, we didn't know where Grenada was. As a matter of fact, when I was told I was going to Grenada I said, "That's great. I've always wanted to go to Spain." And there was a philosophy that the United States would never, ever, ever get involved in a major ground war in the Middle East. Never. That's the environment that we, the Class of '56, graduated into.

A man with far more eloquence than I will ever have stood inside Washington Hall a few years ago and told the Corps of Cadets that ours is the profession of arms, and that our mission would never change. Our mission was to fight our nation's wars. He also told us that we could not fail in that mission.

A lot of people are calling the war we just won the "video game war." People are talking about the great technology. But they've been talking about that since the day we graduated. In the final analysis, you should never forget that the airplanes don't fly, the tanks don't run, the ships don't sail, the missiles don't fire—unless the sons and daughters of America make them do it. It's just that simple.

The mothers and fathers of America will give you their sons and daughters. They will hand you their sons and daughters with the confidence that you will not needlessly waste their lives. And you dare not. You absolutely dare not. That's the burden the mantle of leadership places upon you. And it's lonesome, let me tell you. It's terrible, terribly lonesome to realize that you could be the person who give the orders that will bring about the deaths of thousands and thousands of the young men and women whose lives have been placed in your hands. It is an awesome responsibility, and one that you must prepare yourself for. As MacArthur said, you cannot fail. You dare not fail, because this entire nation will depend upon you at that time.

What kind of a leader must a leader of the 21st Century be? You know, they are having a big discussion about this in America today. They are talking about how the Army turned itself around, how we changed. And they are saving—because there is such a terrible lack of leadership in American industry today—that perhaps the Army should be studied to find our secret formula to get rid of all those lousy, incompetent leaders who could finally win a war. That's bull!

We didn't lose in Vietnam. Not militarily, I've got to tell you. I never was in a single battle in Vietnam that we lost. Not a one. In fact, we kicked the hell out of the VC and the NVA in every battle I was ever in! But we did lose something in Vietnam. We lost our integrity. There was a terrible erosion of integrity within our leadership in Vietnam. Not everybody. I'm not condemning everyone. But I am saying that that is a fact of life—and we just could not allow that to continue. And you can't let it happen on your watch.

To be a 21st-century leader, you must have two things: competence and character.

I've met a lot of leaders that were very, very, very competent. But they didn't have character. For every job they did well in the Army, they sought reward in the form of promotions, in the form of awards and decorations, in the form of getting ahead at the expense of somebody else, in the form of another piece of paper that awarded them another degree. The only reason why they wanted that was because it was a sure road to faster promotion, to somehow get to the top. You see, these were very competent people, but they lacked character.

Now, on the other hand, I've met a lot of leaders who had superb character, but they weren't willing to hold their own feet to the fire. They weren't willing to pay the price of leadership. They were not willing to go the extra mile, to do that extra little bit because that's what it took to be a great leader. And none of those leaders are with us. And none of those leaders would lead in battle. Because the bottom line to everything is, again, when you lead in battle—when you lead in battle-you are leading people. You are leading human beings.

I've seen competent leaders who stood in front of a platoon and saw it as a platoon. But I've seen great leaders who stood in front of a platoon and saw it as a platoon. But I've seen great leaders who stood in front of a platoon and saw it as 44 individuals, each of whom had his hopes, each of whom had his aspirations, each of whom wanted to live, each of who wanted to do good. So, you must have competence and you must have character. Some great man once said that character is seen only when nobody is watching. It's not what people do when they are being watched that demonstrates character; it's what they do when they are not being watched that demonstrates true character. And that's sort of what it's all about. To lead in the 21st Century, to take soldiers, sailors, airmen, marines, coastguardsmen into battle, you will be required to have both competence and character.

Out there among you are cynics. They are the people who scoff at what you are learning here. They are the people who scoff at character. They are the people who scoff at hard work. But they don't know what they are talking about, let me tell you. I can assure you that when the going gets tough and your country needs them, they are not going to be there. They WILL NOT be there. But you will.

What's the magic formula? After Vietnam a whole cottage industry developed, basically in Washington, D.C., that consisted of a bunch that had never been shot at in anger, but who felt fully qualified to comment on the leadership abilities of all the leaders of the United States Army. They were not Monday morning quarterbacks, they were the worst of all possible kinds—Friday afternoon quarterbacks. They felt qualified to criticize us before the game was even played. They talked about great operational concepts and plans and maneuvers, never understanding—never understanding-that the plan goes out the window when you cross the line of departure because there is always some son of a bitch in this choreographed dance you have planned who climbs out of the orchestra pit with a bayonet and chases you around the stage!

They are the same ones who were saying, "My goodness, we have a terrible problem in the Armed Forces because there are no more leaders out there. There are no more combat leaders. Where are the Pattons? Where are the Eisenhowers? Where are the Bradleys? Where are the MacArthurs? Where are the Audie Murphys? They are all gone. We don't have any out there." Coming from a guy who's never been shot at in his entire life, that's a pretty bold statement.

But, you see, leaders were out there. And they are out there. And YOU will be out there. The Pattons and the Bradleys and the Audie Murphys, they aren't running around in peacetime killing people, I hope to hell! it takes a war to demonstrate that we have these people in our ranks, and our ranks are loaded with them. They are loaded with them—and you are going to be one of them when you join our ranks. If there is any doubt in anybody's mind, or was any doubt in anybody's mind, there sure as hell isn't any doubt now, because it took us 100 hours to kick the ass of the fourth largest army in the world! Competence with character. That's what you must have.

Don't ever forget that you are going to lead human beings. Their lives are going to be placed in your hands and you have to measure up. And the only way you are going to measure up is with competence and strong character."

Spiritual Needs I

This is the first in a series of two lessons on soldier's spirituality. This lesson is designed to help you discover your own spirituality and values and how to support and encourage the spirituality of your soldiers. In this lesson, you learn the importance of accommodating the spiritual needs of your subordinates and that this support is vital to achieving a positive ethical command climate, unit cohesion and combat readiness.

The following topics are addressed in this lesson:

- Spirituality;
- Religion;
- Ethical command climate;
- Unit cohesion;
- Combat readiness;
- Religious accommodation; and
- Resources available to assist the leader in meeting subordinates' spiritual needs.

The following Terminal Learning Objective (TLO) is supported in whole or in part by this lesson:

- Accommodate the spiritual needs of subordinates.

Following this lesson you will be able to:

- Assess personal spirituality;
- Analyze personal spirituality as it aligns with Army's core concepts of duty, honor and courage; and
- Describe a leader's obligation to make and support an environment which fosters and accommodates soldier's spirituality.

SPIRITUALITY AND RELIGION

From: http://www.hooah4health.com

How are religion and spirituality related? Some say spirituality is religion, some say it excludes religion: I say it transcends religion. Spirituality is connectedness—vertical and horizontal—interpersonal, intra-personal, and extra-personal. It envelops the intellectual, the emotional and the perceptual.

Spirituality, even though it may not be touched in a tactile sense, can be observed by the activity it produces. Spirit impacts the physical aspects of life, just as the wind makes trees sway on a gusty day.

Brian Luke Seaward, in an article entitled "Reflections on Human Spirituality for the Worksite" published in the January/February 1995 issue of The *American Journal of Health Promotion,* reminds us that spirit is defined the same in every culture. Spirit means breath, as in the breath of life. He expounds, "It was clearly understood ages ago that the health of the human spirit implied an unconditional love of self, shared with all other aspects of creation. That is what it means to be connected. When we are disconnected, we lose our sense of equilibrium and chaos ensues."

Connectedness to humanity and deity alike holds the answer to our question about spirituality's relationship to religion. Jared D. Kass, author of The *Spirituality and Resilience Assessment Packet* (SRA) agrees that spirituality is connectedness. He says that spirituality enhances harmony, productivity, and peace in our everyday lives. Additionally, the stronger one's connectedness, the more resilience or ability to "bounce back" one musters in a crisis. Kass, along with his wife Lynn, developed the SRA to help people measure their heart-felt or intrinsic spirituality which directly impacts their resilience in crisis situations. Since connectedness reduces chaos and increases resilience, harmony in the workplace can be enhanced when employees pursue appropriate interpersonal, intra-personal and extra-personal relationships. The regular practice of true spirituality can make our work environment happier, hardier, and healthier.

Does this pursuit include or exclude religion? Many religions, while exclusive in their beliefs about Deity, share the common principle of, "Unconditional love shared with all other aspects of creation." To love one's self and others in a similar way is well known in Christian circles. This kind of harmony with self, Deity and others is inherent in many other religions as well.

Religion, whether modern or traditional, Eastern or Western, secular or denominational, often addresses the spiritual aspects of our lives. Workers who are spiritually healthy are characterized by the presence of unilateral connectedness and bring harmony, productivity and wellness to our work environments.

Even though some unhealthy religious practices *may* impede spiritual growth, the likelihood of that being widespread has not been determined and is highly unlikely. Even though spirituality transcends religion, religious practices, more often than not, include true spirituality. Religion can be very helpful in focusing spiritual energies toward healthier behaviors. Intrinsic or heartfelt religious practice is a widely acceptable method of applying spirituality to everyday situations.

How are spirituality and religion related? As the practice of spirituality, religion helps apply the concept of connectedness to everyday life. It helps to create an atmosphere wherein spiritual wellness can flourish. Spiritual people exhibit an enhanced resiliency in crisis and are more in tune with themselves and others, and they provide the connectedness and equilibrium needed to promote a healthy atmosphere in which productivity, peace, and harmony reign.

Chaplain (LTC) Gregory L. Black

REALITY CHECK: THE HUMAN AND SPIRITUAL NEEDS OF SOLDIERS AND HOW TO PREPARE THEM FOR COMBAT[1]

by J.W. Brinsfield

> If I learned nothing else from the war, it taught me the falseness of the belief that wealth, material resources, and industrial genius are the real sources of a nation's military power. These are but the stage setting . . . national strength lies only in the hearts and spirits of men.
>
> S.L.A. Marshall[2]

In the quest to reexamine and possibly redefine the Army profession, the key roles, skills, and knowledge required of military leaders are indispensable elements for analysis. No profession can compete with competent outsiders without defining itself, its special expertise requirements, and its solutions to the problems of transformation and change in perceived influence, power allocation, internal organization, and organization of knowledge to support its special claims to jurisdiction.[3]

The historical mission and jurisdiction of the joint military services are to win the nation's wars. All other missions are secondary to this national security responsibility. Yet at the beginning of the twenty-first century, our conception of America's security umbrella has been broadened to include domestic police, fire, and drug enforcement activities as well as international humanitarian and peacekeeping missions—to the detriment, some would say, of the Army's main war-fighting role. In fact, the system of professions within which the Army competes is crowded with American government entities such as the other military services, the State Department, Border Patrol, Drug Enforcement Administration, Federal Bureau of Investigation, Central Intelligence Agency, and Federal Emergency Management Agency. The nation's formerly well-integrated system of professions addressing security has mushroomed "without a commensurate expansion in the legal, cultural, or workplace mechanisms that legitimate each profession's jurisdiction."[4] Mission creep, in other words, has challenged the Army's traditional understanding of its role in the nation's defense.

Moreover, in the quest to establish its professional boundaries, the Army has had to rely on civilian leadership, often with little or no experience in the military, for its mission definition and resources, all the while competing commercially with academia and the marketplace for the hearts and minds of the recruits who may become its future leaders.[5] These challenges, among many others, seem to require a redefinition of and reemphasis on the components of military professionalism and leadership for the future.

Soldiers are the Army's heart, life force, and strength no matter what their mission may be. They define the Army's effectiveness, success, or possible failure. They must respond to the unique demands of the profession of arms: total commitment, unlimited liability, possible lengthy separations from family, community and civilian primary support systems, and total loyalty to a values-based and service-based organization. In time of war, they may be asked to sacrifice themselves for the nation and for one another as guardians of the republic. Any internal analysis and definition of the profession of arms must include, therefore, an appraisal of the soldier's human dimension, lest, to paraphrase the words of one Civil War general, they be asked for more than they could possibly be expected to give.[6]

As part of such an effort, this lesson seeks to analyze the human and spiritual needs of soldiers as part of the special knowledge required by Army leaders to motivate, train, and command their personnel and their units in peace and war. It also suggests some considerations for preparing soldiers psychologically and spiritually for future combat operations.

The working hypothesis is that all soldiers have human needs and most have spiritual needs broadly defined, and that converting these needs into strengths of will and character is an important part of combat leadership—and therefore of Army professionalism. The chapter is composed of three major parts: (1) a definition and discussion of human and spiritual needs, including an analysis of the theory of needs as applied to soldiers; (2) a description of some of the past efforts to capitalize on human and spiritual needs so as to achieve confidence, cohesion, and courage; and (3) a discussion of proposed combat training considerations as related to the human dimension of soldiers in the future. Because certain aspects of human nature cannot be directly observed but must be inferred from observed behavior, the data for analysis rely on multidisciplinary sources which include the humanities as well as the social sciences.

ASSUMPTIONS

Since the subject matter of this analysis deals with the needs of the soldier, a review of sources relating to the individual will be useful before we move to the organizational or profession level. Much of the research data involve individual responses from soldiers in small units rather than Army-wide studies. In taking this approach, it may be assumed that military leaders do and will recognize their dual obligations to complete their missions successfully and to take effective measures to ensure the health and welfare of as many personnel as possible within their commands. This is an ancient canon of the military art, explained by Sun Tzu's *The Art of War* in the early part of the fourth century B.C.:

> And therefore the general who in advancing does not seek personal fame but whose only purpose is to protect the people and promote the best interests of his sovereign, is the precious jewel of the state. Because such a general regards his men as his own sons they will march with him into the deepest valleys. He treats them as his own beloved sons, and they will die with him. If he cherishes his men is this way, he will gain their utmost strength. Therefore The Military Code says: "The general must be the first in the toils and fatigues of the army." [7]

There are, of course, many other authoritative utterances regarding the commander's duty to care for soldiers, but few of such established antiquity. In present literature, if one were to seek guidance for a career in the Army, Field Manual 22-100, *Army Leadership: Be, Know, Do*, states simply, "Accomplish the mission *and* take care of your soldiers." [8]

The second assumption is that a holistic knowledge of the human and spiritual needs of soldiers, yet to be defined, will be of value to the military leader in providing support and resources for meeting these needs, thereby strengthening the capacity of the fighting force to complete its missions successfully. In war, soldiers' comfort, inasmuch as comfort is possible, affects morale and thus combat effectiveness.[9] The Creed of the Noncommissioned Officer includes this concept in the brief declaration that "all soldiers are entitled to outstanding leadership; I will provide that leadership. I know my soldiers and I will always place their needs above my own."[10] Gen. Creighton

Abrams, former Army Chief of Staff, goes to the heart of the matter:

> The Army is not made up of people; the Army is people. They have needs and interests and desires. They have spirit and will, strengths and abilities. They are the heart of our preparedness and this preparedness—as a nation and as an Army—depends upon the spirit of our soldiers. It is the spirit which gives the Army life. Without it we cannot succeed. [11]

If leadership means gaining the willing obedience of subordinates who understand and believe in the mission's purpose, who value their team and their place in it, who trust their leaders and have the will to see the mission through, then leaders must understand two key elements: leadership itself and the people they lead. [12]

DEFINITIONS AND DISCUSSION: RELIGION, SPIRITUALITY, AND HUMAN AND SPIRITUAL NEEDS

On the last page of his classic study of the psychology of soldiers, *The Anatomy of Courage* (1967), Lord Charles Moran approached the subject of religion and spiritual power:

> I have said nothing of religion, though at no time has it been far from my thoughts. General Paget asked me once to talk to officers commanding divisions and corps and armies in the Home Forces. When I had done, they broke up and came to me, one or two at a time, questioning. Often that night I was asked about the importance of religion. Speaking as if they did not know how to put it, they separately told me how faith had come into the lives of many of their men. Is it so strange? Is it not natural that they are fumbling for another way of living, less material, less sterile, than that which has brought them to this pass? What are they seeking? [13]

Lord Moran's questions are well posed, for the separate disciplines of psychology and religion often look to separate sources of authority, separate methodologies, and different language to describe human behavior. Nevertheless, many psychologists, sociologists, anthropologists, and physicians recognize the phenomenology of religion as abstracted from any claims concerning its essence. In other words, religion may be studied and respected as an element of culture without subscription to its content. W.I. Thomas, one of the classic sociologists of the past century, explained that "if a culture believes something to be real, we must respect that belief in dealing with that culture."[14]

Many soldiers in the American Army culture do identify with a specific religious faith—some 299,958 or 64% of active duty soldiers in April 2001—but many are also reluctant to define too closely what they mean by religion, faith, and especially spirituality.[15] Even though spiritual strength is mentioned in many Army publications, including the 1999 edition of the U.S. Army Training and Doctrine Command's *TLS Strategy: Change, Readiness, and the Human Dimension of Training, Leader Development and Soldiers* and the 2001 edition of the Department of the Army's Well-Being Campaign Plan, there are comparatively few useful definitions that have been published. [16]

Part of the reason why soldiers are reluctant to discuss religion openly is their perception that religion is a very personal subject. Professor Morris Janowitz found two generations ago "a tendency among leaders in a political democracy, and especially among the military, to resent being questioned about their religious background." [17] A strong adherence to a particular religious point of view can be perceived as politically divisive and detrimental to unit cohesion. More commonly, religious language itself is not well understood, for the same terms may have different meanings in different faith groups. Military leaders like to have a clear idea of what they are saying and supporting, as do most people.

At the same time, many educational institutions, including the United States Military Academy, have recognized a spiritual domain in their philosophies of comprehensive education. The Cadet Leader Development System, a strategy for total commissioned leader development at West Point, links the spiritual domain to a common quest for meaning in life:

> This [spiritual] domain explicitly recognizes that character is rooted in the very essence of who we are as individuals, and discerning "who we are" is a lifelong search for meaning. Cadet years are a time of yearning, a time to be hungry for personal meaning and to engage in a search for ultimate meaning in life. Formally rec-

ognizing this fundamental aspect of human development is not unique to West Point; educators have long held that individual moral search is an inherent, even vital, component of any robust undergraduate education. In other words, cadets' search for meaning is natural, it will occur, whether or not we explicitly recognize and support it as an institution or not.[18]

For some, the quest for meaning will lead to questions of religion. For others, meaning is found through spirituality, a broader and possibly less distinct category than institutional religion. Is there a useful taxonomy for terms such as religion, spirituality, identity, ultimate meaning, and self-actualization in individual development?

Dr. Jeff Levin, Senior Research Fellow at the National Institute for Healthcare Research and a scholar of religion and medicine, tackles the problem of defining religion and spirituality as follows:

> Historically, "religion" has denoted three things: particular churches or organized religious institutions; a scholarly field of study; and the domain of life that deals with things of the spirit and matters of "ultimate concern." To talk of practicing religion or being religious refers to behaviors, attitudes, beliefs, experiences, and so on, that involve this domain of life. This is so whether one takes part in organized activities of an established religious institution or one has an inner life of the spirit apart from organized religions.
>
> "Spirituality," as the term traditionally has been used, refers to a state of being that is acquired through religious devotion, piety, and observance. Attaining spirituality—union or connection with God or the divine—is the ultimate goal of religion, and is a state not everyone reaches. According to this usage, spirituality is a subset of a larger phenomenon, religion, and by definition is sought through religious participation. [19]

Dr. Levin goes on to observe, however, that in the last thirty years the word "spirituality" has taken on a wider meaning. New Age authors and some news media have limited "religion" to those behaviors and beliefs that occur in the context of organized religious institutions. All other religious expression, particularly private meditation and secular transcendent experiences including feelings of awe and oneness with nature, are now encompassed by the term "spirituality." This wider definition reverses the relationship between religion and spirituality to make the former now the subset of the latter. [20]

Many scholars of world religions agree that Levin's wider definition of spirituality seems to fit the beliefs of many faith groups, even those with non-theistic views. Although the majority of the world's religions do claim to be the vehicles for a personal experience with God, Allah, Brahman, or one of the other of the world's named deities, there are others for whom spirituality is a non-theistic pilgrimage to individual enlightenment, wisdom, and transcendence. For example, in Zen or Ch'an Buddhism, "the highest truth or first principle is inexpressible," that is, the divine is so remote from human perception as to make its essence indescribable, thereby rendering an organized, doctrinal religion impossible; however, a mind-expanding, experiential awakening called "satori" is still available through meditation, mentoring by masters, and self-discipline. [21] In the Shinto religion of Japan, the perception of "kami" may be simply the reverence one has for the awesome power and beauty of nature even though gifts are frequently left at Shinto shrines for the spirits that inhabit such places. [22] The spiritual goal of reaching Nirvana is found in both theistic Hinduism and non-theistic Theravada Buddhism. The Falun Gong meditation which began in China in 1992 consists of spiritual exercises to promote health, cure illnesses, and allow the practitioner to absorb energy from the universe in order to ascend to a higher plane of human existence, but there are no named deities. [23]

Thus, to summarize the period since the 1970s, the context of religious institutions and spiritual practices in America has become enormously more diverse. Although in 1998 approximately 90% of the American people professed to be religious and 63% (169 million) identified themselves as affiliated with a *specific* religious group, the number of separate religious denominations has grown in a sixty-year span from about forty-five in 1940 to more than 2,000 at present. [24] This enlargement of religious and spiritual options suggests that Levin and others are correct to identify spirituality with the individual quest for greater insight, enlightenment, wisdom, meaning, and experience with the numinous or divine. Religion does refer in most current literature to the institutionalization of symbols, rites, practices,

education, and other elements necessary to transmit the specifics of religious culture to the next generation.

However, there is no evidence that the world's major religions are in decline. Indeed, as Samuel Huntington has argued, there is a worldwide revival of interest in traditional faiths, including Christianity in Russia, Buddhism in Japan, and Islam in Central Asia, faiths which offer meaning, stability, identity, assurance, and fixed points of reference in the face of the "clash of civilizations and the remaking of world order." [25] Moreover, in a recent poll taken by Blum and Weprin Associates of New York, which surveyed adults across America, 59% of those polled said that they were *both* religious and spiritual. Only 20% identified themselves as "only spiritual," and only 9% viewed religion in a negative way.[26] Nevertheless, with the growth of communication technologies and the availability of knowledge at the individual level, the spiritual quest for future generations may depend on some traditional religious institutions but will certainly be directed toward meeting individual needs.

THE THEORY OF HUMAN NEEDS APPLIED TO SOLDIERS

The psychological study of soldiers is a relatively new academic endeavor. In the preface to his book, *The Anatomy of Courage*, Lord Moran, who had served as a medical officer in France and Flanders during World War I, explained that "there was no book in the English language on the psychology of the soldier before 1945."[27] *The Anatomy of Courage* was designed to fill that gap. It was an attempt to answer questions about what was happening in men's minds during combat and how they overcame fear. Since 1967, when Moran's book was published, there have been numerous studies on military psychology, military psychiatry, and combat motivation.[28] It was from an analysis of motivation and behavioral theory that the theory of needs as applied to soldiers found its most eloquent proponents.

The nature of the relationship between motivation and human behavior has been a subject of philosophical and psychological interest for centuries. There are multiple modern formulations which seek to explain motivation in general, including hedonistic, cognitive, drive reduction, and needs theories, to mention a few.[29] For more than forty years, a popular theory in U.S. Army literature which outlines both a description of human behavior and of motivation was Dr. Abraham Maslow's concept of *self-actualization* as the driving force of human personality, as set forth in his 1954 book *Motivation and Personality*.[30] Dr. Maslow was associated with the humanistic movement in psychology. Humanistic psychologists emphasize the person and his or her psychological growth.[31] Maslow described self-actualization as the need "to become more and more what one is, to become everything that one is capable of becoming," or, in other words, to be all one can be.[32]

According to Maslow's self-actualizing theory, the components of identity arise from two sources: the individual's unique potential and the different ways the individual copes with impediments placed in the way. Maslow identified two kinds of needs: basic needs arranged in a hierarchy which included physiological safety and security, love and belongingness, and esteem or recognition needs; and metaneeds which included spiritual qualities or metaphysical values such as order, goodness, and unity.[33] Basic needs are deficiency needs and must be fulfilled before a person can turn attention to the metaneeds. Metaneeds are growth needs; if properly satisfied, a person will grow into a completely developed human being—physically, emotionally, and spiritually—and have the potential to become a self-actualized person.[34]

Maslow recognized a spiritual component in the human personality, but argued that it was a natural component which sought meaning in a cause outside oneself and bigger than oneself, something not merely self-centered, something impersonal.[35] Moreover, the spiritual need impelled persons toward vocations, callings, and missions which they described with passionate, selfless, and profound feelings.[36]

Maslow believed that metaneeds or spiritual needs are universal, but that only self-actualized people usually attempted to meet them. "This is to say," he wrote, "that the most highly developed persons we know are metamotivated to a much higher degree, and are basic-need-motivated to a lesser degree than average or diminished people are. The full definition of the person or human nature must then include intrinsic values as part of human nature. These intrinsic values are instinctoid in nature, i.e., they are needed (a) to avoid illness and (b) to achieve fullest humanness or growth. The highest values, the spiritual life, the highest aspira-

tions of mankind are therefore proper subjects for scientific study and research."[37]

Finally, Maslow argued that the spiritual aspirations of the human personality are a natural phenomenon, not a theological construct nor limited to the domain of religious institutions. In his book *Religions, Values, and Peak-Experiences*, Maslow exclaimed, "I want to demonstrate that spiritual values have naturalistic meaning, that they are not the exclusive possession of organized churches, that they do not need supernatural concepts to validate them, that they are well within the jurisdiction of a suitably enlarged science, and that, therefore, they are the general responsibility of all mankind."[38]

The U.S. Army leadership adopted Maslow's theory of basic and metaneeds enthusiastically after 1970. This was due, in part, because it correlated well with observable behavior among soldiers and because it was in consonance with the concept that if missions have requirements and weapons have a basic load, then soldiers must have human requirements and basic needs. In a collection of Bill Mauldin's World War II cartoons titled *Up Front*, G.I. Willie in his torn and dirty fatigues tells a medic, " Just gimme a coupla aspirin, I already got a Purple Heart."[39] Willie's basic needs, in Maslow's terms, clearly claimed priority over his esteem or recognition needs.

The October 1983 edition of Field Manual 22-100, *Military Leadership*, a standard text for thousands of the Army's leaders, incorporated Maslow's hierarchy of needs (physical, security, social) almost verbatim.[40] The manual's authors explained, "As a leader, you must understand these needs because they are powerful forces in motivating soldiers. To understand and motivate people and to develop a cohesive, disciplined, well-trained unit, you must understand human nature."[41]

However, there were three divergencies from Maslow's theory in the 1983 leadership manual. First, rather than discuss the need for esteem or recognition, which is the fourth need in Maslow's hierarchy, the leadership manual addressed "Higher Needs," i.e., the need for religion, the need for increased competence, and the need to serve a worthwhile cause. With regard to the need for religion, the manual's writers explained that historically,

> many people not normally religious
> become so in time of war. The danger and
> chaos of war give rise to the human need

to believe that a greater spiritual being is guiding one's fate for the best, regardless of whether one lives or dies. In this sense it helps soldiers to believe that they are fighting for a cause that is moral and right in the eyes of their religion. This is an important source of motivation for soldiers all over the world.[42]

Although the authors may have reflected their own beliefs accurately, Maslow would have argued that spiritual needs are universal, not dependent upon crises in war except perhaps as one of many catalysts for revealing them and not *always* leading to faith in a greater spiritual power as much as to perhaps a greater potential state of individual spirituality.

In more recent years, the Army has modified its language in describing the needs of soldiers and their families. Part of this was due to advances in medical and behavioral research, notably by the Army Research Institute for the Behavioral and Social Sciences and by the Academy of Health Sciences at Ft. Sam Houston, Texas, among others. Nevertheless, descriptively the human dimension of the soldier is still segmented into roughly the same needs Maslow propounded. The Army Well-Being Strategic Plan of 2001 produced by the Office of the Deputy Chief of Staff for Personnel defined Army well-being as "the personal—physical, material, mental, and spiritual—state of soldiers [Active, Reserve, Guard, retirees, veterans], civilians, and their families that contributes to their preparedness to perform The Army's mission."[43] The spiritual state (of well-being), according to the Army Well-Being Plan, "centers on a person's religious/philosophical needs and may provide powerful support for values, morals, strength of character, and endurance in difficult and dangerous circumstances."[44]

In summary, contemporary psychologists have challenged Maslow's hierarchy of needs, which they describe as "one size fits all," and instead point to a more complex model to explain motivation and behavior. Steven Reiss, a psychologist at Ohio State University, has identified at least fifteen fundamental motivational desires in human beings, including honor, morality, and order. Reiss does not present "spirituality" as a category of human motivation and desire, but he does say that further categories are open to scientific study.[45]

Likewise, but from a different perspective, research in the relationship between spirituality and

healing has increased dramatically in the past ten years. The National Institute for Healthcare Research in Rockville, Maryland, has accumulated more than 200 studies from researchers at such prestigious institutions as Harvard, Duke, Yale, Michigan, Berkeley, Rutgers, and the University of Texas at Galveston showing that religious beliefs and practices benefit health and rates of recovery from illness in many patients.[46] According to one study by Dr. Andrew Newberg, published in 2001 under the title *Why God Won't Go Away*, research on the human brain suggests that a particular area of the brain is activated by prayer and meditation, at least among the subjects involved in the research. This led some interpreters to claim that "the human brain is wired for God."[47]

Yet none of the studies discovered to date claim that *all* people are either spiritual or religious. Levin and Maslow agreed, after sixty years of study between them, that while everyone has a range of needs, not everyone reaches an awareness of innate, or acquired, spiritual needs even though Maslow believed that all human beings are (potentially) motivated by metaneeds to some degree. [48]

What can be demonstrated, and what may be of most import for Army leadership and Army professionalism, is that the American culture, from which the military services draw support, puts a high priority on spirituality, organized religion, religious freedom, and the Constitutional right to the free exercise of religion, a right which both Congress and the Federal courts have applied to military as well as to civilian communities. *The Journal of Family Psychology* reported in 1999 that in America,

many individuals report that religion and spirituality are integral parts of their lives. As many as 95% of American adults express a belief in God, 84% believe God can be reached through prayer, and 86% state religion is important or very important to them. Surveys also suggest religion may play a significant role in many marriages. Religiousness, as reflected by church affiliation or attendance, emerged as a correlate of higher marital satisfaction in early, classic studies on marital adjustment. More recently, greater religiousness has been tied to higher marital satisfaction and adjustment in large, nationally representative samples.[49]

The rate of attendance at religious services at least once a month among a national random sample of 1,000 families as reported by the *Journal of Family Psychology* was 37%, with 25% of the same sample reporting attendance at religious services weekly or more than once a week.[50]

Among Army soldiers in 2001 the rate of identification with one of the seven larger religious faith groups in the Army—Protestant, Catholic, Orthodox, Jewish, Muslim, Buddhist, or Hindu—was 64%, one percentage point higher than the national average.[51] Although chapel attendance figures for soldiers and family members of all faiths in the Army worldwide were not available, the U.S. Army Forces Command reported 10,563 field and chapel worship services conducted in FY 2000 for active duty soldiers.[52] In addition, FORSCOM documented 821 weddings, 611 funerals, 334 memorial services, 2,644 family skill/enhancement classes, and 1,304 separate suicide prevention classes which reached a total population of 89,979 soldiers, retirees, and family members. In a volunteer Army with 65% of its active force soldiers of all ranks married and with 52,000 physically challenged members included in the families, these services were indispensable to soldier welfare and readiness. [53]

Since church attendance by the retiree population has not been separately tabulated, the estimated church attendance figures for active duty soldiers and family members cannot be accurately determined. However, of 12,561 waiting spouses during lengthy separations due to deployments, 30.6% (3,844) reported use of worship programs and services provided by Army chaplains. [54]

Although all relevant inputs have not been considered (e.g., religious activities in the Reserve components), it seems reasonable to conclude that the active duty Army population is a microcosm of American society and culture. The majority of citizens and soldiers profess to be religious. Many more people have an interest in spirituality and religion than attend religious services, at least on a regular basis. However, during periods of prolonged stress to both individuals and families, as exemplified by deployment to a combat zone, most soldiers and spouses indicate that religion is an important support for their pre-deployment readiness, their morale, the well-being of their deploying units, the durability of their marriages, and the welfare of families back home.[55]

THE SOLDIER'S SPIRIT: LEVERAGING THE HUMAN DIMENSION TO BUILD CONFIDENCE, COHESION, AND COURAGE

On 15 June 1941, Gen. George C. Marshall addressed the faculty and students of Trinity College in Hartford, Connecticut, a college linked to the Episcopal Church, on the subject of morale in modern war:

> I know that this association with you here this morning is good for my soul. If I were back in my office I would not have referred to my soul. Instead I should have used the word "morale" and said that this occasion increased my "morale"—in other words was of spiritual benefit to me. One of the most interesting and important phenomena of the last war was the emergence of that French word from comparative obscurity to widespread usage in all the armies of the world. Today as we strive to create a great new defensive force, we are investing the word "morale" with deeper and wider meaning. Underlying all the effort back of this essentially material and industrial effort is the realization that the primary instrument of warfare is the fighting man. We think of food in terms of morale—of clothing, of shelter, of medical care, of amusement and recreation in terms of morale. We want all of these to be available in such quantity and quality that they will be sustaining factors when it comes to a consideration of the soldier's spirit. The soldier's heart, the soldier's spirit, the soldier's soul are everything. Unless the soldier's soul sustains him, he cannot be relied on and will fail himself and his commander and his country in the end.[57]

General Marshall gave a good deal of his personal attention to supporting the soldier's morale, moral behavior, and spiritual strength, supplying more than 550 cantonment chapels and 9,111 chaplains—one for every 1,200 soldiers—to the Army and Army Air Corps.[58]

However, General Marshall recognized that the soldier's spirit—the soldier's morale—included much more and demanded much more than religious support alone. Morale is a disciplined state of mind which embraces confidence in the self and confidence in the unit. It encompasses courage, zeal, loyalty, hope, and at times grim determination to endure to the end.[59]

Morale, élan, esprit de corps,"the will to combat," and the will to win, are the human dimension's most important intangible assets. Strong morale is an emotional bonding of purpose, meaning, common values, good leadership, shared hardship, and mutual respect.[60] Of all of the factors which produce strong morale in a unit—of whatever size—leading by example and unit cohesion are frequently mentioned first.[61] Lord Moran's experiences with unit cohesion in the British regiments during World War I led him to conclude that "there was only one religion in the regular army, the regiment; it seemed to draw out of them the best that was in them."[62] Such morale, such fighting spirit, coupled with faith in their leaders, were important factors in the survival and ultimate victory of soldiers throughout military history.

However, the morale of the soldier and the esprit de corps of the unit may have a short shelf life in extended combat. Like courage, morale is an expendable commodity and needs some replenishment and support to withstand combat stress. John Keegan reflected on the experiences of British and American doctors during World War II in his book *The Face of Battle*. Of all British battle casualties during the active phase of the Battle of France in 1940, "ten to fifteen percent were psychiatric, ten to twenty percent during the first ten days of the Normandy battle and twenty percent during the two latter months, seven to ten percent in the Middle East in the middle of 1942, and eleven percent in the first two months of the Italian campaign."[63] The official American report on combat exhaustion during the same period stated:

> There is no such thing as "getting used to combat." Each moment of combat imposes a strain so great that men will break down in direct relation to the intensity and duration of their exposure [thus] psychiatric casualties are as inevitable as gunshot and shrapnel wounds in warfare. Most men were ineffective after 180 or even 140 days. The general consensus was that a man reached his peak of effectiveness in the first 90 days of combat, that after that his efficiency began to fall off, and that he became steadily less valuable thereafter until he was completely useless. The number of men on duty after 200 to 240 days

of combat was small and their value to their units negligible.[64]

Not only individuals but also whole units became ineffective as a result of fatigue, stress, high casualties, poor leadership, and a loss of hope. In the Tunisian Campaign of 1942, veteran American combat troops joined newer recruits in "going to ground," "burning out," and breaking down. One 1944 report pointed out that in the North African theater nearly all men in rifle battalions not otherwise disabled ultimately became psychiatric casualties even though some of them made it as far as Cassino and Anzio.[65] Other examples of whole units becoming combat ineffective may be gleaned from the experience of some German units on the Eastern Front, American units during the Korean War, and Iraqi units during the Gulf War.[66]

What types of support did the soldiers who were able to endure find helpful in coping with the stresses of combat? John Keegan identifies four critical elements in British armies: moral purpose—believing in the "rightness" of the war; unit cohesion—formed in hard training, sports competitions, and rewards for being the "best"; selfless leadership from first-line officers; and a desire for spiritual or religious fortification before battle.[67]

William Manchester, who served as an enlisted Marine on Okinawa during the most intense fighting in the spring of 1945, wrote of his survival in his book *Goodbye Darkness*:

> You had to know that your whole generation was in this together, that no strings were being pulled for anybody. You also needed nationalism, the absolute conviction that the United States was the envy of all other nations. Today the ascent of Sugar Loaf [on Okinawa] takes a few minutes. In 1945 it took ten days and cost 7,547 Marine casualties. And beneath my feet, where mud had been deeply veined with human blood, the healing mantle of turf [I murmured a prayer: *God*] *take away this murdering hate and give us thine own eternal love*. And then, in one of those great thundering jolts in which a man's real motives are revealed to him, I understood why I jumped hospital and, in violation of orders, returned to the front and almost certain death. It was an act of love. Those men on the line were my family, my home. They were closer to me than I can say,

closer than any friends had been or ever would be. They had never let me down, and I couldn't do it to them. I had to be with them, rather than let them die and me live in the knowledge that I might have saved them. Men, I now know, do not fight for flag or country, for the Marine Corps or glory or any other abstraction. They fight for one another.[68]

If morale is the human dimension's most important tangible asset, cohesion must be the most important single asset for a unit. Cohesion consists psychologically of recognition, stability, and safety.[69] Yet the coping strategies Keegan and Manchester identified, which included cohesion, did not exist as separate components. For Manchester, combat was a spiritual exercise, a willingness to sacrifice for a greater cause (moral purpose) but mostly for his fellow Marines (brotherhood). Moral purpose, selflessness, courage, and spiritual strength in Keegan's list and in Manchester's narration all contributed holistically to unit cohesion and survivability.

American surveys of other World War II combat survivors tended to center on similar coping mechanisms and their relative priorities in importance for survival of the individual. Although the methodologies involved in these surveys may be questioned, the general conclusions that spiritual strength and "not letting others down" were two of their most important motivations for endurance seem to be validated by other observers, not the least of whom were their senior officers.

In November 1945, the Research Branch in the Information and Education Division of the War Department queried a representative group of enlisted men who had returned from combat zones about their experiences in the U.S. Army during World War II. [70] There were few aspects of their experience that elicited positive responses. Most of the soldiers said they were "fed up" with the Army. When asked about coping mechanisms in combat, however, many responded that loyalty to one another and prayer for strength were important coping mechanisms in combat. [71]

In a survey of 1,433 veteran enlisted infantrymen taken in Italy in April of 1945, 84% of the privates and 88% of the noncommissioned officers said that prayer helped them more "when the going got tough" than unit cohesion, the cause they were fighting for, thoughts of finishing the job to get home again, or thoughts of hatred for the enemy.[72] Among company grade infantry officers questioned in the European and Pacific theaters in the spring of 1944, approximately 60 per cent said that prayer helped them a lot in tough circumstances.[73] In both Italy and in the Pacific, at different times, prayer as an aid to adjustment to combat generally ranked higher among enlisted men than did the other personal coping mechanisms listed in the questionnaires. While officers reported being helped by the desire not to let others down, even with them prayer ranked second. [74]

Among very senior officers who expressed religious faith, prayer seemed to be important to remind themselves and their soldiers of their dependence upon a Higher Power, to help senior leaders make decisions calmly, and to help them bear the burdens of their immense responsibilities. Lt. Gen. George Patton recognized the power of spiritual petition when he circulated 250,000 copies of a weather prayer, one for every soldier in the Third Army, during his efforts to relieve Bastogne in December of 1944.[75] President Dwight Eisenhower, in recalling his prayerful decision to launch the Normandy invasion in 1944, reflected that "prayer gives you the courage to make the decisions you must make in a crisis and then the confidence to leave the result to a Higher Power."[76] General of the Army Douglas MacArthur told the cadets at West Point in his "Duty, Honor, Country" address of May 1962:

> The soldier, above all other men, is required to practice the greatest act of religious training—sacrifice. In battle, and, in the face of danger and death, he discloses those divine attributes which his Maker gave when He created man in His own image. No physical courage and no greater strength can take the place of the divine help which alone can sustain him.[77]

In the World War II surveys of combat veterans, prayer was not of itself a sufficient indicator of religious faith; it may have been adopted as an instrument of psychological self-defense. There were no data that could prove a relationship specifically between prayer in battle and formal religion. However, the experience of combat did seem to have an effect on spiritual attitudes, for 79 per cent of combat veterans surveyed in both theaters believed that their Army experience had increased their faith in God.[78] As Lt. Gen. A.A. Vandegrift, Commandant of the United States Marine Corps, reflected on his experiences at Guadalcanal:

The percentage of men who devoted much time to religion might not make a very impressive showing. The average marine, or soldier, or sailor, is not demonstrative about his religion, any more than he is about his patriotism. But I do sincerely believe one thing: every man on Guadalcanal came to sense a Power above himself. There was a reality there greater than any human force. It is literally true—there are no atheists in foxholes—religion is precious under fire.[79]

Thus, from the commander's point of view, the soldier's spirit, the soldier's morale, is not exactly coterminous with the soldier's personal views on, or experience with, religion. The fighting spirit of the soldier may be motivated by any emotion, idea, or complex of ideas that will inspire the soldier to accomplish the mission. These compelling drives may include personal confidence, competence, and pride in self, faith in leaders, unit bonding and cohesion, a belief in the moral necessity and rightness of the cause, a consonance between personal values and national purpose, and a belief that others are depending upon the soldier for success. As the reality of danger increases, however, and casualties pile up, religion seems to provide many soldiers a strong buttress for the spirit and will to endure.

Historically, therefore, religious support for the soldier's spirit has been an important source of strength for many in coping with difficult and dangerous situations, especially over prolonged periods of time. Religious services before battle and the presence of chaplains in the lines, at aid stations, and even in POW camps have helped thousands of soldiers face the uncertainties of war.

For example, during Operation Desert Shield, from August through December 1990, 18,474 soldiers from the XVIII Airborne Corps attended voluntary religious services. The U.S. Army Central Command (ARCENT) sponsored 7,946 religious meetings with an attendance of 341,344 soldiers. Maj. Gen. Barry McCaffrey remarked that "we had the most religious Army since the Army of Northern Virginia during the Civil War."[80]

At midnight on 17 January 1991, Gen. H. Norman Schwarzkopf held a staff meeting with 30 generals and colonels in his war room in Riyadh to read his announcement of the beginning of combat operations. In his message General Schwarzkopf reminded his staff of their purpose, their just cause,

and his total confidence in them. He then asked his chaplain to offer a prayer. The chaplain reflected later that even though it was not discussed as such, the prayer for a quick and decisive victory with few casualties had a unifying, cohesive effect on the staff as they set about the business of war.[81]

In the discussion of spiritual fitness for soldiers in the Army's Health Promotion Program, the term is defined as "the development of those personal qualities needed to sustain a person in times of stress, hardship, and tragedy."[82] No matter how pluralistic the sources for spiritual fitness may be, in the estimation of many senior leaders the ability of the soldier to draw on his or her own spiritual or philosophical resources in times of stress is an undeniable component of readiness. Gen. Gordon Sullivan, former Chief of Staff of the Army, noted a relationship between courage and the spiritual fitness of soldiers in Field Manual 100-1, *The Army*, published in December 1991:

> Courage is the ability to overcome fear and carry on with the mission. Courage makes it possible for soldiers to fight and win. Courage, however, transcends the physical dimension. Moral and spiritual courage are equally important. There is an aspect of courage which comes from a deep spiritual faith which, when prevalent in an Army unit, can result in uncommon toughness and tenacity in combat. [83]

Gen. John Hendrix, a veteran of Operation Desert Storm and Commanding General of U.S. Army Forces Command, stated at a Memorial Day Prayer Breakfast at Ft. McPherson, Georgia, on 22 May 2001:

> Spirituality is an individual matter. We must not cross the line between church and state. But in general spiritual fitness is important to any organization. Spiritual fitness helps shape and mold our character. Spiritual fitness provides each of us with the personal qualities which enable us to withstand difficulties and hardship. When properly exercised, spiritual fitness enhances individual pride in our unit.[84]

Gen. George C. Marshall's comments on the subject to Army chaplains in 1944 in Washington, DC, reinforce the message: "True, physical weapons are indispensable, but in the final analysis it is the human spirit, the spiritual balance, the religious fervor, that wins the victory. It is not enough to fight. . . . It is the spirit which we bring to the fight that decides the issue. The soldier's heart, the soldier's spirit, the soldier's soul, are everything." [85]

TRAINING CONSIDERATIONS: PREPARING SOLDIERS FOR FUTURE COMBAT

Two essential ingredients for success in combat—that is, for creating high morale, unit cohesion, bonding among soldiers, increased personal courage, spiritual strength, and determination to succeed—are inspirational leadership and tough, realistic training. [86] Many officers and noncommissioned officers in the Army, however, have never served in a combat zone. Many others have difficulty envisioning what training for future combat might mean. Therefore we shall glance briefly at the characteristics of the future battlefield and the skills soldiers must possess to prevail. Then, as part of the human dimension, we shall turn to a generalized description of the millennial generation, those Americans born in 1982 and after from whose ranks the Army will recruit its future force. Finally with regard to training, we'll examine a model battalion training program during the Gulf War, noting its holistic approach in utilizing the human dimension for success in future wars.

Battlefield Visualization and Soldier Skills

Army literature on battlefields of the future is complex and copious. For several years at the U.S. Army War College and at the U.S. Army Command and Staff College, among other institutions, numerous subject matter experts prepared briefings, training models, and articles on the Army After Next, on the digitized battlefield, and on Army transformation into a true 21st century fighting force. The purpose of these studies was to prepare the military for future wars and to tailor the reduced forces available to meet changing, possibly asymmetric, threats with a multi-dimensional National Military Strategy.

The Deputy Chief of Staff for Operations and Plans (DCSOPS) has overall responsibility for battlefield visualization. As Lt. Gen. John Miller, former deputy commander, U.S. Army Training and Doctrine Command, explained:

> Battlespace—the use of the entire battlefield and the space around it to apply combat power to overwhelm the enemy—includes not only the physical volume of breadth, depth, and height, but also the operational dimensions of time, tempo, depth, and synchronization. Commanders must integrate other service, nation, and agency assets with their own to apply their effects toward a common purpose. The digitized battle staff—a deputy commander and three planning and operations teams—is one concept to help the commander handle the current battle, the future battle, and sequels to the future battle with an information exchange system that produces virtual collocation between staff and external elements. Emerging technology includes interactive graphics, enemy and friendly force tracking, scalable map displays, three-dimensional terrain visualization, course-of-action analysis, and video-teleconferencing capabilities among other assets.[87]

At the operational and tactical levels, this meant that soldiers would have to be proficient not only with their weapon systems, but also with emerging technologies which would function in all shades of weather, terrain, and illumination. Moreover, dispersal of units, to prevent detection by an enemy with over-the-horizon targeting capabilities, would produce a force with mobile combat power and "just in time" logistics as opposed to the iron mountains of stockpiled equipment familiar on Vietnam-era firebases or on forward-deployed Desert Storm logistical bases.

The specific geography for future engagements is, of course, speculative. In the twentieth century American soldiers have fought in foreign areas on snow-bound tundra, in forests, mountains, deserts, jungles, urban areas, and on sandy beaches. For the future, all of these settings must be considered along with the special problems of homeland defense amidst one's own citizens.

What, then, are the special skills soldiers of the future must possess? In the U.S. Army Training and Doctrine Command's Training, Leader Development and Soldiers Strategy for dealing with change, readiness, and the human dimension, some of these qualities are described:

> First, the leveraging of the human dimension is all about leading change with quality people, grounded on Army values, and

inspired by an American warrior ethos. Adaptive leadership remains an essential aspect. Quality people will need to have the character and interpersonal skills to rapidly integrate individuals and groups of individuals into tailored organizations. They will need to adapt quickly to new situations, and form cohesive teams, and demonstrate competence and confidence operating in complex and ambiguous environments. [88]

In short, the Army will need not just soldiers but soldier-leaders who are committed to the professional ethic, who are talented in small-group facilitation, who are flexible and mentally agile, and who can integrate technological and interpersonal skills in the midst of uncertain and possibly chaotic combat conditions.

Concerning the human dimension, Lieutenant General Miller observed:

> Command of soldiers is, first and foremost, a human endeavor requiring the commander to be a decision-maker and leader. As is the case today, these competent commanders will establish their moral authority by tough, demanding training to standard and by the caring, holistic preparation of their subordinate leaders, soldiers, and units for mission operations. The significance of the bonds of trust and confidence between the leader and the led will grow as the potential for decentralized execution over larger battlespace increases.[89]

Needless to say, with the current shortfall in junior NCOs and company-grade officers, the Army's recruiting and leadership challenges are daunting. One would hope that there are enough time and resources to complete such complex and demanding training before combat operations on a future battlefield become necessary. In the long history of the U.S. Army, however, that has rarely been the case.

The Millennials: What Soldiers for the Future?

From approximately 210 national surveys, interviews, and studies of American young people, prolific authors Neil Howe and William Strauss have formed a description of a group they call The Millennials. These are American young people who were born in 1982 or later, or in other words were 18 or younger in the year 2000. Some characteristics of these young people may be of interest to the Army.

First, they are a large group of approximately 76 million, with 90% native born and about 10% who immigrated to the United States.[90] By the year 2002 they will outnumber the surviving Baby Boomers. They are the most diverse group ethnically in American history, with 36% nonwhite or Latinos in the 1999 youth population.[91] At least one Millennial in five has one immigrant parent, making the Millennials potentially the largest second-generation immigrant group in U.S. history. As the authors point out, their presence will contribute to the irreversible diversification of America.[92]

In terms of religious identity, approximately 20 million are Roman Catholic, which helps account for the growth of the Roman Catholic constituency in the United States from 26.6% of the U.S. Christian population in 1958 (30.6 million) to 38.3% of the U.S. Christian population in 1998 (61.2 million). That is a net increase of 30 million American Roman Catholics in forty years, making the Roman Catholic Church in America four times the size of the Southern Baptist Convention, the largest Protestant denomination.[93]

For many Millennials there is no separation of church and state in their primary education. Two million attend Catholic elementary schools and another two million attend Catholic high schools. Nine in ten private schools in the United States in 2000 had at least a nominal religious affiliation, many with their own mandatory chapel programs. Within the public schools there were no prayer clubs or circles in 1990; now, with the 1995 Federal court ruling that students had a right to organized prayer gatherings as long as they were not official school programs, there are more than 10,000 of them.[94]

Among the Millennials who are over 14, some 65% plan on attending college and 55% go to church regularly as opposed to 45% of Americans as a whole.[95] The ones in high school are bright. They have scored well in science and reading as compared with students from other industrialized countries.[96]

These figures appear even more impressive in light of the report that one-fourth to one-third of all Millennials live in single-parent families. More than half of these single parents, for whatever reason, have unmarried partners living with them.[97] It may not be surprising, then, that about 48% of Millennials have been sexually active as teenagers.[98] The *Chronicle of Higher Education* has reported that, in order to meet the psychological demands of many of these families, there has occurred an increase in "the spiritual dimensions" of social work. Edward R. Canda, a professor of social work at the University of Kansas, noted that "in a crisis or occasion of grief and loss, there is often a shaking of the foundation of one's sense of meaning, who one is, what life is about, and what reality is about. We cannot escape these questions. It would be malpractice to avoid them."[99]

Most importantly, the "war in Kosovo" is the only U.S. military action that most Millennials remember. The oldest young people in this sample were only eight to nine years old during the Gulf War, and the events surrounding the subsequent Oklahoma City Federal building bombing and the Columbine school shootings made greater impressions.[100] The vast majority of this large generation of Americans has no military experience except vicariously at the movies, and unless actively recruited will probably never serve in the armed forces.

Other sources, outside the studies surveyed by Howe and Strauss, paint a less sanguine picture. The State School Superintendent's Office for the state of Georgia reported on 5 May 2001 that of the 116,000 high school freshmen who were enrolled in 1997, only 72,000 graduated in June of 2000. This reflected a high school dropout rate of 38%.[101] Moreover, 47% of Georgia's high school seniors who graduated in the class of 1999 were unable to keep their scholarships as college sophomores because they could not maintain a B average.[102] Finally, United Way reported on 13 May 2001 that there were 230,000 troubled children under some form of care in the state of Georgia—all Millennials under the age of 18. If one assumes that Georgia, with half of its eight million people living in Atlanta, is not too different from many other states, one suspects that the rosy reports by Howe and Strauss were based on the most privileged of the Millennials.

One characteristic which has not been questioned, however, is the growing interest among older young adults in discovering their own interests, vocations, and, in some cases, spiritual insights. Many college students and young business people want to be part of an organization or movement which transcends the ordinary. The Campus Crusade for Christ, for example, has experienced an amazing growth in the past five years among college students looking for meaning in their lives. Campus Crusade has 1,000 college chapters—including one at Harvard—comprising a total of roughly 40,000 students. Donations to Campus Crusade, as reported by The *Chronicle of Higher Education*, exceeded $450 million in the year 2000. "They're bombarded and blasted with all kinds of atheistic teaching from the classroom and they need help," according to William Bright, the lay founder of the movement.[103]

In his recent book, *Capturing the Heart of Leadership*, Professor Gilbert Fairholm of Hampden-Sydney College describes a similar kind of restlessness among young workers:

> Whether we like it or not, work is becoming or has become a prime source of values in our society and our personal lives. American workers are uncomfortable, uncommitted, and adrift. They are searching for new organizational patterns and new paradigms. Integrating the many components of one's work and personal life into a comprehensive system for managing the workplace defines the holistic or spiritual approach. It provides the platform for leadership that recognizes this spiritual element in people and in all of their behavior.[104]

What Fairholm argues is that young people expect leadership to be a relationship, not just a skill or personal attribute. Leaders are leaders only so far as they develop relationships with their followers, relationships that help all concerned to achieve their spiritual as well as economic and social fulfillment.[105] This concept is not far from the Army's definition of the transformational leadership style and may be a constructive bridge in thinking about what "leadership" might mean to the next generation of American soldiers. [106]

A Model for Combat Training

In the summer of 1990, Lt. Col. Gregory Fontenot, commanding the 2nd Battalion, 34th Armor Regiment at Ft. Riley, Kansas, reflected on the training he and his soldiers had received in preparation for their wartime mission. The unit had achieved battle honors and its nickname "Dreadnought" in Vietnam. They had survived their "bloodless combat" exercises at the National Training Center and in REFORGER (Return of Forces to Germany.) But as the rumors of impending war in the Persian Gulf region grew stronger, Fontenot wondered how his current soldiers, untested in combat, would react to fear, stress, and the shock of "seeing the elephant."[108]

As a former assistant professor in the Department of History at West Point, Fontenot did his homework. He read deeply about combat, from fictional accounts such as Stephen Crane's *Red Badge of Courage* to more scholarly studies including Anthony Kellett's *Combat Motivation*. Based on his reading, training, and experience to that time, Fontenot developed the opinion that "unit cohesion stemmed from three general sources: rigorous training to high standards, credible leadership, and soldiers who believed in one another." He added:

> Patriotism and belief in the cause seemed to have little effect on units in combat, though they were important aspects of developing unit cohesion in training prior to combat. None of these conclusions is demonstrable—I came to them via subjective analysis of what I read, heard, and saw. My conclusions are decidedly not the result of objective analysis. In part they stem from my belief that not all human behavior can be reduced to objective and quantifiable data points. Some things must be felt.[109]

Fontenot also believed that the first, and last, emotion to be mastered was fear. He thought that "the stresses of combat are a euphemism for fear. I sought to develop in my soldiers an understanding of what fear would feel like and to eliminate, when possible, the uncertainty that accelerates fear."[110]

In July 1990 Fontenot and members of his color guard participated in a "welcome home" parade for Vietnam-era veterans of the 2nd Battalion, 34th Armor Regiment. It was a reminder of unit pride and tradition just before the Iraqi invasion of Kuwait.

In August it became clear that the United States would fight in the Middle East and that the 2/34 Armor would go to war. Fontenot noted that "each of us had to accept the idea of combat now—not some remote historical event but rather a 'no kidding' fact of life in the immediate present. At this stage, the need to prepare for fear in combat did not drive unit preparation generally or individual psychological preparation specifically. In August, the issue was changing our 'mind-set.' When the mind-set changed, it produced new intellectual and spiritual needs."[111]

For the next five months Fontenot worked to prepare his unit psychologically for combat. He had been working on this training mission since he took command in April of 1989; but as other units began to deploy from Ft. Riley in September, the tasks assumed a new importance and urgency. Fontenot implemented a plan to reinforce unit pride, maximize communication with every soldier in the battalion, provide accurate information, assure complete task understanding, and clarify "the arcane but important" law of war.[112]

He and his staff set up a conference room as a unit history center with slides, videotapes, and actual colors from Vietnam as the centerpiece since "to 18-year-old soldiers in 1989, World War II seemed nearly as distant as the Civil War." New soldier orientations were held in this unit shrine to heroism.

It became Fontenot's goal to meet every soldier in the battalion and to talk frequently to the entire unit from the front of his tank, with chalkboard available, in order to create clear expectations for training and personal relationships with his men. To dispel myths and misinformation about enemy capabilities, qualification gunnery exercises at Ft. Riley's Range Complex were coupled with inspections of the T-72 tank and other Soviet weapons used by the Iraqis. Fontenot required his officers to read a book each month on combat operations from the perspective of a participant and write a critical analysis for him. He personally graded the reports and led discussions on their themes.[113] In November, everyone, including Fontenot, got a "desert haircut," a skin-job which he equated with putting on his Sioux "warfeathers."

At about that time, just prior to deployment in December, Fontenot arranged for a senior chaplain, a personal acquaintance and former colleague who had taught the history of professional ethics in the Department of History at West Point, to come to Fort Riley to present a discussion of just war theory for his officers. The chaplain would himself deploy to Saudi Arabia in December, so he had more than just academic credibility with the officers. Of the chaplain's presentation, Fontenot wrote:

> As esoteric a topic as this might seem, [he] brought to it clarity, wit, and the ability to demonstrate how Thomas Aquinas' thoughts about just war affected tankers and infantrymen today. His talk melded with myriad other preparations we were making and contributed directly to our efforts to strip the coming events of their mystery. [He] showed us another side of the "elephant's" face. [114]

Actually, there were many chaplains involved in both the ethical and spiritual preparations of units for Desert Storm. Twenty of the U.S. Army's training centers had chaplain instructors who were charged strictly not to preach in the classroom, but to discuss professional values, ethics, and leadership. In field units, U.S. Army Forces Command instituted "spiritual fitness training," a command program to address, among other topics, "the full spectrum of moral concerns involving the profession of arms and the conduct of war."[115] The commander's staff officer responsible for conducting the program was the chaplain.

Part of the rationale for tasking chaplains in FORSCOM with the spiritual fitness mission was that they were deployable to combat zones, they could answer questions about morals and morale, they had connections to family support systems back home, they had legal confidentiality so that soldiers could report suspected violations of the law of war to them, as at My Lai in 1968, without fear of recrimination, and they could address the soldier's personal spiritual needs and ethical questions. Although not all chaplains were equally trained in the ethics of war, they helped religious soldiers find the bridge between their spiritual and professional values in a way no other staff officer was expected to do.

By December 1990, the 2/34th Armor was in excess of 100% of its authorized strength—12 tank platoons. The unit moved from the port in Saudi Arabia to tactical assembly area Roosevelt where the lead elements arrived on 12 January 1991. At this point the psychological preparation for combat entered another phase of realism—constant drills, alarms, and alerts for chemical attacks; rehearsals from task force to platoon level; and visits by senior officers to encourage the troops, to exchange information, and to clarify any messages. Maj. Gen. Thomas Rhame, Commander of the 1st Infantry Division, "made sure he laid hands on the troops and commanders. He was enthusiastic and confident, and he communicated that confidence as a senior leader."[116]

As the date approached when the 2/34 would be sent into combat to breach the enemy's prepared defenses, Fontenot began conducting personal chalk talks with primary groups at company and platoon level. He discussed the Clausewitzian triangle of people, state, and army, showing the soldiers how all elements were combined in support of their mission—from the citizens back home to the political leaders to their commanders on the ground. He reminded his soldiers of why the war was being fought and why their mission was important. Finally he discussed fear, how it felt, why it was natural and how it could be useful in stimulating adrenaline and directing the body's blood supply to core functions. "I concluded my discussion by promising them that we would all make mistakes," Fontenot wrote, "however I assured them that we had a technological advantage, superior training, and a good plan of operation, and that our enemies enjoyed none of these benefits."[117]

The 2/34th Armor began its attack on 18 February 1991 against an enemy outpost and fired its last shots on the 28th. The Dreadnoughts destroyed seventy armored vehicles and two dozen trucks, and captured 728 enemy soldiers while participating in night fighting with British and U.S. Air Force support.[118] Of its more than 1,000 soldiers engaged in ten days of combat with enemy tanks and artillery, the 2/34th suffered only two dead and four wounded.[119]

Upon reflection, Fontenot wrote later,

> There is no objective way to demonstrate whether this system of preparation for fear employed in the 2/34 Armor worked. The tolerance of soldiers for miserable conditions and uncertain circumstances remained very high throughout the operation and demonstrated amazing adaptability and patience on their part. There is just no way to ascertain the extent to which ritual, information, discussion, and understanding prepared us for battle. In my experience, commanders at all levels shared the conviction that they bore a responsibility to prepare troops for the stress of combat. The tools to do that included rigorous training, techniques for developing cohesion, clear communication of intent, and addressing the matter of fear forthrightly and on a personal level. [120]

Although Fontenot's account is modest to a fault, the Army was clearly impressed with his insights, not only in past conflicts but also for future integration of strategy, tactics, technology, and the human dimension of leadership. After the Gulf War, he was assigned as the Director, School of Advanced Military Studies, U.S. Army Command and General Staff College, Ft. Leavenworth, Kansas.

CONCLUSION

The purpose of this chapter has been to examine the literature available on the human and spiritual needs of soldiers and how they may be trained for combat in the 21st century. The working hypothesis, that all soldiers have human needs and most have spiritual needs broadly defined, seems to be supported from a wide variety of sources in a number of fields. As Karl von Clausewitz tellingly observed in his treatise *On War*: "All effects in the sphere of mind and spirit have been proven by experience: they recur constantly and must receive their due as objective factors. What value would any theory of war have that ignored them."[121] There also seems no question whether the Army Profession should continue to try to address these needs in the future as part of its leadership doctrine. Indeed, the unique aspects of the profession of arms in requiring the total commitment and unlimited liability of soldiers deployed often in difficult and dangerous situations would seem to mandate such care and concern. Moreover, the Constitution, Congress, and the American people expect and demand it.

A corollary question is to what extent the profession of arms should try to meet the spiritual needs of a military population becoming ever more ethnically, morally, and religiously diverse. At the present time the Army seems to have struck an appropriate balance between facilitating the free exercise of religion and in protecting the freedom of individual conscience for soldiers and their family members. Most religious services and ceremonies are voluntary. The Army's Chaplain Corps, in implementing commanders' religious support programs, currently represents more than 140 different denominations and faith groups in its own ranks. There is no danger that the Army will institutionalize a single religion, nor should it. There is a concern, as a shortage of young ordained clergy grows in both the Roman Catholic and Protestant communities nationally, that there will be a parallel shortage of chaplains for the Army. Part of a solution could lie in the way the Millennial generation chooses to respond to its own spiritual challenges in the 21st century.

The preparation of soldiers for future combat seems to involve more knowledge, more technological skill, and perhaps more maturity on the part of junior leaders than has been the case in the past. Yet the basic principles involved in building relation-ships, unit cohesion, confidence, and courage have not changed very much over the years and may not change markedly in the near future.

There are valid, practical considerations for commanders, staff officers, senior noncommissioned officers, chaplains, surgeons, psychiatrists, and other leaders in preparing soldiers for combat. Some of the more important of these, based on historical experience and analysis, may be summed up as follows:

- Soldiers and family members need to have the most accurate and most current information possible on what they may expect. The importance, necessity, and moral justification of the mission are essential elements of information for the soldiers, their families, and communities if the unqualified support of all affected parties is to be forthcoming.
- Commanders and other leaders need to spend some personal time with soldiers in their primary units to reinforce relationships, cohesion, confidence, and courage. Soldiers must know the commander's intent and their specific jobs to include how they fit into the total effort of the unit.
- Soldiers must have confidence in their leaders, training, equipment, battle plans, and ultimate chance for success. Soldiers should be encouraged to enter into dialogue with their immediate commanders on such subjects as overcoming fear and the means available for supporting one another in the chaos of battle.
- Soldiers need to have time to get their personal affairs in order. This may include time for family, and legal as well as physical, mental, and spiritual preparation.
- Rituals before deployment and before battle based on unit history, esprit de corps, and spiritual preparation are important. These should include voluntary opportunities for religious sacraments, services, or meditation.
- Soldiers need to know that their commanders, senior NCOs, chaplains, and other key personnel are present at every stage during combat operations. The soldiers' morale is strengthened if the total team is demonstrably present and involved.[122]

There is one caveat. War is not a thing which can be seen; it must be thought.[123] No one has ever seen war in all of its dimensions—physical, moral, and spiritual—because each participant sees the event from his or her own narrow, partial perspective. In the distant future, war and the professional skills needed to survive and prevail may be very different with the advent of robotics, information warfare, and even space technologies. Therefore the combat training strategies developed for the first decades of the 21st century may be of short duration, but they will also surely be important for their insights and wisdom in the evolution of future training doctrine and for appreciating the human dimension in Army professionalism.[124]

NOTES

1. The views and opinions expressed in this chapter are those of the author and are not necessarily those of the Department of the Army or any other U.S. government entity.

2. S. L. A. Marshall, *Men Against Fire: The Problem of Battle Command in Future War* (New York: William Morrow Co., 1947), 208, 211.

3. Andrew Abbott, *The System of Professions: An Essay on the Division of Expert Labor* (Chicago, IL: University of Chicago Press, 1988).

4. Don M. Snider and Gale L. Watkins, "The Future of Army Professionalism: A Need for Renewal and Redefinition," *Parameters* 30, 3 (Autumn 2000): 17.

5. Richard A. Gabriel, *To Serve with Honor: A Treatise on Military Ethics and the Way of the Soldier* (Westport, CT: Greenwood Press, 1982), 5-6. Gabriel outlines many of the same handicaps during the Army's shift to the All-Volunteer Force thirty years ago.

6. Attributed to Gen. Robert E. Lee by Douglas S. Freeman as cited in Ken Burns, "The Civil War," PBS video production, 1990, part V.

7. *Sun Tzu: The Art of War,* trans. Samuel B. Griffith (London: Oxford University Press, 1963), 128.

8. FM 22-100, *Army Leadership: Be, Know, Do* (Washington, DC: Headquarters, Department of the Army, 31 August 1999), 3-3.

9. Ibid., 3-4.

10. Ibid., 3-1.

11. Ibid.

12. Ibid., 3-1 and 3-2.

13. Lord Charles Moran, *The Anatomy of Courage* (Boston, MA: Houghton Mifflin, 1967), 202.

14. Interview in Atlanta, Georgia, with James Eric Pierce, former Associate Professor of the Sociology of Religion at Pfeiffer College, on 6 April 2001.

15. Data furnished by Chaplain Michael T. Bradfield, DA Office of the Chief of Chaplains, Washington, DC, 25 April 2001. This is actually a low figure because the 64% of active duty soldiers who profess a specific faith does not count those who belong to faith groups other than the seven largest by population, i.e., Protestant, Catholic, Orthodox, Jewish, Muslim, Buddhist, and Hindu.

16. Task Force TLS, *Training, Leader Development and Soldiers Strategy* (Ft. Leavenworth, KS: U.S. Army Command and General Staff College, 1 October 1999), 75 and slides 14, 17; Lt. Col. Steven W. Shively, Project Officer, DA-ODCSPER, Directorate of Human Resources, *Draft Army Well-Being Campaign Plan*, 5 January 2001, 2.

17. Morris Janowitz, *The Professional Soldier* (New York: The Free Press, 1960), 97.

18. United States Military Academy, Office of Policy, Planning, and Analysis, "Cadet Leader Development System," Draft, July 2001, chapter 3, 3.

19. Jeff Levin, *God, Faith and Health* (New York: John Wiley, 2001), 9-10. Emphasis supplied.

20. Ibid., 10; also see David F. Swenson and Walter Lowrie, trans., *Soren Kierkegaard: Concluding Unscientific Postscript* (Princeton, NJ: Princeton University Press, 1968), 495, for Kierkegaard's condemnation of " faithless religiousness."

21. Robert D. Baird and Alfred Bloom, *Indian and Far Eastern Religious Traditions* (New York: Harper and Row, 1971), 214; and Huston Smith, *The Religions of Man* (New York: Harper and Row, 1958), 149.

22. Geoffrey Parrinder, *World Religions: From Ancient History to the Present* (New York: Facts on File Publications, 1985), 355.

23. Saeed Ahmed, "Falun Gong: Peace of Mind," *Atlanta Journal Constitution*, 19 May 2001, B-1.

24. John W. Wright, ed., *New York Times Almanac 2000* (New York: The Penguin Group, 1999), 414; Levin, 20; and Ron Feinberg, "Amen Corner," *Atlanta Journal Constitution*, 5 May 2001, B-1. This 63% may also be a low figure. The World Christian Encyclopedia published in 2001 reported 192 million Christians in the United States, 32 million more than *The New York Times Almanac* reported in 1998. The difference may be in counting numbers reported by independent congregational churches as opposed to counting only figures from major denominations. See Ron Feinberg, "Report: Christianity Still Largest Religion," *Atlanta Journal Constitution*, 20 January 2001, B-1.

25. Samuel P. Huntingdon, *The Clash of Civilizations and the Remaking of World Order* (New York: Simon and Schuster, 1996), 95-97.

26. A survey of 502 adults from across the country with a 4.5% margin of error as reported in *Atlanta Journal Constitution*, 12 May 2001, B-1.

27. Lord Moran, ix. Lord Moran must not have been as familiar with American sources as he was with British ones, for Yale University Press published William E. Hocking's *Morale and Its Enemies* in 1918.

28. See, e.g., V.V. Shelyag et al., eds., *Military Psychology: A Soviet View* (Washington, DC: Government Printing Office, 1972) ; Richard A. Gabriel, *Military Psychiatry: A Comparative Perspective* (New York: Greenwood Press, 1986); and Anthony Kellett, *Combat Motivation: The Behavior of Soldiers in Battle* (London: Kluwer-Nijhoff Publishing Co., 1982).

29. Robert W. Swezey, Andrew L. Meltzer, and Eduardo Salas, "Some Issues Involved in Motivating Teams," in *Motivation: Theory and Research,* ed. Harold F. O'Neil, Jr., and Michael Drillings (Hillsdale, NJ: Erlbaum Associates, 1994), 141; and Josh R. Gerow, *Psychology: An Introduction* (New York: Longman Publishers, 1997), 360.

30. Gardner Lindzey et al., *Psychology* (New York: Worth Publishers, 1978), 481.

31. Gerow, 360.

32. Lindzey, 481.

33. Ibid.

34. Ibid.

35. Abraham H. Maslow, "A Theory of Metamotivation," in *The Healthy Personality,* eds. Hung-Min Chiang and Abraham H. Maslow (New York: D. Van Nostrand Co., 1969), 29.

36. Ibid.

37. Ibid., 35.

38. Abraham H. Maslow, *Religions, Values, and Peak-Experiences* (New York: Penguin Books, 1970), 4.

39. Bill Mauldin, *Up Front* (New York: W.W. Norton, 2000), 133.

40 Field Manual 22-100, *Military Leadership* (Washington, DC: Headquarters, Department of the Army, 1983), 144-145.

41. Ibid., 135, 144.

42. Ibid., 145.

43. Shively, 2.

44. Ibid., 4.

45. Interview with Chaplain (Major) Daniel Wackerhagen, U.S. Army Chaplain Center and School, Ft. Jackson, SC, 15 May 2001; Steven Reiss, "Toward a Comprehensive Assessment of Fundamental Motivation," *Journal of Psychological Assessment* 10, 2 (June 1998): 97-106.

46. Interview with Dr. Thomas R. Smith, Executive Director for the National Institute for Healthcare Research, Rockville, MD, 4 May 2001; see also Levin, 3-6; and Phyllis McIntosh, "Faith is Powerful Medicine," *Reader's Digest*, October 1999, 151-155.

47. Quoted from a discussion with Col. Eric B. Schoomaker, M.D., former FORSCOM Surgeon and currently Commander of the 30th Medical Brigade in Germany, 11 May 2001.

48. Levin, 9; Maslow, *The Healthy Personality*, 35.

49. Annette Mahoney et al., "Marriage and the Spiritual Realm: The Role of Proximal and Distal Religious Constructs in Marital Functioning," *Journal of Family Psychology* 13, 3 (1999): 321.

50. Ibid., 325.

51. Bradfield.

52. Chaplain (Colonel) Donald Taylor, FORSCOM Command Chaplain, Memorandum for Record, Analysis of FORSCOM Installation Activity Reports for FY 00, Office of the FORSCOM Chaplain, Ft. McPherson, GA, 2 March 2001.

53. Discussion with Dr. Bruce Bell, Army Research Institute, 11 May 2001, who kindly furnished a number of studies used in this paper.

54. U.S. Army Community and Family Support Center, *1995 Survey of Army Families III* (Alexandria, VA: Army Personnel Survey Office, 1995) 5, question 27.

55. James A. Martin et al., eds., *The Military Family: A Practice Guide for Human Service Providers* (Alexandria, VA: The Army Research Institute, 2000), 143,159.

56. Field Manual 22-100, *Army Leadership: Be, Know, Do,* 19.

57. H.A. DeWeerd, ed., *Selected Speeches and Statements of General of the Army George C. Marshall* (Washington, DC: The Infantry Journal, 1945), 121-122.

58. Ibid., 93.

59. Ibid., 123.

60. John Keegan, *The Face of Battle* (New York: Penguin Books, 1976), 274; FM 22-100, *Army Leadership, Be Know, Do*, 3-3.

61. *Sun Tzu: The Art of War*, 128.

62. Lord Moran, 184.

63. Keegan, 335.

64. Ibid., 335-36.

65. Gabriel, 39.

66. John W. Brinsfield, *Encouraging Faith, Supporting Soldiers: A History of the United States Army Chaplain Corps, 1975-1995* (Washington, DC: Headquarters, Department of the Army, Office of the Chief of Chaplains, 1997), part two, 155-156; Russell F. Weigley, *History of the United States Army* (New York: Macmillan Publishing Co., 1967) 519-520.

67. Keegan, 279, 280, 333.

68. William Manchester, *Goodbye Darkness: A Memoir of the Pacific War* (Boston, MA: Little, Brown, 1980), 391, 393.

69. Jonathan Shay, "Trust: Touchstone for a Practical Military Ethos," in *Spirit, Blood, and Treasure: The American Cost of Battle in the 21st Century,* ed.

Donald Vandergriff (Novato, CA: Presidio Press, 2001), E-1-2.

70. Samuel A. Stouffer et al., *The American Soldier: Combat and Its Aftermath* (Princeton, NJ: Princeton University Press, 1949), 611-613.

71. Ibid.

72. Ibid., 177.

73. Ibid., 173.

74. Kellett, 194.

75. John W. Brinsfield, "Army Values and Ethics: A Search for Consistency and Relevance," *Parameters* 28, 3 (Autumn 1998) : 79-82.

76. Ibid.

77. Ibid.

78. Kellett, 195.

79. Ellwood C. Nance, *Faith of Our Fighters* (St. Louis, MO: Bethany Press, 1944), 242.

80. John W. Brinsfield, *Encouraging Faith,* part two, 91.

81. Ibid., 123; interview with Chaplain (Colonel) David P. Peterson, Ft. McPherson, GA, 22 May 2001. Approximately an hour after General Schwarzkopf's staff meeting concluded, President George Bush, Vice President Quayle, General Powell, Secretary Cheney, and most of the President's cabinet attended a prayer service at Ft. Meyer, VA, for the same purpose. The service was also attended by the three Chiefs of Chaplains and by Dr. Billy Graham, the guest speaker. Ibid., 125.

82. Department of the Army Pamphlet 600-63-12, *Fit to Win: Spiritual Fitness* (Washington, DC: U.S. Government Printing Office, 1987), 1.

83. As cited in Brinsfield, "Army Values and Ethics: A Search for Consistency and Relevance," 82.

84. Gen. John W. Hendrix, Personal Notes, Memorial Day Prayer Breakfast Welcoming Address, Ft. McPherson, GA, 22 May 2001, 1.

85. Nance, 190-191. Chaplain Nance, a faculty member at the U.S. Army Chaplain School at Harvard University in 1944, recorded many of Gen. George C. Marshall's comments on the soldier's spirit and the type of chaplains he wanted in the Army. Nance's work was later quoted by Daniel B. Jorgensen, an Air Force chaplain, in *The Service of Chaplains to Army Air Units, 1917-1946* (Washington, DC: Office of the Chief of Air Force Chaplains, 1961), 277; and by Robert L. Gushwa, an Army chaplain, in *The Best and Worst of Times: The United States Army Chaplaincy, 1920-1945* (Washington, DC: Office of the Chief of Chaplains, 1977), 186. Evidently Chaplain (Maj. Gen.) William Arnold in Information Bulletins sent to Army chaplains world-wide as early as August 1941 also regularly quoted General Marshall. See Daniel B. Jorgensen, 146, 299.

86. Field Manual 22-100, *Army Leadership: Be Know, Do,* 20, para. 3-82. Inspirational leadership is intended to combine transformational and transactional leadership styles as indicated in FM 22-100.

87. Lt. Gen. John E. Miller and Maj. Kurt C. Reitinger, "Force XXI Battle Command," *Military Review* 75, 4, (July-August 1995): 6-9.

88. Task Force TLS, 16.

89. Miller and Reitinger, 9.

90. Neil Howe and William Strauss, *Millennials Rising: The Next Great Generation* (New York: Vintage Books, 2000), 14.

91. Ibid., 15.

92. Ibid., 16.

93. Wright, 418; Winthrop S. Hudson, *Religion in America* (New York: Charles Scribner's Sons, 1965), 354.

94. Howe and Strauss, 149, 234.

95. Ibid., 164, 234.

96. Ibid., 144, 164.

97. Chris Roberts, "Number of Single-parent Families Increases 42%," *The State* [Columbia, SC], 23 May 2001, A-1, A-12.

98. Howe and Strauss, 197.

99. D.W. Miller, "Programs in Social Work Embrace the Teaching of Spirituality," *Chronicle of Higher Education*, 18 May 2001, A-12.

100. Howe and Strauss, 19.

101. Reported by Channel 3 Television News, Atlanta, GA, 5 May 2001.

102. *Atlanta Journal Constitution*, 13 May 2001.

103. Beth McMurtrie, "Crusading for Christ, Amid Keg Parties and Secularism," *Chronicle of Higher Education,* 18 May 2001, A-42.

104. Gilbert W. Fairholm, *Capturing the Heart of Leadership: Spirituality and Community in the New American Workplace* (Westport, CT: Praeger Publishers, 1997), 24-25.

105. Ibid., 1.

106. FM 22-100, *Army Leadership: Be, Know, Do,* 19, para. 3-77.

107. William Ernest Hocking, *Morale and Its Enemies* (New Haven, CT: Yale University Press, 1918), 200.

108. Col. Gregory Fontenot, "Fear God and Dreadnought: Preparing a Unit for Confronting Fear," *Military Review* 75, 4 (July-August 1995): 13-24. The account of Colonel Fontenot's preparation for combat with his armor battalion is taken from this article and from his earlier one, "Fright Night: Task Force 2/34 Armor," *Military Review* 73, 1 (January 1993).

109. Fontenot, "Fear God and Dreadnought," 13.

110. Ibid., 13, 14.

111. Ibid.,14,15.

112. Ibid., 18.

113. Ibid., 16.

114. Ibid., 17.

115. U.S. Army FORSCOM Regulation 350-1, 26, para. 3-31, e.

116. Fontenot, "Fear God and Dreadnought," 19.

117. Ibid., 23.

118. Fontenot, " Fright Night: Task Force 2/34 Armor," 39.

119. Ibid.

120. Fontenot, "Fear God and Dreadnought," 24.

121. As cited in Maj. Michael D. Slotnick, "Spiritual Leadership: How Does the Spirit Move You?" Defense Technical Information Center Technical Report AD-A258 523 (Alexandria, VA: DTIC, 1992), 4.

122. A summary of findings from previous references including the U.S. Army Community and Family Support Center, the Army Research Institute, Lord Charles Moran, William E. Hocking, John Keegan, and Gregory Fontenot. For advice to chaplains see Chaplain Milton Haney's "The Duties of a Chaplain" as cited in John W. Brinsfield, "In the Pulpit and in the Trenches," *Civil War Times Illustrated*, September/October 1992, 72-73; and Field Manual 16-1, *Religious Support Doctrine: The Chaplain and the Chaplain Assistant* (Washington, DC: Headquarters, Department of the Army, November 1989), 5-2.

123. Hocking, 49.

124. For assistance in researching and writing this chapter, the author is indebted to Mrs. Teri Newsome and the librarians of the United States Army Chaplain Center and School, the Robert Woodruff Library at Emory University, and the Post Library at Ft. McPherson, GA; as well as to Chaplain Martha Hayes and Chaplain David Colwell at the Office of the Chief of Chaplains; Chaplain Daniel Wackerhagen at the U.S. Army Chaplain Center and School; Chaplain Don Taylor, the Command Chaplain, Headquarters, U.S. Army Forces Command; Chaplain Herb Kitchens, Staff Chaplain, First U.S. Army; Chaplain Kenneth Sampson, the Fifth U.S. Army Chaplain's Office; Chaplain Allen Boatright at the Installation Chaplain's Office, Ft. Stewart, GA; Chaplain Steven Colwell, the Chaplain Instructor, Ft. McCoy, WI; Chaplain Steven Paschall, Third U.S. Army; and those retired chaplains who are cited in the notes; as well as to Dr. Bruce Bell, the Army Research Institute for the Behavioral and Social Sciences; the physicians of the U.S. Army Medical Corps; Ms. Anet Springthorpe, R.N., psychiatric nurse; Dr. Thomas Smith, Director of the National Institute of Healthcare Research; Professor Don Snider of the Department of Social Sciences, USMA; Dr. Daniel Keller, Professor of Philosophy and Ethics, Alabama State University; Mr. David S. Strout of Lakeland, FL; Mrs. Marietta Branson of Atlanta; Mrs. Pat T. Johnson, Chattanooga Baptist Association; Mrs. Debra Yuhas, U.S. Army Forces Command Chaplain's Office; and Gen. John W. Hendrix, Commanding General, U.S. Army Forces Command.

Spiritual Needs II:
The Just War

This is the second of two lessons that deal with spirituality. This lesson provides you with the foundations for understanding the just war and the obligation they have as leaders to help subordinates defend the just war.

The following topics are addressed in this lesson:

- "Just war" tradition;
- Leadership principles derived from the "just war" tradition;
- "Just war" criteria;
  - Just cause
  - Right authority
  - Right intention
  - Formal declaration
  - Last resort
  - Proportionality
  - Discrimination
- *Jus ad bellum;* and
- *Jus in bello*

The following Terminal Learning Objective (TLO) is supported in whole or in part by this lesson:

- Apply "just war" tradition to your service as a leader and the profession of arms.

Following this lesson you will be able to:

- Explain the "just war" tradition;
- Identify the three key leadership responsibilities derived from the "just war" tradition; and
- Apply spiritual tactics to support ethically ambiguous situations.

THE JUST-WAR CRITERIA: A CONTEMPORARY DESCRIPTION

by D.L. Davidson

INTRODUCTION

When Augustine discussed just-war principles, he sought to establish criteria to determine whether or not Christians could morally participate in a war. Though Christians still use the criteria for this reason, the doctrine today is generally applied to evaluate the justification of the war itself. An analogy may be made between the criteria and those moral principles applicable to the use of violence in domestic society.[1] The dictates of conscience, moral reasoning, and common sense agree that indiscriminate killing of persons is wrong and cannot be tolerated. No society can long survive without restraints on criminal acts! Any taking of human life without moral justification is murder; it is intrinsically wrong. The only conditions that justify killing are those necessary for the protection of human life, that is, defense of self and others. Even when justified, however, killing is still subject to moral restrictions and should be avoided if possible. Only the amount of force necessary to restrain aggression is legitimate; and while exercising force, caution must be taken to protect innocent bystanders. These moral principles are reflected in the criminal law codes that regulate civil society.

Similarly, the just-war criteria seeks to determine under what conditions and by what means war is morally justifiable. The doctrine begins with the assumption that the taking of human life even in war is wrong, that it is murder, unless it conforms to the principles of justice. Essentially, war is justifiable only if conducted for defensive purposes. Disproportionate use of force or indiscriminate killing in war is morally wrong. If we return to the thought of Augustine for a moment, we see that just-war doctrine attempts to hold together two claims for those with national responsibility: to protect the lives of citizens through national security and the responsibility to use national security forces morally.

The just-war criteria discussed in the following paragraphs include the *Jus Ad Bellum* principles which identify requisite conditions for resorting to war. These are just cause, right authority, right intention, public declaration, last resort, reasonable hope, and proportionality. Also considered are the *Jus In Bello* principles of proportionality and dis-crimination (noncombatant immunity), the criteria for determining just means. Before turning to them, however, it is helpful to distinguish between "formal" and "substantive" views of the criteria.

Some who discuss just-war theory consider the principles "formal" criteria; others see them as "substantive" proscriptions. A formal view is one that presents a broad outline, or the general form of an idea. A substantive position seeks to specify the content or substance within an idea. According to James Childress the "formal" function of just-war theory is to provide a "framework," or a procedure for analyzing disputes or issues. In this function, the just-war criteria are to be distinguished from policy. They "constitute a formal framework within which different substantive interpretations of justice and morality as applied to war can be debated."[2] A formal theory requires, for example, a just cause before resorting to war but it does not define what constitutes a just cause. This definition requires a substantive theory of justice.

In contemporary discussions among just-war advocates, there is little debate around which criteria to include; that is, there is general agreement on the formal aspects of the theory. Disagreement does exist, however, over substantive issues such as what constitutes justifiable cause, or who is a noncombatant. As we turn now to a discussion of the criteria, their adequacy as to formal framework for debating policy should be assessed; that is, do they identify considerations essential for evaluating war and its means? Also, contemporary views of the criteria should be studied for their contribution toward substantive policies for regulating war.

THE JUST-WAR CRITERIA

Just Cause

What is justice? Though Americans find it hard to agree on specific definitions, we have a general sense of what constitutes justice. It is the impartial distribution of rewards and punishments; justice is "equal opportunity" and "fair treatment." It is, as Aquinas affirmed, "rendering to each one his right." Like "life" and "liberty," justice is a fundamental principle of the nation. The Preamble to the *Constitution* states:

> WE THE PEOPLE of the United States, in Order to form a more perfect Union, *establish Justice,* insure domestic Tranquillity,

provide for the common defense, promote the general Welfare, and secure the Blessings of Liberty to ourselves and our Posterity, do ordain and establish this Constitution for the United States of America.[3] (Underline added.)

Assuming that justice is a regulatory moral principle for domestic and foreign policy, we must then ask, what constitutes a just cause for war? Walzer and Potter affirm that violation of human (and national) rights provide the moral basis for just cause. International law labels such violations crimes of "aggression." Walzer states the case most forcefully: Nothing but aggression can justify war.[4] With Victoria, he concludes that there "is a single and only just cause for commencing a war, namely, a wrong received."[5] The relation between rights and aggression is clear in Walzer's description of aggression:

Aggression is the name we give to the crime of war. We know the crime because of our knowledge of the peace it interrupts—not the mere absence of fighting, but the peace-with-rights, a condition of liberty and security that can exist only in the absence of aggression itself. The wrong the aggressor commits is to force men and women to risk their lives for the sake of their rights. It is to confront them with the choice: your rights or (some of) your lives! Groups of citizens respond in different ways to that choice . . . But they are always justified in fighting; and in most cases, given that harsh choice, fighting is the morally preferred response . . . Aggression is a singular and undifferentiated crime because, in all its forms, it challenges rights that are worth dying for.[6]

Walzer reveals the connection between his views and just-war tradition when affirming the importance of resisting aggression; he writes:

Resistance is important so that rights can be maintained and future aggressors deterred. The theory of aggression restates the old doctrine of the just-war: It explains when fighting is a crime and when it is permissible, perhaps even morally desirable. The victim of aggression fights in self-defense, but he isn't only defending himself, for aggression is a crime against society as a whole.[7]

Like Walzer (and Augustine, Aquinas, Victoria, and Grotius), Potter states that "a just cause for war can only arise out of the necessity to restrain and correct a wrong-doing of others on behalf of the public good."[8]

He specifies three causes which justify war. The first is "to protect the innocent from unjust attack." The nation victimized by unjust aggression has the right to defend itself; that is, "to repel force by force," and to seek alliances with other nations for the purposes of improving its defensive capability. The second cause justifying war, according to Potter, is "to restore rights wrongfully denied." This cause permits a war of "intervention," including crossing another nation's borders to correct a flagrant and persistent denial of justice—as a defense of the innocent. He cites as an example of justifiable intervention coming to the defense of the black community in South Africa should the racist regime governing that country launch an indiscriminate assault on the black population. Walzer also recognizes the justification of intervention in very limited circumstances. He described the Indian invasion of East Pakistan (Bangladesh) in 1971 to stop the aggression of the Bengali people by Pakistani government troops as justifiable intervention.[9] Other examples might include resisting a siege of Berlin or the oppression of Amin in Uganda. The third cause listed by Potter is "to reestablish an order necessary for decent human existence." This cause admits the possibility of "justifiable revolution."[10] Though revolution was not recognized as a right of the people in the Middle Ages, it has been an accepted principle since John Calvin and Locke. Indeed, revolution is the birthright of our own nation, a right documented in the Declaration of Independence:

. . . Governments are instituted among Men, deriving their just powers from the consent of the governed.

. . . But when a long train of abuses and usurpations, pursuing invariably the same Object evinces a design to reduce them under absolute Despotism, it is their right, it is their duty, to throw off such Government, and to provide new Guards for their future security.[11]

Policy makers today face crucial and complex issues concerning intervention and revolution. The modern context is exacerbated in the ideological conflict between democracy and communism. A just war according to Marx-Leninist definition is any war that supports the spread of international communism. A just cause within this ideology is "any class struggle leading to war," especially "liberation war."[12] "Wars of National Liberation" constitute a primary category of communist just wars. Thus, the challenge for American policy makers is to distinguish between wars of revolution, justified because of government oppression, and wars of national liberation instigated by external interference. Just-war theorists disagree when discussing specific cases. The following principles from the just-war tradition can, however, be identified as guidelines relevant to this issue:

(1) Differences in religious or political ideology are not in themselves justification for war or intervention.

(2) Nations should hold strong presumptions against intervening in the internal affairs of other nations or taking sides in a civil war.

(3) Nations are justified in coming to the aid of another nation when that nation is unjustly attacked by a third nation.

(4) Intervention is justified on the request of the government to balance support given by a third nation to an insurrection or insurgency movement.

(5) Intervention is justified in behalf of a revolutionary force seeking to overthrow an extremely oppressive regime, provided that this force has general popular support and has requested intervention.

(6) Intervention is justified to stop massive abuse of human rights.

(7) Intervention is not justified if definitive determination can not be made as to whether or not the unrest in another nation is justifiable revolution with broad popular support or unjustified intervention by a third nation with little popular support.

These principles for intervention, though necessarily somewhat vague and imprecise, seek to hold together the two poles of the right of national self-determination and the justifiable defense of victims of aggression. Crucial in deciding the justification of intervention is the will of the people in the nation experiencing violent conflict.[13]

Two extremely serious problems are associated with the criterion of just cause. The complexity of international relations and, as Walzer says, the lies that governments tell often make it difficult, if not impossible, to determine which side's cause is just.[14] Victoria recognized this dilemma and concluded in such cases that each belligerent should scrupulously adhere to the rules of fighting and seek mutually satisfying terms for peace. Dyck and Potter more closely follow Locke's admonition to seek negotiated or arbitrated settlement.

The second problem with just cause is associated with the first. Wars do not just happen; someone starts them. But determining who is the aggressor is not always easy when international law simply defines the aggressor as the one who "shoots first." Yet, nations sometimes aggress or threaten another nation's security without initiating physical violence, prompting a preemptive strike from the nation challenged. According to international law, preemptive strikes are illegal. Johnson and Walzer object, however, claiming that in certain circumstances they are morally justifiable. Walzer cites the Israeli first strike against Egypt on 5 June 1967 in the Six Day War as a clear example. Egypt had announced a policy of extermination toward Israel. On 14 May the Egyptian government put its military forces on "maximum alert." Four days later Egypt expelled the United Nations Emergency Force from the Sinai and strengthened its forces on the Israeli border. By the end of May, Nasser had announced that he was closing the Straits of Tiran to Israeli shipping and he formed mutual-support treaties with Jordan, Syria and Iraq. The day after the treaty with Iraq was announced the Israelis struck the Egyptian air force on the ground. Walzer concluded that the Israeli strike was justified because it met his criteria for a preemptive strike: (1) a manifest intent to injure, (2) active preparation that makes the intent a positive danger, and (3) a general situation in which the risk of defeat is greatly magnified by the delaying of the fight.[15]

Just cause is the premier criterion of *Jus Ad Bellum*; however, it does not stand-alone. A nation's cause may be just, but still resorting to war may not be moral or prudent. The remaining criteria are necessary for making this determination.

Right Authority

This criterion determines who is to decide whether or not resorting to war is justified. In war between nations, the right authority is the sovereign government of the nation by virtue of its responsibility to provide for the common defense. Certainly a lower authority does not have the right to declare war on another nation. In war within a nation, a rightful authority is one that has substantial popular support before resorting to revolution or civil war. Though just-war theorists commonly advocate this theme, which originated during the Reformation, I have found no one who satisfactorily delineates what constitutes "substantial popular support."[16]

The other side of this question of authority is whether or not citizens ought to support a war declared by the established authority. In the sixteenth century Victoria suggested that the prince ought to seek consultation and be certain that war is justified before turning to hostile action; and the citizen should trust the judgment of the government and support the war effort unless he is certain that the war is unjustified. Childress, for example, affirms that unless a war is "manifestly unjust" the citizen ought to presume "that the authorities, if they are legitimate and have followed proper procedures, have decided correctly."[17] In a democracy like ours, however, where the citizen is both subject and ruler, he concludes that decisions concerning war should have general popular support. Johnson suggests that public consensus on this issue should be forged through a public debate in which the government is responsible for publicizing facts and each citizen is responsible for forming a judgment. Normal political processes should then be followed in which the government's decision on war reflects the will of the people.[18]

Military personnel frequently express the opinion that *Jus Ad Bellum* issues are not the concern of the soldier. The President and Congress have the authority to make decisions concerning war, and the responsibility of the military in this area is to follow orders, not make policy. Arthur Dyck concludes that this view is not fully correct. Officers are policy implementators, not makers. It is the responsibility of military leaders to advise and make policy recommendations, however, and this can be done only if officers are informed on both military and moral issues. Therefore, Dyck affirms that military officers should have competent knowledge in just-war doctrine as well as military capabilities and strategy.[19] It seems reasonable to conclude from the just-war perspective that officers should assume that government decisions are correct, at least until they are firmly convinced otherwise. At this point, however, they should recall that their oath of office compels them to support the *Constitution*, not a government acting contrary to constitutional principles, and to obey "lawful" orders (or those that comply with the *Constitution*).

Right Intention

This criterion focuses on attitudes and goals in war. Augustine suggested that the right attitude was love of neighbors and enemies. Among contemporary writers, Paul Ramsey has continued this theme, at least when addressing other Christians. "It is the work of love and mercy," he says, "to deliver as many as possible of God's children from tyranny, and to protect (them) from oppression."[20] Jesus taught his disciples to turn their own cheek, but he did not instruct them to lift up the face of another oppressed man to be struck on both cheeks. When commenting on the work of Aquinas, Ramsey affirmed: "Profoundly at work in his line of reasoning is what justice transformed by love requires to be extended even to him who wrongfully attacks."[21] According to Ramsey, the principle of "double effect: emphasizes that the right intention of war is to defend life. Taking the life of even an unjust person (i.e., aggressor) should be avoided if possible."[22]

Most of the contemporary discussion around intention concentrates on the attitudes with which war is fought. Ramsey's work lies primarily within the context of *Jus In Bello*. Similar observations, however, can be made in reference to the attitudes prevailing when deciding whether or not to resort to war.[23] The *Jus Ad Bellum* consideration of intentions strongly influenced the rejection of wars for religion, the crusade idea. Contemporary commentaries also tend not to equate love and right intention, unless addressed specifically to religious audiences. The focus is more on the impropriety of the motives of vengeance, cruelty, and hatred. A generalized hatred toward the enemy leads too quickly to events like those at Beirut or My Lai. Once the enemy is viewed as something less than human, atrocities are more likely to occur.

The other major idea discussed under the criterion of right intention is the goals for which war is waged. If aggression constitutes a just cause for war, then a justifiable goal for war is stopping aggression; that is, a restoration of a just peace. During the

Korean War a heated debate emerged between limited war advocates and those who claimed that there is no substitute for victory. Walzer's conclusion on this issue is that "if a just war, its goals properly limited, there is indeed nothing like winning."[24] He recognizes the tension between the importance of winning and justifiable goals. Certainly justice would not be served if a manifestly unjust aggressor achieved victory over a nation justifiably defending itself. From the moral point of view, aggression ought to be defeated! But the other side of this issue is how far you may go in winning. Do you simply stop aggression? Do you also punish the aggressor leaders for their actions? Would you go a step further and dictate a regime to govern the defeated aggressor nation? In other words, what are justifiable goals in waging war? In responding to this question, Walzer concludes:

> The theory of ends in war is shaped by the same rights that justify the fighting in the first place—most importantly, by the right of nations, even of enemy nations, to continue national existence and, except in extreme circumstances, to the political prerogatives of nationality.[25]

He agrees with Locke that establishing a perpetual rule over the defeated nation is not a justifiable goal for war. He does recognize the propriety of punishing the leaders of the aggressor nation and insists that "it is vitally important that they not be allowed to benefit" from their "crimes."[26] The goals of stopping aggression, punishing the leaders of aggression to deter future aggression, and establishing temporary (though not permanent) occupational forces were validated by Nuremberg and appear consistent with just-war tradition.

A related issue is how and when to terminate hostilities? This question involves a *Jus In Bello* consideration of goals. John Rawls expresses a view that has wide currency among contemporary writers:

> The aim of war is a just peace, and therefore the means employed must not destroy the possibility of peace or encourage a contempt for human life that puts the safety of ourselves and of mankind in jeopardy.[27]

Generally, the just-war tradition argues against total destruction of the enemy and unconditional surrender. Just-war writers also warn against rushing so quickly toward a cessation of combat that an "unjust" peace is established. Walzer concurs with the American negotiators in the Korean War who refused to accede to North Korean demands for forcible repatriation of prisoners as a condition for cease-fire. Although their decision prolonged the fighting, the American negotiators "insisted on the principle of free choice, lest the peace be as coercive as war itself."[28] A just peace, the proper goal of war, is one that lays the foundation for future harmonious relations between belligerents, rather than leaving conditions and attitudes that abet future wars.[29]

Formal Declaration

This criterion states that the legitimate authority of a nation should formally declare its intentions before resorting to war. American law also requires a formal declaration to invoke a "legal" status between belligerent nations. "The Law of Land Warfare" (U.S. Army Manual, FM 27-10) records: "The Contracting Powers recognize that hostilities between themselves must not commence without previous and explicit warning, in the form either of a reasoned declaration of war or of an ultimatum with conditional declaration of war." The manual then adds the interpretive comment that surprise is still possible because "nothing in the foregoing rule requires that any particular length of time shall lapse between a declaration of war and the commencement of hostilities."[30] This interpretation seems to nullify what Potter sees as the purposes of this criterion: (1) to indicate to a potential enemy how war can be avoided; (2) to give notice to other nations so that they may assess the justice of the cause and conduct themselves accordingly; and (3) to establish with certainty that war is being waged on the initiative of the will of the people rather than a small clique.[31] Potter's views are consistent with the just-war tradition; however, there is not a clear consensus on this criterion among contemporary writers. Childress indicates that a formal declaration may not always be appropriate; and Johnson considers this criterion unimportant today because of the movement to apply the laws of war in all armed conflict, not just in conditions of officially declared war.[32] The Egyptian-Israeli Six Day War, discussed above under the principle of just cause, appears to be a legitimate example of when an advanced formal declaration would be inappropriate. The objective of this criterion is sound, however, and if publication in advance is not practical, still there is a need to declare intentions and to state the conditions acceptable for ending hostilities.

Last Resort

When one reflects on the vast destruction, death, and injury that accompany modern war, there is a compulsion to recoil from any use of violence. Yet, heinous atrocities (e.g., Dachau, Bataan, Warsaw), marshal driving impulses to rescue sufferers and punish aggressors. The just-war doctrine attempts to hold both of these poles in tension rather than siding completely with either one. In discussing this tension Potter concludes:

> Moral power belongs to those who affirm both the obligation to contend for justice and the ideal not to harm. The two claims must be held together . . . There is a constant temptation to relieve the tension by scanting one claim or the other and thus by simplifying the moral situation.[33]

The criterion of just cause admits the propriety of defending human rights, by force if necessary. The principle of last resort emphasizes that recourse to force is moral only when truly necessary, and when other viable alternatives are not available. Last resort reminds us of our moral duty not to harm, that resorting to war must be done reluctantly. Just cause is not license and should lead to war only as a last resort. When possible, conflict between and within nations should be resolved by means other than war, such as negotiation, arbitration, appeal to international institutions, and economic sanctions. The Catholic moralist Francis J. Connell states the thesis of last resort as follows:

> . . . rulers of nations may not declare war against another nation unless they are sure they are in the right, and have first tried all peaceful measures that might contribute toward righting the wrong inflicted by this other nation.[34]

The principle of last resort does not insist that every conceivable alternative to war be attempted. The nature of some aggressive acts may preclude some alternatives. It does require, however, that all realistic options be considered before deciding on the alternative of war.

Proportionality

The principle of proportionality evaluates the effects or ends of war. It does this by calculating the value of expected results. In this regard, proportionality is "counting the costs," or cost-benefit analysis. In ethical decision making there is frequently a tension between "ends" and "means," between the "good" result desired and conceptions of what is "right" action. Those who consider results the only valid criterion for selecting a course of action are in effect saying that "the ends justify the means." The just-war tradition attempts to incorporate both elements, good results and right action, in making decisions about war. In the *Jus Ad Bellum* sense this principle insists that there be "due proportion, that is, less evil following from acting rather than not acting in the manner contemplated."[35] War is not justifiable if it will produce more destruction that it prevents. In the language of the limited-war idea, proportionality means that "the costs of the war must not outweigh the benefits."[36] Understood this way, proportion has the potential for overriding just cause. In just-war doctrine, a nation may have just cause, right intentions, justifiable goals, and may consider war as a last resort, and still may not be morally justified in going to war if the results on balance, are negative. Ramsey writes:

> It can never be right to resort to war, no matter how just the cause, unless a proportionality can be established between military/ political objectives and their price, or unless one has reason to believe that in the end more good will be done than undone or a greater measure of evil prevented.[37]

The principle of proportionality is related to another concept, which at times is discussed as a separate criterion. This concept resolves that under most conditions nations should not go to war unless there is a reasonable hope of success. Political leaders "are stewards of the welfare of the nation and the life of each citizen."[38] Lives and goods are to be defended, but not squandered. If there is not reasonable expectation of success, or a balance of good to be achieved in war, then resort to war squanders the lives and resources of the nation. Therefore, it is possible for war to be a moral option only if there is due proportion and a reasonable hope of success.

The principle of proportionality also has been applied to *Jus In Bello* issues in the modern era. In this context the principle states that the means of fighting, including tactics and weapons, should be proportionate to the provocation and the mission; namely, one does not use a sledge hammer to kill a fly! It is not right to cause unnecessary suffering. Proportionality in the conduct of combat is related to the principle of war called "economy of force."[39] Both suggest that assets be judiciously employed to achieve victory with minimum loss of lives and resources. Economy of force, however, is primarily concerned with the efficient use of resources, whereas proportionality seeks to determine how much force is justified in response to particular cases of aggression. Even if resources were ample and sufficient means were available, still it would be morally wrong to destroy a village by air strikes and artillery because of fire from a single sniper. Critics frequently cited such cases in Vietnam as illustrations of disproportionate means. Some antagonists moved from the combat context to *Jus Ad Bellum* conclusions. If effect, they were saying that disproportionate means overrode the justice of the cause, that "overkill" destroyed more values than the war was preserving.

The essence of the principle of due proportion is to proscribe unnecessary suffering. This principle is reflected in the international laws of war in the prohibitions against such acts on undefended buildings or towns, use of poisons, torture, and unnecessary destruction of food, property, and other domestic resources.[40]

Discrimination

One distinction between just-war theory and the limited-war idea is that in the latter proportionality, in the terms of "cost-benefit analysis," has more prominence. Just-war theory places greater emphasis on protecting the innocent, or "discriminating" between warriors and noncombatants. Many just-war theorists tend to view noncombatant immunity as an "absolute" principle, whereas limited-war advocates more frequently consider the principle a "relative" concept. Ramsey insists on the priority of immunity over proportionality.[41] Johnson, however, considers Ramsey's emphasis on the absoluteness and priority of discrimination an "extreme" position within the just-war tradition.[42]

Of all the just-war criteria, the principle of noncombatant immunity is most frequently represented in the international laws of war. Walzer observes:

The war convention rests first on a certain view of combatants, which stipulates their battlefield equality. But it rests more deeply on a certain view of noncombatants, which holds that they are men and women with rights and that they cannot be used for some military purpose, even if it is a legitimate purpose.[43]

Virtually every moral commentary on war since World War II, whether focused on the air battle or ground combat, has discussed the problem of noncombatant immunity. The issue is not whether noncombatants should be immune to attack; there has been general agreement on this point since classical times. Rather, the problem is deciding "who" is a noncombatant; that is, the problem of discrimination. The difficulty of differentiating between combatants and noncombatants has escalated with each stage in the development of modern warfare: the advent of conscript armies and large standing armies in Napoleon's era, new weaponry developed in the industrial revolution, the mobilization of whole societies in major wars, the large scale employment of guerrilla or insurgency war and terrorism, and the invention of weapons of mass destruction.

Traditionally, noncombatants have been distinguished either in terms of their "function" during war or their "class." This last method identifies noncombatants as those persons belonging to certain classes or professions, such as medical personnel, the clergy, farmers, merchants, and others designated as "protected persons." The functional method of discrimination classifies as noncombatants those who do not "contribute directly" to fighting the war. Writers vary, however, in specifying what constitutes direct participation. The elderly, infirm, and infants are normally considered noncombatants. Soldiers in uniform are combatants, unless they wear certain distinctive symbols which identify them as noncombatants, or they have been rendered incapable of hostile acts. For example, medical personnel and chaplains wear distinctive symbols; prisoners of war and soldiers with incapacitating wounds are incapable of hostile action, and, thus, are noncombatants. Persons who violate their noncombatant status are subject to attack.[44] Among civilians, those who make war decisions or produce war materials are generally considered as direct contributors to the war effort and, thus, are combatants. Those who perform services or produce goods necessary for living are noncombatants, even though military personnel may use their services or goods. This line of reasoning, for example, allows bombardment of munitions factories, but not canneries. In describing whom a combatant could attack, Anscombe stated:

> But people whose mere existence and activity supporting existence by growing crops, making clothes, etc., constitutes an impediment to him—such people are innocent and it is murderous to attack them, or make them a target for an attack which he judges will help him towards victory. For murder is the deliberate killing of the innocent, whether for its own sake or as a means to some further end.[45]

Anscombe maintains that noncombatants can be distinguished, at least a large portion of them, for "even in war, a very large number of the enemy population are just engaged in maintaining the life of the country, or are sick, or aged, or children."[46] Our experience in Vietnam, however, demonstrates how complex identifying noncombatants can be. Is a child carrying live munitions, for example, a combatant or noncombatant? Nevertheless, in insurgency warfare, where a principal goal is winning the allegiance of the populace, noncombatant immunity is even more crucial. Also it should be remembered that unconventional war, as its name implies, is not a paradigm for all warfare.

Another serious dilemma associated with the principle of noncombatant immunity is the issue of "military necessity." This asks if moral rules (and legal statutes) can be set aside for the sake of accomplishing a legitimate military objective. Is it right for a defending nation to employ proscribed means if these are necessary to avoid defeat by an aggressor?

Answers to this question vary, depending on one's concept of moral principles and the rule of military necessity. Those who view moral principles as absolutes oppose overriding the principle of immunity in cases of military necessity. Those who conceive of principles as general guides are more inclined to set aside norms when they conflict with objectives. The latter suggest that the laws of war and just-war principles do not impede military effectiveness, because they do not preclude any action militarily necessary in war.[47]

A third position[48] falls between these two. It describes ethical principles as "ideal" (or *prima facie*) duties. They are always "actual" duties except in contexts where one ideal duty conflicts with another. In such cases both can not be honored, and the context strongly influences which duty one should fulfill. When an ideal duty is set aside, it still retains its importance and should be restored as soon as possible. In the question of military necessity, the duty not to harm noncombatants conflicts with the duty to protect human life by defeating aggression. For an action to qualify as a military necessity, however, the context must be one in which defeat is truly an issue. In circumstances where these two duties actually conflict, ethicists who hold this view of moral principles generally accept the validity of military necessity.

Military necessity, however, has often been invoked in the past to justify violations of immunity, which were not essential to victory, as the German doctrine of *Kriegsraison*, illustrates. In summary, this doctrine stated that military necessity "overrides and renders inoperative the ordinary laws and customs of war."[49] With this doctrine in World War II, Germans claimed as "military necessity" the extermination of millions of Poles, Russians, Gypsies, and Jews; medical experiments on prisoners; and the deportation of citizens of occupied territories to slave labor.[50] Many ethicists also criticize the Allied fire bombing of Dresden and Tokyo and the atomic bombing of Nagasaki and Hiroshima as violations of the principle of immunity and abuse of the concept of military necessity.

The international lawyers McDougal and Feliciano suggest that in the view reflected in the doctrine of *Kriegsraison*, military necessity has come to mean "relative expediency and comparative convenience and advantageousness."[51]

Walzer rejects this thinking in even stronger language:

> The doctrine justifies not only whatever is necessary to win the war, but also whatever is necessary to reduce the risks of losing, or simply to reduce losses in the course of the war. In fact, it is not about necessity at all; it is a way of speaking in code, or a hyperbolic way of speaking, about probability and risk.

Walzer rejects some applications of military necessity but not the basic concept.

How then shall we evaluate claims of military necessity? A good starting point is Potter's general affirmation that "the principles governing the right and wrong use of force cannot be broken with (moral) immunity. There is a high cost to defying each and every one."[52] Therefore, our predisposition must favor adhering to the principle of noncombatant immunity. That a proposed action really is a military necessity always requires substantiation. Next, the principle of immunity should shape our policies for fighting, and especially target selection. Ramsey insists at this point that warfare ought to be "counter-force," that is, directed at combatants. Noncombatants, he says, are never legitimate targets in themselves for direct attack.[53] Actual military necessity may permit the harming of noncombatants, according to Johnson, but only at the point where the *Jus In Bello* principle of immunity has become a *Jus Ad Bellum* emergency; that is, when necessary to enable a nation with just cause to avoid defeat at the hands of an unjust aggressor.[54] Walzer states this position clearly. Kant insisted that we do no injustice "though the heavens fall."[55] Walzer rephrases Kant in his maxim: "do justice unless the heavens are (really) about to fall."[56] He explains:

> These, then are the limits of the realism of necessity. Utilitarian calculation can force us to violate the rules of war only when we are face-to-face not merely with defeat but with a defeat likely to bring disaster to a political community. But these calculations have no similar effects when what is at stake is only the speed or the scope of victory. They are relevant only to the conflict between winning and fighting well, not to the internal problems of combat itself.[57]

Walzer thus admits that immunity can be overridden in cases of "supreme emergency," or when a nation's political survival is at stake. He allows military necessity in its extreme form, only when there are *Jus Ad Bellum* consequences.

The question in the case of military necessity is where to draw the line. It is certainly reasonable to draw this line well short of the *Kriegsraison* doctrine. However, this does not mean that the principles are absolute and the rules should never be overridden. Troop commanders are rightly concerned for the welfare of their personnel in combat. Indeed, they are morally and legally responsible for their safety.

Therefore, I would draw the line as follows: Combat commanders can take actions necessary to avoid the destruction of their personnel, even if it may mean indirectly harming civilians as long as due proportion is not exceeded. This premise runs great risk of abuse, and must, therefore, be applied with exacting moral discipline. An example of the circumstances I have in mind is that a commander could call in close-air support to avoid being overrun by the enemy, even though he knew that civilians would be killed in the process. Such action is allowed under the principle of "double effect" (cf. Aquinas, above) in that intended targets of the air attack would be enemy troops. The innocent civilians would be unintended victims. This kind of action remains subject to the restraints of due proportion and noncombatant immunity continues in principle. Combat decisions such as this must also consider the fact that soldiers are legitimate targets of attack, noncombatants are not.

CONCLUSION

We have now concluded our description of the just-war criteria. One final word is in order before we consider more directly the issues associated with nuclear weapons. Walzer stated: "War is always judged twice, first with reference to the reasons states have for fighting, secondly with reference to the means they adopt."[58] He is affirming that both *Jus Ad Bellum* and *Jus In Bello* criteria are essential for a complete moral doctrine of just war. The position of Dyck, Potter, Johnson, Childress, and Walzer is that each of the just-war criteria are necessary.[59] They have evolved over the centuries because theologians and philosophers have recognized their moral rightness, but also because statesmen and soldiers have acknowledged their practical value. It is not to the commander's advantage if civilians turn to underground subversion or "fifth column" terrorism because of abusive treatment. War is even more violent when enemy troops "fight to the death" because they are more afraid of becoming prisoners of war. And certainly, in the age of modern weaponry, opting for war is prudent only for a justifiable cause and as a last resort when there is a reasonable hope of defeating aggression and restoring a just peace.

NOTES

1. Analogies similar to the one which follows are presented by Childress in "Just-War Theories: The Bases, Interrelations, Priorities, and Functions of Their Criteria," *Theological Studies* 39 (September 1978): 428-31; Potter, "The Moral Logic of War," *McCormick Quarterly* 23 (May 1970): 203f; Walzer, *Just and Unjust Wars: A Moral Argument with Historical Illustrations* (New York: Basic Books, Inc., 1977), pp. 53-62.

2. James F. Childress, "Just-War Criteria," in *War or Peace? The Search for New Answers*, ed. Thomas A. Shannon (Maryknoll, New York: Orbis Books, 1980), p. 51. James T. Johnson, interview, Rutgers University, 5 January 1982.

3. Henry Steele Commager, ed., *Documents of American History*, 5th ed. (New York: Appleton-Century-Crafts, Inc., 1949), p. 139.

4. Walzer, *Just and Unjust Wars*, p. 62.

5. Ibid.

6. Ibid., pp. 51 and 53.

7. Ibid., p. 59.

8. Potter, "The Moral Logic of War," p. 207.

9. Walzer, *Just and Unjust Wars*, p. 108.

10. The three causes for war are discussed by Potter in "The Moral Logic of War," pp. 207-16.

11. Commager, *Documents of American History*, pp. 100-101.

12. For further discussion see "The Poverty of Philosophy" and "The Communist Manifesto" by Marx, reprinted in *Karl Marx: Selected Writings,* edited by David McLellan, especially pp. 215 and 246. Paul Ramsey provides an extended discussion of revolution in *War and the Christian Conscience,* Chapter 6, "Justifiable Revolution," and in *The Just War,* p. 189, from which the quotation in the text is cited. Here Ramsey is quoting from Y.A. Korovin, et. al., Academy of Sciences of U.S.S.R., *International law* (Moscow: Foreign Languages Publishing House), p. 402. Support of liberation movements is fundamental to the "Brezhnev Doctrine and the 1977 Soviet Constitution."

13. See Walzer, *Just and Unjust Wars*, Chapter 6, "Interventions."

14. Ibid., p. 74.

15. Ibid., p. 81.

16. See for example James Turner Johnson, "What Guidance Can Just-War Tradition Provide for Contemporary Moral Thought about War," *New Catholic World* 226 (March-April 1982):83.

17. Childress, "Just-War Theories," p. 436. Ramsey and Johnson generally concur with Childress.

18. James T. Johnson, personal interview, Fort Monmouth, New Jersey, 9 April 1982. See also "Just War Theory: What's the Use?," *Worldview* 19 (July-August 1976).

19. Personal Interview, Cambridge, Massachusetts, 7 February 1981.

20. Ramsey, *The Just War,* p. 143.

21. Ramsey, *War and the Christian Conscience*, pp. 43-44.

22. Ibid., p. 43.

23. See Johnson, "Just War Theory: What's the Use?," p. 43.

24. Walzer, *Just and Unjust Wars*, p. 122.

25. Ibid., p. 123.

26. Ibid.

27. Rawls, *A Theory of Justice* (Cambridge, Massachusetts: The Belknap Press of Harvard University Press, 1971), p. 379.

28. Walzer, *Just and Unjust Wars*, p. 123.

29. See Childress, "Just-War Theories," pp. 438-39.

30. See U.S. Army Field Manual 27-10: The Law of Land Warfare, 15 July 1956, p. 15. This law is a Hague Convention protocol.

31. Potter, "The Moral Logic of War," p. 219.

32. Johnson, "Toward Reconstructing The *Jus Ad Bellum*," *The Monist* 57 (October 1973):487, note 46.

33. Potter, *War and Moral Discourse,* p. 53.

34. Connell, "Is the H-bomb Right or Wrong," *The Sign* (March 1950): 11-13; quoted from Ramsey, *War and The Christian Conscience*, p. 78.

35. Dyck, "Ethical Bases of the Military Profession," p. 44.

36. See Johnson, *Just War Tradition,* pp. 204f. Johnson also discusses here the often noted difficulty in proportionality and utilitarian theory in general of accurate calculation of effects, or end results.

37. Ramsey, *The Just War,* p. 195.

38. Potter, "The Moral Logic of War," p. 219.

39. See U.S. Army Field Manual 100-1: The Army, 14 August 1981, p. 15.

40. See U.S. Army Field Manual 27-10: The Law of Land Warfare, passim.

41. Ramsey believes that questions of justice take precedence. Therefore, he emphasizes that the principle of protecting the innocent, which is manifested in the criteria of just cause and discrimination, should be considered prior to discussions of effects. That is, a nation should determine if it is "right" to resort to war or use certain weapons in the protection of the innocent from aggression before asking if these actions are proportionate responses. This does not mean for Ramsey that proportionality may not rule out these proposed actions. See Ramsey, *War and The Christian Conscience,* Chapter One, and pp. 143-45, 154, 351, passim; Ramsey, *The Just War,* p. 155.

42. See Johnson, *Just War Tradition,* Chapter Seven. Johnson points out that noncombatant immunity was an idea emphasized more by chivalry than theology in the Middle Ages. He views Walzer's position which allows discrimination to be overridden, but only in "supreme emergencies," as more characteristic of the tradition than Ramsey's absolutist position. It is worth noting, however, that many contemporary theological and philosophical writers also consider this principle absolute, or at least nearly so; cf. Richard Wasserstrom, Thomas Nagel, Jeffrie Murphy, Alan Donagan, and others. See discussion below.

43. Walzer, *Just and Unjust Wars*, p. 137.

44. For example, persons in civilian clothing carrying weapons, chaplains carrying weapons, prisoners who

seek to escape or commit hostile acts, and wounded soldiers who attempt hostile acts are combatants.

45. Elizabeth Anscombe, "War and Murder," originally published in 1961, cited from Wakin, *War, Morality, and the Military Profession* (Boulder: Westview Press, 1979), p. 289.

46. Ibid., p. 297.

47. This view is congruent with the limited-war concept and with utilitarian ethical theory, even the "rule" kind.

48. This position has been developed from the theory of the British philosopher Sir David Ross. This view considers ethical principles to be *prima-facie* duties, rather than absolute or relative guidelines. They are intrinsically right, but not always fitting. This view is a modification of the traditional deontic theory of ethics and should not be confused with "situation ethics." For further discussion, see Childress, "Just-War Theories," and William K. Frankena, *Ethics*, 2nd edition (Englewood Cliffs, New Jersey: Prentice-Hall, Inc., 1973), pp. 55-56.

49. Myres S. McDougal and Florentino P. Feliciano, *Law and Minimum World Public Order: The Legal Regulations of International Coercion* (New Haven: Yale University Press, 1961), p. 672.

50. These ruthless acts were claimed as acts of "military necessity" by various Germans in the war crimes tri-

als following World War II; cf. McDougal and Feliciano, pp. 676-677.

51. Ibid., p. 672.

52. Potter, "The Moral Logic of War," p. 225.

53. Ramsey, *War and The Christian Conscience*, pp. 68, 70, 148-49, 228-29, 320-23, passim. Ramsey's "counter-force" strategy rejects "Counter-Value Strategy," which advocated the targeting of nuclear weapons on enemy cities. Ramsey insists that only enemy forces (including war industries) are legitimate targets.

54. For Walzer and Brandt, Hitler's Germany is the paradigmatic example of an aggressor against whom a nation could morally override the principle of immunity, if necessary, to avoid defeat.

55. Cited from Murphy in Wakin, *War, Morality, and the Military Profession*, p. 354.

56. Walzer, *Just and Unjust Wars*, p. 231.

57. Ibid., p. 268.

58. Ibid., p. 21.

59. As noted earlier, Johnson, who has taken on the task of restoring to international recognition the *Jus Ad Bellum* criteria, does not emphasize "public declaration"; this omission, however, results from his position that all military conflict is subject to these moral principles, not legally declared wars only.

Consideration of Others I

This is the first in a set of two lessons on the Army's policies on Equal Opportunity and Prevention of Sexual Harassment. You will explore the Army's EO and POSH programs through review of the *VEILS System,* the Virtual Experience Interactive Learning Software.

The following topics are addressed in this lesson:

- Consideration of Others (COO) program;
- Equal Opportunity (EO) program;
- Prevention of Sexual Harassment (POSH) program;
- Consideration of Others and organizational climate; and
- relationship of organizational climate to individual and unit mission effectiveness.

The following Terminal Learning Objective (TLO) is supported in whole or in part by this lesson:

- Understand basic knowledge of Consideration of Others (CO)) and human diversity.

Following this lesson you will be able to:

- Identify behaviors that are inappropriate or disrespectful.
- Describe the impact of disrespectful behavior on unit cohesion and morale; and
- Identify possible steps to correct inappropriate or disrespectful behavior.

RACISM AND SEXISM

by D.L. Davidson

Racism and sexism are forms of discrimination that are very similar. Sexism is based on gender while racism is based on race or color.

1. DEFINITION. Personal racism or sexism is an attitude of superiority, coupled with an act to subordinate an individual, because of their race or gender.

2. FACTORS IN THE DEVELOPMENT OF RACISM AND SEXISM.

   a. *Contact between racial and ethnic groups is nearly as old as human life itself.* People have always migrated from area to area. These migrations were for various reasons, but regardless of the reasons, these migrations resulted in contacts with different cultures.

   b. *Social visibility.* With contact, comes social visibility. Society likes to categorize things, to include people. The easiest way to categorize people is through obvious traits. Something visual, such as skin color; names, i.e. Jewish, Hispanic, Polish; language, or other features such as folds of the eyes, are all traits that make categorizing people simple to do. Cultural habits such as what we eat, how we prepare meals, celebrations, what utensils we use, all can play a factor in social visibility differences. It is common to take the position that "different means wrong."

   c. *Unequal power.* Whoever has the power can control resources and make policies. The group in control develops a feeling of superiority.

   d. *Ethnocentrism* is a belief that one's own ethnic group is superior to all other groups. If this group also holds the power—likely the majority—then this belief can become even more damaging to the minority groups.

   e. *Competition.* When everyone wants a piece of the pie, some are likely to get a bigger piece than others. Generally, it will be the group in power who gets the bigger piece.

   f. *Stereotypes.* We learn our stereotypes from parents, schools, peers, and the media. Stereotypes maintain prejudice.

   g. *Sex-role socialization.* This is the process by which males and females learn to display appropriate behavior for their sex. In learning these roles during sex-role socialization, we also acquire attitudes and values associated with these roles.

3. PERSONAL RACIST AND SEXIST BEHAVIORS. Some behaviors that we observe on a daily basis are actually racist and sexist behaviors. Let's look at a few of these behaviors and discuss their impact on minorities and women.

   a. *Paternalism.* This behavior takes the form of acting 'fatherly' or over-protective of someone. Frequently, this behavior will take place toward a female, and when it does, can be a form of sexism. It may imply that the woman is incapable of doing her job, or surviving without the man taking her under his wing and helping her along.

   b. *Ignoring.* Discounting what an individual says because they are a minority or a female.

   c. *Speaking for.* Not letting people speak for themselves. When someone asks him or her a direct question the person guilty of racism interrupts him/her and answers the question himself.

   d. *Testimonials.* "I am not prejudice, some of my best friends are black" (or women or any other minority group).

   e. *Ethnic, racist, or sexist jokes.* This area is pretty self-explanatory and does not require elaboration or clarification. They only continue to reinforce stereotypes.

   f. *Frequent interruptions.* This indicates that you don't take what someone is saying as being important. You have a 'better grasp' or understanding of the points they may be making and feel compelled to make sure you make it clear what 'needs' to be said.

   g. *Stereotypical language.* Speaking in terms that use statements, which indicate or reinforce the stereotypes about the group you are talking about. A statement like: "all women are just too emotional to handle the stress filled command environment."

h. *Titles and ranks.* Calling minorities and women by their first names while addressing majority members (males) by their titles or rank.

i. *Denying opportunities.* Simply put, providing more beneficial jobs, positions, or assignments to majority members than to minority members.

4. FACTORS THAT SUPPORT RACISM AND SEXISM.

a. *Reference groups.* Groups or association with like attitudes and like values. Examples include the Ku Klux Klan and some fraternal organizations. These reference groups enable people to associate with people that have the same attitudes as they do.

b. *Conformity to norms.* Some individuals find it easier to conform to the standard norm of the group than it is to challenge the attitude.

c. *Self-fulfilling prophecy.* We can influence the behavior of another person by expressing our expectations of that person. If we assume that because a person is a minority, they will not achieve the same level of competence as a majority member, frequently, that is exactly what appears to happen. While there are many factors that may factor into this phenomenon, the whole concept is called the 'self-fulfilling prophecy'.

d. *Pro-sexism.* Accommodating sexist behavior by reinforcing it, rather than questioning, checking, or opposing it.

5. STRATEGIES FOR COMBATING RACISM AND SEXISM. While nothing is likely to completely eradicate racism and sexism, there are things we can do to minimize their affect on our units.

a. *Awareness.* To make a difference in these areas, we must be aware the potential for both racism and sexism exist. We must also make a conscious effort to look for problems or problem areas in which either or both could happen.

b. *Education.* Education empowers people to recognize behaviors related to racism and sexism. Individuals can then reflect and check their own behaviors and attitudes.

c. *Legislation.* This not only refers to the 'laws of the land' relevant to racism and sexism, but also to the standards and policies implemented within your unit.

d. *Participation.* This refers to taking part in activities in which you interact with members of different races and genders.

e. *Self-analyze.* Often, one of the hardest things a person must do is to be honest with themselves. If we harbor prejudices and fears about other groups, it is best to be able to acknowledge that to ourselves. Only then can we figure out what steps we need to take to overcome these attitudes and beliefs we hold.

f. *Acknowledging and understanding differences.* We are each different. This holds true among our own race and gender, we well as between races and genders. If we can simply accept that we are different, and that one characteristic isn't necessarily wrong or better, then we'll be well on the road to having a better understanding of those who are different than ourselves.

g. *Commander's responsibility.* The commander is responsible for his or her command climate. He or she needs to know if there are incidents of racism or sexism in order to take appropriate actions.

PREVENTION OF SEXUAL HARASSMENT

The elimination of sexual harassment has been a long-standing goal of the Army. During recent years the issue of sexual harassment has received significant media and political attention in both government and in private sectors. This heightened awareness on the causes of sexual harassment has intensified national debate on prevention strategies. Sexual harassment affects everyone. It detracts from a positive unit climate that promotes individual growth and teamwork, vital to combat readiness. Sexual Harassment victimizes males as well as females and can occur at any time, and is not limited to the workplace. For these reasons sexual harassment cannot and will not be tolerated.

1. POLICY: Sexual harassment is a form of gender discrimination that involves unwelcome sexual advances, requests for sexual favors, and other verbal or physical conduct of a sexual nature when:

   a. submission to, or rejection of, such conduct is made either explicitly or implicitly a term or condition of a person's job, pay, or career, or

   b. submission to, or rejection of, such conduct by a person is made as a basis for career or employment decisions affecting that person, or

   c. such conduct has the purpose or effect of unreasonably interfering with an individual's work performance or creates an intimidating, hostile, or offensive work environment.

   Any person in a supervisory or command position who uses or condones implicit or explicit sexual behavior to control, influence, or affect the career, pay, or job of a soldier or civilian employee is engaging in sexual harassment. Similarly, any soldier or civilian employee who makes deliberate or repeated unwelcome verbal comments, gestures, or physical contact of a sexual nature is also engaging in sexual harassment.

2. TYPES OF SEXUAL HARASSMENT. Soldiers and civilians need to have a clear understanding of some of the basic principles which are critical to identifying types of behavior which constitute sexual harassment. Two of these include "quid pro quo" and "hostile environment." Also, soldiers and civilians should understand "unwelcome" as viewed by a "reasonable woman" standard, and the relevancy of impact versus intent.

   a. Quid Pro Quo. "Quid pro quo" which is a Latin term essentially means "this for that." This term refers to conditions placed on a person's career or terms of employment in return for sexual favors. It involves threats of adverse actions if the victim does not submit or promises of favorable actions if the person does submit. Incidents of quid pro quo can also have an adverse effect on third persons. It can result in allegations of sexual favoritism, or gender discrimination when a person feels unfairly deprived of recognition, advancement, or other career opportunities due to favoritism shown to another soldier or civilian employee based on a sexual relationship.

   b. Hostile environment. A "hostile environment" occurs when soldiers or civilians are subjected to offensive, unwanted, and unsolicited comments and behavior of a sexual nature. If these behaviors have the potential of unreasonably interfering with their performance, then the environment is classified as hostile

   Examples of a hostile environment: Feminine terms in describing unsatisfactory male performance such as wimp, sissy, or mama's boy; jody calls during physical training; posting of sexually oriented cartoons and pictures in the work area; telling of sexually explicit jokes and sharing sexist attitudes and opinions.

3. RELATED ELEMENTS OF SEXUAL HARASSMENT. In addition to the two basic categories of "Quid Pro Quo" and Hostile Environment, soldiers and civilian employees need to be aware of other related elements to identify behavior that constitutes sexual harassment.

   a. Impact vs Intent. Soldiers and civilians must understand that what they may consider to be joking or horseplay must be evaluated on its appropriateness and offensiveness as perceived by the recipient. When attention of a sexual nature is neither wanted, initiated, nor solicited, it is considered "unwelcome." In determining whether such behavior constitutes sexual harassment, a primary concern is the impact of the act upon the victim, not the intent of the alleged harasser. An excuse such as, "I was only joking" is irrelevant."

b. Reasonable person and reasonable woman standards. Another variable in assessing the impact or expected reaction to sexual harassment is measured by the "reasonable person standard" or the "reasonable woman standard." These standards are used to predict the expected reaction to or impact of perceived offensive behaviors on the recipient. They ensure adequate sensitivity to a person's feelings and perspective while avoiding extremes. The purpose of adopting a "reasonable woman's standard" is to avoid the issue of male bias which could exist in a "reasonable person's standard."

4. CATEGORIES OF SEXUAL HARASSMENT. Sexual harassment behavior is a major factor for determining hostile environment and can be categorized into four basic forms: verbal comments, nonverbal gestures, printed material and physical contact. The following are common examples:

a. Verbal comments. Examples of verbal comments include telling sexual jokes and using profanity, threats; sexually oriented jody calls, sexual comments, whistling, describing certain sexual attributes about one's physical appearance, and referring to soldiers or coworkers by honey, baby, sweetheart or dear. Initially this form of harassment appears innocent until someone demands that his or her appropriate title be used. When the victim's request is not honored and the behavior is repeated or escalated to another form, it can be classified as creating a hostile environment.

b. Nonverbal gestures. Examples of nonverbal sexual harassment include staring at someone (giving the person "the eye" or "once over"), blowing kisses, licking lips, or winking in a suggestive manner. Nonverbal sexual harassment also includes sexually oriented pictures, faxes, screen savers, and e-mail. Nonverbal forms of sexual harassment may take on a more hostile appearance after the victim has rejected the advances of the harasser.

c. Physical contact. Examples of physical contact are touching, patting, hugging, pinching, grabbing, cornering or blocking a doorway, unsolicited back and neck rubs, or unsolicited clothing adjustments.

5. VICTIM IMPACT. Soldiers and civilians must understand the devastating affect sexual harassment can have on a victim and on unit readiness. Problems due to sexual harassment can manifest themselves in a number of ways. Some are very obvious, while others may be well hidden and not so visible. The first and most obvious impact sexual harassment has on victims is that it interferes with their work performance. A soldier or civilian employee who has to fend off offensive and repeated sexual attacks cannot perform quality work. Sexual harassment also creates a hostile environment by placing unreasonable stress on the victim. Sexual harassment promotes a negative form of stress that can affect everyone in the workplace. The impact of this form of stress on the victim can be devastating. It can affect not only the victim's ability to perform effectively on the job but can also have an adverse impact on off duty time. Sexual harassment also puts a high degree of fear and anxiety into the workplace. When the harassment is quid pro quo, the fear of loss of job or career opportunities can undermine a unit's teamwork and morale. The bottom line is this: Anyone who is sexually harassed will be less productive, and the command climate will likely suffer. Soldiers and civilian employees can only reach their full potential in an environment that fosters dignity and respect.

6. SEXUAL HARASSMENT CHECKLIST. Use the following checklist to assess whether an incident or behavior is sexual harassment;

- Is the behavior inappropriate for the workplace?
- Is the behavior sexual in nature or connotation?
- Is the conduct unwanted, unwelcome, or unsolicited?

- Do the elements of power, control, or influence exist?
- Does the situation indicate a quid pro quo relationship?
- Does the behavior create a hostile or offensive environment?
- Is the behavior repeated as it relates to gender treatment?
- How would a "reasonable person" or "reasonable woman" be affected?

7. REPORTING SEXUAL HARASSMENT. All soldiers and their family members have the right to prompt and thorough redress of sexual harassment complaints without fear of intimidation or reprisal. Refer to AR 600-20, which contains detailed information on the Army's EO complaint process in Appendix E. The chain of command is the primary channel for handling and correcting allegations of sexual harassment. Although a number of alternate channels are available, soldiers and DA civilians are encouraged to bring their complaints to the first line supervisor for resolution at the lowest possible level. Should complainants feel uncomfortable in bringing their concerns to the chain of command or the allegation of sexual harassment is against a member of the chain, a number of alternate agencies are available to assist in the complaint process. Complaints of sexual harassment may be filed formally or informally.

   a. An informal complaint is one in which the complainant does not wish to file his or her grievance in writing. In attempting to resolve the problem at the lowest possible level, it may not be necessary to involve the commander or other members of the chain of command.

   b. Soldiers, family members, or civilians who wish to file a formal complaint must submit a sworn statement using DA Form 7279-R. The complainant is responsible for providing all pertinent information to include a detailed description of the incident and the names of witnesses and other involved parties. Complainants have 60 calendar days from the date of the alleged incident in which to file a formal complaint of sexual harassment. The comman-

der who acknowledges the complaint has 14 calendar days to resolve the complaint or provide written feedback to the complainant. An extension of additional 30 calendar days may be required in special circumstances. At the conclusion of the commander's inquiry or investigation, the complainant will be informed in writing as to whether his or her complaint was substantiated and the appropriate action taken. Should the complainant disagree with the findings or actions taken to resolve the complaint, the complainant may file an appeal. Appeals must be submitted within 7 calendar days of being notified as to the final disposition of the complaint. The appeal should be filed with the commander who processed the complaint, next higher commander within the chain, or with the commander who has General Court-Martial convening authority. Should complainants feel that they are victims of intimidation or reprisal actions, they must report such incidents to the chain of command or other alternate agencies.

8. RECOMMENDED TECHNIQUES FOR DEALING WITH SEXUAL HARASSMENT. All soldiers and civilian employees have a responsibility to help resolve acts of sexual harassment and are encouraged to report them to the chain of command or appropriate agencies. There are certain actions victims can take to help them deal with sexual harassment situations. This following list is prioritized to denote a victim's increased involvement.

   a. Diary. Keeping a record of daily events is a way to help victims clarify situations and events that affect them emotionally. Like a diary, the information that is recorded should resemble a journal of personal notes. These notes should be factual and include details to include time, location, and names of those present during each incident. Those who elect to use this strategy, however, should be cautioned not to keep their diary in the work area nor should they let others see or read their notes. In the event the victim decides to file a complaint, the diary can be useful in recalling specifics on who, what, when, and where.

b. Intermediary. A victim may want to take a more direct approach in attempting to stop a sexual harassment situation. However, he or she may feel intimidated, apprehensive or reluctant to speak to the harasser directly. In such cases, a coworker, supervisor, or another leader can serve as an intermediary and speak to the offender on behalf of the victim. Hopefully, the person who is asked to be an intermediary is not also intimidated. If so, chances for success by this means are minimal at best. An intermediary does not speak for the victim, but relates what behavior the victim wants stopped.

c. Letter. Another strategy for confronting sexual harassment is to write the harasser a letter. The letter should be professional, polite, and specific about what behaviors are offensive and unwelcome. The letter should contain at least three parts: first, an objective description of the behavior or incident(s) without evaluating the harasser or providing editorial comments; second, a description of how the victim is affected by the behavior; and finally, what the victim wants the harasser to do to correct the problem. The advantages of this technique is that it gives the victim a chance to handle the situation, it avoids formal charges and public confrontations, and it gives the harasser an opportunity to look at the impact of his or her behavior. Victims should be warned that a letter also could be interpreted by the harasser as a sign of weakness or intimidation. Therefore, the victim should be prepared to report the incident should the harassment continue.

d. Confronting. Confronting the harasser directly can be an effective method for dealing with unwanted, offensive behavior. Soldiers and civilian employees are encouraged to take this course of action whenever it is appropriate to do so. However, depending on the severity of the act and victim's own confidence for success, direct confrontation may not be appropriate in all circumstances. Victims should be aware that successful confrontation involving severe forms of harassment does not preclude reporting the harassment to the chain of command. Victims of sexual harassment should be encouraged to confront their harasser at the time of the act or very soon thereafter and do so in a professional manner. The victim should tell the harasser exactly what behavior is offensive and unwanted. However, the victim should be cautioned when using this approach not to verbally attack the harasser, but calmly describe the behavior. Finally, victims should let the harasser know how they feel and that his or her behavior will be reported to the chain of command if the behavior is continued or repeated.

e. Reporting. The decision to report an incident of sexual harassment is often viewed as a last resort by most victims. This is due to their fear of involvement, fear of reprisal, or fear of being identified as one who complains. Reporting does have its place even when the victim has been successful in stopping the harassment. Depending on the severity of the incident, "reporting" may be the appropriate first course of action. Reporting may also be the final choice when prior coping efforts have failed and no alternative remains. Reporting must deal with facts so that the commander or other leaders can address specific issues and talk to valid witnesses.

Consideration of Others II

This is the second of two lessons on the Army's Equal Opportunity and Prevention of Sexual Harassment policies. In this lesson, you learn about the Army's policies for filing complaints.

The following topics are addressed in this lesson:

- Consideration of Others (COO) program;
- Equal Opportunity (EO) program;
- Prevention of Sexual Harassment (POSH) program; and
- Army procedures for filing complaints against EO and POSH violations.

The following Terminal Learning Objective (TLO) is supported in whole or in part by this lesson:

- Understand basic knowledge of Consideration of Others (COO) and human diversity.

Following this lesson you will be able to:

- Describe the Army's Consideration of Others (COO) program;
- Recognize the leader's role related to taking action against inappropriate or disrespectful behaviors;
- Develop personal strategies for how to deal with these COO issues; and
- Develop organizational strategies (regulations and policies) for how to deal with these COO issues.

EQUAL OPPORTUNITY COMPLAINT PROCEDURES

The EO complaints processing system addresses complaints that allege unlawful discrimination or unfair treatment on the basis of race, national origin, color, gender, and/or religious affiliation, or sexual harassment. Attempts should always be made to solve the problem at the lowest possible level within an organization.

PART I: TYPES OF COMPLAINTS

The Army has two types of EO complaints within its EO complaint process. They are informal and formal.

   a. ***Informal Complaints.*** An informal complaint is any complaint that a soldier, family member or DA civilian does not wish to file in writing. Informal complaints may be resolved directly by the individual, with the help of another unit member, the commander or other person in the complainant's chain of command. Typically, those issues that can be taken care of informally can be resolved through discussion, problem identification, and clarification of the issues. An informal complaint is not subject to time suspense nor is it reportable.

   b. ***Formal Complaints.*** A formal complaint is one that a complainant files in writing and swears to the accuracy of the information. Formal complaints require specific actions, are subject to timelines, and require documentation of the actions taken. An individual files a formal complaint using a DA Form 7279-R, Equal Opportunity Complaint Form.

   (1) In Part I of DA Form 7279-R, the complainant will specify the alleged concern, provide the names of the parties involved and witnesses, describe the incident(s)/behavior(s), and indicate the date(s) of the occurrence(s). The complainant will also state the equal opportunity basis of the complaint (e.g., unlawful discrimination based upon gender, race, color, national origin, religious affiliation, or sexual harassment). Complainant will be advised of the importance of describing the incident(s) in as much detail as possible to assist in the investigative process.

   (2) Soldiers have 60 calendar days from the date of the alleged incident in which to file a formal complaint. This time limit is established to set reasonable parameters for the inquiry or investigation and resolution of complaints, to include ensuring the availability of witnesses, accurate recollection of events, and timely remedial action. If a complaint is received after 60 calendar days, the commander may conduct an investigation into the allegations or appoint an investigating officer. In deciding whether to conduct an investigation, the commander should consider the reason for the delay, the availability of witnesses, and whether a full and fair inquiry or investigation can be conducted.

PART II: ALTERNATIVE AGENCIES

Although handling EO complaints through the chain of command is strongly encouraged, this is not the only channel. Should the soldier feel uncomfortable in filing a complaint with the chain of command, or should the complaint be against a member of the chain of command, a number of alternative agencies.

The following are frequently used agencies with a brief description of each agency:

   a. ***Equal Opportunity Adviser (EOA):*** The EOA is trained to receive, process, and conduct inquiries into complaints of discrimination and sexual harassment.

   b. ***Chaplain:*** The chaplain is the subject matter expert on addressing issues concerning religious discrimination or accommodation.

   c. ***Provost Marshal (PM):*** Is primarily responsible for receiving and investigating violations of the UCMJ, which are criminal in nature.

   d. ***Staff Judge Advocate (SJA):*** The SJA serves as an advisor and may receive complaints about discrimination in legal proceedings.

   e. ***Housing Referral Office (HRO):*** Is responsible for monitoring and administering the installation's housing referral program. The HRO will receive and investigate complaints of discrimination in rental or sale of off-post residents.

f. ***Inspector General (IG):*** The IG's office is the principal agency for receiving and investigating complaints about command environment and leadership. The timelines and procedures outlined in this lesson plan do not apply to complaints filed with the IG. Complaints filed with the IG will be processed outside of EO channels in accordance with AR 20-1.

g. ***EO Hotline:*** In addition to the alternative agencies, each installation has an EO Hotline. This hotline is normally used to provide information on discrimination and sexual harassment. EO complaints cannot be received over the phone.

PART III: ENTERING THE EO COMPLAINT PROCESS

Submission of EO complaints to the chain of command is strongly encouraged. Regardless of what agency handles a formal complaint, the complainant must be sworn to the complaint on DA Form 7279-R.

Complaints filed with the IG's office will be processed as an Inspector General Action Requests (IGARS) IAW AR 20-1. No timeline will be imposed on conducting the investigation or feedback to the complainant.

Regardless of what agency or commander receives the complaint, the chain of command has 14 calendar days in which to resolve or refer it to a higher echelon commander. The commander who has the responsibility for resolving the complaint may request an extension of up to 30 additional calendar days after the initial 14-day suspense.

Receipt of complaints will be annotated in writing on a DA Form 7279-R, Part Id. If the receiving agency decides not to investigate but to refer the complaint to another agency or, back to the appropriate commander, the referral must be made within 3 calendar days with the written acknowledgment of the commander or agency receiving the referral (DA Form 7279-R, Part 10a).

The commander will provide written feedback to the complainant not later than the 14th calendar day after receiving the complaint and then provide updates every 14-calendar days until final resolution.

PART IV: THE RIGHT TO APPEAL

If the complainant perceives the investigation failed to reveal all relevant facts to substantiate the allegations, or that the actions taken by the command on his or her behalf were insufficient to resolve the complaint, the complainant has the right to appeal to the next higher commander in his or her chain of command. The complainant may not appeal the action taken against the perpetrator, if any is taken.

The appeal must be presented within 7 calendar days following notification of the results of investigation and acknowledgment of the actions of the command to resolve the complaint. The complainant must provide a brief statement that identifies the basis of the appeal. This will be done in writing on the DA Form 7279-R, Part IV, and the complaint form will be returned to the commander in the chain of command who either conducted the investigation or appointed the investigating officer.

Once the complainant initiates the appeal, the commander has 3 calendar days to refer the appeal to the next higher unit commander. The commander to which the appeal is made has 14 calendar days to review the case and act on the appeal (i.e. approve it, deny it, or conduct an additional investigation). Not later than the 14th calendar day following receipt of the appeal this commander shall provide written feedback, consistent with Privacy Act and FOIA limitations, to the complainant on the results of the appeal. Complaints that are not resolved at brigade level may be appealed to the General Courts-Martial Convening Authority. The only exception to this is where organizations have Memorandums of Understanding or Support that delegate Uniform Code of Military Justice authority to a local commander. Decisions at this level are final.

Ethical Decision Making I

This is the first in a series of two lessons on ethical decision-making, and part of a ten-lesson set on the role values and ethics have on the development of leadership. This lesson is designed to help you discover your own values and how they affect an ethical decision-making process.

The following topics are addressed in this lesson:

- Personal value system;
- Effect of values on decision making;
- Army values support of national values;
- Relationship of personal values to Army and national values;
- Obligation as leaders to make ethical decisions; and
- Obligation to foster an ethical climate.

The following Terminal Learning Objective (TLO) is supported in whole or in part by this lesson:

- Apply Army Values and Ethical Requirements that Guide Leader Behavior.

Following this lesson you will be able to:

- Define and differentiate the following terms pertaining to ethics and morality: attitude, belief, custom, duty, ethics, moral, professional ethics, right, values, virtue, wrong;
- Clarify personal values as they relate to making ethical decisions; and
- Describe a leader's obligation to make and support ethical decisions.

THE ETHICS OF MILITARY LEADERSHIP

DEFINITIONS

Attitude—A way of thinking or behaving. (Attitudes are often reflections of beliefs and values.)

Belief—Something accepted as true or real. (Beliefs may or may not have emotional components. Beliefs that elicit an emotional response are probably values.)

Custom—A usual way of behaving or of doing something. (Customs may result from values or beliefs, and they almost always reflect values or beliefs.)

Duty—The conduct or action required of a person on moral grounds.

Ethics—Moral principles [used to guide correct and honorable behavior]; the philosophical study of moral choice and moral reasoning.

Ethos—The character, attitude, or beliefs peculiar to a specific culture, group, or person.

Moral—Of or concerned with the goodness and badness of human character or with the principles of what is right and wrong in conduct. Conforming to a standard of right behavior.

Professional Ethics—Ideals and practices that grow out of one's professional privileges, responsibilities, and social contract. Professional ethics apply to certain groups, define situations that otherwise remain uncertain, and direct the moral consciousness of members of the profession to its peculiar problems.

Right—Conforming to ethical or moral standards. The term is used when speaking of acts.

Values—Standards or principles considered precious or important in life. Relative worth or utility. (Values help provide standards for governing behavior. Moral values are a subset of the larger concept of values.)

Virtue—Moral excellence, goodness, a particular form of this.

Wrong—Deviating from moral rectitude as prescribed by law or by conscience; immoral; not just, proper, or equitable according to a standard or code.

THE BASES FOR MORALITY

What is the source of moral principles? What makes some moral principles more dearly held than others?

If you were to survey humankind and ask a single question: "What do you value most?," a great many answers would result. An underlying theme to most of these answers would probably be the preservation and promotion of humanity.

We view behaviors that help meet the needs of individuals and societies, as good. These behaviors include not just those that secure the physical requirements for survival, such as food, water, and shelter, but also the less tangible requirements for growth and enjoyment. Conversely, we view behaviors that hinder the preservation and promotion of humanity as bad. So important and dearly held is our existence, that the words "good" and "bad," as used here, don't just mean desirable or undesirable, rather, they are morally evaluative terms. A person and/or behavior that facilitate humanity's survival and growth are generally considered morally good, and the individual or behavior that hinders or harms survival and growth is considered morally bad.

The basic moral principle of preserving and promoting humanity underlies all morally sound values, although the exact expression of these values may differ from person to person as a result of the individual's experiences and environment. For example, work that provides for the physical needs of one's family clearly functions to preserve humanity. However, one person might prefer to provide for his or her family by working as a computer programmer while another prefers to work as a farmer. The valued occupation differs but the core value remains the same.

While the exact expression of values may differ from person to person and nation to nation, there is widespread agreement on fundamental values related to the preservation and promotion of humanity. This agreement is well illustrated in Army Field Manual 27-10, *The Law of Land Warfare*. This manual provides authoritative guidance to American military personnel on the conduct of warfare. It is largely based on the Hague Conventions of 1907 and the 1949 Geneva Conventions for the Protection of War Victims. The stated goal of the law of land warfare is, "to diminish the evils of war by: a. Protecting both combatants and noncombatants from unnecessary suffering; b. Safeguarding certain fundamental human rights of persons who fall into the hands of the enemy, particularly prisoners of war, the wounded and sick, and civilians; and c. Facilitating the restoration of peace." Thus, even war is restricted by the desire to preserve humanity.

Specific to the U.S. Army are the ethical values expressed in FM 1, *The Army*, and FM 100-5, *Operations*. FM 100-5 states:

> "The nation expects its Army to adhere to the highest standards of professional conduct and to reflect the ideals of American values. The American people demand a high-quality Army that honors the core values of the Constitution it is sworn to uphold—a strong respect for the rule of law, human dignity, and individual rights."

This statement reflects our society's expectation that the Army is to be a repository of American values. FM 22-102, *Soldier Team Development*, says that we must adhere to our national values even when waging war; because to violate the basic principles of American life while defending that way of life would lead to a hollow victory. When we enter military service, we swear an oath to safeguard our national values against all threats. These fundamental American values are embedded into our professional Army ethos: subordination to political authority, loyalty, duty, selfless service, courage, integrity, respect for human dignity, sense of justice. Clearly, the values that underlie the Army ethos serve to preserve and promote society.

Many of our values and ethical principles are concerned with interpersonal behaviors. Typical values are honesty, fairness, equity, and integrity. It is easy to see that these are principles that tend to promote the successful functioning of social systems. Since societies combine the talents and resources of many people to produce a superior existence for all, the maintenance of societies is directly related to humanity's survival and growth.

Even people, who are not able to articulate this fundamental concern for the preservation of humanity, often have a subconscious understanding of this basic ethic. Malham Wakin, in his book, *War, Morality, and the Military Profession*, provides insight into this subconscious understanding. Wakin points out that people commonly cite medicine and

law as the "noblest callings in our society." Doctors protect life itself and restore its quality; lawyers and judges provide justice. Thus, both professions are very directly related to the preservation and promotion of humanity. It is easy to see that the military profession is also a noble calling, because the military is charged with defending our very way of life. Wakin describes this hypothetical situation:

> "One can easily imagine a professor at a civilian institution calling her local newspaper to report that several of her students had cheated on a homework assignment, only to be disappointed by the editor's reaction that her story was not newsworthy. But a service-academy cheating episode makes headlines, causes national investigative committees to be appointed, precipitates reassignments for superintendents and commandants, and may even generate massive curriculum changes."

Why do people react so strongly to cheating at a military academy and so mildly to cheating at a civilian institution? One obvious answer is that consciously or subconsciously we are aware of and value the critical life-preserving role of the military. When something threatens the ability of the military to execute its mission, we feel it as a threat to our safety—a threat to a central value.

THE IMMORALITY OF INCOMPETENCE

Do we have a moral imperative to be professionally competent? That is, if a military member accepts responsibility, which he is unequipped to discharge competently, is he guilty of immoral behavior?

Malham Wakin believes that members of the military, like members of other noble professions, do have a moral obligation to be competent. He says that many types of personal failures and inabilities normally have no moral implications. For example the failure of a school course or the inability to play the violin well enough to gain a symphony position aren't immoral. However, when the activity or profession affects the " ... survival of society, loss of human life, and use of national treasure, it seems clear ... [that we have] ... entered the moral realm."

Doctors, legal professionals, and military personnel and other professionals are given special authority by society to perform functions crucial to the preservation of the society. Such professionals have entered into a public trust. Members of professions are expected to have mastered extensive bodies of professional knowledge and to be skilled in the performance of their functions. Society expects these professionals to adhere to a higher standard of performance, dedication, and ethics, and to police their own ranks of those who are incapable or unwilling to perform to these higher standards. Professional membership is only granted after a prolonged period of education, training, and testing, and is signified by licensing, ordination, commissioning, or similar official act of bestowing authority to practice the profession. Because professionals have such potential to harm others, society wants to make sure that only the most competent and trustworthy are given the authority to practice. As a profession's ability to do harm increases, society becomes more concerned with the competence of the profession's practitioners, entry requirements into the profession are made more stringent, and the moral obligation to be professionally competent increases.

Wakin describes the weight of the moral obligation to be competent in this fashion:

> "It is obvious that an incompetent physician may, in a lifetime of practicing bad medicine, harm many of his patients, perhaps even cause some deaths. It is also disheartening to contemplate the damage that an incompetent junior high school teacher may do to developing young minds. But the incompetent military leader may bring about needless loss of life and indeed, at the extreme, may have at his fingertips, the ability to destroy humanity, as we know it. Given this critical uniqueness of the role of military leaders, no nation can afford to have them be intellectually incompetent or morally insensitive."

As Wakin points out, no other profession has the potential to inflict as much harm as the military profession. It seems clear, therefore, that no other profession has a stronger moral imperative to be competent than does the military profession.

HOW WE DEVELOP MORALLY:

We can all think of people who differ in the moral quality of their behavior and reasoning. History gives us examples of moral extremes such as Gandhi and Lincoln at one end of the continuum and Hitler and Stalin at the opposite end. How do people come to be so widely different in the moral aspects of their reasoning and behavior? Two modern developmental theories help to explain the moral differences that we see between people.

Kohlberg's Stage Theory of Moral Development

Lawrence Kohlberg, of Harvard University, has focused his research not on the goodness or badness of people's behaviors, but rather on the characteristics of the moral reasoning that led to the behaviors. According to Kohlberg, it isn't the nature of a person's behavior that makes the person moral or immoral, it is the reasoning that the person employs to reach his or her decision on how to act. Generally, the more sophisticated and principled the thought process, the higher is the person's level of moral development. Kohlberg's theory is thus called a cognitive–developmental theory because of its focus on development of the reasoning process.

Kohlberg says that there are six stages of moral development that people may progress through. According to Kohlberg, as we grow, we must pass through the stages in the order shown; we can't skip a stage. Furthermore, most people do not progress to the highest stage of moral reasoning. He divides these six stages into three levels with two stages in each level.

Moral reasoning in the **preconventional level** is governed by the self-centered interests of avoiding punishment (stage 1 reasoning) or gaining benefits (stage 2 reasoning). Guilt, shame, and concern for others do not function at this level. The primary motivating forces are self-centered fear of punishment and desire for reward. Stage one reasoning is usually characteristic of children aged ten and under, and stage two reasoning is typical of children twelve and above.

In the **conventional level**, moral reasoning is influenced by the desire to win the approval (honor) and avoid the disapproval (dishonor) of others. Honor is brought about by properly discharging one's duties and dishonor comes from failing in one's duties. Feelings of guilt and concern for the physical well being of others are important motivating forces at this level. Initially the approval of other individuals is sought and their disapproval is avoided (stage 3 reasoning), and later the approval of society or segments of society is sought and society's disapproval is avoided (stage 4 reasoning). Conventional level reasoning usually emerges in adolescence. Most adults never progress beyond conventional moral reasoning.

In the **postconventional level**, moral reasoning is guided by internalized fundamental and universal ethical principles that may surpass society's laws in importance. The individual is concerned about the maintenance and loss of the respect of others (stage 5 reasoning), or the maintenance and loss of self-respect (stage 6 reasoning), as a result of following or violating personally accepted ethical principles. Only only a minority of adults reaches post conventional reasoning.

The level of moral development that an individual reaches is clearly dependent upon several factors. First, the person's intelligence determines how sophisticated his or her reasoning process is capable of being. The education, knowledge base, and experiences of the person affect the direction and limit the content of the reasoning. Finally, personality, beliefs, values, attitudes, customs, and situation all influence the direction and nature of the individual's moral reasoning.

Social Learning Theory

Social learning theory maintains that people tend to do things that result in rewards and avoid doing things that result in punishments or aversive outcomes. However, social learning theory goes beyond simple directly experienced rewards and punishments and embraces the notion of learning by observing others (observational learning). The other person that we observe and learn from is often called a behavioral model or simply a model.

The essential steps in social learning are: 1. Observe the behavior of another person, 2. Remember the behavior and its consequences, 3. Decide whether to imitate the behavior, and 4. Act on the decision to behave in a similar way or not. There are a number of factors that influence this process.

First, we are limited to observing the behaviors of behavioral models to which we are exposed. Exposure to another person can take the form of direct observation or it can take place through one of the media (movie, television, book, conversation, etc.). While it may sound simplistic, it is important to remember that we can't imitate the behavior of models that we aren't exposed to in some form. So, for example, if we aren't exposed to another's altruistic behavior, we can't imitate altruistic behavior.

Sometimes, behavioral models exist in our environment but we don't attend to them. This is because not all models have the same attractiveness. If a person is well-known, well-liked, powerful, physically attractive, flamboyant, etc. we are more likely to pay attention to him or her. Our inclination and ability to watch television, go to movies, read books and news papers, listen to the radio, and talk to others also helps to determine the models that we attend to. It is, of course, essential that we attend to the model if we are to learn form the model.

Our observations of the model focus on two aspects, the actual behaviors executed by the model and the consequences of the behavior. It is important that the consequences be noted because they act as vicarious reinforcement or punishment and help to determine whether we will seek to act in the same way or avoid similar behaviors.

The determination of whether or not we will behave like the behavioral model did is largely a function of the consequences of the model's behavior. If the model was rewarded for the behavior and we believe that we would also be similarly rewarded, then we are more likely to imitate the model. Conversely, if the outcomes for the model were aversive and we think that they would be aversive for us as well, then we are less likely to imitate the model.

There are, however, factors that confound the influence of observed rewards and punishments. For example, if the model is held in very high regard, the model's behaviors might be imitated even if the consequences of the model's behavior were aversive. Presumably, in such a case, the rewarding properties of just being like the model outweigh the aversive consequences of the behavior. In an opposite vein, we might not imitate the behavior of a model held in low regard even if the outcomes of the model's behavior were favorable. Another factor that helps determine our response to observed behaviors is the influence of countervailing models. That is, the lessons we gain from one model might counterbalance or overwhelm those from another model.

Eventually, we decide to act or not act in a fashion similar to our models. As stated earlier, if we are rewarded for this behavior we will tend to continue behaving in a similar fashion, and if we are punished for the behavior, we will tend to discontinue the behavior.

Social learning theory, of course, is a general theory of how we learn. Although the theory isn't limited to the learning of ethical behavior, it fully encompasses this type of learning and it has important implications for our behavior as leaders and for fostering the ethical growth of others and ourselves.

The Nature of Ethical Dilemmas:

An ethical dilemma occurs when we are faced with choosing between two or more good values. The closer the competing values are in their importance to us, the more difficult it is to choose among them, and the more strongly felt is the dilemma.

Sometimes concern for our personal well-being conflicts with the institutional values of the nation, the Army, and our unit that we have accepted. A soldier, aware of the ethical impropriety of a superior, may feel compelled to report the wrongdoing on one hand, but fear covert career-ending revenge from the superior or his friends on the other hand. Such fears may seem justified in light of stories of "whistle-blowers" who found themselves reassigned to relatively meaningless positions or driven out of the organization entirely. Advice from more experienced soldiers to "pick your battles carefully" and to not "fall on your sword over the small things" also serves to increase this type of concern.

Some ethical conflicts involve competing organizational (nation, Army, unit, legal) values.

Another type of ethical dilemma is often subtle. In fact, it is so subtle that we may not even experience it as a strong internal conflict that causes us to stop and struggle. Sometimes we know that a contemplated action is wrong, but we convince ourselves that it is acceptable, in this particular case, because it is such a seemingly small ethical violation, and it probably will not have any detrimental results. Such dilemmas are usually only felt as a slight passing twinge of concern, which we quickly rationalize away. This kind of decision often results in the erosion of our ethical sensibility and may lead us to the point where we no longer feel even the slight twinge of conscience mentioned earlier. Additionally, the apparently innocuous ethical compromises that we make today may come back to

haunt us in the form of a similar situation but with greater stakes that we aren't willing to risk. Each compromise today erodes our ethical foundation for the future.

FM 22-100, *Military Leadership*, lists some leader behaviors and attitudes to be avoided since they frequently place subordinates in ethical binds:

- I don't care how you get it done—just do it!
- There is no excuse for failure!
- Can do!
- Zero defects.
- Covering up errors to look good.
- Telling superiors what they want to hear.
- Making reports say what your leader wants to see.
- Setting goals that are impossible to reach (missions without resources).
- Loyalty up—not down.

ETHICAL DECISION MAKING

The ethical decision making process employs the same six problem solving steps that we use to solve other types of problems:

- Define the problem.
- Gather information.
- Search for possible solutions.
- Analyze possible solutions.
- Pick the best solution.
- Implement the solution.

The following questions will help guide you in the ethical decision making process. Attempt to answer them before making a moral decision:

1. Have you defined the problem accurately?
2. How would you define the problem if you stood on the other side of the fence?
3. What are the conflicting values that created the dilemma?
4. What are the sources of the conflicting values (personal, organizational, religious, etc.)?
5. What do laws, regulations, customs, orders, standards, basic national values, traditional Army values, unit operating values, your values, and institutional pressures indicate?
6. What is the normal behavior in the Army and in American society relative to your action?
7. What does your conscience say?
8. How did this situation occur in the first place?

9. To whom and to what do you give your loyalty as a person and as a member of your profession?

10. What are the implications of your oath of office on this decision?

11. What is your motive or intention in making this decision?

12. What means are you planning to use to implement the decision?

13. What will the consequences of implementing the plan be for you, for others, for the organization, and for society?

14. Whom could your decision or action injure?

15. Would it be appropriate to discuss the problem with the affected parties before you make your decision?

16. Are you confident that your decision will be as valid over a long period of time as it seems now?

17. Does your decision put you in a weaker position to enforce the ethical principle(s) involved in the future?

18. Could you disclose, without qualm, your decision or action to your boss, your commander, the Joint Chiefs of Staff, your family, society as a whole? If not, are your reasons justifiable?

19. How would it look if a story about your decision was printed on the front page of the New York Times?

20. What is the symbolic potential of your action if understood? If misunderstood?

21. Under what conditions would you allow exceptions to your position?

PART I: JOINT ETHICS REGULATION (JER)

BASIC OBLIGATION OF PUBLIC SERVICE

a) *Public service is a public trust.* Each employee has a responsibility to the United States Government and its citizens to place loyalty to the constitution, laws and ethical principles above private gain. To ensure that every citizen can have complete confidence in the integrity of the Federal Government, each employee shall respect and adhere to the principles of ethical conduct set forth in this section, as well as the implementing standards contained in this part and in supplemental agency regulations.

b) *General principles.* The following general principles apply to every employee and may form the basis for the standards contained in this part. Where a situation is not covered by the standards set forth in this part, employees shall apply the principles set forth in this section in determining whether their conduct is proper.

1. Public service is a public trust, requiring employees to place loyalty to the Constitution, the laws and ethical principles above private gain.

2. Employees shall not hold financial interests that conflict with the conscientious performance of duty.

3. Employees shall not engage in financial transactions using nonpublic government information or allow the improper use of such information to further any private interest.

4. An employee shall not, except as permitted by subpart B of this part, solicit or accept any gift or other item of monetary value form any person or entity seeking official action from, doing business with, or conducting activities regulated by the employee's agency, or whose interests may be substantially affected by the perfor-mance or nonperformance of the employee's duties.

5. Employees shall put forth honest effort in the performance of their duties.

6. Employees shall not knowingly make unauthorized commitments or promises of any kind purporting to bind the Government.

7. Employees shall not use public office for private gain.

8. Employees shall act impartially and not five preferential treatment to any private organization or individual.

9. Employees shall protect and conserve Federal property and shall not use it for other than authorized activities.

10. Employees shall not engage in outside employment or activities, including seeking or negotiating for employment that conflict with official Government duties and responsibilities.

11. Employees shall disclose waste, fraud, abuse, and corruption to appropriate authorities.

12. Employees shall satisfy in good faith their obligations as citizens, including all just financial obligations, especially those—such as Federal, State, or local taxes—that are imposed by law.

13. Employees shall adhere to all laws and regulations that provide equal opportunity for all Americans regardless of race, color, religion, sex, national origin, age, or handicap.

14. Employees shall endeavor to avoid any actions creating the appearance that they are violating the law or the ethical standards set forth in this part. Whether particular circumstances create an appearance that the law or these standards have been violated shall be determined from the perspective of a reasonable person with knowledge of the relevant facts.

Ethical Decision Making II

This is the second in a series of two lessons focusing on the Army's doctrine on ethical decision making. This lesson is designed to help you learn the six-step process to ethical decision-making and to provide you with opportunities to practice applying the process when faced with morally ambiguous situations.

The following topics are addressed in this lesson:

- Effect of values on decision making;
- Application of the ethical decision making process;
- Obligation as leaders to make ethical decisions; and
- Obligation to foster an ethical climate.

The following Terminal Learning Objective (TLO) is supported in whole or in part by this lesson:

- Resolve an Ethical Problem.

Following this lesson you will be able to:

- Analyze a case study involving ethical decision-making; and
- Apply the ethical decision making process to a morally ambiguous situation.

Respect

This is the first lesson of a two-part series that reduces the topic to its essential ingredient—Respect. The purpose of this lesson is to develop the understanding of the Army's *Consideration of Others* program.

The following topics are addressed in this lesson:

- The meaning of dignity and respect; and
- How consideration of others epitomizes the Warrior Ethos.

The following Terminal Learning Objective (TLO) is supported in whole or in part by this lesson:

- Apply Army values and ethical requirements that guide leader behavior.

Following this lesson you will be able to:

- Define respect;
- Identify disrespectful attitudes and behaviors; and
- Describe the effects of prejudice and disrespect on the effectiveness of a unit.

Respect in Action

This is the second in a series of two lessons on Respect. The purpose of this lesson is to further reinforce that the value of *Respect* is an essential component for the development of cohesive war fighting units.

The following topics are addressed in this lesson:

- What inspires soldiers to "Follow Me";
- What happens when respect is absent; and
- Negative effects of a lack of respect.

The following Terminal Learning Objective (TLO) is supported in whole or in part by this lesson:

- Apply Army Values and Ethical Requirements that Guide Leader Behavior.

Following this lesson you will be able to:

- Analyze unit situations to identify instances of disrespect and discrimination; and
- Develop ways to address instances of disrespect or discrimination found in a unit.

MODULE V

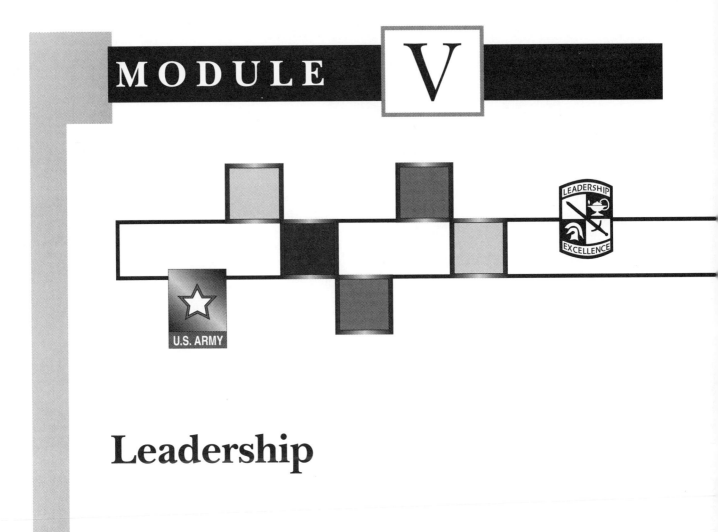

Leadership

This module consists of thirteen lessons. The first five lessons review general principles of Army leadership doctrine found in FM 22-100 *Army Leadership: Be, Know, Do.* The module also examines Army leadership doctrine at the direct level of leadership. The remaining eight lessons address key leadership topics in greater depth by consulting the findings of more than fifty years of leadership research. These key topics include such issues as power and influence; personality; leader assessment and development; adult development; transactional and transformational leadership; followership; and group cohesion, dysfunction, and conflict. While these lessons do address leadership theory and research findings, the primary emphasis of the lessons is on the practical application of leadership concepts as promoted by theory and as indicated by research.

Army Leadership:
Be-Know-Do

This lesson is the first in a series of thirteen lessons dealing with leadership. This and the next four lessons focus your attention on an examination of basic Army leadership doctrine.

The following topics are addressed in this lesson:

- The Army Leadership Framework;
- Leader actions that affect unit success;
- Leadership defined;
- Be, Know, & Do dimensions of leadership;
- Levels of leadership;
- Leaders of leaders;
- Leadership and command;
- Subordinates; and
- The payoff: Excellence.

The following Terminal Learning Objective (TLO) is supported in whole or in part by this lesson:

- Demonstrate an understanding of Army leadership doctrine.

Following this lesson you will be able to:

- Define leadership according to Army Field Manual 22-100, *Army Leadership;*
- Describe the Army leadership framework;
- Describe the concept of leading leaders and its implications for the exercise of leadership; and
- Describe the role and behavior expected of subordinates.

Army Leadership:
Character and Competence

This lesson is the second in a series of thirteen lessons dealing with leadership. This lesson continues and expands your examination of basic Army leadership doctrine.

The following topics are addressed in this lesson:

- Army Leadership Framework;
- Leader attributes and skills that affect unit success;
- Character: what a leader must be;
    - Army values
    - Leader attributes
    - Focus on character
- Competence: what a leader must know; and
- Leadership: what a leader must do
    - Influencing
    - Operating
    - Improving.

The following Terminal Learning Objective (TLO) is supported in whole or in part by this lesson:

- Demonstrate an understanding of Army leadership doctrine.

Following this lesson you will be able to:

- Differentiate between the two components of character: values and attributes;
- Describe the mental, physical, and emotional attributes critical to Army leaders;
- Relate the warrior ethos to the accomplishment of the Army's mission; and
- Describe the four categories of skills that an Army leader must know.

Army Leadership: The Human Dimension

This lesson is the third in a series of thirteen lessons dealing with leadership. This lesson continues and expands your examination of basic Army leadership doctrine. The lesson employs a student questionnaire, discussion, and brainstorming exercise to facilitate exploration of the human dimension of direct leadership, with emphasis on the issues of stress and stress management.

The following topics are addressed in this lesson:

- Definition of stress;
- Basic physiological and psychological effects of stress;
- Stressors likely to be encountered in the Army;
- Actions that individuals can take to manage their own stress;
- Actions that leaders can take to help their unit members manage stress;
- People, the team, and the institution;
- Combat stress;
- The stress of change;
- Climate and culture;
- Leadership styles; and
- Intended and unintended consequences.

The following Terminal Learning Objective (TLO) is supported in whole or in part by this lesson:

- Demonstrate an understanding of Army leadership doctrine.

Following this lesson you will be able to:

- Describe the sources of psychological stress in the Army;
- Describe the leader's role in establishing, maintaining, and changing unit climate and culture; and
- Relate leadership style to task and situation characteristics.

Army Leadership: Direct Leadership Skills

This lesson is the fourth in a series of thirteen lessons dealing with leadership. This lesson continues and expands your examination of basic Army leadership doctrine. The lesson employs small group work, cadet briefings, and discussion to familiarize you with the direct leadership skills that are important for success as a newly commissioned Army lieutenant.

The following topics are addressed in this lesson:

- Direct leadership skills important for success;
  - Interpersonal skills
  - Conceptual skills
  - Technical skills
  - Tactical skills
- Self-assessment of direct leadership skill set and proficiency; and
- Planning for direct leadership self-development.

The following Terminal Learning Objective (TLO) is supported in whole or in part by this lesson:

- Demonstrate an understanding of Army leadership doctrine.

Following this lesson you will be able to:

- Describe the interpersonal, conceptual, technical, and tactical skills that direct leaders must master and develop;
- Relate ethical reasoning to the Army problem-solving process; and
- Describe methods of self-assessment and self-development of direct leadership skills.

Army Leadership: Direct Leadership Action

This lesson is the fifth in a series of thirteen lessons dealing with leadership, and the final lesson dealing with Army leadership doctrine at the direct level of leadership. This lesson continues and expands your examination of basic Army leadership doctrine.

The following topics are addressed in this lesson:

- Influencing actions;
- Operating actions; and
- Improving actions.

The following Terminal Learning Objective (TLO) is supported in whole or in part by this lesson:

- Demonstrate an understanding of Army leadership doctrine.

Following this lesson you will be able to:

- Describe leader actions that influence subordinates' motivation;
- Relate assessment methods to unit effectiveness; and
- Describe leader actions that develop subordinates and build teams.

Leadership Framework

This lesson is the sixth in a group of thirteen lessons dealing with leadership. This lesson provides several perspectives, designed to help you, analyze and organize leadership concepts. It also promotes the understanding that it is possible to develop yourself as a leader.

The following topics are addressed in this lesson:

- Concept and definition of leadership;
- Leader-Follower-Situation (L-F-S) Model;
- Spiral of experience;
- Leadership as an art and science;
- Relationship of leadership and followership; and
- How to learn leadership.

The following Terminal Learning Objective (TLO) is supported in whole or in part by this lesson:

- Apply leadership theory & principles.

Following this lesson you will be able to:

- Define leadership;
- Describe the interactional framework for analyzing leadership; and
- Describe the development of leadership through the Action-Observation-Reflection (AOR) model.

WHAT IS LEADERSHIP?

by R.L. Huges, R.C. Ginnett, and G.J. Curphy

What *is* leadership? People who do research on leadership actually disagree more than you might think about what leadership really is. Most of this disagreement stems from the fact that **leadership** is a complex phenomenon involving the leader, the followers, and the situation. Some leadership researchers have focused on the personality, physical traits, or behaviors of the leader; others have studied the relationships between leaders and followers; still others have studied how aspects of the situation affect the ways leaders act. Some have extended the latter viewpoint so far as to suggest there is no such thing as leadership; they argue that organizational successes and failures often get falsely attributed to the leader, but the situation may have a much greater impact on how the organization functions than does any individual, including the leader (Meindl & Ehrlich, 1987).

Perhaps the best way for you to begin to understand the complexities of leadership is to see some of the ways leadership has been defined. Leadership researchers have defined leadership in the following different ways:

- The creative and directive force of morale (Munson, 1921).
- The process by which an agent induces a subordinate to behave in a desired manner (Bennis, 1959).
- The presence of a particular influence relationship between two or more persons (Hollander & Julian, 1969).
- Directing and coordinating the work of group members (Fiedler, 1967).
- An interpersonal relation in which others comply because they want to, not because they have to (Merton, 1969; Hogan, Curphy, & Hogan, 1994).
- Transforming followers, creating visions of the goals that may be attained, and articulating for the followers the ways to attain those goals (Bass, 1985; Tichy & Devanna, 1986).
- The process of influencing an organized group toward accomplishing its goals (Roach & Behling, 1984).
- Actions that focus resources to create desirable opportunities (Campbell, 1991).

- The leader's job is to create conditions for the team to be effective (Ginnett, 1996).

As you can see, these definitions differ in many ways, and these differences have resulted in various researchers exploring very different aspects of leadership. One's definition of leadership might also influence just *who* is considered an appropriate leader for study. For example, researchers who adopted Merton's definition might not be interested in studying Colin Powell's leadership as an army general. They might reason that the enormous hierarchical power and authority of an army general makes every order or decision a "have to" response from subordinates. Thus, each group of researchers might focus on a different aspect of leadership, and each would tell a different story regarding the leader, the followers, and the situation.

Although such a large number of leadership definitions may seem confusing, it is important to understand that there is no single correct definition. The various definitions can help us appreciate the multitude of factors that affect leadership, as well as different perspectives from which to view it. For example, in Bennis's definition, the word *subordinate* seems to confine leadership to downward influence in hierarchical relationships; it seems to exclude informal leadership. Fiedler's definition emphasizes the directing and controlling aspects of leadership, and thereby may deemphasize emotional aspects of leadership. The emphasis Merton placed on subordinates' "wanting to" comply with a leader's wishes seems to exclude coercion of any kind as a leadership tool. Further, it becomes problematic to identify ways in which a leader's actions are really leadership if subordinates voluntarily comply when a leader with considerable potential coercive power merely asks others to do something without explicitly threatening them. Similarly, Campbell used the phrase *desirable opportunities* precisely to distinguish between leadership and tyranny.

All considered, we believe the definition provided by Roach and Behling (1984) to be a fairly comprehensive and helpful one. Therefore, this lesson also defines leadership as "the process of influencing an organized group toward accomplishing its goals." There are several implications of this definition which are worth further examination.

LEADERSHIP IS BOTH A SCIENCE AND AN ART

Saying leadership is both a science and an art emphasizes the subject of leadership as a field of scholarly inquiry, as well as certain aspects of the practice of leadership. The scope of the science of leadership is reflected in the number of studies—approximately 8,000—cited in an authoritative reference work, *Bass & Stogdill's Handbook of Leadership: Theory, Research, & Managerial Applications* (Bass, 1990). However, being an expert on leadership research is neither a necessary nor a sufficient condition for being a good leader. Some managers may be effective leaders without ever having taken a course or training program in leadership, and some scholars in the field of leadership may be relatively poor leaders themselves.

This is not to say that knowing something about leadership research is irrelevant to leadership effectiveness. Scholarship may not be a prerequisite for leadership effectiveness, but understanding some of the major research findings can help individuals better analyze situations using a variety of perspectives. That, in turn, can give leaders insight about how to be more effective. Even so, because the skill in analyzing and responding to situations varies greatly across leaders, leadership will always remain partly an art as well as a science.

LEADERSHIP IS BOTH RATIONAL AND EMOTIONAL

Leadership involves both the rational and emotional sides of human experience. Leadership includes actions and influences based on reason and logic as well as those based on inspiration and passion. We do not want to cultivate leaders like Commander Data of *Star Trek: The Next Generation,* who always responds with logical predictability. Because people differ in their thoughts and feelings, hopes and dreams, needs and fears, goals and ambitions, and strengths and weaknesses, leadership situations can be very complex. Because people are both rational and emotional, leaders can use rational techniques and/or emotional appeals in order to influence followers, but they must also weigh the rational and emotional consequences of their actions.

A full appreciation of leadership involves looking at both these sides of human nature. Good lead-

ership is more than just calculation and planning, or following a "checklist," even though rational analysis can enhance good leadership. Good leadership also involves touching others' feelings; emotions play an important role in leadership too. Just one example of this is the civil rights movement of the 1960s. It was a movement based on emotions as well as on principles. Dr. Martin Luther King, Jr., *inspired* many people to action; he touched people's hearts as well as their heads.

Aroused feelings, however, can be used either positively or negatively, constructively or destructively. Some leaders have been able to inspire others to deeds of great purpose and courage. On the other hand, as images of Adolf Hitler's mass rallies or present-day angry mobs attest, group frenzy can readily become group mindlessness. As another example, emotional appeals by the Reverend Jim Jones resulted in approximately 800 of his followers' volitionally committing suicide.

The mere presence of a group (even without heightened emotional levels) can also cause people to act differently than when they are alone. For example, in airline cockpit crews, there are clear lines of authority from the captain down to the first officer (second in command) and so on. So strong are the norms surrounding the authority of the captain that some first officers will not take control of the airplane from the captain even in the event of impending disaster. Foushee (1984) reported a study wherein airline captains in simulator training intentionally feigned incapacitation so that the response of the rest of the crew could be observed. The feigned incapacitations occurred at a predetermined point during the plane's final approach in landing, and the simulation involved conditions of poor weather and visibility. Approximately 25 percent of the first officers in these simulated flights allowed the plane to crash. For some reason, the first officers did not take control even when it was clear the captain was allowing the aircraft to deviate from the parameters of a safe approach. This example demonstrates how group dynamics can influence the behavior of group members even when emotional levels are *not* high. (Believe it or not, airline crews are so well trained, this is *not* an emotional situation.) In sum, it should be apparent that leadership involves followers' feelings and nonrational behavior as well as rational behavior. Leaders need to consider *both* the rational and the emotional consequences of their actions.

LEADERSHIP AND MANAGEMENT

In trying to answer "What is leadership?" it is natural to look at the relationship between leadership and management. To many, the word **management** suggests words like *efficiency, planning, paperwork, procedures, regulations, control,* and *consistency.* Leadership is often more associated with words like *risk taking, dynamic, creativity, change,* and *vision.* Some say leadership is fundamentally a value-choosing, and thus a value-laden, activity, whereas management is not. Leaders are thought to *do the right things,* whereas managers are thought to *do things right* (Bennis, 1985; Zaleznik, 1983). Here are some other distinctions between managers and leaders (Bennis, 1989):

- Managers administer; leaders innovate.
- Managers maintain; leaders develop.
- Managers control; leaders inspire.
- Managers have a short-term view; leaders, a long-term view.
- Managers ask how and when; leaders ask what and why.
- Managers imitate; leaders originate.
- Managers accept the status quo; leaders challenge it.

Zaleznik (1974, 1983) goes so far as to say these differences reflect fundamentally different personality types, that leaders and managers are basically different kinds of people. He says some people are managers *by nature;* other people are leaders *by nature.* This is not at all to say one is better than the other, only that they are different. Their differences, in fact, can be quite useful, since organizations typically need both functions performed well in order to be successful. For example, consider again the civil rights movement in the 1960s. Dr. Martin Luther King, Jr., gave life and direction to the civil rights movement in America. He gave dignity and hope of freer participation in our national life to people who before had little reason to expect it. He inspired the world with his vision and eloquence, and changed the way we live together. America is a different nation today because of him. Was Dr. Martin Luther King, Jr., a leader? Of course. Was he a manager? Somehow that does not seem to fit, and the civil rights movement might have failed if it had not been

for the managerial talents of his supporting staff. Leadership and management complement each other, and both are vital to organizational success.

With regard to the issue of leadership versus management, we take a middle-of-the-road position. We think of leadership and management as closely related but distinguishable functions. Although some of the functions performed by leaders and managers may be unique, there is also an area of overlap.

LEADERSHIP AND FOLLOWERSHIP

One aspect of our text's definition of leadership is particularly worth noting: Leadership is a social influence process shared among *all* members of a group. Leadership is not restricted to the influence exerted by someone in a particular position or role; followers are part of the leadership process, too. In recent years, both practitioners and scholars have emphasized the relatedness of leadership and **followership.** As Burns (1978) observed, the idea of "one-man leadership" is a contradiction in terms.

Thus, the question *What is leadership?* cannot be separated from the question *What is followership?* There is no simple line dividing them; they merge. The relationship between leadership and followership can be represented by borrowing a concept from topographical mathematics: the Möbius strip. You are probably familiar with the curious properties of the Möbius strip: When a strip of paper is twisted and connected, it proves to have only one side. You can prove this to yourself by putting a pencil to any point on the strip and tracing continuously. Your pencil will cover the entire strip (i.e., both "sides"), eventually returning to the point at which you started. In order to demonstrate the relevance of this curiosity to leadership, cut a strip of paper. On one side write *leadership,* and on the other side write *followership.* Then twist the strip and connect the two ends in the manner of the figure. You will have created a leadership/followership Möbius strip wherein the two concepts merge one into the other, just as leadership and followership can become indistinguishable in organizations (adapted from Macrorie, 1984).

This does not mean leadership and followership are the same thing. When top-level executives were asked to list qualities they most look for and admire in leaders and followers, the lists were similar but not identical (Kouzes & Posner, 1987). Ideal leaders were characterized as honest, competent, forward looking, and inspiring; ideal followers were described as honest, competent, dependent, and cooperative. The differences could become critical in certain situations, as when a forward-looking and inspiring subordinate perceives a significant conflict between his own goals or ethics and those of his superiors. Such a situation could become a crisis for the individual and the organization, demanding choice between leading and following.

LEADERSHIP ON STAGES LARGE AND SMALL

Great leaders sometimes seem larger than life. Charles de Gaulle, a leader of France during and after World War II, was such a figure (see Highlight 29–1). Not all good leaders are famous or powerful, however, and we believe leadership can be best understood if we study a broad range of leaders, some famous and some not so famous. Most leaders, after all, are not known outside their own particular sphere or activity, nor should they be. Here are a few examples of leadership on the small stage, where individuals influenced and helped their respective groups attain their goals.

- An elderly woman led an entire community's effort to organize an advocacy and support group for parents of mentally ill adult children and provide sheltered living arrangements for these people. She helped these families while also serving an invaluable role in educating state legislators and social agencies about the needs of this neglected constituency. There had been numerous parents with mentally ill children in this community before, but none had had the idea or took the initiative to organize among themselves. As a result of this woman's leadership, many adults live and work in more humane conditions than they did before.

- A seasoned air force sergeant took two young, "green" enlistees under her wing after they both coincidentally reported for duty on the same day. She taught them the ropes at work and took pride as they matured. One of them performed so well that he went on to be commissioned as an officer. Unfortunately, the sergeant discovered the other pilfering cash from the unit gift fund. Though it pained her to do so, the sergeant took action for the enlistee to be discharged

Highlight 29–1

THE STATELINESS OF CHARLES DE GAULLE

Certain men have, one might almost say from birth, the quality of exuding authority, as though it were a liquid, though it is impossible to say precisely of what it consists. In his fascinating book *Leaders,* former president Richard Nixon described the French president Charles de Gaulle as one of the great leaders he had met. Following are several aspects of de Gaulle's leadership based on Nixon's observations.

- *He conveyed stately dignity.* De Gaulle had a resolute bearing that conveyed distance and superiority to others. He was at ease with other heads of state but never informal with anyone, even close friends. His tall stature and imperious manner conveyed the message he was not a common man.

- *He was a masterful public speaker.* He had a deep, serene voice and a calm, self-assured manner. He used the French language grandly and eloquently. According to Nixon, "He spoke so articulately and with such precision that his message seemed to resonate apart from his words" (p. 59).

- *He played the part.* De Gaulle understood the role of theater in politics, and his meetings with the press (a thousand at a time!) were like audiences with royalty. He staged them in great and ornate halls, and he deftly crafted public statements that would be understood differently by different groups. In one sense, perhaps, this could be seen as a sort of falseness, but that may be too narrow a view. Nixon reflected on this aspect of de Gaulle's leadership: "General de Gaulle was a facade, but not a false one. Behind it was a man of incandescent intellect and a phenomenal discipline. The facade was like the ornamentation on a great cathedral, rather than the flimsy pretense of a Hollywood prop with nothing behind it" (p. 60).

Source: R. Nixon, *Leaders* (New York: Warner Books, 1982).

Highlight 29–2

THE ROMANCE OF LEADERSHIP

This text is predicated on the idea that leaders can make a difference. Interestingly, though, while people in the business world generally agree, not all scholars do.

People in the business world attribute much of a company's success or failure to its leadership. One study counted the number of articles appearing in *The Wall Street Journal* that dealt with leadership and found nearly 10 percent of the articles about representative target companies addressed that company's leadership. Furthermore, there was a significant positive relationship between company performance and the number of articles about its leadership; the more a company's leadership was emphasized in *The Wall Street Journal*, the better the company was doing. This might mean the more a company takes leadership seriously (as reflected by the emphasis in *The Wall Street Journal*), the better it does.

However, the authors were skeptical about the real utility of leadership as a concept. They suggested leadership is merely a romanticized notion, an obsession people want and need to believe in. Belief in the potency of leadership may be a sort of cultural myth, which has utility primarily insofar as it affects how people create meaning about causal events in complex social systems. The behavior of leaders, the authors contend, does not account for very much of the variance in an organization's performance. Nonetheless, people seem strongly committed to a sort of basic faith that individual leaders shape organizational destiny for good or ill.

Source: J. R. Meindl, S. B. Ehrlich, and J. M. Dukerich, "The Romance of Leadership." *Administrative Science Quarterly* 30 (1985), pp. 78–102.

---

from the service. Leadership involves significant intrinsic rewards such as seeing others blossom under your tutelage, but with its rewards also goes the responsibility to enforce standards of conduct.

- The office manager for a large advertising agency directed its entire administrative staff, most of whom worked in the reception area. His engaging personality and concern for others made everyone feel important. Morale in the office was high, and many important customers credit their positive "first impression" of the whole agency to the congeniality and positive climate among the office staff. Leaders set the tone for the organization, and followers often model the behaviors displayed by the leader. This leader helped create an office mood of optimism and supportiveness that reached outward to everyone who visited.

These examples are representative of the opportunities every one of us has to be a leader. To paraphrase John Fitzgerald Kennedy, we all can make a difference and each of us should try. However, this lesson is more than an exhortation for each of us to play a more active leadership role on the various stages of our lives. It is a review of what is known about leadership from available research, a review we hope is presented in a way that will foster leadership development. We are all more likely to make the kind of difference we want if we understand what leadership is and what it is not, how you get it, and what improves it (see Highlight 29–2 for a contrasting view of how much of a difference leaders really make). Toward that end, we will look at leaders on both the large and the small stages of life throughout the book. We will look at leaders on the world stage like Albright, Powell, and Matsushita; and we will look at leaders on those smaller stages closer to home like principals, coaches, and managers at the local store. You also might want to see Highlight 29–3 for a listing of women leaders throughout history from many different stages.

Highlight 1–3

WOMEN AND LEADERSHIP A FEW WOMEN LEADERS THROUGHOUT HISTORY

69 B.C.   Cleopatra, Queen of Egypt, is born and ascends the throne at age 17.

1429   Joan of Arc is finally granted an audience with Charles the Dauphin of France and subsequently captains the army at the siege of Orleans.

1492   Queen Isabella of Spain finances Columbus's voyage to the New World.

1638   Religious dissident Anne Hutchinson leads schismatic group from Massachusetts Bay Colony into wilderness and establishes Rhode Island.

1803–1806   Sacajawea leads the Lewis and Clark expedition.

1837   Educator Mary Lyons founds Mount Holyoke Female Seminary (later Mount Holyoke College), the first American college exclusively for women.

1843   Dorothea Dix reports to Massachusetts legislature on treatment of criminally insane, resulting in a significant reform of American mental institutions.

1849   Harriet Tubman escapes from slavery and becomes one of the most successful "conductors" on the Underground Railroad. She helps more than 300 slaves to freedom.

1854   Florence Nightingale, the founder of modern nursing, organizes a unit of women nurses to serve in the Crimean War.

1869   Susan B. Anthony is elected president of the National American Woman Suffrage Association.

1900   Carry Nation gains fame destroying saloons as head of the American Temperance Movement.

1919   Mary Pickford becomes the first top-level female executive of a major film studio.

1940   Margaret Chase Smith is the first woman elected to Congress.

1966   National Organization of Women (NOW) is founded by Betty Friedan.

1969   Golda Meir is elected prime minister of Israel.

1979   Mother Teresa receives Nobel Prize for her three decades of work leading the Congregation of Missions of Charity in Calcutta, India.

1979   Margaret Thatcher becomes the United Kingdom's first female prime minister.

1981   Jeane Kirkpatrick is appointed U.S. ambassador to the United Nations.

1981   Sandra Day O'Connor is first woman appointed to the U.S. Supreme Court.

1988   Benazir Bhutto is elected first female prime minister of Pakistan.

1994   Christine Todd Whitman becomes governor of New Jersey, later appointed to cabinet by President Bush in 2001.

1996   Madeleine Albright is appointed U.S. secretary of state.

Source: Originally adapted from the *Colorado Education Association Journal,* February–March 1991. Based on original work by the Arts and Entertainment Network.

LOOKING AT LEADERSHIP THROUGH SEVERAL LENSES

by R.L. Huges, R.C. Ginnett, and G.J. Curphy

Leadership is defined as the process of influencing an organized group toward accomplishing its goals. We will expand on this definition by introducing and describing a three-factor framework of the leadership process. We find this framework to be a useful heuristic both for analyzing various leadership situations and for organizing various leadership theories and supporting research. Therefore, this reading is devoted to providing an overview of the framework.

In attempting to understand leadership, scholars understandably have spent much of their energy studying successful and unsuccessful leaders in government, business, athletics, and the military. Sometimes scholars have done this systematically by studying good leaders as a group (see Bennis & Nanus, 1985; Astin & Leland, 1991), and sometimes they have done this more subjectively, drawing lessons about leadership from the behavior or character of an individual leader such as Martin Luther King, Jr., Lee Iacocca, or Golda Meir. The latter approach is similar to drawing conclusions about leadership from observing individuals in one's own life, whether it be a high school coach, a mother or father, or one's boss. It may seem that studying the characteristics of effective leaders is the best way to learn about leadership, but such an approach tells only part of the story.

Consider an example. Suppose a senior minister was told by one of his church's wealthiest and consistently most generous members that he should not preach any more prochoice sermons on abortion. The wealthy man's contributions were a big reason a special mission project for the city's disadvantaged youth had been funded, and we might wonder whether the minister would be influenced by this outside pressure. Would he be a bad leader if he succumbed to this pressure and did not advocate what his conscience dictated? Would the minister be a bad leader if his continued public stand on abortion caused the wealthy man to leave the church and withdraw support for the youth program?

Although we can learn much about leadership by looking at leaders themselves, the preceding example suggests that studying only leaders provides just a partial view of the leadership process. Would we really know all we wanted to about the preceding example if we knew everything possible about the minister himself? His personality, his intelligence, his interpersonal skills, his theological training, his motivation? Is it not also relevant to understand a bit more, for example, about the community, his parishioners, the businessman, and so on? This points out how leadership depends on several factors, including the situation and the followers, not just the leader's qualities or characteristics. Leadership is more than just the kind of person the leader is or the things the leader does. Leadership is the process of influencing others toward the achievement of group goals; it is not just a person or a position.

If we use only leaders as the lens for understanding leadership, then we get a very limited view of the leadership process. We can expand our view of the leadership process by adding two other complementary lenses: the followers and the situation. However, using only the followers or the situation as a lens also would give us an equally limited view of the leadership process. In other words, the clearest picture of the leadership process occurs only when we use all three lenses to understand it.

THE INTERACTIONAL FRAMEWORK FOR ANALYZING LEADERSHIP

Perhaps the first researcher formally to recognize the importance of the leader, follower, and situation in the leadership process was Fred Fiedler (1967). Fiedler used these three components to develop his contingency model of leadership. Although we recognize Fiedler's contributions, we owe perhaps even more to Hollander's (1978) transactional approach to leadership. We call our approach the **interactional framework.**

There are several aspects of this derivative of Hollander's (1978) approach that are worthy of additional comment. First, the framework depicts leadership as a function of three elements—the **leader,** the **followers,** and the **situation.** Second, a particular leadership scenario can be examined using each level of analysis separately. Although this is a useful way to understand the leadership process, we can have an even better understanding of the process if we also examine the interactions among the three elements, or lenses. For example, we can better understand the leadership process if we not only look at the leaders and the followers but also examine how leaders and followers affect each other in the leadership process.

Similarly, we can examine the leader and the situation separately, but we can gain even further understanding of the leadership process by looking at how the situation can constrain or facilitate a leader's actions and how the leader can change different aspects of the situation in order to be more effective. Thus, a final important aspect of the framework is that leadership is the result of a complex set of interactions among the leader, the followers, and the situation. These complex interactions may be why broad generalizations about leadership are problematic; there are many factors that influence the leadership process.

An example of one such complex interaction between leaders and followers is evident in what has been called in-groups and out-groups. Sometimes there is a high degree of mutual influence and attraction between the leader and a few subordinates. These subordinates belong to the **in-group** and can be distinguished by their high degree of loyalty, commitment, and trust felt toward the leader. Other subordinates belong to the **out-group.** Leaders have considerably more influence with in-group followers than with out-group followers. However, this greater degree of influence also has a price. If leaders rely primarily on their formal authority to influence their followers (especially if they punish them), then leaders risk losing the high levels of loyalty and commitment followers feel toward them. There is even a theory of leadership called **Leader-Member Exchange Theory** that describes these two kinds of relationships and how they affect the types of power and influence tactics leaders use (Graen & Cashman, 1975).

THE ACTION-OBSERVATION-REFLECTION MODEL

by R.L. Huges, R.C. Ginnett, and G.J. Curphy

We have discussed the importance of using multiple perspectives to analyze various leadership situations. Moreover, we argued that it is relatively difficult for leaders to develop this method of analysis on their own and that formal education is one of the best ways to develop multiple perspectives on leadership. Given the importance of formal education and experience in leadership development, this reading reviews some of the ways you can better learn about leadership. As an overview, we begin this reading by presenting a general model that describes how we learn from experience. Next, we describe how perceptions can affect a leader's interpretation of, and actions in response to, a particular leadership situation and why reflection is important to leadership development. In addition, this reading reveals how the people you work with and the task itself can help you become a better leader, and reviews some of the typical content and pedagogy found in many formal leadership education programs. Finally, we discuss how to evaluate and choose between the many different kinds of leadership programs available.

Consider for a moment what a young person might learn from spending a year working in two very different environments: as a staff assistant in the U.S. Congress or as a carpenter on a house construction crew. Each activity has a rich store of leadership lessons there for the taking. Working in Congress, for example, would provide opportunities to observe political leaders both onstage in the public eye and backstage in more private moments. It would provide opportunities to see members of Congress interacting with different constituencies, to see them in political defeat and political victory, and to see a range of leadership styles. A young person could also learn a lot by working on a building crew as it turned plans and materials into the reality of a finished house: watching the coordination with subcontractors, watching skilled craftsmen train younger ones, watching the leader's reactions to problems and delays, watching the leader set standards and assure quality work. At the same time, a person could work in either environment and *not* grow much if he or she is not disposed to. Making the most of experience is key to developing one's

leadership ability. In other words, leadership development depends not just on the kinds of experiences one has but also on how one uses them to foster growth. A study of successful executives found that one key quality that characterized them was an "extraordinary tenacity in extracting something worthwhile from their experience and in seeking experiences rich in opportunities for growth" (McCall, Lombardo, & Morrison, 1988, p. 122).

But how does one do that? Is someone really more likely to get the lessons of experience by looking for them? Why is it not enough just to be there? Experiential learning theorists, such as Kolb (1983), believe people learn more from their experiences when they spend time thinking about them. These ideas are extended to leadership in the **action-observation-reflection** (A-O-R) **model**, which shows that leadership development is enhanced when the experience involves three different processes: action, observation, and reflection. If a person acts but does not observe the consequences of her actions or reflect on their significance and meaning, then it makes little sense to say she has learned from an experience. Because some people neither observe the consequences of their actions nor reflect on how they could change their actions to become better leaders, leadership development through experience may be better understood as the growth resulting from repeated movements through all three phases rather than merely in terms of some objective dimension like time (e.g., how long one has been on the job). We believe the most productive way to develop as a leader is to travel along the **spiral of experience**.

Perhaps an example from Colin Powell's life will clarify how the spiral of experience pertains to leadership development. In 1963, Powell was a 26-year-old officer who had just returned to the United States from a combat tour in Vietnam. His next assignment would be to attend a month-long advanced airborne Ranger course. Near the end of the course, he was to parachute with other troops from a helicopter. As the senior officer on the helicopter, Powell had responsibility for assuring it went well. Early in the flight he hollered for everyone to make sure their static lines were secure, the cables which automatically pulled the chutes open when you jump. Nearing the jump site, he yelled for the men to check their hook-ups one more time. Here are his words describing what happened next:

Then, like a fussy old woman, I started checking each line myself, pushing my way through the crowded bodies, running my hand along the cable and up to each man's chute. To my alarm, one hook belonging to a sergeant was loose. I shoved the dangling line in his face, and he gasped . . . This man would have stepped out of the door of the helo and dropped like a rock. (Powell, 1995, p. 109)

So what did Powell learn from this experience? Again, in his own words:

Moments of stress, confusion, and fatigue are exactly when mistakes happen. And when everyone else's mind is dulled or distracted the leader must be doubly vigilant. "Always check small things" was becoming another one of my rules. (p. 109)

Let us now examine this incident in light of the A-O-R model. *Action* refers to Powell's multiple calls for the parachutists to check their lines. We might speculate from his self-description ("like a fussy old woman") that Powell might have felt slightly uncomfortable with such repeated emphasis on checking the lines, even though he persisted in the behavior. Perhaps you, too, sometimes have acted in a certain manner (or were forced to by your parents!) despite feeling a little embarrassed about it; and then, if it was successful, felt more comfortable the next time acting the same way. That seems to be just what happened with Powell here. The *observation* phase refers to Powell's shocked realization of the potentially fatal accident that would have occurred had he *not* double-checked the static lines. And the *reflection* phase refers to the lesson Powell drew from the experience: "Always check the small things." Even though it was obviously not a totally new insight, its importance was strongly reinforced by this experience. In a very real sense, Powell was "spiraling" through a lesson he'd learned from other experiences too, but embracing it even more this time, making it part of his style.

We also should note how Powell himself described his learning in a manner consistent with our interactional framework. He emphasized the situational importance of the leader's attention to detail, especially during moments of stress, confusion, and fatigue, when mistakes may be most likely to happen. Finally, it's worth noting that throughout Powell's autobiography he discusses many lessons he learned from experience. One of the keys to his success was his ability to keep learning throughout his career.

Power and Influence

This lesson is the seventh in a group of thirteen lessons dealing with leadership. This lesson examines the concepts of interpersonal power and interpersonal influence tactics, as well as the relationship between these concepts.

This lesson also gives you practice in applying the concepts of power and influence to situations where you may need to understand or exert influence. An additional outcome of this lesson is an increased sensitivity and awareness of the pervasive existence and use of interpersonal power and interpersonal influence tactics in a variety of settings.

The following topics are addressed in this lesson:

- French & Raven's five sources of power;
- Yukl's outcomes of influence attempts; and
- Application of influence methods.

The following Terminal Learning Objective (TLO) is supported in whole or in part by this lesson:

- Apply leadership theory & principles.

Following this lesson you will be able to:

- Differentiate the outcomes of influence attempts;
- Describe the sources of interpersonal power; and
- Describe interpersonal influence tactics according to current leadership theory.

POWER AND INFLUENCE

by R.L. Huges, R.C. Ginnett, and G.J. Curphy

We begin by examining the phenomenon of power. Some of history's earliest characterizations of leaders concerned their use of power. Shakespeare's plays were concerned with the acquisition and failing of power (Hill, 1985), and Machiavelli's The Prince has been described as the "classic handbook on power politics" (Donno, 1966). Current scholars have also emphasized the need to conceptualize leadership as a power phenomenon (Gardner, 1986; Hinkin & Schriesheim, 1989). Power may be the single most important concept in all the social sciences (Burns, 1978), though scholars today disagree on precisely how to define power or influence. But it's not just scholars who have different ideas about power. The concept of power is so pervasive and complex that each one of us probably thinks about it a little differently.

What comes to your mind when you think about power? Do you think of a person wielding enormous authority over others? Do you think of high office? Do you think of making others do things against their will? Is power ethically neutral, or is it inherently dangerous as Lord Acton said? ("Power corrupts, and absolute power corrupts absolutely.") Do you think a leader's real power is always obvious to others? What sorts of things might enhance or detract from a leader's power? What are the pros and cons of different ways of trying to influence people? These are the kinds of issues we will explore in this reading.

SOME IMPORTANT DISTINCTIONS

Power has been defined as the capacity to produce effects on others (House, 1984), or the potential to influence others (Bass, 1990). While we usually think of power belonging to the leader, it is actually a function of the leader, the followers, and the situation. Leaders have the potential to influence their followers' behaviors and attitudes. However, followers also can affect the leader's behavior and attitudes. Even the situation itself can affect a leader's capacity to influence his followers (and vice versa). For example, leaders who can reward and punish followers may have a greater capacity to influence followers than those leaders who cannot use rewards or punishments. Similarly, follower or situational characteristics may diminish a leader's potential to influence

followers, as when the latter belong to a strong, active union.

Several other aspects of power also are worth noting. Gardner (1986) made an important point about the exercise of power and its effects. He stated that "power does not need to be exercised in order to have its effect—as any hold-up man can tell you" (Gardner, 1986, p. 5). Thus, merely having the capacity to exert influence can often bring about intended effects, even though the leader may not take any action to influence his or her followers. For example, some months after the end of his term, Eisenhower was asked if leaving the White House had affected his golf game. "Yes," he replied, "a lot more people beat me now." Alternatively, power represents an inference or attribution made on the basis of an agent's observable acts of influence (Schriesheim & Hinkin, 1990). Power is never directly observed but rather attributed to others on the basis and frequency of influence tactics they use and on their outcomes.

Many people use the the terms *power, influence,* and *influence tactics* synonymously (Bass, 1990), but it is useful to distinguish between them. **Influence** can be defined as the change in a target agent's attitudes, values, beliefs, or behaviors as the result of influence tactics. **Influence tactics** refer to one person's actual behaviors designed to change another person's attitudes, beliefs, values, or behaviors. Although these concepts are typically examined from the leader's perspective (e.g., how a leader influences followers), we should remember that followers can also wield power and influence over leaders as well as over each other. Leadership practitioners can improve their effectiveness by reflecting on the types of power they and their followers have and the types of influence tactics that they may use or that may be used *on* them.

Whereas power is the *capacity* to cause change, influence is the degree of *actual change* in a target person's attitudes, values, beliefs, or behaviors. Influence can be measured by the behaviors or attitudes manifested by followers as the result of a leader's *influence tactics.* For example, a leader may ask a follower to accomplish a particular task, and whether or not the task is accomplished is partly a function of the leader's request. (The follower's ability and skill as well as access to the necessary equipment and resources are also important factors.) Such things as subordinates' satisfaction or motivation, group cohesiveness and climate, or unit performance indices can be used to measure the effectiveness of leaders' influence attempts. The degree to which leaders can change the level of satisfaction, motivation, or cohesiveness among followers is a function of the amount of power available to both leaders and followers. On the one hand, leaders with relatively high amounts of power can cause fairly substantial changes in subordinates' attitudes and behaviors; for example, a new and respected leader who uses rewards and punishments judiciously may cause a dramatic change in followers' perceptions about organizational climate and the amount of time followers spend on work-related behaviors. On the other hand, the amount of power followers have in work situations can also vary dramatically, and in some situations particular followers may exert relatively more influence over the rest of the group than the leader does. For example, a follower with a high level of knowledge and experience may have more influence on the attitudes, opinions, and behaviors of the rest of the followers than a brand-new leader. Thus, the amount of change in the attitudes or behaviors of the targets of influence is a function of the agent's capacity to exert influence and the targets' capacity to resist this influence.

Highlight 30–1

GESTURES OF POWER AND DOMINANCE

We can often get clues about relative power just by paying attention to behaviors between two people. There are a number of nonverbal cues we might want to pay attention to.

The phrase **pecking order** refers to the status differential between members of a group. It reminds us that many aspects of human social organization have roots, or at least parallels, in the behavior of other species. The animal kingdom presents diverse and fascinating examples of stylized behaviors by which one member of a species shows its relative dominance or submissiveness to another. There is adaptive significance to such behavioral mechanisms since they tend to minimize actual physical struggle and maintain a stable social order. For example, lower-ranking baboons step aside to let a higher-status male pass; they become nervous if he stares at them. The highest-status male can choose where he wants to sleep and whom he wants to mate with. Baboons "know their place." As with humans, rank has its privileges.

Our own stylized power rituals are usually so second-nature we aren't conscious of them. Yet there is a "dance" of power relations among humans just as among other animals. The following are some of the ways power is expressed nonverbally in humans.

Staring. In American society, it is disrespectful for a person of lower status to stare at a superior, though superiors are not bound by a similar restriction. Children, for example, are taught not to stare at parents. And it's an interesting comment on the power relationship between sexes that women are more likely to avert their gaze from men than vice versa.

Pointing. Children are also taught it's not nice to point. However, adults rarely correct each other for pointing because more than mere etiquette, pointing seems to be a behavior that is acceptable for high-status figures or those attempting to assert dominance. An angry boss may point an index finger accusingly at an employee; few employees who wanted to keep their jobs would respond in kind. The same restrictions apply to frowning.

Touching. Invading another person's space by touching the person without invitation is acceptable when one is of superior status but not when one is of subordinate status. It's acceptable, for example, for bosses or teachers to put a hand on an employee's or a student's shoulder, but not vice versa. The disparity also applies to socioeconomic status; someone with higher socioeconomic status is more likely to touch a person of lower socioeconomic status than vice versa.

Interrupting. Virtually all of us have interrupted others, and we have all been interrupted ourselves. Again, however, the issue is who was interrupting whom? Higher-power or -status persons interrupt; lower-power or -status persons are interrupted. A vast difference in frequency of behaviors also exists between the sexes in American society. Men interrupt much more frequently than women do.

Source: D. A. Karp and W. C. Yoels, *Symbols, Selves, and Society* (New York: Lippincott, 1979).

Leaders and followers typically use a variety of tactics to influence each other's attitudes or behaviors (see Highlight 30–1 for a description of some nonverbal power cues common to humans). Influence tactics are the overt behaviors exhibited by one person to influence another. They range from emotional appeals, to the exchange of favors, to threats. The particular tactic used in a leadership situation is probably a function of the power possessed by both parties. Individuals with a relatively large amount of power may successfully employ a wider variety of influence tactics than individuals with little power. For example, a well-respected leader could make an emotional appeal, a rational appeal, a personal appeal, a legitimate request, or a threat to try to modify a follower's behavior. The follower in this situation may only be able to use ingratiation or personal appeals in order to change the leader's attitude or behavior.

At the same time, because the formal leader is not always the person who possesses the most power in a leadership situation, followers often can use a wider variety of influence tactics than the leader to modify the attitudes and behaviors of others. This would be the case if a new leader were brought into an organization in which one of his or her subordinates was extremely well liked and respected. In this situation, the subordinate may be able to make personal appeals, emotional appeals, or even threats to change the attitudes or behaviors of the leader, whereas the new leader may be limited to making only legitimate requests to change the attitudes and behaviors of the followers.

POWER AND LEADERSHIP

We began this reading by noting how an understanding of power has long been seen as an integral part of leadership. Several perspectives and theories have been developed to explain the acquisition and exercise of power. In this section we will first examine various *sources* of power. Then we will look at how individuals vary in their personal *need* for power.

SOURCES OF LEADER POWER

Where does a leader's power come from? Do leaders *have* it, or do followers *give* it to them? As we shall see, the answer may be both . . . and more.

Something as seemingly trivial as the arrangement of furniture in an office can affect perceptions of another person's power. One vivid example comes from John Ehrlichman's (1982) book, *Witness to Power*. Ehrlichman described his first visit to J. Edgar Hoover's office at the Department of Justice. The legendary director of the FBI had long been one of the most powerful men in Washington, D.C., and as Ehrlichman's impressions reveal, Hoover took every opportunity to reinforce that image. Ehrlichman was first led through double doors into a room replete with plaques, citations, trophies, medals, and certificates jamming every wall. He was then led through a second room, similarly decorated, then into a third trophy room, and finally to a large but bare desk backed by several flags and still no J. Edgar Hoover. The guide opened a door behind the desk, and Ehrlichman went into a smaller office, which Hoover dominated from an impressive chair and desk that stood on a dais about six inches high. Erhlichman was instructed to take a seat on a lower couch, and Mr. Hoover peered down on Ehrlichman from his own loftier and intimidating place.

On a more mundane level, many people have experienced a time when they were called in to talk to a boss and left standing while the boss sat behind the desk. Probably few people in that situation misunderstand the power messages there. In addition to the factors just described, other aspects of office arrangements also can affect a leader's or follower's power. One factor is the shape of the table used for meetings. Individuals sitting at the ends of rectangular tables often wield more power, whereas circular tables facilitate communication and minimize status differentials. However, specific seating arrangements even at circular tables can affect participants' interactions; often individuals belonging to the same cliques and coalitions will sit next to each other. By sitting next to each other, members of the same coalition may exert more power as a collective group than they would sitting apart from each other. Also, having a private or more open office may not only *reflect* but also *affect* power differentials between people. Individuals with private offices can dictate to a greater degree when they want to interact with others by opening or closing their doors or by giving instructions about interruptions. Individuals with more open offices have much less power to control access to them. By being aware of dynamics like these, leaders can somewhat influence others' perceptions of their power relationship.

Prominently displaying symbols like diplomas, awards, and titles also can increase one's power. This was shown in an experiment in a college setting where a guest lecturer to several different classes was introduced in a different way to each. To one group he was introduced as a student; to other groups he was introduced as a lecturer, senior lecturer, or professor, respectively. After the presentation, when he was no longer in the room, the class estimated his height. Interestingly, the same man was perceived by different groups as increasingly taller with each increase in academic status. The "professor" was remembered as being several inches taller than the "student" (Wilson, 1968).

This finding demonstrates the generalized impact a seemingly minor matter like one's title can have on others. Another study points out more dramatically how dangerous it can be when followers are overly responsive to the *appearances* of title and authority. This study took place in a medical setting and arose from concern among medical staff that nurses were responding mechanically to doctors' orders. A researcher made telephone calls to nurses' stations in numerous different medical wards. In each, he identified himself as a hospital physician and directed the nurse answering the phone to prescribe a particular medication for a patient in that ward. Many nurses complied with the request despite the fact it was against hospital policy to transmit prescriptions by phone. Many did so despite never even having talked to the particular

Highlight 30–2

THE MILGRAM STUDIES

One intriguing way to understand power, influence, and influence tactics is to read a synopsis of Stanley Milgram's classic work on obedience and to think about how this work relates to the concepts and theories discussed in the present lesson. Milgram's research explored how far people will go when directed by an authority figure to do something that might injure another person. More specifically, Milgram wanted to know what happens when the dictates of authority and the dictates of one's conscience seem incompatible.

The participants were men from the communities surrounding Yale University. They were led to believe they were helping in a study concerning the effect of punishment on learning; the study's legitimacy was certainly enhanced by being conducted on the Yale campus itself. Two subjects at a time participated in the study, one as a teacher and the other as learner. The roles apparently were assigned randomly. The teacher's task was to help the learner memorize a set of word pairs by providing electric shocks whenever the learner (who would be in an adjacent room) made a mistake.

A stern experimenter described procedures and showed participants the equipment for administering punishment. This "shock generator" looked ominous, with rows of switches, lights, and warnings labeled in 15-volt increments all the way to 450 volts. Various points along the array were marked with increasingly dire warnings such as *extreme intensity* and *danger: severe.* The switch at the highest level of shock simply was marked XXX. Every time the learner made a mistake, the teacher was ordered by the experimenter to administer the next-higher level of electric shock.

In actuality, there was only one true subject in the experiment—the teacher. The learner was really a confederate of the experimenter. The supposed random assignment of participants to teacher and learner conditions had been rigged in advance. The real purpose of the experiment was to assess how much electric shock the teachers would administer to the learners in the face of the latter's increasingly adamant protestations to stop. This included numerous realistic cries of agony and complaints of a heart condition, all standardized, predetermined, tape-recorded messages delivered via the intercom from the learner's to the teacher's room. If the subject (i.e., the teacher) refused to deliver any further shocks, the experimenter prodded him with comments such as "The experiment requires that you go on" and "You have no other choice; you must go on."

Before Milgram conducted his experiment, he asked mental health professionals what proportion of the subjects would administer apparently dangerous levels of shock. The consensus was that only a negligible percentage would do so, perhaps 1 or 2 percent of the population. Milgram's actual results were dramatically inconsistent with what any of the experts had predicted. Fully 70 percent of the subjects carried through with their orders, albeit sometimes with great personal anguish, and delivered the maximum shock possible—450 volts!

Source: S. Milgram, "Behavioral Study of Obedience," *Journal of Abnormal and Social Psychology* 67 (1963), pp. 371–78.

"physician" before the call—and despite the fact that the prescribed medication was dangerously excessive, not to mention unauthorized. In fact, 95 percent of the nurses complied with the request made by the most easily falsifiable symbol of authority, a bare title (Cialdini, 1984). (Also see Highlight 30–2.)

Even choice of clothing can affect one's power and influence. Uniforms and other specialized clothing have long been associated with authority and status, including their use by the military, police, hospital staffs, clergy, and so on. In one experiment, people walking along a city sidewalk were stopped by someone dressed either in regular clothes or in the uniform of a security guard and told this: "You see that guy over there by the meter? He's overparked but doesn't have any change. Give him a dime!" Whereas fewer than half complied when the requestor was dressed in regular clothes, over 90 percent did when he was in uniform (Bickman, 1974). This same rationale is given for having personnel in certain occupations (e.g., airline crew members) wear uniforms. Besides more easily identifying them to others, the uniforms increase the likelihood that in emergency situations their instructions will be followed. Similarly, even the presence of something as trivial as tattoos can affect the amount of power wielded in a group. One of the authors of this text had a friend named Del who was a manager in an international book-publishing company. Del was a former merchant marine whose forearms were adorned with tattoos. Del would often take off his suit coat and roll up his sleeves when meetings were not going his way, and he often exerted considerably more influence by merely exposing his tattoos to the rest of the group.

A final situational factor that can affect one's potential to influence others is the presence or absence of a crisis. Leaders usually can exert more power during a crisis than during periods of relative calm. Perhaps this is because during a crisis leaders are willing to draw on bases of power they normally forgo. For example, a leader who has developed close interpersonal relationships with followers generally uses her referent power to influence them. During crises or emergency situations, however, leaders may be more apt to draw on their legitimate and coercive bases of power to influence subordinates. That was precisely the finding in a study of bank managers' actions; the bank managers were more apt to use legitimate and coercive power during crises than during noncrisis situations (Mulder,

de Jong, Koppelar, & Verhage, 1986). This same phenomenon is observable in many dramatizations. In the television series *Star Trek, the Next Generation,* for example, Captain Picard normally uses his referent and expert power to influence subordinates. During emergencies, however, he will often rely on his legitimate and coercive power. Another factor may be that during crises followers are more willing to accept greater direction, control, and structure from leaders, whatever power base may be involved.

A Taxonomy of Social Power

French and Raven (1959) identified five sources, or bases, of power by which an individual can potentially influence others. These five sources include one that is primarily a function of the leader; one that is a function of the relationship between leaders and followers; one that is primarily a function of the leader and the situation; one that is primarily a function of the situation; and finally, one that involves aspects of all three elements. Understanding these bases of power can give leadership practitioners greater insight about the predictable effects—positive or negative—of various sorts of influence attempts. Following is a more detailed discussion of French and Raven's (1959) five bases of social power.

Expert Power

Expert power is the power of knowledge. Some people are able to influence others through their relative expertise in particular areas. A surgeon may wield considerable influence in a hospital because others depend on her knowledge, skill, and judgment, even though she may not have any formal authority over them. A mechanic may be influential among his peers because he is widely recognized as the best in the city. A longtime employee may be influential because his corporate memory provides a useful historical perspective to newer personnel. Legislators who are expert in the intricacies of parliamentary procedure, athletes who have played in championship games, and soldiers who have been in combat before are valued for the lessons learned and wisdom they can share with others.

Because expert power is a function of the amount of knowledge one possesses relative to the rest of the members of the group, it is possible for followers to have considerably more expert power than leaders in certain situations. For example, new leaders often possess less knowledge of the jobs and tasks performed in a particular work unit than the followers do, and in this case the followers can potentially wield considerable influence when decisions are made regarding work procedures, new equipment, or the hiring of additional workers. Probably the best advice for leaders in this situation is to ask a lot of questions and perhaps seek additional training to help fill this knowledge gap. So long as different followers have considerably greater amounts of expert power, it will be difficult for a leader to influence the work unit on the basis of expert power alone.

Referent Power

One way to counteract the problems stemming from a lack of expertise is to build strong interpersonal ties with subordinates. Referent power refers to the potential influence one has due to the strength of the relationship between the leader and the followers. When people admire a leader and see her as a role model, we say she has referent power. For example, students may respond positively to advice or requests from teachers who are well liked and respected, while the same students might be unresponsive to less-popular teachers. This relative degree of responsiveness is primarily a function of the strength of the relationship between the students and the different teachers. We knew one young lieutenant who had enormous referent power with the military security guards working for him due to his selfless concern for them, evident in such habits as bringing them hot chocolate and homemade cookies on their late-night shifts. The guards, sometimes taken for granted by other superiors, understood and valued the extra effort and sacrifice this young supervisor put forth for them. When Buddy Ryan was fired as head coach of the Philadelphia Eagles football team, many of the players expressed fierce loyalty to him. One said, "We'd do things for Buddy that we wouldn't do for another coach. I'd sell my body for Buddy" (Associated Press, January 9, 1991). That is referent power.

Another way to look at referent power is in terms of the role friendships play in making things happen. It is frequently said, for example, that many people get jobs based on who they know, not what they know. The fact is, there is some truth to that. But we think the best perspective on this issue was offered by David Campbell, who said, "It's not who you know that counts. It's what who you know *knows about you* that counts!" (personal communication).

Referent power often takes time to develop. Furthermore, it can have a downside in that a desire to *maintain* referent power may limit a leader's actions in particular situations. For example, a leader who has developed a strong relationship with a follower may be reluctant to discipline the follower for poor work or chronic tardiness, as these actions could disrupt the nature of the relationship between the leader and the follower. Thus, referent power is a two-way street; the stronger the relationship, the more influence leaders and followers exert over each other. Moreover, just as it is possible for leaders to develop strong relationships with followers and, in turn, acquire more referent power, it is also possible for followers to develop strong relationships with other followers and acquire more referent power. Followers with relatively more referent power than their peers are often the spokespersons for their work units and generally have more latitude to deviate from work-unit norms. Followers with little referent power have little opportunity to deviate from group norms. For example, in an episode of the television show *The Simpsons*, Homer Simpson was fired for wearing a pink shirt to work (everybody else at the Springfield nuclear power plant had always worn white shirts). Homer was fired partly because he "was not popular enough to be different."

Legitimate Power

Legitimate power depends on a person's organizational role. It can be thought of as one's formal or official authority. Some people make things happen because they have the power or authority to do so. The boss can assign projects; the coach can decide who plays; the colonel can order compliance with uniform standards; the teacher assigns the homework and awards the grades. Individuals with legitimate power exert influence through requests or demands deemed appropriate by virtue of their role and position. In other words, legitimate power means a leader has authority because he or she has been assigned a particular role in an organization (and the leader has this authority only as long as he or she occupies that position and operates within the proper bounds of that role).

It is important to note that legitimate authority and leadership are not the same thing. Holding a position and being a leader are not synonymous, despite the relatively common practice of calling position holders in bureaucracies the leaders. The head of an organization may be a true leader, but he also may not be. Effective leaders often intuitively realize they need more than legitimate power to be successful. Before he became president, Dwight Eisenhower commanded all Allied troops in Europe during World War II. In a meeting with his staff before the Normandy invasion, Eisenhower pulled a string across a table to make a point about leadership. He was demonstrating that just as you can pull a string, not push it, officers must lead soldiers and not push them from the rear.

It is also possible for followers to use their legitimate power to influence leaders. In these cases, followers can actively resist a leader's influence attempt by only doing work specifically prescribed in job descriptions, bureaucratic rules, or union policies. For example, many organizations have job descriptions that limit both the time spent at work and the types of tasks and activities performed. Similarly, bureaucratic rules and union policies can be invoked by followers to resist a leader's influence attempts. Often the leader will need to change the nature of his or her request or find another way to resolve the problem if these rules and policies are invoked by followers. If this is the case, then the followers will have successfully used legitimate power to influence their leader.

Reward Power

Reward power involves the potential to influence others due to one's control over desired resources. This can include the power to give raises, bonuses, and promotions; to grant tenure; to select people for special assignments or desirable activities; to distribute desired resources like computers, offices, parking places, or travel money; to intercede positively on another's behalf; to recognize with awards and praise; and so on. Many corporations use rewards extensively to motivate employees. At McDonald's, for example, there is great status accorded the All-American Hamburger Maker, the cook who makes the fastest, highest-quality hamburgers in the country. At individual fast-food restaurants, managers may reward salespersons who handle the most customers during rush periods. Tupperware holds rallies for its salespeople. Almost everyone wins something, ranging from pins and badges to lucrative prizes for top performers (Peters & Waterman, 1982). Schools pick teachers of the year, and professional athletes are rewarded by selection to all-star teams for their superior performance.

The potential to influence others through the ability to administer rewards is a joint function of the leader, the followers, and the situation. Leaders vary considerably in the types and frequency in which they mete out rewards, but the position they fill also helps to determine the frequency and types of rewards administered. For example, employees of the month at Kentucky Fried Chicken are not given new cars; the managers of these franchises do not have the resources to offer such awards. Similarly, leaders in other organizations are limited to some extent in the types of and frequency with which they can administer awards. Nevertheless, leadership practitioners can enhance their reward power by spending some time reflecting on the followers and the situation. Often a number of alternative or innovative rewards can be created, and these rewards, along with ample doses of praise, can help a leader overcome the constraints his or her position puts on reward power.

Although using the power to administer rewards can be an effective way to change the attitudes and behaviors of others, there are several situations where a leader's use of reward power can be problematic. For example, the perception that a company's monetary bonus policy is handled equitably may be as important in motivating good work (or avoiding morale problems) as the amount of the bonus itself. Moreover, a superior may mistakenly assume that a particular reward is valued when it is not. This would be the case if a particular subordinate were publicly recognized for her good work when she actually dislikes public recognition. Leadership practitioners can avoid the latter problem by developing good relationships with subordinates and administering rewards that they, not the leader, value. Another potential problem with reward power is that it may produce compliance but not other desirable outcomes like commitment (Yukl, 1989). In other words, subordinates may perform only at the level necessary to receive a reward and may not be willing to put forth the extra effort needed to make the organization better. An overemphasis on rewards as payoff for performance may also lead to resentment and feelings by workers of being manipulated, especially if it occurs in the context of relatively cold and distant superior-subordinate relationships. Extrinsic rewards like praise, compensation, promotion, privileges, and time off may not have the same effects on behavior as intrinsic rewards such as feelings of accomplishment, personal growth, and development. There is evidence that under some conditions extrinsic rewards can decrease intrinsic motivation toward a task and make the desired behavior less likely to persist when extrinsic rewards are not available (Deci, 1972; Ryan, Mims, & Koestner, 1983). Overemphasis on extrinsic rewards may instill an essentially contractual or economic relationship between superiors and subordinates, diluting important aspects of the relationship like mutual loyalty or shared commitment to higher ideals (Wakin, 1981).

All these cautions about reward power should not cloud its usefulness and effectiveness, which is very real. As noted previously, top organizations make extensive use of both tangible and symbolic rewards in motivating their workers. Furthermore, some of the most important rewards are readily available to all leaders—sincere praise and thanks to others for their loyalty and work. The bottom line is that leadership practitioners can enhance their ability to influence others based on reward power if they (a) determine what rewards are available, (b) determine what rewards are valued by their subordinates, and (c) establish clear policies for the equitable and consistent administration of rewards for good performance.

Finally, because reward power is partly determined by one's position in the organization, some people may believe followers have little, if any, reward power. This may not be the case. If followers have control over scarce resources, then they may use the administration of these resources as a way of getting leaders to act in the manner they want. Moreover, followers may reward their leader by putting out a high level of effort when they feel their leader is doing a good job, and they may put forth less effort when they feel their leader is doing a poor job. By modifying their level of effort, followers may in turn modify a leader's attitudes and behaviors. And when followers compliment their leader (e.g., for running a constructive meeting), it is no less an example of reward power than when a leader compliments a follower. Thus, leadership practitioners should be aware that followers can also use reward power to influence leaders.

Coercive Power

Coercive power, the opposite of reward power, is the potential to influence others through the administration of negative sanctions or the removal of positive events. In other words, it is the ability to control others through the fear of punishment or the loss of valued outcomes. Like reward power, coercive power is partly a function of the leader, but the situation often limits the coercive actions a leader can take. Examples of coercive power include policemen giving tickets for speeding, the army court-martialing AWOL soldiers, a teacher detaining disruptive students after school, employers firing lazy workers, and parents spanking children (Klein, 1991). Even presidents resort to their coercive powers. Historian Arthur Schlesinger, Jr., for example, described Lyndon Johnson as having a "devastating instinct for the weaknesses of others." Lyndon Johnson was familiar and comfortable with the use of coercion; he once told a White House staff member, "Just you remember this. There's only two kinds at the White House. There's elephants and there's ants. And I'm the only elephant" (Barnes, 1989).

Coercive power, like reward power, can be used appropriately or inappropriately. It is carried to its extreme in harsh and repressive totalitarian societies. One of the most tragic instances of coercive power was in the cult led by Jim Jones, which tragically and unbelievably self-exterminated in an incident known as the Jonestown massacre (Conway & Siegelman, 1979). Virtually all of the 912 who died there drank, at Jones's direction, from large vats of a flavored drink containing cyanide. The submissiveness and suicidal obedience of Jones's followers during the massacre were due largely to the long history of rule by fear Jones had practiced. For example, teenagers caught holding hands were beaten, and adults judged slacking in their work were forced to box for hours in marathon public matches against as many as three or four bigger and stronger opponents. Jim Jones ruled by fear, and his followers became self-destructively compliant.

Perhaps the preceding example is so extreme that we can dismiss its relevance to our own lives and leadership activities. On the other hand, it does provide a dramatic reminder that reliance on coercive power has inherent limitations and drawbacks. This is not to say the willingness to use disciplinary sanctions is never necessary. Sometimes it is. Informal coercion, as opposed to the threat of formal punishment, can also be used to change the attitudes and behaviors of others. Informal coercion is usually expressed implicitly, and often nonverbally, rather than explicitly. It may be the pressure employees feel to donate to the boss's favorite charity, or it may be his glare when they bring up an unpopular idea. One of the most common forms of coercion is simply a superior's temperamental outbursts. The intimidation caused by a leader's poorly controlled anger is usually, in its long-term effects, a dysfunctional style of behavior for leaders.

It is also possible for followers to use coercive power to influence their leader's behavior. For example, a leader may be hesitant to take disciplinary action against a large, emotionally unstable follower. Followers can threaten leaders with physical assaults, industrial sabotage, or work slowdowns and strikes, and these threats can serve to modify a leader's behavior. In all likelihood, followers will be more likely to use coercive power to change their leader's behavior if they have a relatively high amount of referent power with their fellow co-workers. This may be particularly true if threats of work slowdowns or strikes are used to influence a leader's behavior.

Concluding Thoughts about French and Raven's Power Taxonomy

On the basis of all this, can we reach any conclusions about what base of power is best for a leader to use? As you might have anticipated, we must say that's an unanswerable question without knowing more facts about a particular situation. For example, consider the single factor of whether or not a group is facing a crisis. This might affect the leader's exercise of power simply because leaders usually can exert *more* power during crises than during periods of relative calm. Perhaps this is because during a crisis leaders are willing to draw on bases of power they normally forgo. For example, a leader who has developed close interpersonal relationships with followers generally uses her referent power to influence them, but during crises or emergency situations leaders may be more apt to draw on their legitimate and coercive bases of power to influence subordinates. That was precisely the finding in a study of bank managers' actions; the bank managers were more apt to use legitimate and coercive power during crises than during noncrisis situations (Mulder, de Jong, Koppelar, & Verhage, 1986). Furthermore, it may be that during crises followers are more *eager* to receive direction and control from leaders.

But can't we make *any* generalizations about using various sources of power? Actually, there has been considerable research looking at French and Raven's ideas, and generally the findings indicate that leaders who relied primarily on referent and expert power had subordinates who were more motivated and satisfied, were absent less, and performed better (Yukl, 1981). However, Yukl (1981) and Podsakoff and Schriesheim (1985) have criticized these findings, and much of their criticism centers on the instrument used to assess a leader's bases of power. Hinkin and Schriesheim (1989) developed an instrument that overcomes many of the criticisms, and future research should more clearly delineate the relationship between the five bases of power and various leadership effectiveness criteria.

Even though much of the research to date about the five bases of power may be flawed, four generalizations about power and influence still seem warranted. First, effective leaders typically take advantage of *all* their sources of power. Effective leaders understand the relative advantages and disadvantages of different sources of power, and they selectively emphasize one or another depending on their particular objectives in a given situation. Second, whereas leaders in well-functioning organizations have strong influence over their subordinates, *they are also open to being influenced by them.* High degrees of reciprocal influence between leaders and followers characterize the most effective organizations (Yukl, 1989). Third, leaders vary in the extent to which they share power with subordinates. Some leaders seem to view their power as a fixed resource that, when shared with others (like cutting a pie into pieces), reduces their own portion. They see power in zero-sum terms. Other leaders see power as an expandable pie. They see the possibility of increasing a subordinate's power without reducing their own. Needless to say, which view a leader subscribes to can have a major impact on the leader's support for power-sharing activities like delegation and participative management. A leader's support for power-sharing activities (or, in today's popular language, *empowerment*) is also affected by the practice of holding leaders responsible for subordinates' decisions and actions as well as their own. It is, after all, the coach or manager who often gets fired when the team loses (Hollander & Offermann, 1990; Pfeffer, 1977). Fourth, effective leaders generally work to *increase* their various power bases (i.e., whether expert, referent, reward, or legitimate) or become more willing to *use* their coercive power.

TYPES OF INFLUENCE BEHAVIOR

by R.L. Huges, R.C. Ginnett, and G.J. Curphy

In recent years, researchers have begun to examine the specific types of behavior used to exercise influence, rather than focusing exclusively on power as a source of potential influence. The most common form of influence behavior in organizations is a "simple request" based on legitimate power. Target compliance is likely for a simple request that is clearly legitimate, relevant for the work, and something the target person knows how to do. However, if the requested action would be unpleasant, inconvenient, irrelevant, or difficult to do, the targets reaction is likely to be resistance. Target commitment is an unlikely outcome for a simple request, except under the most favorable of conditions. For many types of influence attempts it is necessary to use another form of influence behavior called a "proactive influence tactic."

A number of studies have identified distinct types of proactive influence tactics (Kipnis, Schmidt, & Wilkinson, 1980; Mowday, 1978; Porter, Mien, & Angle, 1981; Schilit & Locke, 1982; Schriesheim & Hinkin, 1990; YukI & Falbe, 1990). Building on the earlier work, Yukl and his colleagues (e.g.. Yukl &

Falbe, 1990; Yukl, Lepsinger, & Lucia, 1992; Yukl & Tracey, 1992) have identified 11 proactive influence tactics that are relevant for influencing subordinates, peers, and superiors in large organizations. Each tactic will be explained briefly, and the conditions favoring its use will be described.

RATIONAL PERSUASION

Rational persuasion involves the use of explanations, logical arguments, and factual evidence to show that a request or proposal is feasible and relevant for attaining task objectives. A weak form of rational persuasion may include only a brief explanation of the reason for a request, or an undocumented assertion that a proposed change is desirable and feasible. Stronger forms of rational persuasion include a detailed explanation of the reasons why a request or proposed change is important, and presentation of concrete evidence that a proposal is feasible.

Rational persuasion is most appropriate when the target person shares the same task objectives as the manager but does not recognize the proposal is the best way to attain the objectives, lithe agent and target person have incompatible objectives, then rational persuasion is unlikely to be successful for

---

Definition of the Proactive Influence Tactics

Rational Persuasion: The agent uses logical arguments and factual evidence to show a proposal or request is feasible and relevant for attaining important task objectives.

Apprising: The agent explains how carrying out a request or supporting a proposal will benefit the target personally or help advance the target person's career.

Inspirational Appeals: The agent makes an appeal to values and ideals or seeks to arouse the target person's emotions to gain commitment for a request or proposal.

Consultation: The agent encourages the target to suggest improvements in a proposal, or to help plan an activity or change for which the target person's support and assistance are desired,

Exchange: The agent offers an incentive, suggests an exchange of favors, or indicates willingness to reciprocate at a later time if the target will do what the agent requests.

Collaboration: The agent offers to provide relevant resources and assistance if the target will carry out a request or approve a proposed change.

Personal Appeals: The agent asks the target to carry out a request or support a proposal out of friendship, or asks for a personal favor before saying what it is.

Ingratiation: The agent uses praise and flattery before or during an influence attempt or expresses confidence in the target's ability to carry out a difficult request.

Legitimating Tactics: The agent seeks to establish the legitimacy of a request or to verify authority to make it by referring to rules, formal policies, or official documents.

Pressure: The agent uses demands, threats, frequent checking, or persistent reminders to influence the target person.

Coalition Tactics: The agent seeks the aid of others to persuade the target to do something or uses the support of others as a reason for the target to agree.

obtaining target commitment or even compliance. Along with facts and logic, a rational appeal usually includes some opinions or inferences that the agent asks the target person to accept at face value because there is insufficient evidence to verify them. Thus, the success of the influence attempt also depends in part on whether the target person perceives the agent to he a credible and trustworthy source of information, inferences, and predictions.

APPRISING

With this tactic the agent explains why a request or proposal is likely to benefit the target person as an individual. One type of benefit involves the target person's career, which could be aided by opportunities to learn new skills, meet important people, or gain more visibility and a better reputation. Another type of benefit is to make the target person's job easier or more interesting. Like rational persuasion, apprising often involves the use of facts and logic, but the benefits described are for the target person rather than for the organization. Unlike exchange tactics, the benefits to be obtained by the target person are a by-product of doing what the agent requests, not something the agent will provide. Use of apprising is more likely to be successful if the agent understands the target's needs and how a request or proposal may be relevant for satisfying them. Agent credibility is also required for successful use of this tactic.

INSPIRATIONAL APPEALS

This tactic involves an emotional or value-based appeal, in contrast to the logical arguments used in rational persuasion. An inspirational appeal is an attempt to develop enthusiasm and commitment by arousing strong emotions and linking a request or proposal to a person's needs, values, hopes, and ideals. Some bases for appealing to most people include their desire to be important, to feel useful, to develop and use their skills, to accomplish something worthwhile, to perform an exceptional feat, to be a member of the best team, or to participate in an exciting effort to make things better. Some ideals that may be the basis for an inspirational appeal include patriotism, loyalty, liberty, freedom, self-fulfillment, justice, fairness, equality, love, tolerance, excellence, humanitarianism, and progress. For example, soldiers are asked to volunteer for a dan-

gerous mission as an expression of their patriotism, or a group of employees is asked to work extra hours on a special project because it may save many lives. No tangible rewards are promised, only the prospect that people will feel good as a result of doing something that is noble and just, making an important contribution, performing an exceptional feat, or serving God and country.

Inspirational appeals vary in complexity, from a brief explanation of the ideological benefits from a proposed project or change, to a major speech that articulates an appealing vision of what the organization could accomplish or become. The appropriate level of complexity depends on the size of the task to be undertaken, the amount of effort and risk involved, and the extent to which people are asked to deviate from established, traditional ways of doing things. To formulate an effective appeal, the agent must have insight into the values, hopes, and fears of the person or group to be influenced. Effectiveness also depends on communication skills, such as the agent's ability to use vivid imagery and metaphors, manipulate symbols, and employ voice and gestures to generate enthusiasm and excitement.

CONSULTATION

Consultation occurs when the target person is invited to participate in planning how to carry out a request or implement a proposed change. There are several reasons for using consultation as a decision procedure but when used as a proactive influence tactic, the primary purpose is to influence the target person to support a decision already made by the agent. Consultation can take a variety of forms when used as an influence tactic. In one common form of consultation, the manager presents a proposed policy or plan to a person who will be involved in implementing it to discover if the person has any doubts or concerns. In the discussion, which is really a form of negotiation and joint problem solving, the manager tries to find ways to modify the proposal to deal with the person's major concerns. In another common variation of consultation, the manager presents a general strategy or objective to the other person rather than a detailed proposal and asks the person to suggest specific action steps for implementing it. The suggested action steps are discussed until there is agreement by both parties.

EXCHANGE

This type of influence tactic involves the explicit or implicit offer to provide something the target person wants in return for carrying out a request. This tactic is especially useful when the target person is indifferent or reluctant about complying with a request because it offers no important benefits and would involve considerable effort and inconvenience. Exchange tactics are a way to increase the benefits enough to make it worthwhile for a target person to comply with the request. An essential condition for effective use of this tactic is control over something the target person desires enough to justify compliance. The incentive may involve a wide range of tangible or intangible benefits (e.g., a pay increase or promotion, scarce resources, information, assistance on another task, assistance in advancing the target's career). Sometimes the promise may be implicit rather than explicit. That is, the agent suggests returning the favor in some unspecified way at a future time. An offer to exchange benefits will not be effective unless the target person perceives that the agent is able and willing to carry out the agreement.

COLLABORATION

This influence tactic involves an offer to provide necessary resources or assistance if the target person will carry out a request or approve a proposal. Collaboration may seem similar to exchange in that both tactics involve an offer to do something for the target person. However, there are important differences in the underlying motivational processes and facilitating conditions. Exchange involves increasing the benefits to be obtained by carrying out a request, and it is especially appropriate when the benefits of compliance would otherwise be low for the target person. Collaboration involves reducing the difficulty or costs of carrying out a request, and it is especially appropriate when compliance would be difficult for the target person. Exchange usually involves an impersonal trade of unrelated benefits whereas collaboration usually involves a joint effort to accomplish a task or objective.

PERSONAL APPEALS

A personal appeal involves asking someone to do a favor out of friendship or loyalty to the agent. This influence tactic is not feasible when the target person dislikes the agent or is indifferent about what happens to the agent. The stronger the friendship or loyalty, the more one can ask of the target person. Of course, if referent power is very strong, a personal appeal should not be necessary. Personal appeals are most likely to be used when asking for something that is not part of the target person's regular job responsibilities (e.g., provide assistance, do a personal favor).

INGRATIATION

Ingratiation is behavior that makes the target person feel better about the agent. Examples include giving compliments, doing unsolicited favors, acting deferential and respectful, and acting especially friendly. When ingratiation is perceived to be sincere, it tends to strengthen positive regard and make a target person more willing to consider the agent's request. However, ingratiation is likely to be viewed as manipulative when it is used just before asking for something. Therefore, ingratiation is less useful for an immediate influence attempt than as a longer-term strategy to improve relationships with people (Liden & Mitchell, 1988; Wayne & Ferris, 1990).

LEGITIMATING TACTICS

Legitimating tactics involve attempts to establish one's legitimate authority or right to make a particular type of request. Compliance is more likely when a request is viewed as legitimate and proper. Legitimacy is unlikely to be questioned for a routine request that has been made and complied with many times before. However, legitimacy is more likely to be questioned when you make a request that is unusual, when the request clearly exceeds your authority, or when the target person does not know who you are or what authority you have.

There are several different types of legitimating tactics, most of which are mutually compatible. Examples include providing evidence of prior precedent, showing consistency with organizational policies and rules, showing consistency with professional role expectations, and showing that the request was approved by someone with proper authority.

PRESSURE

Pressure tactics include threats, warnings, and assertive behavior such as repeated demands or frequent checking to see if the person has complied with a request. Pressure tactics are sometimes successful in inducing compliance with a request, particularly if the target person is just lazy or apathetic rather than strongly opposed to it. However, pressure tactics are unlikely to result in commitment, and they may have serious side effects. There are hard and soft forms of pressure. The hard forms (e.g., threats, warnings, demands) are likely to cause resentment and undermine working relationships. The target person may try to avoid you, discredit you, or restrict your power. Sometimes hard pressure tactics are necessary to obtain compliance with a rule or policy that is important to the organization, such as safety rules and ethical practices. However, in most cases, the softer forms (e.g., persistent requests, reminders that the person promised to do something) are more likely to gain compliance without undermining your relationship with the person.

COALITION TACTICS

Coalition tactics involve getting help from other people to influence the target person. The coalition partners may be peers, subordinates, superiors, or outsiders. When assistance is provided by the superior of the target person, the tactic is usually called an "upward appeal." Another distinct type of coalition tactic is to use a prior endorsement by other people to help influence the target person to support your proposal. To be helpful, the endorsements should come from people whom the person likes or respects. Coalition tactics are usually used in combination with one or more of the other influence tactics. For example, you may bring along a supporter when meeting with the target person, and both agents may use rational persuasion to influence the target person.

OTHER TYPES OF INFLUENCE BEHAVIOR

The 11 influence tactics just described are used in proactive influence attempts to motivate someone to carry out a request, perform a task, or support a proposal. Some other types of influence behavior are reactive rather than proactive. These behaviors are typically used after a target person has already complied with a request or has failed to observe rules and regulations. Examples include giving praise and rewards to reinforce desirable behavior, and using coercive power to punish unacceptable behavior. Still other managerial behaviors influence target behavior primarily by guiding or facilitating it rather than by energizing it. Examples include modeling proper behavior, showing a subordinate how to do a task, providing coaching, setting performance goals or standards, and providing resources needed to complete a task. There has been little research to investigate how proactive influence tactics are related to other aspects of leadership behavior.

POWER AND INFLUENCE BEHAVIOR

Studies using survey questionnaires (Hinkin & Schriesheim, 1990; Kapoor & Ansari, 1988) or influence incidents (Yukl, Kim, & Falbe, 1996) find that power and influence behavior are distinct constructs. However, the relationship between specific forms of power, specific influence behaviors, and influence outcomes is not understood very well yet. Five types of effects are possible, and they are not mutually exclusive.

Agent power may directly affect the agent's choice of influence tactics (as depicted by arrow #1). Some tactics require a particular type of power to be effective, and a leader with relevant power is more likely to use these tactics. For example, exchange tactics require reward power, which provides an agent with something of value to exchange with the target person. Strong forms of pressure such as warnings and threats are more likely to be used by an agent who has some coercive power over the target person. Rational persuasion is more likely to be used when the agent has the knowledge necessary to explain why a request is important and feasible.

Some influence tactics may have a direct effect on target attitudes or behavior, regardless of the agent's power. However, in the majority of influence attempts, it is likely that power acts as a moderator variable to enhance or diminish the effectiveness of the tactics used by the agent. This moderator effect of power is most likely to occur for types of power directly relevant to the tactics used in an influence attempt. For example, expert power probably moderates the effect of rational persuasion. A proposal explaining why it is important to change operating procedures is more likely to be successful if made by someone perceived to have relevant expertise. A similar moderating effect probably occurs for reward power and exchange tactics. An agent with high reward power is likely to have more success offering an exchange than an agent with little reward power. Note that the target person's perception of agent reward power is more important than the agent's actual control over rewards. In a classic movie theme, a shabbily dressed millionaire offers a stranger a lot of money to do something, and the stranger refuses, believing that the agent is poor. In contrast, well-dressed con artists with little money are sometimes able to influence people to extend credit or lend valuable items on the (unfulfilled) hope they will result in later purchases.

It is also possible that agent power can enhance the success of influence tactics for which the power is not directly relevant. An agent with strong referent power may be more successful when using rational persuasion to gain support for a proposal. An agent with strong coercive power may be more successful in gaining compliance with a simple request, even though no pressure or exchange tactics are used. Strong expert power may increase the credibility of a request unrelated to the agent's expertise. For example, a famous scientist influences people to participate in a risky financial venture.

Another possibility is that agent power can influence the target person regardless of whether the agent makes any overt influence attempt. For example, people may cooperate more with an agent who has substantial reward power in the hopes of getting some rewards in the future. A classic example is provided by the case of relatives who are especially friendly and helpful to a rich old uncle, but ignore another uncle whom they believe to be poor. In organizations, people act more deferentially toward somebody who has high position power, because they are aware of the possibility that the person can affect their job performance and career advancement. People are less likely to criticize or contradict a powerful agent, because they do not want to risk the agent's displeasure. People are more likely to cooperate with an agent who has strong referent power, even though the agent does nothing to encourage such behavior.

There has been little research to investigate the relationships between power and influence. There is only limited evidence for the proposition that power influences the choice of influence tactics. There is no supporting evidence that power moderates the effectiveness of a specific influence tactic. There is only anecdotal evidence that power increases compliance or changes target behavior independently of the use of tactics based on this power. Clearly these important research questions deserve more attention.

Personality and Leadership

This lesson is the eighth in a group of thirteen lessons dealing with leadership. This lesson examines the relationship of personality to leadership success and failure. This lesson also examines the relationship between persoanlity of both successful and unsuccessful leadership.

The following topics are addressed in this lesson:

- The "Great Man" theory of leadership;
- Linkage between the L-F-S Model and leader personality;
- Personality and leader effectiveness;
- The "Big Five" personality traits; and
- Dysfunctional personality traits, often associated with leadership failure.

The following Terminal Learning Objective (TLO) is supported in whole or in part by this lesson:

- Apply leadership theory & principles.

Following this lesson you will be able to:

- Describe the Five Factor Model (FFM) of personality;
- Employ personality instrument to self-assess personality according to the FFM;
- Relate personality traits to leadership success; and
- Describe dark-side personality traits.

PERSONALITY TRAITS AND LEADERSHIP

by R.L. Huges, R.C. Ginnett, and G.J. Curphy

> Powell's Rules for Picking People: Look for intelligence and judgment and, most critically, a capacity to anticipate, to see around corners. Also look for loyalty, integrity, a high energy drive, a balanced ego, and the drive to get things done.
>
> Colin Powell

One question that leadership researchers have tried to answer over the past 100 years is whether certain personal attributes or characteristics help or hinder the leadership process. In other words, does athletic ability, height, personality, intelligence, or creativity help a leader to influence a group? Put in the context of three leaders, are Colin Powell, Madeleine Albright, or Konosuke Matsushita smarter, more creative, more ambitious, or more outgoing than their less successful counterparts? Do these three leaders act in fundamentally different ways than their followers, and are these differences in behavior due to differences in their innate intelligence, certain personality traits, or creative ability? If so, then could these same characteristics also be used to differentiate successful from unsuccessful leaders, executives from first-line supervisors, or leaders from individual contributors? It was questions like these that led to what was perhaps the earliest theory of leadership, the **Great Man theory** (Stogdill, 1974).

The roots of the Great Man theory can be traced back to the early 1900s, when many leadership researchers and the popular press maintained that leaders and followers were fundamentally different. This led to hundreds of research studies that looked at whether certain personality traits, physical attributes, intelligence, or personal values differentiated leaders from followers. Stogdill (1948) was the first leadership researcher to summarize the results of these studies, and he came to two major conclusions. First, leaders were not qualitatively different than followers; many followers were just as tall, smart, outgoing, and ambitious as the people who were leading them. Second, some characteristics, such as intelligence, initiative, stress tolerance, responsibility, friendliness, and dominance, were modestly related to leadership success. In other words, people who were smart, hardworking, conscientious, friendly, or willing to take charge were often more successful in influencing a group to accomplish its goals than people who were less smart, lazy, impulsive, grumpy, or did not like giving orders. Having "the right stuff" in and of itself was no guarantee of leadership success, but it did improve the odds of successfully influencing a group toward the accomplishment of its goals.

Subsequent reviews by Mann (1959) and Stogdill (1974) involving hundreds of more sophisticated studies came to the same two conclusions. Although these three reviews provided ample evidence that people with the right stuff were more likely to be successful as leaders, many leadership researchers focused solely on the point that leaders were not fundamentally different than followers. They erroneously concluded that personal characteristics could not be used to predict future leadership success; as a result most of the subsequent research shifted toward other leadership phenomena. It was not until the publication of seminal articles by Lord, DeVader, and Allinger (1986) and Hogan, Curphy, and Hogan (1994) that intelligence and personality regained popularity with leadership researchers. Because of these two articles and subsequent leadership research, we now know a lot about how intelligence and various personality traits help or hinder leaders in their efforts to influence others. This research also provided insight on the role that various situational and follower characteristics have in affecting how a leader's intelligence and personality play out in the workplace. The purpose of this reading is to summarize what we currently know about personality, intelligence, and leadership. As an overview, this chapter defines personality, intelligence, creativity, and emotional intelligence, reviews some of the key research findings for these concepts, and discusses the implications of this research for leadership practitioners.

WHAT IS PERSONALITY?

> There is an optical illusion about every person we ever meet. In truth, they are all creatures of a given temperament, which will appear in a given character, whose boundaries they will never pass: but we look at them, they seem alive, and we presume there is impulse in them. In the

moment, it seems like an impulse, in the year, in the lifetime, it turns out to be a certain uniform tune, which the revolving barrel of the music box must play.

Ralph Waldo Emerson

Despite its common usage, Robert Hogan (1991) noted that the term **personality** is fairly ambiguous, and has at least two quite different meanings. One meaning refers to the impression a person makes on others. This view of personality emphasizes a person's *social reputation* and reflects not only a description but also an evaluation of the person in the eyes of others. From the standpoint of leadership, this view of personality addresses two distinct issues: "What kind of leader or person is this?" and "Is this somebody I would like to work for or be associated with?" In a practical sense, this view of personality comes into play whenever you describe the person you work for to a roommate or friend. For example, you might describe him or her as pushy, honest, outgoing, impulsive, decisive, friendly, and independent. Furthermore, whatever impression this leader made on you, chances are others would use many of the same terms of description. In that same vein, many people would probably say that Colin Powell is self-confident, friendly, conventional, outgoing, and achievement-oriented, and that he handles pressure well.

The second meaning of personality emphasizes the underlying, unseen structures and processes inside a person that explain why we behave the way we do; why each person's behavior tends to be relatively *similar across different situations,* yet also *different from another person's behavior.* Over the years psychologists have developed many theories to explain how such unseen structures may cause individuals to act in their characteristic manner. For example, Sigmund Freud (1913) believed that the intrapsychic tensions among the id, ego, and superego caused one to behave in characteristic ways even if the real motives behind the behaviors were unknown (i.e., unconscious) to the person. Although useful insights about personality have come from many different theories, most of the research addressing the relationship between personality and leadership success has been based on the **trait approach,** and that emphasis is most appropriate here.

"**Traits** refer to recurring regularities or trends in a person's behavior" (R. Hogan, 1991, p. 875), and the trait approach to personality maintains that people behave the way they do because of the strengths of the traits they possess. Although traits cannot be seen, they can be inferred from consistent patterns of behavior and reliably measured by personality inventories. For example, the personality trait of dependability differentiates leaders who tend to be hardworking and rule abiding from those who do not like to work hard and are more prone to break rules. Leaders getting higher scores on the trait of dependability on a personality inventory would be more likely to come to work on time, do a thorough job in completing work assignments, and rarely leave work early. We would also infer that leaders getting lower scores on the trait of dependability would be late to work more often, make impulsive decisions, or fail to follow through with commitments.

Personality traits are useful concepts for explaining why people act fairly consistently from one situation to the next. This cross-situational consistency in behavior may be thought of as analogous to the seasonal weather patterns in different cities (Hogan, Hogan, & Roberts, 1996; Roberts, 1996). We know that it is extremely cold and dry in Minneapolis in January, and hot and humid in Hong Kong in August. Therefore, we can do a pretty good job predicting what the weather will generally be like in Minneapolis in January, even though our predictions for any particular day will not be perfect. Although the average temperature in Minneapolis hovers around 20°F, the temperature ranges from −30°F to 30°F on any single day in January. Similarly, knowing how two people differ on a particular personality trait can help us predict more accurately how they will tend to act in a variety of situations.

Just as various climate factors can affect the temperature on any single day, so can external factors affect a leader's behavior in any given situation. The trait approach maintains that a leader's behavior reflects an interaction between his or her personality traits and various situational factors (see, for example, Highlight 31–1. Traits play a particularly important role in determining how people behave in unfamiliar, ambiguous, or what we might call **weak situations.** On the other hand, situations that are governed by clearly specified rules, demands, or organizational policies—**strong situations**—often minimize the effects traits have on behavior (Curphy, 1997a, c; 1996b).

Highlight 31–1

PERSONALITY AND THE PRESIDENCY

Traits are unseen dispositions that can affect the way people act. Their existence can be inferred by a leader's consistent pattern of behaviors. One way of examining a leader's standing on the trait of achievement orientation is to examine one's achievements and accomplishments over the life span. Leaders with higher levels of achievement orientation tend to set high personal goals and are persistent in the pursuit of these goals. When considering the following leader's achievements and accomplishments, think about this person's standing on this personality trait, and try to guess who this person might be:

Age 23: lost a job.

Age 23: was defeated in bid for state legislature.

Age 24: failed in business venture.

Age 25: was elected to legislature.

Age 26: sweetheart died.

Age 27: experienced several emotional problems.

Age 27: was defeated in bid to be speaker of the house.

Age 34: was defeated for nomination to Congress.

Age 37: was elected to Congress.

Age 39: lost renomination to Congress.

Age 40: was defeated in bid for land office.

Age 45: was defeated in bid for U.S. Senate.

Age 47: was defeated for nomination to be vice president.

Age 49: was defeated in bid for Senate a second time.

Age 51: was elected president of the United States.

The person was Abraham Lincoln.

The strength of the relationship between personality traits and leadership effectiveness relationship is often inversely related to the relative strength of the situation (i.e., leadership traits are more closely related to leadership effectiveness in weak situations). Given the accelerated pace of change in most organizations today, it is likely that leaders will be facing even more unfamiliar and ambiguous situations in the future. Therefore, personality traits may play an increasingly important role in a leader's behavior. If organizations can accurately identify those personality traits and the individuals who possess them, then they should be able to do a better job promoting the right people into leadership positions. And if the right people are in leadership positions, the odds of achieving organizational success should be dramatically improved. The next section describes some of the efforts researchers have taken to identify those personality traits related to leadership effectiveness.

THE FIVE FACTOR MODEL OF PERSONALITY

Although personality traits provide a useful approach to describing distinctive, cross-situational behavioral patterns, one potential problem is the sheer number of traitlike terms available to describe another's stereotypical behaviors. As early as 1936 Allport and Odbert identified over 18,000 trait-related adjectives in a standard English dictionary. Despite this large number of adjectives, research has shown that most of the traitlike terms people use to describe others' behavioral patterns could be reliably categorized into five broad personality dimensions. Historically, this five-dimension model was first identified by Webb in 1915 (Deary, 1996) and independently verified by Thurstone (1934), but over the years a number of researchers using very diverse samples and assessment instruments have noted similar results (see Hogan, Curphy, & Hogan, 1994). Given the robustness of the findings, there

Table 31–1   The Five Factor Model of Personality

FIVE FACTOR DIMENSIONS	TRAITS	BEHAVIORS/ITEMS
Surgency	*Dominance*	I like having responsibility for others.
	Sociability	I have a large group of friends.
Agreeableness	*Empathy*	I am a sympathetic person.
	Friendly	I am usually in a good mood.
Dependability	*Organization*	I usually make "to do" lists.
	Credibility	I practice what I preach.
	Conformity	I rarely get into trouble.
	Achievement orientation	I am a high achiever.
Adjustment	*Steadiness*	I remain calm in pressure situations.
	Self-acceptance	I take personal criticism well.
Intellectance		I like traveling to foreign countries.

appears to be a compelling body of evidence to support these five dimensions of personality. These dimensions are referred to in the personality literature as the **Five Factor Model (FFM) of personality**, and most modern personality researchers endorse some version of this model (Azar, 1995; Barrick & Mount, 1996; Curphy, 1998b; Hogan, 1991; Hogan, Hogan, & Roberts, 1996; Barrick, 1999; Quirk & Fondt, 2000).

At its core, the FFM of personality is a categorization scheme. Most, if not all, of the personality traits that you would use to describe someone else could be reliably categorized into one of the FFM personality dimensions. A description of the model can be found in Table 31–1. The five major dimensions include surgency, dependability, agreeableness, adjustment, and intellectance. Perhaps the easiest way to understand this categorization scheme is to describe how our three world leaders would fall into each of the FFM categories.

Surgency (also referred to as dominance, self-confidence, the need for power, or dynamic) involves patterns of behavior often exhibited in group settings and generally concerned with getting ahead in life (Michel & Hogan 1996; Hogan, 2000). Such behavioral patterns often appear when someone is trying to influence or control others. Individuals higher in surgency are outgoing, competitive, decisive, impactful, and self-confident.

Individuals lower in surgency prefer to work by themselves and have relatively little interest in influencing or competing with others.

Because leaders' decisiveness, competitiveness, and self-confidence can affect their ability to successfully influence a group, it is not surprising that leaders often have higher surgency scores than nonleaders (Barrick, 1999; Hurtz & Donovan, 2000). Given the behaviors associated with surgency, it is likely that our three world leaders would have higher surgency scores than most other people. Moreover, Colin Powell, and Madeleine Albright would probably have higher surgency scores than Konosuke Matsushita because the former two leaders appear outwardly more assertive and outspoken than Matsushita.

Another FFM personality dimension is **agreeableness** (also known as empathy, friendliness, or the need for affiliation). This personality dimension concerns how one gets along with, as opposed to getting ahead of, others (Hogan, 2000). Individuals high in agreeableness tend to be empathetic, approachable, and optimistic; those lower in agreeableness are more apt to appear insensitive, distant, and pessimistic.

Because teamwork and cooperation are important components of group functioning, it should not be surprising that leaders often have higher agreeableness scores than people in individual contributor roles

(Barrick, 1999; Sandal, Endressen, Vaernes, & Ursin, 1999). Chances are that Colin Powell and Konosuke Matsushita have fairly high agreeableness scores—both project warm, down-to-earth, and approachable images and appear to be genuinely concerned about others. Madeleine Albright would probably have average agreeableness scores—she can be extremely charming when she wants to, but at other times can appear distant, aloof, and difficult to get along with.

Dependability (also known as conscientiousness) does not involve interacting with others but rather concerns those behavioral patterns related to one's approach to work. Leaders who are higher in dependability tend to be planful and hardworking, follow through with their commitments, and rarely get into trouble. Those who are lower in dependability tend to be more spontaneous, creative, and rule bending, and less concerned with following through with commitments.

In many ways dependability may be more concerned with management than leadership tendencies. Although leaders with higher scores are planful, organized, goal oriented, and prefer structure, they also tend to be risk averse, uncreative, somewhat boring, and dislike change. Again, the situation will determine whether these tendencies can help or hinder a leader's ability to influence a group toward the accomplishment of its goals. For our three world leaders, Colin Powell would likely have the highest dependability scores; Madeleine Albright and Konosuke Matsushita might have somewhat lower scores.

Adjustment (also known as emotional stability or self-control) is concerned with how people react to stress, failure, or personal criticism. Leaders higher in adjustment tend to be calm and tend not to take mistakes or failures personally, whereas those lower in adjustment may become tense, anxious, or exhibit emotional outbursts when stressed or criticized.

Followers often mimic a leader's emotions or behaviors under periods of high stress, so leaders who are calm under pressure and thick-skinned can often help a group stay on task and work through difficult issues. Unfortunately, the opposite is also true. With his calm demeanor and high stress tolerance, Konosuke Matsushita would probably have the highest adjustment scores of our three world leaders. Colin Powell would also have fairly high scores. Madeleine Albright is known to have a tem-

per and be prone to occasional emotional outbursts; therefore, she would likely have lower than average adjustment scores.

Those behavioral patterns dealing with how one reacts to new experiences are related to the personality dimension of **intellectance** (also known as openness to experience). Leaders higher in intellectance tend to be imaginative, broad-minded, and curious; they seek out new experiences through travel, the arts, movies, sports, reading, going to new restaurants, or learning about new cultures. Individuals lower in intellectance tend to be more practical and have narrower interests; they like doing things the tried-and-true way rather than experimenting with new ways. It is important to note that intellectance is not the same thing as intelligence—smart people are not necessarily intellectually curious. Our three world leaders all appear to be open to new experiences and intellectually curious. All are well traveled and seem to have a broad set of interests; therefore, they would all have higher than average intellectance scores.

IMPLICATIONS OF THE FIVE FACTOR MODEL

The trait approach and the FFM provide leadership researchers and practitioners with several useful tools and insights. For one, personality traits provide researchers and practitioners with an explanation for leaders' and followers' tendencies to act in consistent ways over time. They help us to understand why some leaders are dominant versus deferent, outspoken versus quiet, planful versus spontaneous, warm versus cold, and so forth. It is also important to note that the behavioral manifestations of personality traits are often exhibited automatically and without much conscious thought. People high in surgency, for example, will often maneuver to influence or lead whatever groups or teams they are a part of without even thinking about it. Although personality traits predispose us to act in certain ways, we can nonetheless learn to modify our behaviors through experience, feedback, and reflection.

Personality traits are one of the key components of behavior and are relatively difficult to change. Moreover, because personality traits tend to be stable over the years and the behavioral manifestations of traits occur somewhat automatically, it is extremely important for leaders, and leaders to be, to have insight into their personalities. For example, consider a leader who is relatively low in the trait of adjustment, but also is deciding whether to accept a high-stress/high-visibility job. On the basis of his personality trait scores alone, we might predict that this leader could be especially sensitive to criticism, as well as moody and prone to emotional outbursts. If the leader understood that he may have issues dealing with stress and criticism, then he could choose not to take the position, modify the situation to reduce the level of stress, or learn techniques for effectively dealing with these issues. A leader who lacked this self-insight would probably make poorer choices and have more difficulties coping with the demands of this position (Curphy, 1996a).

Personality traits tend to be stable over the years and the behavioral manifestations of traits occur somewhat automatically, it is extremely important for leaders, and leaders to be, to have insight into their personalities. For example, consider a leader who is relatively low in the trait of adjustment, but also is deciding whether to accept a high-stress/high-visibility job. On the basis of his personality trait scores alone, we might predict that this leader could be especially sensitive to criticism, as well as moody and prone to emotional outbursts. If the leader understood that he may have issues dealing with stress and criticism, then he could choose not to take the position, modify the situation to reduce the level of stress, or learn techniques for effectively dealing with these issues. A leader who lacked this self-insight would probably make poorer choices and have more difficulties coping with the demands of this position (Curphy, 1996a).

The FFM has proved to be very useful in several different ways. It is fairly robust, and most personality researchers currently embrace some form of the Big Five model (Azar, 1995; Barrick, 1999; Mount, Barrick, & Strauss, 1994; Barrick & Mount, 1996; Curphy, 1998b; Hogan, Hogan, & Roberts, 1996; Howard & Howard, 1995; Hurtz & Donovan, 2000). Furthermore, the model has proved to be a very useful scheme for categorizing the findings of the personality-leadership performance research.

Another advantage of the FFM is that it is a useful method for profiling people. For example, Mumford, Zaccaro, Johnson, Diana, Gilbert, and Threlfall (2000) reported that a unique set of personality traits differentiated senior leaders in operational units compared with those in staff functions in the U.S. Army. Heckman and Roberts (1997) showed that engineers and accountants tended to be lower in the trait of surgency but higher in the trait of dependability. On the other hand, marketing and sales place a premium on creativity and on influencing others, and people in these occupations tended to be higher in surgency but lower in dependability. There is a compelling body of evidence showing that surgency, agreeableness, dependability, and adjustment are all positively correlated with leadership success—the higher the scores on these four FFM dimensions, the more likely an individual will be an effective leader (Curphy, 2001; Hogan, Curphy, & Hogan, 1994; Barrick, 1999; Quirk & Fandt, 2000; Hurtz & Donovan, 2000; Judge, Higgens, Thoresen, & Barrick, 1999). The intellectance–leadership performance relationship is more tenuous; higher scores on intellectance are related to a leader's willingness to learn and look for a new job when downsized (Barrick, 1999; Boudreau, Boswell, Judge, & Bretz, 2001), but do not appear to be consistently related to leadership success (Hogan, Curphy, & Hogan, 1994). Some of the more recent research also showed that surgency is the best predictor of a leadership job offer after an interview and successful completion of an overseas leadership assignment (Caldwell & Burger, 1998; Caliguiri, 2000). Agreeableness is also a key factor in completing an overseas leadership assignment and working in tightly confined team situations, such as submarine crews (Sandal, Endressen, Vaernes, & Ursin, 1999). Dependability is related to the amount of time people take to prepare for an interview and their overall job satisfaction; lower scores increase their likelihood of engaging in counterproductive work behaviors (Barrick, 1999, Caldwell & Burger, 1998; Hurtz & Donovan, 2000; Sarchione, Cuttler, Muchinsky, & Nelson-Grey, 1998). Higher adjustment scores also helped leaders to complete an overseas assignment, successfully cope with change, and report positive earnings per share after an initial public offering (Judge, Thoresen, Pucik, & Welbourne, 1999; Welbourne & Cyr, 1999). In a similar vein, Blake (1996) reported some interesting findings for military cadets who were higher in agreeableness and surgency. His research indicated that higher agreeableness was positively related to performance ratings during the freshman and sophomore years but that higher surgency was more strongly related to performance ratings over the last two years at the U.S. Coast Guard Academy. Apparently getting along with others and developing strong social supports are very important during the first two years of a military cadet's life, but getting ahead becomes more important over the last two years. It may be that it takes a couple of years to develop strong social networks and supports, and once they have been established, other personality traits, such as surgency, become more important.

Another advantage of the Five Factor Model is that it appears universally applicable across cultures (Curphy, 1997a, 1996b; Hogan, Hogan, & Roberts, 1996; Schmidt, Kihm, & Robie, 2000; Salgado, 1997). People from Asian, Western European, Middle Eastern, Eastern European, or South American cultures seem to use the same five personality dimensions to categorize, profile, or describe others.

While the categorization schemes seem to be the same, however, some cultures do place varying importance on different personality dimensions. For example, Barrick and Mount (1996; Barrick, 1999) reported that dependability was positively related to job performance across *all* jobs in the United States. No matter what the job, it seems that people who are more planful, rule abiding, goal oriented, and reliable are generally higher performers than people who lack these attributes. These same findings for dependability hold true for employees in European countries, but in Europe higher-performing employees also had higher adjustment scores (Salgado, 1997).

WHY DO SOME LEADERS FAIL? THE DARK SIDE OF PERSONALITY

It goes without saying that not all leaders are successful, and some fail miserably. Why do leaders fail? Failure can occur for a variety of reasons, some of which are beyond the leader's or anyone else's control. Sometimes, however, leaders fail for personal, rather than situational, reasons—they may simply lack the abilities or experience needed to be successful. At other times, they may possess these assets but still fail. When this happens it is often because the leaders have been promoted to positions where they can no longer rely on themselves to do all the work but must instead succeed through others. Such leaders generally lack the

ability to form cohesive, goal-oriented teams, and this deficit can be the result of one or more dark-side personality traits. **Dark-side personality traits** are irritating or counterproductive behavioral tendencies that interfere with a leader's ability to form cohesive teams and that cause followers to exert less effort toward goal accomplishment. Several aspects of dark-side traits are worth noting. First, typical measures of personality are designed to detect bright-side traits, and dark-side traits are usually not assessed or detected with interviews, personality inventories, or assessment center techniquese (Brinkmeyer & Hogan, 1997; Brown, 1997; Curphy, 1997d; Curphy, Gibson, Asiu, Horn, & Macomber, 1994; Hogan, Curphy, & Hogan, 1994; McDaniel, 1999; Rybicki & Klippel, 1997). Second, some dark-side traits are strongly related to higher FFM dimension scores. For example, perfectionism is often associated with very high dependability scores. Argumentativeness, impulsivity, and narcissism are related to higher surgency scores (McDaniel, 1999). Although higher surgency, agreeableness, dependability, and adjustment scores are related to leadership success, companies may also have a greater proportion of leaders with dark-side tendencies if they use FFM personality inventories as part of the hiring process. Third, these counterproductive tendencies typically become apparent only after a leader has been in the position for some period of time. Candidates possessing dark-side traits may do very well in interviews but be poor performers once on the job. Table 31–2 provides descriptions of some of the more common dark-side traits.

The behaviors associated with dark-side traits can occur anywhere in an organization. Many times organizations put up with these tendencies because an individual is smart, is experienced, or possesses unique skills. Nevertheless, leaders manifesting dark-side traits tend to leave a longer and longer trail of bruised people, and it is often only a matter of time before these tendencies catch up with them. As seen in Highlight 31–2, these tendencies can and often do have tragic consequences. See if you can pick out which dark-side traits this individual exhibited.

Table 31–2 Dark-Side Personality Traits

Argumentative. This trait identifies leaders who are suspicious, are overly sensitive to criticism, and expect to be mistreated. Leaders possessing this trait do not take personal criticism well and are apt to start arguments and have a hard time ending them.

Interpersonal Insensitivity. Leaders possessing this trait tend to be aloof and unaware of how they come across to others, and to have difficulties putting themselves in "other peoples' shoes."

Narcissism. Leaders with this trait tend to be overly self-confident, self-centered, and extremely ambitious. They grossly overestimate their abilities, have a strong sense of entitlement, and often hold others in contempt. Extremely arrogant, they are always right and not afraid to tell you so. Such individuals often exploit followers for their own self-aggrandizement.

Fear of Failure. These individuals make poor leaders because they dread being criticized. As a result, they tend to be overly cautious and reluctant decision-makers. When forced to make decisions, they often impose old solutions to problems even when it is obvious that they will not work.

Perfectionism. This dark-side trait identifies leaders who are conscientious and methodical but also attend so closely to details that they have trouble setting and maintaining priorities. They maintain extremely high standards for themselves and their followers, and their inflexibility, nit-picking, and micromanaging tendencies can be extremely irritating.

Impulsivity. As leaders, these individuals are hedonistic and often ignore the feelings of followers when in pursuit of their own pleasure. They enjoy testing limits, may fail to keep promises and commitments, and often neglect to consider the consequences of their actions.

Highlight 31–2

AN EXAMPLE OF DARK-SIDE PERSONALITY TRAITS

The subject in this case is a CEO of a $2 billion book publishing company who was dismissed as part of a corporate buyout. The individual started his career with the company as a book salesman over 30 years ago and reigned as the CEO for over 15 years. His leadership credo was "business is conflict. . . You don't get excellence by saying yes. You get love, but you don't get excellence. This company has raised the hurdles of excellence every bloody day."

According to his staff, the subject ruled by intimidation and fear. His profane harangues were an industry legend. Scores of former employees tell of meetings at which he publicly threatened to lop off people's hands or private body parts or tear out their throats for failure to perform. Whenever something went wrong or a goal wasn't achieved, the subject always saw it as a personal matter rather than the result of the business situation. As a result, the subject always placed personal blame for failure and the staff quickly learned not to come forward with problems. He rarely went through a single meeting without going after someone, and people saw his use of degradation and humiliation as a way of controlling his staff.

Many of his staff saw the buyout as the only way to get rid of the CEO. He had been in place for over 15 years and played a key role in making the company a multibillion-dollar organization. Nevertheless, after the buyout the parent organization faced the specter of mass resignations if the subject was allowed to remain as CEO. As a result of the discontent of his staff, the CEO was asked to resign. Unfortunately, even to this day the CEO has no idea why he was let go, and seems genuinely despondent over the decision. When confronted with stories of abuse and intimidation, he either denies that they ever took place or claims that they were blown all out of proportion.

Source: R. T. Hogan, G. J. Curphy, and J. Hogan, "What Do We Know about Leadership: Effectiveness and Personality," *American Psychologist* 49 (1994) pp. 493–504.

LESSON THIRTY-TWO

Leadership Assessment and Development

This lesson is the ninth in a group of thirteen lessons dealing with leadership. This lesson focuses on self-development and the production of Developmental Action Plans that can be used to guide self-development efforts

The following topics are addressed in this lesson:

- How to conduct a self-assessment;
- Process of self-development;
- Peer feedback; and
- Developmental Action Plans.

The following Terminal Learning Objectives (TLO) are supported in whole or in part by this lesson:

- Conduct self-assessment.
- Apply self-development techniques.

Following this lesson you will be able to:

- Describe personal strengths and weaknesses related to leadership; and
- Design a personal plan of leadership self-development.

LEARNING FROM EXPERIENCE

by R.L. Huges, R.C. Ginnett, and G.J. Curphy

Leadership practitioners can enhance the learning value of their experiences by *(a)* creating opportunities to get feedback, *(b)* taking a 10 percent stretch, *(c)* learning from others, *(d)* keeping a journal of daily leadership events, and *(e)* having a developmental plan.

CREATING OPPORTUNITIES TO GET FEEDBACK

It may be difficult for leaders to get relevant feedback, particularly if they occupy powerful positions in an organization. Yet leaders often need feedback more than subordinates do. Leaders may not learn much from their leadership experiences if they get no feedback about how they are doing. Therefore, they may need to create opportunities to get feedback, especially with regard to feedback from those working for them.

First of all, leaders should not assume they have invited feedback merely by saying that they have an open-door policy. A mistake some bosses make is presuming that others perceive them as open to discussing things just because they say they are open to discussing things. How truly open a door is, clearly, is in the eye of the beholder. In that sense, the key to constructive dialogue (i.e., feedback) is not just expressing a policy but also being perceived as approachable and sincere in the offer.

Some of the most helpful information for developing your own leadership can come from asking for feedback from others about their perceptions of your behavior and its impact on your group's overall effectiveness. Leaders who take psychological tests and use periodic surveys or questionnaires will have greater access to feedback than leaders who fail to systematically solicit feedback from their followers. Unless leaders ask for feedback, they may not get it.

TAKING A 10 PERCENT STRETCH

Learning always involves stretching. Learning involves taking risks and reaching beyond one's comfort zone. This is true of a toddler's first unsteady steps, a student's first serious confrontation with divergent worlds of thought, and leadership development. The phrase *10 percent stretch* conveys the idea of voluntary but determined efforts to improve leadership skills. It is analogous to physical exercise, though in this context stretching implies extending one's behavior, not muscles, just a bit beyond the comfort zone. Examples could include making a point to converse informally with everyone in the office at least once each day, seeking an opportunity to be chairman of a committee, or being quieter than usual at meetings (or more assertive, as the case may be). There is much to be gained from a commitment to such ongoing "exercise" for personal and leadership development.

Several positive outcomes are associated with leaders who regularly practice the 10 percent stretch. First, their apprehension about doing something new or different gradually decreases. Second, leaders will broaden their repertoire of leadership skills. Third, because of this increased repertoire, their effectiveness will likely increase. And finally, leaders regularly taking a 10 percent stretch will model something very valuable to others. Few things will send a better message to others about the importance of their own development than the example of how sincerely a leader takes his or her own development.

One final aspect of the 10 percent stretch is worth mentioning. One reason the phrase is so appealing is that it sounds like a measurable yet manageable change. Many people will not offer serious objection to trying a 10 percent change in some behavior, whereas they might well be resistant (and unsuccessful) if they construe a developmental goal as requiring fundamental change in their personality or interpersonal style. Despite its nonthreatening connotation, though, an actual 10 percent change in behavior can make an enormous difference in effectiveness. In many kinds of endeavor the difference between average performers and exceptional performers is 10 percent. In baseball, for example, many players hit .275, but only the best hit over .300—a difference of about 10 percent.

LEARNING FROM OTHERS

Leaders learn from others, first of all, by recognizing they *can* learn from others and, importantly, from *any* others. That may seem self-evident, but in fact people often limit what and whom they pay attention to, and thus what they may learn from. For example, athletes may pay a lot of attention to how coaches handle leadership situations. However, they may fail to realize they could also learn a lot by watching the director of the school play and the band conductor. Leaders should not limit their learning by narrowly defining the sorts of people they pay attention to.

Similarly, leaders also can learn by asking questions and paying attention to everyday situations. An especially important time to ask questions is when leaders are new to a group or activity and have some responsibility for it. When possible, leaders should talk to the person who previously had the position to benefit from his or her insights, experience, and assessment of the situation. In addition, observant leaders are able to extract meaningful leadership lessons from everyday situations. Something as plain and ordinary as a high school car wash or the activities at a fast-food restaurant may offer an interesting leadership lesson. Leaders can learn a lot by actively observing how others react to and handle different challenges and situations, even very common ones.

KEEPING A JOURNAL

Another way leaders can mine experiences for their richness and preserve their learning is by keeping a journal (Csikszentmihalyi, 1990). Journals are similar to diaries, but they are not just accounts of a day's events. A journal should include entries that address some aspect of leaders or leadership. Journal entries may include comments about insightful or interesting quotes, anecdotes, newspaper articles, or even humorous cartoons about leadership. They may also include reflections on personal events, such as interactions with bosses, coaches, teachers, students, employees, players, teammates, roommates, and so on. Such entries can emphasize a good (or bad) way somebody handled something, a problem in the making, the differences between people in their reactions to situations, or people in the news, a book, or a film. Leaders should also use their journals to "think on paper" about leadership readings from textbooks or formal leadership programs or to describe examples from their own experience of a concept presented in a reading.

There are at least three good reasons for keeping a journal. First, the very process of writing increases the likelihood that leaders will be able to look at an event from a different perspective or feel differently about it. Putting an experience into words can be a step toward taking a more objective look at it. Second,

leaders can (and should) reread earlier entries. Earlier entries provide an interesting and valuable autobiography of a leader's evolving thinking about leadership and about particular events in his or her life. Third, journal entries provide a repository of ideas that leaders may later want to use more formally for papers, pep talks, or speeches. As seen in Highlight 32-1, good journal entries provide leaders with a wealth of examples that they may use in speeches, presentations, and so on.

HAVING A DEVELOPMENTAL PLAN

Leadership development almost certainly occurs in ways and on paths that are not completely anticipated or controlled. That is no reason, however, for leaders to avoid actively directing some aspects of their own development. A systematic plan outlining self-improvement goals and strategies will help leaders take advantage of opportunities they otherwise might overlook. Developing a systematic plan also will help leaders prioritize the importance of different goals so that their efforts can be put into areas with the greatest relative payoffs. Leaders who carefully choose which seminars and conferences to attend may help themselves maximize their contribution to their personal developmental goals. Leaders should look for opportunities on the job or in volunteer work for responsibilities that may further their growth. Leaders should recognize, however, that they may experience conflict—both internal and external—between doing more of what they already do well and stretching developmentally.

The following is an example of such a conflict. Suppose Sheila is an accountant who has just joined the board of a local charity. Because handling financial records is something many people do not enjoy, and because Sheila has a demonstrable knack for and interest in it, others on the board may well ask her to become the treasurer. Almost certainly Sheila would do as good a job as anyone else on the board. But suppose Sheila's personal goals included developing her public speaking skills. In such a case, doing what she does best (and what others want her to do) might stand in the way of growth in another area.

Sheila has several alternatives. She could refuse the job of treasurer because she has had her fill of accounting. Alternatively, she could accept the job of treasurer and look for yet another activity in

I went skiing this weekend and saw the perfect example of a leader adapting her leadership style to her followers and situation. While putting on my skis I saw a ski instructor teaching little kids to ski. She did it using the game "red light, green light." The kids loved it and seemed to be doing very well. Later that same day, as I was going to the lodge for lunch, she was teaching adults, and she did more demonstrating than talking. But when she talked she was always sure to encourage them so they did not feel intimidated when some little kid whizzed by. She would say to the adults that it's easier for children, or that smaller skis are easier. She made the children laugh and learn, and made the adults less self-conscious to help them learn too . . .

Today may not exactly be a topic on leadership, but I thought it would be interesting to discuss. I attended the football game this afternoon and could not help but notice our cheerleaders. I was just thinking of their name in general, and found them to be a good example (of leadership). Everyone gets rowdy at a football game, but without the direction of the cheerleaders there would be mayhem. They do a good job of getting the crowd organized and the adrenaline pumping (though of course the game is most important in that too!). It's just amazing to see them generate so much interest that all of the crowd gets into the cheering. We even chant their stupid-sounding cheers! You might not know any of them personally, but their enthusiasm invites you to try to be even louder than them. I must give the cheerleaders a round of applause . . .

I've been thinking about how I used to view/understand leadership, trying to find out how my present attitudes were developed. It's hard to remember past freshman year, even harder to go past high school. Overall, I think my father has been the single most important influence on my leadership development—long before I even realized it. Dad is a strong "Type A" person. He drives himself hard and demands a great deal from everyone around him, especially his family and especially his only son and oldest child. He was always pushing me to study, practice whatever sport I was involved in at the time, get ahead of everybody else in every way possible.

which to develop her public speaking skills. Unfortunately, both of these options may present their own problems. Still another alternative would be to negotiate to expand the role of treasurer to allow greater opportunity to blend the role with her own developmental goals. For example, Sheila might choose to make regular oral reports to the board instead of submitting solely written reports. Additionally, she might take on a larger share of speaking at local service clubs for the purpose of public education about the charity and her own expert view of its needs with regard to fund-raising and financial support. The point here is that leaders simply need to be deliberate in seeking opportunities to put their personal development plans into action. Leaders should exercise control over events to the extent they can; they should not let events exercise a counterproductive control over them.

A leader's first step in exercising control over his personal development is to identify what his goals actually are. The example above presumed Sheila already had identified public speaking as a skill she

wanted to improve. But what if a leader is uncertain about what he or she needs to improve? As described earlier, leaders should systematically collect information from a number of different sources. One place a leader can get information about where to improve is through a review of current job performance, if that is applicable. Ideally, leaders will have had feedback sessions with their own superiors, which should help them identify areas of relative strength and weakness. Leaders should treat this feedback as a helpful perspective on their developmental needs. Leaders also should look at their interactions with peers as a source of ideas about what they might work on. Leaders should especially take notice if the same kind of problem comes up in their interactions with different individuals in separate situations. Leaders need to look at their own role in such instances as objectively as they can; there might be clues about what behavioral changes might facilitate better working relationships with others. Still another way to identify developmental objectives is to look ahead to what new skills are needed to function effectively at a higher level in the organization, or in a different role than the leader now has. Finally, leaders can use formal psychological tests and questionnaires to determine what their relative strengths and weaknesses as a leader may be.

On a concluding note, there is one activity leaders should put in their developmental plans whatever else might be included in them: a program of personal reading to broaden their perspectives on leadership. This reading can include the classics as well as contemporary fiction, biographies and autobiographies of successful leaders, essays on ethics and social responsibility, and assorted self-improvement books on various leadership and management issues. A vital part of leadership development is intellectual stimulation and reflection, and an active reading program is indispensable to that. Leaders might even want to join (or form) a discussion group that regularly meets to exchange ideas about a book everyone has read.

REFLECTION AND LEADERSHIP DEVELOPMENT

by R.L. Huges, R.C. Ginnett, and G.J. Curphy

Perhaps the most important yet most neglected component of the action-observation-reflection model is reflection. Reflection is important because it can provide leaders with a variety of insights into how to frame problems differently, look at situations from multiple perspectives, or better understand subordinates. However, most managers spend relatively little time on this activity, even though the time spent reflecting about leadership can be quite fruitful.

One reason the reflection component is often neglected may be time pressure at work. Leaders are usually very busy people working in pressure-filled situations and often do not have time to ponder all the possible consequences of their actions or reflect on how they could have accomplished a particular action better. Sometimes it takes an out-of-the-ordinary experience to focus one's attention on developmental challenges. In addition, some leaders may not be aware of the value of reflection in leadership development. Hopefully, this section will clarify the value of reflection, and in so doing can complement the emphasis, throughout the remainder of the book, on looking at leadership from different perspectives.

SINGLE- AND DOUBLE-LOOP LEARNING

It is difficult for leaders to fundamentally change their leadership style without engaging in some kind of reflection. Along these lines, Argyris (1976) described an intensive effort with a group of highly successful chief executive officers who became even better leaders through increased self-awareness. Argyris's model for conceptualizing this growth is applicable to any level of leader and is worth considering in more detail.

Argyris (1976) said that most people interact with others and the environment on the basis of a belief system geared to manipulate or control others, and to minimize one's own emotionality and the negative feelings elicited from others. This belief system also tends to create defensive interpersonal relationships and limits risk taking. People "programmed" with this view of life (as most of us are, according to Argyris) produce group and organizational dynamics charac-terized by avoidance of conflict, mistrust, conformity, intergroup rivalry, misperceptions and miscommunications with others, ineffective problem solving, and poor decision making. Most important for our purposes here, it generates a certain kind of learning that Argyris called **single-loop learning.**

Single-loop learning describes a kind of learning between the individual and the environment in which learners seek relatively little feedback that may significantly confront their fundamental ideas or actions. There is relatively little public testing of ideas against valid information. Consequently, an actor's belief system becomes self-sealing and self-fulfilling, and little time is spent reflecting about the beliefs. Argyris used the term *single-loop learning* because it operates somewhat like a thermostat; individuals learn only about subjects within the "comfort zone" of their belief systems. They might, for example, learn how well they are achieving a designated goal. They are far less likely, however, to question the validity of the goal or the values implicit in the situation, just as a thermostat does not question its temperature setting. That kind of self-confrontation would involve **double-loop learning.**

Double-loop learning involves a willingness to confront one's own views and an invitation to others to do so, too. It springs from an appreciation that openness to information and power sharing with others can lead to better recognition and definition of problems, improved communication, and increased decision-making effectiveness. Mastering double-loop learning can be thought of as learning how to learn. With considerable collective work, including the difficult task of working through personal blind spots, Argyris's group of leaders did move to this stage. In other words, through reflection they learned how to change their leadership styles by questioning their assumptions about others, their roles in the organization, and their underlying assumptions about the importance of their own goals and those of the organization.

Konosuke Matsushita seems to have perfected the art of double-loop learning despite never thinking of it in such a formal way. Early in his career Matsushita learned, as he said, to "subject my own methods of management to careful scrutiny, finding that there were many ways in which they could be improved" (quoted in Kotter, 1997, p. 83). He always stressed the importance of an open mind, expecting that he could learn something valuable from everyone he met. He was also quite successful in infusing his whole company with a similar value, which made it an extremely adaptive organization. He pushed not only himself but others as well out of comfortable routines. He believed that his company's success depended upon a humble commitment to continuous improvement rather than a corporate culture that was arrogant and rigid.

THINKING FRAMES AND MULTIPLE PERSPECTIVES

Another way to conceptualize reflection in leadership development involves **thinking frames,** which refer to the tactics and strategies people use to organize their thinking and to construe the meaning of events (Perkins, 1986). Thinking frames are our mental tools, and they may or may not be useful, just as a hammer or saw may or may not be useful depending on the task at hand. In addition, just as a child with a hammer perceives that the whole world needs hammering, our thinking frames can also represent limits on the ways we can (conceptually) operate on our environment. Leadership development can be thought of as the process of developing more complex and differentiated frames for organizing one's thinking (and hence action) about leadership. Moreover, because some thinking frames are relatively subtle, their development may be better assisted through structured educational experiences. For example, most people would not have thought of the action-observation-reflection model on their own. The development of multiple frames, or perspectives, may be one of the greatest contributions a formal course in leadership can make to a leader's development. The overarching idea in discussing the different definitions and theories of leadership in this text is to help you to develop different frames or perspectives for interpreting leadership situations, which in turn may help you to better influence others to achieve organizational goals. Perhaps one key to leadership success is having a variety of tools to choose from and knowing when and where to use them. We hope the theories and concepts described in this text will give you the tools, and by reflecting about your experiences as a leader, you should begin to gain some insight on when and where to use them.

SETTING GOALS

by R.L. Huges, R.C. Ginnett, and G.J. Curphy

> Goals Should Be Specific and Observable
> Goals Should Be Attainable but Challenging
> Goals Require Commitment
> Goals Require Feedback

The Roman philosopher Seneca wrote, "When a man does not know what harbor he is making for, no wind is the right wind." Setting goals and developing plans of action to attain them are important for individuals and for groups. For example, the purpose or goal is often the predominant norm in any group. Once group goals are agreed on, they serve to induce member compliance, act as a criterion for evaluating the leadership potential of group members, and become the criteria for evaluating group performance (Bass, 1990).

Perhaps the most important step in accomplishing a personal or group goal is stating it right in the first place. The reason many people become frustrated with the outcomes of their New Year's resolutions is not any character flaw on their part (e.g., "I don't have any willpower"), but that their resolutions are so vague or unrealistic they are unlikely to ever lead to demonstrable results. It is possible to keep New Year's resolutions, but one must set them intelligently. In a more general sense, some ways of writing goal statements increase the likelihood that someone will successfully achieve the desired goals. Goals should be specific and observable, attainable and challenging, based on top-to-bottom commitment, and designed to provide feedback to personnel about their progress toward them. The following is a more detailed discussion of each of these points.

GOALS SHOULD BE SPECIFIC AND OBSERVABLE

Research provides strong support for the idea that specific goals lead to higher levels of effort and performance than general goals. General goals do not work as well because they often do not provide enough information regarding which particular behaviors are to be changed or when a clear end-state has been attained. This may be easiest to see with a personal example.

Assume that a student is not satisfied with her academic performance and wants to do something about it. She might set a very general goal, such as "I will do my best next year" or "I will do better in school next year." At first, such a goal may seem fine; after all, as long as she is motivated to do well, what more would be needed? However, on further thought you can see that "do my best" or "do better" are so ambiguous as to be unhelpful in directing her behavior and ultimately assessing her success. General goals have relatively little impact on energizing and directing immediate behavior, and they make it difficult to assess, in the end, whether someone has attained them or not. A better goal statement for this student would be, for example, to attain a B average or to get no deficient grades this semester. Specific goals like these make it easier to chart one's progress. A more business-oriented example might deal with improving productivity at work. Specific goal statements in this case might include a 20 percent increase in the number of products being produced by the work unit over the next three months or a 40 percent decrease in the number of products being returned by quality control next year.

The idea of having specific goals is closely related to that of having observable goals. It should be clear to everyone when the goal has or has not been reached. It is easy to say your goal is to go on a diet, but a much better goal is "to lose 10 pounds by March." Similarly, it is easy to say the team should do better next season, but a better goal is to say the team will win more than half of next season's games. It is important to note that specific, observable goals are also time limited. Without time limits for accomplishing goals, there would be little urgency associated with them. Neither would there be a finite point at which it is clear a person or group has or has not accomplished the goals. For example, it is better to set a goal of improving the next quarter's sales figures than just improving sales.

GOALS SHOULD BE ATTAINABLE BUT CHALLENGING

Some people seem to treat goals as a sort of loyalty oath they must pass, as if it would be a break with one's ideals or be a reflection of insufficient motivation if any but the loftiest goals were set for oneself or one's organization. Yet to be useful, goals must be realistic. The struggling high school student who sets a goal of getting into Harvard may be unrealistic; but it may be realistic to set a goal of getting into the local state university. A civil rights activist may wish to eliminate prejudice completely, but a more attainable goal might be to eliminate racial discrimination in the local housing project over the next five years. A track team is not likely to win every race, but it may be realistic to aim to win the league championship.

The corollary to the preceding point is that goals should also be challenging. If goals merely needed to be attainable, then there would be nothing wrong with setting goals so easy that accomplishing them would be virtually guaranteed. Setting easy goals does not result in high levels of performance; higher levels of performance come about when goals stretch and inspire people toward doing more than they thought they could. Goals need to be challenging but attainable to get the best out of oneself and others.

GOALS REQUIRE COMMITMENT

There is nothing magical about having goals; having goals per se does not guarantee success. Unless supported by real human commitment, goal statements are mere words. Organizational goals are most likely to be achieved if there is commitment to them at both the top and the bottom of the organization. Top leadership needs to make clear that it is willing to put its money where its mouth is. When top leadership sets goals, it should provide the resources workers need to achieve the goals and then should reward those who do. Subordinates often become committed to goals simply by seeing the sincere and enthusiastic commitment of top leadership to them. Another way to build subordinate acceptance and commitment to goals is to have subordinates participate in setting the goals in the first place. Research on the effects of goal setting demonstrates that worker acceptance and satisfaction tend to increase when workers are allowed to participate in setting goals (Erez, Earley, & Hulin, 1985; Locke, Latham, & Erez, 1987).

On the other hand, research is less conclusive about whether participation in goal setting actually increases performance or productivity. These mixed findings about participation and performance may be due to various qualities of the group and the leader. In terms of the group, groupthink may cause highly cohesive groups to commit to goals that are unrealistic and unachievable. Group members may not have realistically considered equipment or resource constraints, nor have the technical skills needed to successfully accomplish the goal. In addition, group members may not have any special enthusiasm for accomplishing a goal if the leader is perceived to have little expert power or is unsupportive, curt, or inept (House, 1984; Latham & Lee, 1986; Locke, Latham, & Erez, 1987). However, if leaders are perceived to be competent and supportive, then followers may have as much goal commitment as they would if they had participated in setting the goal. Thus, participation in goal setting often leads to higher levels of commitment and performance if the leader is perceived to be incompetent, but it will not necessarily lead to greater commitment and performance than is achieved when a competent leader assigns a goal. Again, these findings lend credence to the importance of technical competence in leadership effectiveness.

GOALS REQUIRE FEEDBACK

One of the most effective ways to improve any kind of performance is to provide feedback about how closely a person's behavior matches some criterion, and research shows that performance was much higher when goals were accompanied by feedback than when either goals or feedback were used alone. Goals that are specific, observable, and time limited are conducive to ongoing assessment and performance-based feedback, and leaders and followers should strive to provide and/or seek feedback on a fairly regular basis. Moreover, people should seek feedback from a variety of sources or provide feedback using a variety of criteria. Often, different sources and criteria can paint very different pictures about goal progress, and people can get a better idea of the true level of their progress by examining the information provided and integrating it across the different sources and criteria.

Adult Development

This lesson is the tenth in a group of thirteen lessons dealing with leadership. This lesson focuses on the leader and follower components of the interactional framework of leadership (the L-F-S model) by addressing the stages and associated issues of adult development.

The following topics are addressed in this lesson:

- Leader-Follower-Situation leadership model
- Leader self-development process
- Stages of adult development and associated intrapersonal issues
- Developmental theories

The following Terminal Learning Objective (TLO) is supported in whole or in part by this lesson:

- Apply leadership theory & principles.

Following this lesson you will be able to:

- List the stages of adult development;
- Describe typical themes and issues of each stage of adult development; and,
- Relate knowledge of adult development to leadership.

ADULT DEVELOPMENT

Many developmental psychologists believe that adults develop in predictable ways across their life-spans. Some psychologists have proposed conceptual frameworks or theories of adult development composed of distinct stages or periods of development, each of which is marked by characteristic issues, priorities, and questions. The issues, priorities, and questions of each stage have a powerful influence on the motivations of individuals in the stage. Since understanding the motivations and concerns of followers can help leaders' attempts to influence followers and make decisions that affect followers, it is important that leaders understand the progress of adult development. In addition, understanding the characteristic issues of each stage can give leaders useful insights into their own behaviors, feelings, and motivations.

LEVINSON'S STAGES OF SOCIAL DEVELOPMENT

Psychologist Daniel Levinson proposed that life can be divided into four "eras," which he named Preadulthood (conception to about age 22), Early Adulthood (about age 17–45), Middle Adulthood (about age 40–65), and Late Adulthood (about age 60 to death). Each era overlaps with the next in a transition period which lasts approximately five years. The transition period ends the previous era and begins the next. Levinson further divided the Early and Middle Adulthood eras into developmental periods as shown below.

The development that takes place across the span of the adult years relates to the individual's life structure. In Levinson's conceptualization, life structure refers to the important components of an individual's life and how these components are related

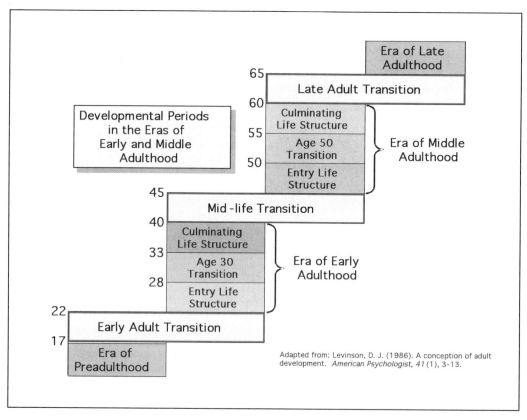

Adapted from: Levinson, D. J. (1986). A conception of adult development. *American Psychologist, 41* (1), 3-13.

FIGURE 33–1

to one another. He believes that, "the primary components of a life structure are the person's *relationships* with various others in the external world."[1] Relationships are broadly conceived and may be with living individuals, historical figures, fictional figures, groups, organizations, and even social movements. As the person develops across the lifespan, these relationships evolve and thus, the life structure evolves. Although an individual's life structure may contain many components and many relationships, usually one or two components fill the dominant central role in the life structure. The components that most often fill the central role are marriage/family and occupation.

The life structure evolves through alternating periods of structure-building and structure-changing. In structure-building periods, the individual makes significant decisions about the desired character and direction of key life components, and then develops and pursues a course of action to shape the life components as conceived. In the structure-changing periods, the individual critically examines the adequacy of the existing structure, explores alternative structures and ways of being, and develops commitment toward new preferred structures and ways of being. The new commitments of the structure-changing period give direction to the next structure-building period that follows. The choices and tasks of the developmental periods of Levenson's model are as follows:

Early Adult Transition (age 17-22). The individual in this period must terminate the adolescent life structure and make commitments to various ways of being that will shape the course of the early adult years. This is the time when many individuals go to college, become independent of their families, and make initial decisions about careers. It is typically a time of exploration, experimentation, and practice. For many, this is a period of instability, doubt, and concern over the necessity of committing to ways of being without the benefit of adult life experience that would make such commitments seem more certain and less risky.

Entry Life Structure for Early Adulthood (age 22-28). The key task of this period is to make and act on the choices which will establish the initial adult life structure. These choices include career, marriage, friendships, values, activities, ways of

behaving, and so on. Once basic life structure choices are made, the individual works to elaborate and build on the choices so as to become established in a distinctive way of being. This means that the individual may invest significant effort in beginning a career and gaining initial career advancement. The individual may also exert a great deal of effort in building a marriage and establishing a family.

Age 30 Transition (age 28-33). The age 30 transition offers an opportunity to examine the structure, direction, and accomplishments of the previous period to determine if the initial decisions of the early adulthood era were appropriate and satisfying. If these decisions are found wanting, the age 30 transition becomes a time of adjustment and redirection. If the initial decisions are found to be sound and satisfying, the age 30 transition results in renewed commitment to the chosen life course and a feeling of having attained a more mature adult status. Some experience the age 30 transition as a time of crisis or panic. These individuals have a sense of being on the wrong path in life and having little time to get on the right path. Individuals may question career decisions, marital commitments, and lifestyle.

Culminating Life Structure for Early Adulthood (age 33-40). This is a period of increased productivity and stability. Individuals have incorporated the changes of the age 30 transition into their life plans and are now seeking to advance in their careers and other aspects of life. Growth, security, and stability within the key components of the life plan are the themes and goals of this period.

Midlife Transition (age 40-45). The midlife transition marks the termination of the early adulthood era and beginning of the middle adulthood era. During this period, individuals examine the life structure that they established and pursued during their 30s. The individual takes stock by comparing the actual accomplishments of the previous periods to the fantasies and ambitions that drove them. This is often a period of crisis in which many conclude that the accomplishments of the previous decade did not justify the sacrifices that they required. The person may feel a sense of panic over having "wasted" their time and efforts and now having little time to get their lives on the right track. The individual may realign her or his priorities, often in a direction that gives increased emphasis to interpersonal relationships. Career, marriage, and lifestyle changes are common during this period.

Entry Life Structure for Middle Adulthood (age 45–50). This period is focused on establishing the redirected life structure that emerges from the midlife transition. It is a period of building, making decisions, and acting to achieve stability in the new life structure.

Age 50 Transition (age 50–55). This period offers another opportunity to evaluate the decisions and life structure pursued in the previous period, and to make any needed course corrections.

Culminating Life Structure for Middle Adulthood (age 55–60). This is another period of stability and building as the individual pursues the life structure decided in the previous period.

ERIK ERICKSON'S THEORY OF PSYCHOSOCIAL DEVELOPMENT

Erik Erickson's theory of psychosocial development proposes that people pass through eight distinct stages of psychosocial development during their lifespans. Successful progress through each of the stages requires the adequate (but not necessarily total) resolution of a psychosocial conflict that is characteristic of the stage. Failure to adequately resolve a stage may leave the individual preoccupied, enmeshed, and developmentally stuck in the negative outcomes of the stage. The name of each of the eight stages describes the successful and unsuccessful outcomes of the stage's conflict. The eight stages and the ages at which they characteristically occur are as follows:

Erickson's Stages of Psychosocial Development		
STAGE	**STAGE NAME**	**AGE SPAN**
1	trust versus mistrust	birth – 1½ years
2	autonomy versus shame and doubt	1½ – 3 years
3	initiative versus guilt	3 – 6 years
4	industry versus inferiority	6 – 12 years
5	identity versus role confusion	adolescence
6	intimacy versus isolation	early adulthood
7	generativity versus stagnation	middle adulthood
8	ego integrity versus despair	late adulthood

Since we are concerned with the leadership of individuals in late adolescence and adulthood (the ages found in the Army), only stages five through eight are described below.

Stage 5—Identity versus Role Confusion. Individuals in this stage are constantly experimenting and testing different personal identities or ways of being. This behavior is often apparent in high school students and is also displayed by some college students. Almost like changing outfits, these individuals may jump from one social group to another as they search for a way of being that fits.

They are searching for their role in life by looking for evidence of who they are, what makes them unique, what their skills and talents are, and what direction they should take in life. If the conflict is adequately resolved, a suitable role is adopted, an adequate self-concept is developed, and the individual has a sense of personal identity and purpose in life. If the conflict is not resolved and a suitable role is not adopted, the individual may feel directionless, have difficulty in interpersonal relationships, and even engage in socially unacceptable behavior.

Stage 6—Intimacy versus Isolation. The primary aim of this period is to learn how to successfully form close interpersonal relationships. Individuals in this stage wonder if they are able to form close and lasting relationships with others or whether they are unable to form such relationships and are therefore destined to live life in isolation and loneliness. Erikson believed that individuals who had not established an adequate personal identity in stage 5 would not be able to form the close interpersonal relationships needed to resolve stage 6.

Stage 7—Generativity versus Stagnation. In this period, individuals examine the accomplishments and contributions of their lives and form conclusions as to their worth. At the same time, individuals in stage 7 seek to maximize their productivity and contributions. Contributions at all social levels, family, community, work, and society as a whole, are examined. The focus is on helping future generations and ensuring the survival and success of family and society. If this self-assessment results in positive conclusions, the individual experiences contentment and the sense of having done one's share. If, on the other hand, this self-assessment results in negative conclusions, the individual may develop a sense of meaninglessness, triviality, failure, and stagnation.

Stage 8—Ego Integrity versus Despair. Persons in this stage examine the successes and failures of their lives and seek to achieve self-acceptance. They try to resolve past conflicts and unfinished business to achieve closure and satisfaction. Those who successfully resolve the issues of this stage develop a sense of accomplishment, wisdom, and contentment. Those who do not resolve the issues of this stage may suffer from a sense of regret, failure, bitterness, and despair.

ENDNOTE

[1]Levinson, D. J. (1986). A conception of adult development. *American Psychologist, 41*(1), P.6

Followership

This lesson is the eleventh in a group of thirteen lessons dealing with leadership. This lesson examines the role that followers play in organizational effectiveness and the characteristics of good followers. The lesson is centered around Kelley's model of followership and the similarities between good followership and good leadership.

The following topics are addressed in this lesson:

- Critical incidents of followership exercise to identify productive and counter-productive followership;
- Kelly's five followership styles;
- Relation of followership to French and Raven's five sources of power; and
- Group member relationships.

The following Terminal Learning Objective (TLO) is supported in whole or in part by this lesson:

- Apply leadership theory & principles.

Following this lesson you will be able to:

- Relate follower characteristics to task and organizational outcomes; and
- Describe five followership styles and the circumstances that lead to their adoption.

FOLLOWERS AND FOLLOWSHIP

by R.L. Huges, R.C. Ginnett, and G.J. Curphy

Perhaps no single researcher has studied followers and followership more than Robert Kelley (1988, 1992). According to Kelley's own account, this has not been without considerable misunderstanding, if not ridicule, from others. He recounts a typical conversation from an encounter as he worked on this project while traveling as an airline passenger (1992, pp. 11–12):

> "What are you working on?" (asks a fellow passenger).
> "Followership," I say.
> "What? Run that by me again."
> "Followership—the flip side of leadership," I explain.
> "Oh, you mean the people who need to be told what to do. The sheep?"

Before we provide Kelley's rejoinder to this statement, you might ask yourself at this point, "How do I view followership?" To make the question a little more personal, ask the question this way: "What would be my parents' reaction if I came home and told them I had been elected the best follower in my class?" To the degree your parents are like many of the adults we (your authors) work with in our roles helping to develop leadership, I expect the response would be less than overwhelming. To take this questioning one step further, you might even be asking yourself right now, "How did these ideas on followership even get into this book? I thought this book was about leaders and leadership." There are several reasons we feel the reader should consider these elements important in the quest for understanding leadership. First of all, there simply is no such thing as leaders without followers. It would be like trying to understand gravity without considering mass. One makes no sense without the other. Second, as we shall see, many of the characteristics of good leadership are also found in highly effective followers. It is also the case that we serve as followers for most of our organizational lives, *even when we may also be serving as leaders.*

Organizational successes and failures often get unfairly attributed to leaders, although followers may have been the true reason for successes and failure (Meindl & Ehrlich, 1987). For example, when

professional sports teams are doing well or poorly, the success or failure is often unfairly attributed to the coach. Coaches are often lauded for being the key to a team's successes and are often the first to be dismissed after an abysmal season. However, a team loaded with talented players may have been successful regardless of the coach; conversely, a team with below-average players may be unsuccessful (at winning games) despite having a great coach. Thus, followers play a key role in the fate of an organization, but their contributions are often overlooked or erroneously attributed to leaders.

As we mentioned above, it is important to remember that even when one is identified as a leader, the same person often holds a complementary follower role. Almost all leaders answer to someone else; school coaches answer to athletic directors; principals answer to school superintendents, who in turn answer to school board members; managers answer to directors, who answer to vice presidents, who answer to presidents; colonels answer to generals, and so on. Most individuals will spend more time as followers than as leaders, and it is not at all uncommon to switch between being a leader and being a follower several times over the course of a day. In fact, our research on high performance teams has shown us that in the most successful teams, there is a great deal of role switching among the "followers" concerning who is serving a leadership role at any given time.

Unfortunately, the follower role has been studied very little. Research efforts have focused instead on the characteristics associated with individuals in leadership roles; relatively little research has looked at what makes successful followers. Moreover, there does not appear to be a perfect and direct relationship between good followership and good leadership. Not all good leaders were necessarily good followers, and not all good followers become good leaders. The Center for Creative Leadership has used the term *derailment* to describe what happens to individuals who eventually fail as leaders despite performing well for a long time in followership and junior leadership roles (McCall & Lombardo, 1983). It might be that such individuals fail to reflect sufficiently on their followership experiences and on the potential lessons for their own development.

In sum, because leadership is not a one-way street, and because most individuals are both leaders and followers, this examines the leadership process by focusing on followers. More specifically, this chapter looks at followers from a number of different perspectives: the influence relationships between leaders and followers; effects of followers' individual characteristics on leadership; follower styles, partnering, and SYMLOG analysis of interactions within a team. The chapter concludes with a look ahead to the world of stewardship and the concurrent requirement for courageous followership.

Transactional and Transformational Leadership

This lesson is the twelfth in a group of thirteen lessons dealing with leadership. This lesson focuses on the important concepts of transactional and transformational leadership.

The following topics are addressed in this lesson:

- Definitions and difference between transactional and transformational leadership;
- Maslow's hierarchy of needs; and
- L-F-S Model and conditions promoting transformational outcomes.

The following Terminal Learning Objective (TLO) is supported in whole or in part by this lesson:

- Apply leadership theory & principles.

Following this lesson you will be able to:

- Differentiate transactional and transformational leadership;
- Describe leader, follower, and situational characteristics associated with charismatic and transformational leadership; and
- Describe the relationship between the Five Factor Model dimensions of personality and transformational leadership.

THE EMOTIONAL APPROACH TO ORGANIZATIONAL CHANGE: CHARISMATIC AND TRANSFORMATIONAL LEADERSHIP

by R.L. Huges, R.C. Ginnett, and G.J. Curphy

Although the rational approach provides a straightforward model for organizational change, it seems like many of the large-scale political, societal, or organizational changes were not this formulaic. For example, it is doubtful that Jesus Christ, Muhammad, Joan of Arc, Vladimir Lenin, Adolf Hitler, Mahatma Gandhi, Mao Zedong, Martin Luther King, Jr., the Ayatollah Khomeini, or Nelson Mandela followed some change formula or plan, yet these individuals were able to fundamentally change their respective societies. Although these leaders differ in a number of important ways, one distinct characteristic they all share is charisma. Charismatic leaders are passionate, driven individuals who are able to paint a compelling vision of the future. Through this vision they are able to generate high levels of excitement among followers and build particularly strong emotional attachments with them. The combination of a compelling vision, heightened emotional levels, and strong personal attachments often compels followers to put forth greater effort to meet organizational or societal challenges. The enthusiasm and passion generated by charismatic leaders seems to be a dual-edged sword, however. Some charismatic movements can result in positive and relatively peaceful organizational or societal changes; some more recent examples might include the Falun Gong movement in China, Louis Farrakhan's Million Man March, or Gloria Steinem's feminist movement. On the downside, when this passion is used for selfish or personal gains, history mournfully suggests it can have an equally devastating effect on society. Examples here might include David Koresh of Waco infamy, Adolf Hitler, or the Serbian leader Slobodan Milosevic.

So what is it about charismatic leadership that causes followers to get so excited about future possibilities that they may willingly give up their lives for a cause? Even though many people conjure up images of charismatic individuals when thinking about leadership, the systematic investigation of charismatic leadership is relatively recent. The remainder of this lesson provides a historical review of the research on charismatic leadership and the leader-follower-situation components of charismatic leadership.

CHARISMATIC LEADERSHIP: A HISTORICAL REVIEW

Prior to the mid-1970s charismatic leadership was studied primarily by historians, political scientists, and sociologists. Of this early research, Max Weber (1947) arguably wrote the single most important work. Weber was a sociologist interested primarily in how authority, religious, and economic forces affected societies over time. Weber maintained that societies could be categorized into one of three types of authority systems: traditional, legal-rational, and charismatic.

In the **traditional authority system,** the traditions or unwritten laws of the society dictate who has authority and how this authority can be used. The transfer of authority in such systems is based on traditions such as passing power to the first-born son of a king after the king dies. Historical examples would include the monarchies of England from the 1400s to 1600s or the dynasties of China from 3000 B.C. to the 1700s. Although few nations are currently ruled by monarchies, there are a number of modern-day examples of the traditional authority system. Many CEOs in privately held companies or publicly traded companies that are controlled by a majority shareholder are often the children or relatives of the previous CEO. Examples include Ford, Anheuser-Busch, Coors, Amway, and Carlson Companies (owners of T.G.I.F. restaurants and Radisson Hotels). In the **legal-rational authority system** a person possesses authority not because of tradition or birthright, but because of the laws that govern the position occupied. For example, elected officials and most leaders in nonprofit or publicly traded companies are authorized to take certain actions because of the position they occupy. The power is in the position itself, rather than in the person who occupies the position.

These two authority systems can be contrasted to the **charismatic authority system,** in which persons derive authority because of their exemplary characteristics. Charismatic leaders are thought to possess superhuman qualities or powers of divine origin that set them apart from ordinary mortals. The locus of authority in this system rests with the individual possessing these unusual qualities; it is not derived from birthright or laws. According to Weber, charismatic leaders come from the margins of society and emerge as leaders in times of great social crisis. These leaders serve to focus society both on the problem it faces and on the revolutionary solutions proposed by the leader. Thus, charismatic authority systems are usually the result of a revolution against the traditional and legal-rational authority systems. Examples of these revolutions might be the overthrow of the shah of Iran by the Ayatollah Khomeini, the ousting of the British in India by Mahatma Gandhi, and the success of Martin Luther King, Jr., in changing the civil rights laws in the United States. Unlike traditional or legal-rational authority systems, charismatic authority systems tend to be short-lived. Charismatic leaders must project an image of success in order for followers to believe they possess superhuman qualities; any failures will cause followers to question the divine qualities of the leader and in turn erode the leader's authority.

A number of historians, political scientists, and sociologists have commented on various aspects of Weber's conceptualization of charismatic authority systems. Of all these comments, however, probably the biggest controversy surrounding Weber's theory concerns the locus of charismatic leadership. Is charisma primarily the result of the situation or social context facing the leader, the leader's extraordinary qualities, or the strong relationships between charismatic leaders and followers? A number of authors argued that charismatic movements could not take place unless the society was in a crisis (Blau, 1963; Chinoy, 1961; Wolpe, 1968). Along these lines, Friedland (1964), Gerth and Mills (1946), and Kanter (1972) argued that before a leader with extraordinary qualities would be perceived as charismatic, the social situation must be such that followers recognize the relevance of the leader's qualities. Others have argued that charismatic leadership is primarily a function of the leader's extraordinary qualities, not the situation (Tucker, 1968; Dow, 1969). These qualities include having extraordinary powers of vision, the rhetorical skills to communicate this vision, a sense of mission, high self-confidence and intelligence, and setting high expectations for followers. Finally, several authors have argued that the litmus test for charismatic leadership does not depend on the leader's qualities or the presence of a crisis, but rather on followers' reactions to their leader (Clark, 1972; Deveraux, 1955; Downton, 1973; Marcus,

1961; Shils, 1965). According to this argument, charisma is attributed only to those leaders who can develop particularly strong emotional attachments with followers.

The debate surrounding charismatic leadership shifted dramatically with the publication of James MacGregor Burns's, *Leadership* (1978). Burns was a prominent political scientist who had spent a career studying leadership in the national political arena. He believed that leadership could take one of two forms. **Transactional leadership** occurred when leaders and followers were in some type of exchange relationship in order to get needs met. The exchange could be economic, political, or psychological in nature, and examples might include exchanging money for work, votes for political favors, loyalty for consideration, and so forth. Transactional leadership is very common but tends to be transitory, in that there may be no enduring purpose to hold parties together once a transaction is made. Burns also noted that while this type of leadership could be quite effective, it did not result in organizational or societal change and instead tended to perpetuate and legitimize the status quo.

The second form of leadership is **transformational leadership,** which serves to change the status quo by appealing to followers' values and their sense of higher purpose. Transformational leaders articulate the problems in the current system and have a compelling vision of what a new society or organization could be. This new vision of society is intimately linked to the values of both the leader and the followers; it represents an ideal that is congruent with their value systems. According to Burns, transformational leadership is ultimately a moral exercise in that it serves to raise the standard of human conduct. This implies that the acid test for transformational leadership might be the answer to the question, "Do the changes advocated by the leader advance or hinder the development of the organization or society?" Transformational leaders are also adept at **reframing** issues; they point out how the problems or issues facing followers can be resolved if they fulfill the leader's vision of the future. These leaders also teach followers how to become leaders in their own right and incite them to play active roles in the change movement (see Highlight 35–1).

It is important to note that all transformational leaders are charismatic, but not all charismatic leaders are transformational. Transformational leaders

---

Highlight 35–1

AN EXAMPLE OF A TRANSFORMATIONAL LEADER: NELSON MANDELA

South Africa was ruled by a white minority government for much of the past 200 years. Although blacks made up over 75 percent of the populace, whites owned most of the property, ran most of the businesses, and controlled virtually all of the country's resources. Moreover, blacks did not have the right to vote and often worked under horrible conditions for little or no wages. Seeing the frustration of his people, Nelson Mandela spent 50 years working to overturn white-minority rule. He started by organizing the African National Congress, a nonviolent organization that protested white rule through work stoppages, strikes, and riots. Several whites were killed in the early riots, and in 1960 the police killed or injured over 250 blacks in Sharpeville. Unrest over the Sharpeville incident caused 95 percent of the black workforce to go on strike for two weeks, and the country declared a state of emergency. Mandela then orchestrated acts of sabotage to further pressure the South African government to change. The organization targeted installations and took special care to ensure no lives were lost in the bombing campaign. Mandela was arrested in 1962 and spent the next 27 years in prison. While in prison he continued to promote civil unrest and majority rule, and his cause eventually gained international recognition. He was offered but turned down a conditional release from prison in 1985. After enormous international and internal pressure, South African President F. W. de Klerk "unbanned" the ANC and unconditionally released Nelson Mandela from prison. Nonetheless, South Africa remained in turmoil, and in 1992 four million workers went on strike to protest white rule. Because of this pressure, Mandela forced de Klerk to sign a document outlining multiparty elections. Mandela won the 1994 national election and was the first truly democratically elected leader of the country.

Sources: M. Fatima, *Higher than Hope: The Authorized Biography of Nelson Mandela* (New York: Harper & Row, 1990); S. Clark, *Nelson Mandela Speaks: Forming a Democratic, Nonracist South Africa* (New York: Pathfinder Press, 1993).

---

are charismatic because they are able to articulate a compelling vision of the future and form strong emotional attachments with followers. However, this vision and these relationships are aligned with followers' value systems and help them get their needs met. Charismatic leaders who are *not* transformational can convey a vision and form strong emotional bonds with followers, but they do so in order to get their own (i.e., the leader's) needs met. Both charismatic and transformational leaders strive for organizational or societal change; the difference is whether the changes are for the benefit of the leader or the followers. This distinction can be appreciated more fully by reading Highlight 13–2. Finally, transformational leaders are always controversial. Charismatic leadership almost inherently raises conflicts over values or definitions of the social "good." Controversy also arises because the people with the most to lose in any existing system will put up the most resistance to a transformational change initiative. The emotional levels of those resisting the transformational leadership movement are often just as great as those who embrace it, and this may be the underlying cause for the violent ends to Martin Luther King, Jr., John F. Kennedy, Mahatma Gandhi, Joan of Arc, or Jesus Christ.

Burns stated that transformational leadership always involves conflict and change, and transformational leaders must be willing to embrace conflict, make enemies, exhibit a high level of self-sacrifice, and be thick-skinned and focused in order to perpetuate the cause.

Yukl (1999), Hunt (1999) and Conger and Hunt (1999) all maintained that the publication of *Leadership* (Burns, 1978) played a key role in renewing interest in the topic of leadership. As a result, research over the past 25 years has explored cross-cultural, gender, succession, leader, follower, situational, and performance issues in charismatic or transformational leadership. From these efforts we now know that charismatic or transformational leadership is both common and rare. It is common because it can occur in almost every social stratum across every culture. For example, a high school student leader in France, a military cadet leader at the United States Air Force Academy, a Kenyan community leader, an Indonesian hospital leader, or a Russian business executive could all be perceived as charismatic or transformational leaders (Bass, 1999; Den Hartog, Hanges, Dorfman, Ruitz-Quintana & Associates, 1999). But it is also rare because most people in positions of authority are not perceived to

Highlight 35–2

AN EXAMPLE OF A CHARISMATIC LEADER: DAVID KORESH

In April 1993 approximately 85 people died at a religious compound outside Waco, Texas. Many of them died from the fire that consumed the compound, but a single shot in the head had killed others. Twenty-five of the deceased were children. How did this happen? The story of David Koresh is a classic example of what can go wrong when the situational, follower, and leadership elements necessary for charismatic leadership are in place but the leader exploits followers for his own selfish purposes. As a child, David's nickname was Sputnik—he was smart, inquisitive, energetic, but also had a strong need for security. When David turned nine his mother decided to attend the local Seventh-day Adventist church. Apparently David loved church and religion—he would be spellbound during sermons and spend hours listening to religious programs on the radio. David had a strong need to be the center of attention and spent time convincing others that he was special and worthwhile. He did so by reciting long passages of Scripture during church meetings and by telling others that God was talking to him. He eventually joined the Branch Davidians, a splinter group of the Seventh-day Adventists. Over the next four years David consolidated his hold on leadership, and convinced his fellow sect members that he was a living prophet and that Armageddon was at hand. To meet the challenge of Armageddon, he and fellow Branch members acquired a large cache of handguns, assault weapons, and explosives. During this time David's behavior became increasingly temperamental and violent. He made fellow members watch violent war movies, listen to his rock and roll sessions, and put them through long fasts and strange diets. This bizarre behavior continued until the Alcohol, Tobacco, and Firearms raid in February 1993.

Source: K.R. Samples; E.M. deCastro; R. Abanes; and R.J. Lyle, *Prophets of the Apocalypse: David Koresh and Other American Messiahs* (Grand Rapids, MI: Baker Books, 1994).

be charismatic or transformational leaders. We also know that females such as Margaret Thatcher, Mary Kay Ash, or Anita Roddick tend to be perceived as more charismatic than their male counterparts, and that transformational leadership results in higher group performance than transactional leadership (Eagly, 1987; Rosener, 1990; Druskat, 1994; Bass, Avolio, & Atwater, 1996; Ross & Offermann, 1991; Avolio & Bass, 2000; Bass, 1999, 2000; Waldman, Ramirez, House, & Puranam, 2001). Although charismatic or transformational leadership often results in large-scale organizational change and higher organizational performance, there is little evidence that these changes remain permanent in business settings after the leader moves on (Conger, 1999).

As a result of this research, we also have three newer theories of charismatic or transformational leadership. Conger and Kanungo (1998) used a stage model to differentiate charismatic from noncharismatic leaders. Charismatic leaders begin by thoroughly assessing the current situation and pinpointing problems with the status quo. They then articulate a vision that represents a change from the status quo. This vision represents a challenge to and is a motivating force for change for followers. The vision must be articulated in such a way that

increases dissatisfaction with the status quo and compels followers to take action. In the final stage, leaders build trust in their vision and goals by personal example, risk taking, and their total commitment to the vision. The theory developed by House and his colleagues (House, 1977; House & Shamir, 1993; Shamir, House, & Arthur, 1993) describes how charismatic leaders achieve higher performance by changing followers' self-concepts. Charismatic leaders are believed to motivate followers by changing their perceptions of work itself, offering an appealing vision of the future, developing a collective identity among followers, and increasing their confidence in getting the job done. Avolio and Bass's (2000) theory of transactional and transformational leadership is essentially an extension of Burns's theory. Unlike Burns, who viewed transactional and transformational leadership as the extremes of a single continuum, Avolio and Bass viewed these two concepts as independent leadership dimensions. Thus, leaders can be transformational and transactional, transactional but not transformational, and so on. Transformational leaders are believed to achieve stronger results because they heighten followers' awareness of goals and the means to achieve them, they convince followers to take action for the collective good of the group, and their vision of the future helps followers satisfy higher-order needs. Because Avolio and Bass created a questionnaire to assess a leader's standing on transactional and transformational leadership, this theory is by far the most thoroughly researched and will be discussed in more detail later in this lesson.

WHAT ARE THE COMMON CHARACTERISTICS OF CHARISMATIC AND TRANSFORMATIONAL LEADERSHIP?

by R.L. Huges, R.C. Ginnett, and G.J. Curphy

Although there are some important differences in the theories offered by Conger and Kanungo (1998), House (1977), and Avolio and Bass (2000), in reality they are far more similar than different. It is also important to note that these researchers either do not differentiate charismatic from transformational leadership, or see charisma as a component of transformational leadership. Therefore, we will use the terms somewhat interchangeably in the next section, although we acknowledge the fundamental difference between these two types of leadership. A review of the common leader, follower, and situational factors from Burns and the three more recent theories. Like the past debates surrounding charismatic leadership, modern researchers are divided on whether charismatic leadership is due to the leader's superhuman qualities, a special relationship between leaders and followers, the situation, or some combination of these factors. Irrespective of the locus of charismatic leadership, the research does provide overwhelming support for the notion that transformational leaders are effective at large-scale societal or organizational change.

LEADER CHARACTERISTICS

Leadership researchers have spent considerably more time and effort trying to identify the unique characteristics of charismatic leaders than they have exploring follower or situational factors (Conger, 1999). This is partly because some researchers believe that it is possible to drive higher levels of organizational change or performance through the selection or training of charismatic leaders (Avolio & Bass, 1998, 2000; Bass, 1999; Hooijberg & Choi, 2000; Ross & Offermann, 1997; Zacharatos, Barling, & Kelloway, 2000). Although some scholars have argued that the leader's personal qualities are the key to charismatic or transformational leadership (Boal & Bryson, 1987; C. W. Hill, 1984, Kets de Vries, 1977, 1993; Sashkin, 1988; Zeleznik, 1974), we do not believe the leader's qualities alone result in charismatic leadership. We do, however, acknowledge several common threads in the behavior and

style of both charismatic and transformational leaders, and these include their vision and values, rhetorical skills, ability to build a particular kind of image in the hearts and minds of their followers, and personalized style of leadership.

Vision

Both transformational and charismatic leaders are inherently future-oriented. They involve helping a group move "from here to there." Charismatic leaders perceive fundamental discrepancies between the way things are and the way things can (or should) be. They recognize the shortcomings of a present order and offer an imaginative vision to overcome them. Several aspects of vision are worth elaboration. First, vision is not limited to grand social movements; leaders can use vision to help drive organizational change and performance in any kind or level of organization. Second, both Bennis and Nanus (1985) and Tichy and Devanna (1986) reported that the leader's vision of the future is often a collaborative effort; the genius of the leader is his or her ability to synthesize seemingly disparate issues and problems and develop a vision that ties all of these concerns together. Paradoxically, the magic of a leader's vision is often that the more complicated the problem, the more people may be drawn to simplistic solutions. Third, values play a key role in the leader's vision, and serve as a moral compass for aligning the actions of leaders and followers with change initiatives (Ket de Vries, 1993; Shamir, Arthur, & House, 1994; Shamir, House, & Arthur, 1993; Bass, 1999; Bass & Steidlmeier, 1999). As noted previously, this is one way transformational leaders differ from "mere" charismatic leaders: the former builds a vision based on *followers'* values whereas the latter's vision is based solely on their *own* values. Fourth, the leader's vision helps followers interpret events and actions in terms of a common perceptual framework (Wofford & Goodwin, 1994; Fairhurst & Sarr, 1996; Gardner & Avolio, 1998). Fifth, Berlew (1974, 1992) maintained that the vision of the charismatic leader had both a stimulating and a unifying effect on the efforts of followers. These effects can help drive greater organizational change and higher performance levels by followers.

Rhetorical Skills

In addition to *having* vision, charismatic leaders are gifted in *sharing* their vision. As discussed earlier, charismatic and transformational leaders have superb

rhetorical skills that heighten followers' emotional levels and inspire them to embrace the vision. As it turns out, both the content of a transformational leader's speeches and the way they are delivered are vitally important. Charismatic leaders make extensive use of metaphors, analogies, and stories rather than abstract and colorless rational discourse to reframe issues and make their points. Moreover, these stories and metaphors can be particularly effective when they invoke potent cultural symbols and elicit strong emotions. Transformational leaders are adept at tailoring their language to particular groups, thereby better engaging them mentally and emotionally. Many transformational or charismatic religious and political leaders effectively use speech techniques like repetition, rhythm, balance, and alliteration to strengthen the impact of their messages (Conger, 1989; Holladay & Coombs, 1994; Shamir, Arthur, & House, 1994; Den Hartog & Verburg, 1997; Awamleh & Gardner, 1998; Berson, Shamir, Avolio, & Popper, 2001; Gargiulo, 2001). Often the delivery of the speech is even more important than the content itself, as poor delivery can detract from compelling content. Adolf Hitler mastered his delivery techniques so well that his speeches can have a hypnotizing power even to people who do not understand German (Willner, 1984). Similarly, many people consider Martin Luther King, Jr.'s "I Have a Dream" speech one of the most moving speeches they have ever heard. Note his use of different speech techniques and his masterful evocation of patriotic and cultural themes in the excerpt presented in Highlight 35–3.

Image and Trust Building

Transformational leaders build trust in their leadership and the attainability of their goals through an image of seemingly unshakable self-confidence, strength of moral conviction, personal example and self-sacrifice, and unconventional tactics or behavior (House, 1977; Conger, 1989; Bass & Avolio, 1994; Bass, 1997; Gardner & Avolio, 1998; Bass & Steidlmeier, 1999; Conger, 1999; Yorges, Weiss, & Strickland, 1999; Choi & Mai-Dalton, 1999). They are perceived to have unusual insight and ability and act in a manner consistent with their vision and values. Some charismatic leaders even seem to place more importance on creating the *appearance* of success than on success per se (House, 1977). Whereas transformational leaders **build trust** by showing commitment to followers' needs over self-interest, some charismatic leaders are not beyond taking credit for others' accomplishments or exaggerating their expertise (Conger, 1989).

Personalized Leadership

One of the most important aspects of charismatic and transformational leadership is the personal nature of the leader's power. These leaders share strong, personal bonds with followers, even when the leader occupies a formal organizational role (Yagil, 1998; Conger, 1999; Avolio & Bass, 2000). It is this **personalized leadership** style that seems to be responsible for the feelings of empowerment notable among followers of charismatic or transformational leaders, and it has three important com-

---

Highlight 35–3

I HAVE A DREAM

This will be the day when all of God's children will be able to sing with new meaning—"my country 'tis of thee, sweet land of liberty, of thee I sing; land where my fathers died, land of the pilgrim's pride; from every mountain side, let freedom ring"—and if America is to be a great nation, this must become true. So let freedom ring from the prodigious hilltops of New Hampshire. Let freedom ring from the mighty mountains of New York. Let freedom ring from the snow-capped Rockies of Colorado. Let freedom ring from the curvaceous slopes of California. But not only that. Let freedom ring from Stone Mountain of Georgia. Let freedom ring from Lookout Mountain of Tennessee. Let freedom ring from every hill and molehill of Mississippi, from every mountainside, let freedom ring. And when we allow freedom to ring, when we let it ring from every village and every hamlet, from every state and every city, we will be able to speed up that day when all of God's children—Black and White men, Jews and Gentiles, Protestants and Catholics—will be able to join hands and to sing in the words of the old Negro spiritual: "Free at last, free at last; thank God Almighty, we are free at last."

Source: Martin Luther King, Jr., "I Have a Dream" speech.

ponents. First, charismatic leaders are more sensitive to the emotional states of followers (Judge & Bono, 2000). They seem to be more adept at picking up social cues and tailoring their messages accordingly. Second, they also tend to be emotionally expressive, especially through such nonverbal channels as their eye contact, posture, movement, gestures, tone of voice, and facial expressions (Bass, 1990; Den Hartog & Verburg, 1997). It is partly through their ability to pick up on emotional cues and their nonverbal behaviors that some people are perceived to have a "magnetic" personality. Third, transformational leaders empower followers by building their self-efficacy. They do this by giving followers tasks that lead to successively greater success experiences and heightened self-confidence, encouraging followers to continually upgrade their skills, and creating an environment of heightened expectations and positive emotions (Larmore & Ayman, 1998; Bass, 1997; Bass & Avolio, 1994; Conger & Kanungo, 1998; Rost, 1991).

FOLLOWER CHARACTERISTICS

If charismatic leadership were defined solely by a leader's characteristics, then it would be relatively easy to identify those individuals with good visioning, rhetorical, and impression management skills, and place them in leadership positions. Over time we would expect that a high percentage of followers would embrace and act on the leader's vision. However, a number of leaders appear to possess these attributes, yet are not seen as charismatic. They may be good, competent leaders in their own right, but they seem unable to evoke strong feelings in followers or to get followers to do more than they thought possible. In reality, charisma is probably more a function of the followers' reactions to a leader than of the leader's personal characteristics. If followers do not accept the leader's vision or become emotionally attached to the leader, then the leader simply will not be perceived to be either charismatic or transformational. Thus, **charisma** is in the eyes and heart of the beholder; it is a particularly strong emotional reaction to, identification with, and belief in some leaders by some followers. It is important to note that this definition is value-free—leaders seen as charismatic may or may not share the same values as their followers or meet Burns's criteria for transformational leadership. Many of the more popular conceptualizations of

charisma and charismatic leadership today also define charisma in terms of followers' reactions to the leader (Bass, 1985, 1997; Avolio & Bass, 2000; Conger & Kanungo, 1998; Shamir, House, & Arthur, 1993; Howell, 1988; Willner, 1984). Defining charisma as a reaction that followers have toward leaders makes it reasonable to turn our attention to the four unique characteristics of these reactions.

Identification with the Leader and the Vision

Two of the effects associated with charismatic leadership include a strong affection for the leader and a similarity of follower beliefs with those of the leader. These effects describe a sort of bonding or **identification with the leader** personally, and a parallel psychological investment to a goal or activity (a "cause") bigger than oneself. Followers bond with a leader because they see the implementation of the vision as a solution to all of their problems. Followers may be intensely dissatisfied with the status quo but unsuccessful in developing a satisfactory solution on their own. Charismatic leaders capitalize on this dissatisfaction and on the belief that most people want to make a difference in their organizations or society. Followers' identities or self-concepts also become defined in terms of the leader. Being like the leader, or approved by the leader, becomes an important part of one's self-worth (Ehrhart & Klein, 2001; Lord & Brown, 2001). Effects like these go well beyond what might be expected from the typical contractual or exchange relationships between most supervisors and subordinates.

Heightened Emotional Levels

Charismatic leaders are able to stir followers' feelings, and this **heightened emotional level** results in increased levels of effort and performance. Emotions are often the fuel driving large-scale initiatives for change, and charismatic leaders will often do all they can to maintain them, including getting followers to think about their dissatisfaction with the status quo or making impassioned appeals directly to followers. There are several dangers with increasing followers' emotional levels, however. The leader must ensure that followers' emotions are channeled toward the change initiative, otherwise followers will find some other outlet for their feelings and efforts. In addition, the people alienated by a charismatic leader and the movement can have emotions just as intense as those of the followers of the vision.

This polarizing effect of charismatic leaders may be one reason why they tend to have violent deaths, as those alienated by a charismatic leader are just as likely to act on their emotions as followers within the movement (House, Woycke, & Fodor, 1988).

Willing Subordination to the Leader

Whereas the preceding factor dealt with followers' emotional and psychological closeness to the leader, **willing subordination to the leader** involves their deference to his or her authority. Charismatic leaders often seem imbued with superhuman qualities. As a result, followers often naturally and willingly submit to the leader's apparent authority and superiority. Followers seem to suspend their critical thinking skills; they have few if any doubts about the intentions or skills of the leader, the correctness of the vision or change initiative, or the actions they need to take in order achieve the vision.

Feelings of Empowerment

Followers of charismatic leaders are moved to expect more of themselves, and they work harder to achieve these higher goals. Charismatic leaders capitalize on the Pygmalion Effect: They set high expectations while boosting the self-confidence of followers by expressing confidence in their abilities and providing ongoing encouragement and support (Dvir, Eden, Avolio, & Shamir, 1999; Larmore & Ayman, 1998; Bass & Avolio, 1994). Somewhat paradoxically, followers feel stronger and more powerful at the same time they willingly subordinate themselves to the charismatic leader. Charismatic leaders are able to make their followers feel more powerful without any diminution or threat to their own status. These **feelings of empowerment,** when combined with heightened emotional levels and a leader's vision of the future, often result in increases in organ-izational, group, or team performance or significant social change.

SITUATIONAL CHARACTERISTICS

Most of the research up to now has focused on identifying the leader attributes associated with charismatic leadership. There is considerably more to learn about the underlying attributes of followers and the situational characteristics of charismatic or transformational leadership (Beyer, 1999; Conger, 1999). Despite this gap in knowledge, some researchers believe that situational factors do play

an important role in determining whether a leader will be perceived as charismatic (Bradley, 1987; Roberts & Bradley, 1988; Westley & Mintzberg, 1988; Gardner & Avolio, 1998; Conger, 1999; Hunt, Boal, & Dodge, 1999; Shamir & Howell, 1999; Waldman, Ramirez, House, & Puranam, 2001). It may be that individuals possessing the qualities of charismatic leaders will be perceived as charismatic *only when confronting certain types of situations.* It may also be that the more favorable the situation is for charismatic leadership, the fewer qualities leaders will need before they are perceived to be charismatic (Conger, 1999). Because the situation may play an important role in the attribution of charisma, it will be useful to review some of the situational factors believed to affect charismatic leadership (see also Highlight 35–4).

Crises.

Perhaps the most important situational factor associated with charismatic leadership is the presence or absence of a **crisis.** Followers who are content with the status quo are relatively unlikely to perceive a need for a charismatic leader or be willing to devote great effort to fundamentally change an organization or society. On the other hand, a crisis—whether reflected by the failure of traditional social institutions or a corporation's imminent financial failure—often creates a "charisma hunger" in followers; they are looking for a leader to alleviate or resolve their crisis (Madsen & Snow, 1983; Trice & Beyer, 1986). Leaders are given considerably more latitude and autonomy and may temporarily (or sometimes permanently) suspend accepted rules, policies, and procedures in order to pull the organization out of the crisis. Some researchers even believe that some leaders purposely create or manufacture crises to increase followers' acceptance of their vision, the range of actions they can take, and followers' level of effort (Pawar & Eastman, 1997; Avolio & Bass 1988; Boal & Bryson, 1987; Kets de Vries, 1977). Although a crisis situation does not necessarily make every leader look charismatic, such a situation may "set the stage" for particular kinds of leader behaviors to be effective (Hunt, Boal, & Dodge, 1999; Waldman, Ramirez, House, & Puranam, 2001).

Task Interdependence

It may be easier for leaders to be seen as charismatic when the tasks performed by their followers require a high level of interdependent rather than indepen-

---

Highlight 35–4

SAVING CONTINENTAL AIRLINES

By all accounts, Continental Airlines was ready to go under in 1993. The company ranked last in customer service of the 10 major airlines, it lost $600 million in 1994, and employees were so disgrunted that they tore the Continental Airlines logos off their uniforms. The company had gone through 10 CEOs in as many years, and had no vision or strategy in place to pull out of its nosedive. Because of the crisis facing the company, Gordon Berthune from Boeing and Greg Brenneman from Bain & Company were asked in early 1994 to be the next in line to turn Continental Airlines around. Fortunately for the customers, employees, and shareholders, these two leaders have been remarkably successful with their change efforts. But how were they able to turn around such a company facing such a crisis? They did so through a combination of rational and emotional change approaches. They started with a thorough assessment of the situation facing the company. They then built a vision and implemented a set of strategies to improve financial and customer service results. Some of these strategies included changing the Continental Airlines brand, eliminating nonprofitable routes, improving maintenance and operational performance, tracking cash flow, building employee trust and morale through constant communication and numerous "town hall" meetings, eliminating 7,000 positions (of 50,000 employees), and aligning the compensation system around desired employee behaviors. None of these changes were easy—Brenneman likened them to having a 12-hour surgery without anesthesia. However, during the time that these two leaders were on board, Continental Airlines' revenues doubled, the company made a profit every year from 1995 to 2000, stock prices increased fivefold, employee morale soared, and customer satisfaction ratings placed the airline among the best in the industry.

Source: G. Brenneman, *Right Away and All at Once: How We Saved Continental.* Reprint No. 98503 (Boston: Harvard Business School Publishing Division, 1998).

---

dent effort (Curphy, 1991a, 1992a). With **task interdependence,** for example, it may be easier for leaders to be perceived as charismatic when they are leading a software design team rather than a sales team because each individual programmer's code could be affected by the code developed by the other programmers. However, a sales representative with a defined territory will probably not be affected by efforts of the other sales representatives on the team.

Other Situational Characteristics

Several other situational characteristics may help or hinder the emergence of a charismatic leader. Howell and Avolio (1993) found that organizations placing a premium on innovation were much more supportive of transformational leadership than those less committed to innovation. Another situational factor that may affect charismatic leadership is organizational downsizing. In the minds of many peoples, downsizing has destroyed the implicit contract between employer and employee, and left many employees disillusioned with corporate life (Church, 1994). On the one hand, because charismatic or transformational leadership is intensely relational in nature, destroying the implicit contract between leaders and followers could greatly diminish the odds of charis-

matic leadership emergence. On the other hand, this disillusionment has caused many talented managers to leave large organizations to form their own companies. Employees are drawn to these start-up organizations precisely because the company's vision is consistent with their own personal values. But of all the situational variables affecting charismatic leadership, perhaps the most important and overlooked variable is time. Charismatic or transformational leadership does not happen overnight. It takes time for leaders to develop and articulate their vision, heighten followers' emotional levels, build trusting relationships with followers, and direct and empower followers to fulfill the vision. It may be that a crisis compresses the amount of time while relatively stable situations lengthen the amount of time needed for charismatic leadership to emerge.

CONCLUDING THOUGHTS ABOUT THE CHARACTERISTICS OF CHARISMATIC AND TRANSFORMATIONAL LEADERSHIP

Several final points about the characteristics of charismatic leadership need to be made. First, although we defined charisma as a quality attributed to certain leaders based on the relationships they share with followers, charismatic leadership is most fully understood when we also consider how leader and situational factors affect this attribution process. The special relationships charismatic leaders share with followers do not happen by accident; rather, they are often the result of interaction between the leader's qualities, leader and follower values, and the presence of certain situational factors. Second, it seems unlikely that all the characteristics of charismatic leadership need to be present before charisma is attributed to a leader. The bottom line for charisma seems to be the relationships certain leaders share with followers, and there may be a variety of ways in which these relationships can develop. This also implies that charisma may be more of a continuum than an all-or-nothing phenomenon. Some leaders may be able to form particularly strong bonds with a majority of followers, others with a few followers, and still others may get along with most but not form particularly strong bonds with any followers. Third, it does seem that charismatic leadership can happen anywhere—schools, churches, communities, businesses, government organizations, and nations—and does not happen only on the world stage.

Fourth, given that there are a number of ways to develop strong emotional attachments with followers, one important question is whether it is possible to attribute charisma to an individual based solely on his or her position or celebrity status (Etzioni, 1961; Hollander, 1978; Bass, 1990). Some individuals in positions of high public visibility and esteem (e.g., film stars, musicians, athletes, television evangelists, and politicians) can develop (even cultivate) charismatic images among their fans and admirers. In these cases, it is helpful to recognize that charismatic leadership is a two-way street. Not only do followers develop strong emotional bonds with leaders, but leaders also develop strong emotional bonds with followers and are concerned with follower development (Burns, 1978; Dvir, Eden, Avolio, & Shamir, 1999). It is difficult to see how the one-way communication channels of radio and television can foster these two-way relationships or enhance follower growth. Thus, although we sometimes view

certain individuals as charismatic based on media manipulation and hype, this is not transformational leadership in the truest sense.

So what can leadership practitioners take from this research if they want to use an emotional approach to drive organizational change? They will probably be more successful at driving organizational change if they capitalize on or create a crisis. They also need to be close enough to their followers to determine the sources of discontent and ensure their vision is aligned with followers' values and paints a compelling picture of the future. Leaders must passionately articulate their vision of the future; it is difficult to imagine followers being motivated toward a vision that is unclear or presented by a leader who does not seem to really care about it. Leadership practitioners also need to understand that they alone cannot make the vision a reality; they need their followers' help and support to create organizational or societal changes. Along these lines, they will need to be a role model and coach followers on what they should (and should not) be doing, provide feedback and encouragement, and persuade followers to take on more responsibilities as their skills and self-confidence grow. Finally, leadership practitioners using this approach to organizational change also need to be thick skinned, resilient, and patient. They will need to cope with the polarization effects of charismatic leadership and understand that it takes time for the effects of this type of leadership to yield results. However, the rewards appear to be well worth the efforts. There appears to be overwhelming evidence that charismatic or transformational leaders are more effective than their noncharismatic counterparts, whether they be presidents of the United States (Deluga, 1998), CEOs (Waldman, Ramirez, House, & Puranam, 2001), military cadets and officers (Bass, 2000; Curphy, 1991a; Clover, 1990; Adams, Price, Instone, & Rice, 1984), college professors (Labak, 1973), or first-line supervisors and middle-level managers in a variety of public and private sector companies (Avolio & Bass, 2000).

Group and Cohesion Dysfunction

This lesson is the last in a group of thirteen lessons dealing with leadership. This lesson examines various aspects of group cohesion including the factors that enhance group cohesion, dysfunctional aspects of group cohesion.

The following topics are addressed in this lesson:

- Concepts of groups, group cohesion, and intra-group conflict;
- Methods and factors that increase and decrease group cohesion;
- Dysfunctional cohesion ("groupthink"); and
- Seven common sources of conflict.

The following Terminal Learning Objective (TLO) is supported in whole or in part by this lesson:

- Apply leadership theory & principles.

Following this lesson you will be able to:

- Differentiate the terms group, team, and organization;
- Describe the functional and dysfunctional roles of group members;
- Describe antecedents and indicators of group cohesion;
- Describe potential dysfunctional outcomes of high group cohesion; and
- Apply methods to reduce groupthink.

GROUP COHESION DEFINED

from Military Leadership: PL300 Course Guide

A group's effectiveness is partially determined by the mix of appropriate skills and abilities. Yet there's more to effectiveness than the talents of individual members. The group needs to work as a team. More precisely, the group needs to show cohesiveness—defined as the power of a group to think and act as a single unit in pursuit of a common objective.[1] Expanding on this definition, D. Cartwright, an organizational psychologist, noted that:

> . . . the members of a highly cohesive group, in contrast with one with a low level of cohesiveness, are more concerned with their membership and are therefore more strongly motivated to contribute to the group's welfare, to advance its objectives, and to participate in its activities. Cohesiveness contributes to a group's potency and vitality; it increases the significance of membership for those who belong to the group.[2]

In essence, cohesiveness is the glue that keeps the group together.

Factors that increase group cohesiveness include the following:[3]

- **Agreement on group goals.** This binds the group together and structures interaction patterns toward successful outcomes.
- **Frequency of interaction** *among group members.* This increases the chances for closeness to develop.
- **Personal attractiveness to one another.** This helps members overcome obstacles to goal accomplishment and personal growth and development.
- **Intergroup competition.** This brings the group closer together.
- **Favorable evaluation of group performance.** This serves to elevate the prestige and worthiness of the group in the eyes of its members and other members of the organization.

Conversely, factors found to decrease group cohesiveness include:[4]

- **Disagreement on goals.** This causes conflict and infighting.
- **Group size.** As the size of the group increases, the frequency of interaction between members decreases.
- **Unpleasant experiences with the group.** This lessens the attraction level, resulting in a lack of trust.
- **Intragroup competition.** This causes conflict and infighting.
- **Domination.** When one or more of the members dominate, cliques tend to develop.

So what's the nature of the relationship between group cohesiveness and performance? If a group has a high degree of cohesiveness and a norm that favors high performance, we can expect a high level of performance. If, on the other hand, a highly cohesive group favors low performance, we can expect a decrease in performance. For groups with low cohesion, group norms don't have as much influence on performance as they would in groups with high cohesion.

ENDNOTES

1 Walker, C.R., R.H. Guest, and A.N. Turner, "Work Groups on the Assembly Line," in *Organizational Behavior and the Practice of Management,* eds. David R. Hampton, Charles E . Summer, and Ross A. Webber (Glenville, Ill.: Scott, Foresman, 1968), pp. 329-332.

2 Cartwright, D., "The Nature of Group Cohesiveness," in *Group Dynamics,* eds. Dorwin Cartwright and Alvin Zander (New York: Harper & Row, 1968), p. 91.

3 Ivancevich, Szlagyi, and Wallace, *op cit,* pp. 216-217.

4 *Ibid.,* pp. 217-218.

COHESION IN MILITARY GROUPS

from Military Leadership: PL300 Course Guide

In their classic study of the German *Wehrmacht* in WWII, Shils and Janowitz (1948) focused much of their efforts towards trying to understand why German combat units were effective fighting forces even in the last days of the war when it became apparent that they would suffer defeat. They concluded:

For the ordinary German soldier the decisive fact was that he was a member of a squad or section which maintained its structural integrity and which coincided roughly with the social unit which satisfied some of his major primary needs. He was likely to go on fighting, provided he had the necessary weapons, as long as the group possessed leadership with which he could identify himself, and as long as he gave affection to and received affection from the other members of his squad and platoon. In other words, as long as he felt himself to be a member of his primary group and therefore bound by the expectations and demands of its other members, his soldierly achievement was likely to be good.

The degree to which members are attracted to and remain in a group is often called *cohesion*. In other words cohesion is the strength by which a group is "glued together." We should expect that those units that are highly cohesive would show greater levels of mutual respect, trust, confidence and understanding. These are intangibles that are difficult to observe and measure. However, since a highly cohesive group is one that is "glued" tightly together, we should observe members showing greater care about the group and stronger commitment to it. From this we would expect that these members place more energy, both physical and psychological, into group activities. With more energy from members, these groups would have more collective resources to devote to group activities, efforts and goals. Out of these observations are derived the common indicators of group cohesion. Let's explore each one of them individually.

GREATER INTERACTION AND COMMUNICATION

We would expect that members of a close-knit group would communicate more with each other. Because they value the group, they are more willing to take part in the group's efforts and activities and this normally causes more interaction (although this is task dependent). It has been shown that the greater the cohesion, the greater the communication activity between members in the group. Cohesive groups also meet more and this naturally adds to the communication and interaction of members.

In highly cohesive groups, all members participate more and participation is spread more equally among members. The quality of communication is characterized by greater cooperation and friendliness, and is oriented towards keeping the group tight. In low-cohesive groups, members are less cooperative, tend to keep comments that relate to group performance to themselves, and are more aggressive in the way they respond to group interaction. BG S.L.A. Marshall's renowned work, *Men Against Fire*, gives numerous accounts of soldiers in highly cohesive units constantly keeping horizontal and vertical communication channels open, and tells how such channels had a pronounced effect on their psychological well-being which in turn brought them much closer to their unit. Such communication patterns also allowed soldiers to more quickly and effectively teach each other new skills and abilities as well as provide accepted feedback on performance. Hence, there is also a reciprocal relationship between a group's communication and interaction processes. The more cohesive a group is, the greater the quantity and quality of its communications. This, then, builds even greater cohesion.

POWER OF THE GROUP OVER ITS MEMBERS

When members are committed to their group, they are more willing to make personal changes, and sacrifices, to remain an active part of the group. This allows the group to have power over the opinions and behavior of its members. Highly cohesive groups exert strong pressure on group members to conform to the group's opinions, attitudes and behaviors.

Another interesting facet of the group's power over its members is that highly cohesive groups increase their members' ability to resist external pressures, as well as internal pressures placed on them. In regard to military organizations, this is a critical point. When a unit is very cohesive, it can tolerate more resistance, stress, and even internal rebellion without risking disintegration. Less cohesive groups disintegrate more quickly under both internal and external scrutiny. Studies of the German Army in 1943 and 1944 on the Eastern Front illustrate the degree of hardship, failure, misery, fatigue and stress that can be sustained by highly cohesive units. These effects stem from the understanding that in highly cohesive groups, members value their belonging to the group to the point of a great willingness to change themselves and tolerate others to remain in the group.

GOAL ATTAINMENT

It is somewhat intuitive that highly cohesive groups will be more successful at directing group efforts and energy towards attainment of group goals. Experience on the "fields of friendly strife" tells us that a team's cohesiveness can make the difference between winning and losing. That is why one of the fundamentals of unit training is building teamwork. The 1st Marine Division's gallant attack into a vastly numerically superior Chinese force at the Chosin Reservoir in Korea in 1951, in order to prevent being encircled, is a classic example of what a cohesive unit can do in the face of adversity and great difficulty.

However, groups don't always set goals that the organization desires. If a highly cohesive group sets productivity and successful organizational performance as group goals, then these goals will be attained to a much higher degree than low-cohesive groups. However, as leaders, we must be wary of cohesive groups that choose dysfunctional norms and performance standards as their goals. A leader's greatest challenge may be redirecting a highly cohesive group with dysfunctional performance norms towards organizationally desired performance norms.

MEMBER SATISFACTION

When there is much interaction and friendly cooperative communications between group members, there is bound to be a sense of member satisfaction from being part of the group. In those moments of triumph when we belong to a group in which everybody pulls together to accomplish some difficult mission, there is indeed great satisfaction. Witness a reunion of WWII veterans from Patton's Third Army or from the 101st Airborne Division to see that for many of these veterans, belonging to the group continues to be a source of deep and intense satisfaction and lasting fulfillment.

Of course, it is possible for members to be attracted and committed to the group because of its goals or other aspects of the group without being satisfied with the group as a whole. Generally however, the greater the cohesion, the greater member satisfaction with being part of the group and satisfaction with the group's goals and efforts.

GROUP LOYALTY AND IDENTIFICATION

Quite naturally, groups that offer great satisfaction and which invoke power over members' opinions and actions also invoke and inspire greater loyalty from their members. This in turn leads the group to spend less effort in maintaining its membership (effort which in turn can be directed towards goal accomplishment). Military history is full of examples of soldiers from highly cohesive units fighting tenaciously because of their unit's lineage and tradition. At the battle of Rorke's Drift in 1879 (*Zulu-British War*), in which 11 Victoria Crosses were awarded (Britain's highest award for combat bravery), 139 British soldiers withstood and defeated a Zulu force of over 4000 warriors. During the battle the British colors were the rallying point for the small surrounded British garrison and many soldiers gave their lives keeping the colors up in plain view on the battlefield.

There is also a reciprocal process between loyalty and identification. When members render loyalty to their group, they develop greater psychological identification with that group. This identification then elicits greater loyalty from its members.

ELABORATE GROUP NORMS AND PRACTICES

When a group achieves high cohesion, we begin to see extensive behavioral routines and practices that members perform together to express the group's uniqueness and identification. Examples might be informal initiations such as the famous Prop Blasts that airborne units conduct for their new officers, inside jokes and ways of kidding one another. Often there are enigmatic rituals and symbols that group members adopt to represent themselves. Just go on a PT run with a ranger unit to see evidence of this: socks rolled precisely the same; elbows held at exactly 90 degree angles; strict adherence to not wiping sweat from one's head while running. These norms and practices help members to establish a psychological "we-they" boundary between themselves and the rest of the world. We again see, much like in the other common indicators, that there is a circular relationship here. As the group becomes more cohesive, it creates and develops these unique norms and practices. These unique norms and practices in turn fuel cohesion.

> What makes a soldier capable of obedience and direction in action ... includes ... confidence in his comrades and fear of their reproaches and retaliation if he abandons them in danger; his desire to go where others go without trembling more than they ... Self-esteem is unquestionably one of the most powerful motives which moves our men. They do not wish to pass for cowards in the eyes of their comrades. ... We are all proud people, but people who would skulk in battle if we were not seen, and who consequently must always be seen, and act in the presence of our comrades and the officers who supervise us.
>
> ARDANT DuPICQ

TASK AND SOCIAL COHESION

Similar to distinguishing between task and social leaders, it is also useful to distinguish between task and social cohesion. We may tend to focus on the social aspect of cohesion—how well people get along in a group, while task cohesion may be more important depending on the nature of the group. Task cohesion is cohesion that allows a group to work well together on a given task. In many groups it is more important that they are able to accomplish a given task, and less important that they get along together. How would we know which form of cohesion is more important? It depends on the purpose of the group. If the group's primary focus is to complete certain tasks, then obviously task cohesion is more important, but if the group is organized for social reasons, then social cohesion is more important. However, both forms of cohesion are important in most groups. Social cohesion supports the completion of group tasks, and successful completion of group tasks can enhance social cohesion.

The indicators of cohesion, and leader actions to build cohesion we have discussed thus far related to both task and social cohesion. However, in the Army, we should place additional emphasis on training as the primary means of building task cohesion. Naturally, we also want everyone to get along and build social cohesion, but this is not enough unless we have also built task cohesion through effective training. It is imperative that military units be able to function together as a team—each soldier knows their role and is able to coordinate with the other members of their team—task cohesion.

Task cohesion begins with a good socialization program that orients soldiers to their role in the unit and attends to their social needs. Task cohesion is maintained through battle focused training that causes soldiers to work as teams and sustains their ability to fight under stressful circumstances. During the stress of combat, soldiers typically respond according to how they are trained, in the ways their leaders direct them, and/or in accordance with what the rest of their team is doing. We must train soldiers how to respond properly to the rigors of combat, be there to lead them, and build teams that give soldiers support to accomplish their combat mission. The ultimate indicator of cohesion is how a group reacts to adversity. A truly cohesive unit uses adversity to come together, while adversity may tear apart a less cohesive group. Building task cohesion allows your unit to stick together and continue the mission under the most stressful circumstances.

Additional means of building social cohesion in the military include: military ceremonies, unit sports programs, unit social functions, and attending to soldiers spiritual needs. These activities help build social cohesion in a unit and support task cohesion, but are not enough to make up for the lack of an effective training program to build task cohesion. In fact, an effective training program can help build social cohesion through the pride and confidence a unit derives from the knowledge that they can get the job done in combat and the trust that each soldier will perform their job as part of the team.

> Three times in 40 years I served in superb units. All three were excellent because of the cohesion we built by demanding unit training and leadership that developed the soldiers' confidence in themselves, their leaders and in each other ...
>
> GENERAL DON A. STARRY

THE NATURE OF GROUPS

by R.L. Huges, R.C. Ginnett, and G.J. Curphy

Understanding the unique characteristics that make individual followers tick is useful to leaders, but not enough. Leaders also need to understand how followers as a group represent something that cannot be understood solely in terms of the group members' collective individual characteristics. While both leadership and followership often have been conceptualized in terms of characteristics of individuals, it is interesting to note that a survey of 35 texts on organizational behavior found that in each one, the chapter on leadership is in the section on group behavior, not in the section on individual behavior (Ginnett, 1992). This should not be terribly surprising since groups (even as small as two people) are essential if leaders are to impact anything beyond their own behavior. What may be surprising is that the concept of groups is sometimes omitted entirely from books on leadership. The whole can be greater than the sum of its parts, and the **group perspective** looks at how different group characteristics can affect relationships both with the leader and among followers.

This reading will begin by examining some of the characteristic of groups that uniquely differentiate them from individual phenomena. Given the high interest in organizational team work, we will move from the group to the team and conclude with a model developed to help leaders design, diagnose, and leverage high-impact factors to create the conditions which foster team effectiveness.

Perhaps we should begin by defining what a **group** is. A group can be thought of as "two or more persons who are interacting with one another in such a manner that each person influences and is influenced by each other person" (Shaw, 1981). Three aspects of this definition are particularly important to the study of leadership. First, this definition incorporates the concept of reciprocal influence between leaders and followers, an idea considerably different from the one-way nature of influence implicit in the dictionary's definition of followers. Second, group members interact and influence each other. Thus, people waiting at a bus stop would not constitute a group, as there generally is neither interaction nor influence between the various individuals. On the other hand, eight people meeting to plan a school bond election would constitute a group, as there

probably would be a high level of mutual interaction among the attendees. Third, the definition does not constrain individuals to only one group. Everyone belongs to a number of different groups; an individual could be a member of various service, production, sports, religious, parent, and volunteer groups simultaneously.

It is important to realize that though people belong to many groups, just as they do to many organizations, groups and organizations are not the same thing (groups, of course, can exist within organizations). Organizations can be so large that most members do not know most of the other people in the organization. In such cases there is relatively little intermember interaction and reciprocal influence. Similarly, organizations typically are just too large and impersonal to have much effect on anyone's feelings, whereas groups are small and immediate enough to impact both feelings and self-image. People often tend to identify more with the groups they belong to than with the organizations they belong to; they are more psychologically "invested" in their groups. Also, certain important psychological needs (e.g., social contact) are better satisfied by groups than by organizations.

Perhaps an example will clarify the distinction between groups and organizations. Consider a church so large that it may fairly be described as an organization: so large that multiple services must be offered on Sunday mornings; so large that dozens of different study classes are offered each week; so large there are numerous different choirs and musical ensembles. In so large a church, the members hardly could be said to interact with or influence each other except on an occasional basis. Such size often presents both advantages and disadvantages to the membership. On the one hand, it makes possible a rich diversity of activities; on the other hand, such size can make the church itself (i.e., the overall organization) seem relatively impersonal. It may be difficult to identity with a large organization other than in name only (e.g., "I belong to First Presbyterian Church"). In such cases many people identify more with particular groups within the church than with the church itself; it may be easier to *feel* a part of some smaller group such as the high school choir or a weekly study group.

Although groups play a pervasive role in society, in general people spend very little time thinking about the factors that affect group processes and

intragroup relationships. Therefore, the rest of this section will describe some group characteristics that can affect both leaders and followers. Much of the research on groups goes well beyond the scope of this chapter (see Gibbard, Hartman, & Mann, 1978; Shaw, 1981; Hackman, 1990), but six concepts are so basic to the group perspective that they deserve our attention. These six concepts are group size, stages of group development, roles, norms, communication, and cohesion. Five of them will be addressed in sections below. The sixth, communication, permeates them all.

GROUP NORMS

by R.L. Huges, R.C. Ginnett, and G.J. Curphy

Norms are the informal rules groups adopt to regulate and regularize group members' behaviors. Although norms are only infrequently written down or openly discussed, they nonetheless often have a powerful and consistent influence on behavior (Hackman, 1976). That is because most people are rather good at reading the social cues that inform them about existing norms. For example, most people easily discern the dress code in any new work environment without needing written guidance. People also are apt to notice when a norm is violated, even though they may have been unable to articulate the norm before its violation was apparent. For example, most students have expectations (norms) about creating extra work for other students. Imagine the reaction if a student in some class complained that not enough reading was being assigned each lesson or that the minimum length requirements for the term paper needed to be substantially raised.

Norms do not govern all behaviors, just those a group feels are important. Norms are more likely to be seen as important and apt to be enforced if they *(a)* facilitate group survival; *(b)* simplify, or make more predictable, what behavior is expected of group members; *(c)* help the group avoid embarrassing interpersonal problems; or *(d)* express the central values of the group and clarify what is distinctive about the group's identity (Feldman, 1984).

One irony about norms is that an outsider to a group often is able to learn more about norms than an insider. An outsider, not necessarily subject to the norms himself, is more apt to notice them. In fact, the more "foreign" an observer is, the more likely it is the norms will be perceived. If a man is accustomed to wearing a tie to work, he is less likely to notice that men in another organization also wear ties to work, but is *more* likely to note that the men in a third organization typically wear sweaters and sweatshirts around the office.

GROUP COHESION

by R.L. Huges, R.C. Ginnett, and G.J. Curphy

Group cohesion is the glue that keeps a group together. It is the sum of forces that attract members to a group, provide resistance to leaving it, and motivate them to be active in it. Highly cohesive groups interact with and influence each other more than do less cohesive groups. Furthermore, a highly cohesive group may have lower absenteeism and lower turnover than a less cohesive group, and low absenteeism and turnover often contribute to higher group performance; higher performance can, in turn, contribute to even higher cohesion, thus resulting in an increasingly positive spiral.

However, greater cohesiveness does not always lead to higher performance. A highly cohesive but unskilled team is still an unskilled team, and such teams will often lose to a less cohesive but more skilled one. Additionally, a highly cohesive group may sometimes develop goals that are contrary to the larger organization's goals. For example, members of a highly cohesive research team at a particular college committed themselves to working on a problem that seemed inherently interesting to them. Their nearly zealous commitment to the project, however, effectively kept them from asking, or even allowing others to ask, if the research aligned itself well with the college's stated objectives. Their quite narrow and basic research effort deviated significantly from the college's expressed commitment to emphasize applied research. As a result, the college lost some substantial outside financial support.

Other problems also can occur in highly cohesive groups. Researchers (Alderfer, 1977; Ginnett, 1987) have found that some groups can become so cohesive they erect what amount to fences or boundaries between themselves and others. Such **overbounding** can block the use of outside resources that could make them more effective. Competitive product development teams can become so overbounded (often rationalized by security concerns or inordinate fears of "idea thieves") that they will not ask for help from willing and able staff within their own organizations.

One example of this problem was the failed mission to rescue U.S. embassy personnel held hostage in Iran during the Carter presidency. The rescue itself was a rather complicated mission involving many different sorts of U.S. military forces. Some of these forces included sea-based helicopters. The helicopters and their crews were carried on regular naval vessels, though most sailors on the vessels knew nothing of the secret mission. Senior personnel were so concerned that some sailor might leak information, and thus compromise the mission's secrecy, that maintenance crews aboard the ships were not directed to perform increased levels of maintenance on the helicopters immediately before the critical mission. Even if a helicopter was scheduled for significant maintenance within the next 50 hours of flight time (which would be exceeded in the rescue mission), crews were not told to perform the maintenance. According to knowledgeable sources, this practice did impact the performance of at least one of the failed helicopters, and thus the overall mission.

Janis (1982) discovered still another disadvantage of highly cohesive groups. He found that people in a highly cohesive group often become more concerned with striving for unanimity than in objectively appraising different courses of action. Janis labeled this phenomenon **groupthink** and believed it accounted for a number of historic fiascoes, including Pearl Harbor and the Bay of Pigs invasion. It may have played a role in the *Challenger* disaster, and it also occurs in other cohesive groups ranging from business meetings to air crews, and from therapy groups to school boards.

What is groupthink? Cohesive groups tend to evolve strong informal norms to preserve friendly internal relations. Preserving a comfortable, harmonious group environment becomes a hidden agenda that tends to suppress dissent, conflict, and critical thinking. Unwise decisions may result when concurrence seeking among members overrides their willingness to express or tolerate deviant points of view and think critically. Janis (1982) identified a number of symptoms of groupthink, which can be found in Highlight 36–1.

A policy-making or decision-making group displaying most of the symptoms in Highlight 36–1 runs a big risk of being ineffective. It may do a poor job of clarifying objectives, searching for relevant information, evaluating alternatives, assessing risks, and anticipating the need for contingency plans. Janis (1982) offered the following suggestions as ways of reducing groupthink and thus of improving the quality of a group's input to policies or decisions. First, leaders should encourage all group members to take on the role of critical evaluator. Everyone in the group needs to appreciate the importance of airing doubts and objections. This includes the leader's willingness to listen to criticisms of his or her own ideas. Second, leaders should create a climate of open inquiry through their own impartiality and objectivity. At the outset, leaders should refrain from stating personal preferences or expectations, which may bias group discussion. Third, the risk of groupthink can be reduced if independent groups are established to make recommendations on the same issue. Fourth, at least one member of the group should be assigned the role of devil's advocate, an assignment that should rotate from meeting to meeting.

One final problem with highly cohesive groups may be what Shephard (1991) has called **ollieism.** Ollieism, a variation of groupthink, occurs when illegal actions are taken by overly zealous and loyal subordinates who believe that what they are doing will please their leaders. It derives its name from the actions of Lieutenant-Colonel Oliver North, who among other things admitted he lied to the U.S. Congress about his actions while working on the White House staff during the Iran-Contra affair. Shephard cited the slaying of Thomas à Becket by four of Henry II's knights and the Watergate break-in as other prime examples of ollieism. Ollieism differs from groupthink in that the subordinates' illegal actions usually occur without the explicit knowledge or consent of the leader. Nevertheless, Shephard pointed out that although the examples cited of ollieism were not officially sanctioned, the responsibility for them still falls squarely on the leader. It is the leader's responsibility to create an ethical climate within the group, and leaders who create highly cohesive yet unethical groups must bear the responsibility for the group's actions.

After reading about the uncertain relationships between group cohesion and performance, and the problems with overbounding, groupthink, and ollieism, one might think that cohesiveness should be something to avoid. Nothing, however, could be further from the truth. First of all, problems with overly cohesive groups occur relatively infrequently and, in general, leaders will be better off thinking of ways to create and maintain highly cohesive teams than not developing these teams out of concern for potential groupthink or overbounding situations. Second, perhaps the biggest argument for developing cohesive groups is to consider the alternative—

Highlight 36–1

SYMPTOMS OF GROUPTHING

An illusion of invulnerability, which leads to unwarranted optimism and excessive risk taking by the group.

Unquestioned assumption of the group's morality and therefore an absence of reflection on the ethical consequences of group action.

Collective rationalization to discount negative information or warnings.

Stereotypes of the opposition as evil, weak, or stupid.

Self-censorship by group members from expressing ideas that deviate from the group consensus due to doubts about their validity or importance.

An illusion of unanimity such that greater consensus is perceived than really exists.

Direct pressure on dissenting members, which reinforces the norm that disagreement represents disloyalty to the group.

Mindguards, who protect the group from adverse information.

Source: Adapted from I. L. Janis, *Groupthink,* 2nd ed. (Boston: Houghton Mifflin, 1982).

Highlight 36–2

THE ABILENE PARADOX

That July afternoon in Coleman, Texas (population 5,607), was particularly hot—104 degrees according to the Rexall's thermometer. In addition, the wind was blowing fine-grained West Texas topsoil through the house. But the afternoon was still tolerable—even potentially enjoyable. A fan was stirring the air on the back porch; there was cold lemonade; and finally, there was entertainment. Dominoes. Perfect for the conditions. The game requires little more physical exertion than an occasional mumbled comment, "Shuffle 'em," and an unhurried movement of the arm to place the tiles in their appropriate positions on the table. All in all, it had the makings of an agreeable Sunday afternoon in Coleman. That is, until my father-in-law suddenly said, "Let's get in the car and go to Abilene and have dinner at the cafeteria."

I thought, "What, go to Abilene? Fifty-three miles? In this dust storm and heat? And in an unairconditioned 1958 Buick?"

But my wife chimed in with, "Sounds like a great idea. I'd like to go. How about you, Jerry?" Since my own preferences were obviously out of step with the rest, I replied, "Sounds good to me," and added, "I just hope your mother wants to go."

"Of course I want to go," said my mother-in-law. "I haven't been to Abilene in a long time."

So into the car and off to Abilene we went. My predictions were fulfilled. The heat was brutal. Perspiration had cemented a fine layer of dust to our skin by the time we arrived. The cafeteria's food could serve as a first-rate prop in an antacid commercial.

Some four hours and 106 miles later, we returned to Coleman, hot and exhausted. We silently sat in front of the fan for a long time. Then, to be sociable and to break the silence, I dishonestly said, "It was a great trip, wasn't it?"

No one spoke.

Finally, my mother-in-law said, with some irritation, "Well, to tell the truth, I really didn't enjoy it much and would rather have stayed here. I just went along because the three of you were so enthusiastic about going. I wouldn't have gone if you all hadn't pressured me into it."

I couldn't believe it. "What do you mean 'you all'?" I said. "Don't put me in the 'you all' group. I was delighted to be doing what we were doing. I didn't want to go. I only went to satisfy the rest of you. You're the culprits."

My wife looked shocked. "Don't call me a culprit. You and Daddy and Mama were the ones who wanted to go. I just went along to keep you happy. I would have had to be crazy to want to go out in heat like that."

Her father entered the conversation with one word. "Shee-it." He then expanded on what was already absolutely clear: "Listen, I never wanted to go to Abilene. I just thought you might be bored. You visit so seldom I wanted to be sure you enjoyed it. I would have preferred to play another game of dominoes and eat the leftovers in the icebox."

After the outburst of recrimination, we all sat back in silence. Here we were, four reasonably sensible people who—of our own volition—had just taken a 106-mile trip across a godforsaken desert in furnace-like heat and a dust storm to eat unpalatable food at a hole-in-the-wall cafeteria in Abilene, when none of us had really wanted to go. To be concise, we'd done just the opposite of what we wanted to do. The whole situation simply didn't make sense.

At least it didn't make sense at the time. But since that day in Coleman, I have observed, consulted with, and been a part of more than one organization that has been caught in the same situation. As a result, the organizations have either taken side trips or, occasionally, terminal journeys to Abilene, when Dallas or Houston or Tokyo was where they really wanted to go. And for most of those organizations, the negative consequences of such trips, measured in terms of both human misery and economic loss, have been much greater than for our little Abilene group.

I now call the tendency for groups to embark on excursions that no group member wants "the Abilene paradox." Stated simply, when organizations blunder into the Abilene paradox, they take actions in contradiction to what they really want to do and therefore defeat the very purpose they are trying to achieve. Business theorists typically believe that managing conflict is one of the greatest challenges faced by an organization, but a corollary of the Abilene paradox states that the inability to manage agreement may be the major source of organization dysfunction.

Source: Jerry B. Harvey, "The Abilene Paradox: The Management of Agreement," *Organizational Dynamics*, Summer 1974. Reprinted by permission of the publisher. American Management Association New York. http:www.amanet.org. All rights reserved.

groups with little or no cohesiveness. In the latter groups, followers would generally be dissatisfied with each other and the leader, commitment to accomplishing group and organizational goals may be reduced, intragroup communication may occur less frequently, and interdependent task performance may suffer (Robbins, 1986). Because of the problems associated with groups having low cohesiveness, leadership practitioners need to realize that developing functionally cohesive work groups is a goal they all should strive for.

In summary, the group perspective provides a complementary level of analysis to the individual perspective presented earlier in this chapter. A follower's behavior may be due to his or her values, traits, or experience (i.e., the individual perspective), or this behavior may be due to the followers' roles, the group norms, the group's stage of development, or the group's level of cohesiveness (i.e., the group perspective). Thus, the group perspective can also provide both leaders and followers with a number of explanations of why individuals in groups behave in certain ways. Moreover, the six group characteristics just described can give leaders and followers ideas about *(a)* factors that may be affecting their ability to influence other group members and *(b)* what to do to improve their level of influence in the group.

It is important to note that sometimes the hardest people to be assertive with are friends, family, and peers. Leaders who fail to be assertive with friends and peers run the risk of becoming victims of the Abilene paradox (see Highlight 36–2 on the previous page). The **Abilene paradox** (Harvey, 1974) occurs when someone suggests that the group engage in a particular activity or course of action, and no one in the group really wants to do the activity (including the person who made the suggestion). However, because of the false belief that everyone else in the group wants to do the activity, no one behaves assertively and voices an honest opinion about it. Only after the activity is over does anyone voice an opinion (and it is usually negative). For example, someone in your group of friends may suggest that the group go to a particular movie on a Friday night. No one in the group really wants to go, yet because of the false belief everyone else is interested, no one points out the movie is not supposed to be very good and the group should do something else instead. If group members' true opinions surface only *after* the movie, then the group has fallen victim to the Abilene paradox. Leaders can avoid the Abilene paradox by being assertive when suggestions about group decisions and activities are first made.

There are several things everyone can do to help themselves behave more assertively. These things include *(a)* using "I" statements, *(b)* speaking up for what you need, *(c)* learning to say no, *(d)* monitoring your inner dialogue, and *(e)* being persistent.

RESOURCES

URLs ACCESSED DURING THIS COURSE

Blackboard: *http://rotc.blackboard.com/*

http://www.epolicyinstitute.com/e_policies/

http://www.wordsintime.co.uk/articles/article-howtowriteemails.html

http://www.cgsc.army.mil/cal/values/values2/

http://www.alvincyork.org/Biography.htm

http://call.army.mil/products/spc_prod/cofs/wickham.htm

http://www.cgsc.army.mil/cal/values/values2/

http://www.hooah4health.com/spirit/religion.htm

http://www.hooah4health.com/spirit/resiliency.htm

http://www-tradoc.monroe.army.mil/schools.htm

Branch Newsletter: *https://www.perscomonlin.army.mil*

COPYRIGHT ACKNOWLEDGMENTS

Grateful acknowledgment is made to the following sources for permission to reprint material copyrighted or controlled by them:

MODULE II

Lesson Three

Tubbs, S., and Moss, S. "Nonverbal Communication" in *Human Communication* (8th edition). New York:McGraw-Hill, 2000. Chapter 4, pp. 101–104; 105–127; and pp. 129–131.

Lesson Four

The ePolicy Handbook by Nancy Flynn, © 2001.

Copyright © WordsIntime Ltd, 2002 (from *www.wordsintime.co.uk/articles/article-how-towriteemails.html)* Reproduced with permission from *Training Journal,* May 1998.

Taken From the *Information Literacy Competency Stds for Higher Education* by Assoc. of College & Reasearch Libraries. *http://www.ala.org/acrl/i/intro.html*

MODULE IV

Lesson Fifteen

Maihafer, H. J. *Brave Decisions.* Brassey's Inc., 1999. Chapter 12, Decision in Korea. Pp. 179–195.B32

Lesson Sixteen

Brinsfield, John W. "Reality Check: The Human and Spiritual Needs of Soldiers and How to Prepare Them for Combat" in *The Future of the Army Profession.* Boston: McGraw-Hill Primis Custom Publishing, 2002. Chapter 19, pages 397–424.

Lesson Seventeen

Johnson, James Turner. "The Just-War Idea and the Ethics of Intervention" in *The Leader's Imperative.* West Lafayette, IN: Purdue University Press. 2001.

Makin, Malham M. (ed.), *War, Morality, and the Military Profession,* Westview Press, 1986.

Davidson, LTC Donald L., "The Just War Criteria: A Contempory Description." in *Nuclear Weapons and American Churches,* Strategic Studies Institute, U.S. Army War College, Carlise Barracks, PA.

Lesson Eighteen

Racism and Sexism, has been adapted from the Consideration of Others Handbook, available at: *http://www.odcsper.army.mil/default.asp?pageid = 51f*

Prevention of Sexual Harassment, has been adapted from the Consideration of Others Handbook, available at: *http://www.odcsper.army.mil/default.asp?pageid = 51f*

Lesson Nineteen

Equal Opportunity Complaint Procedures, has been adapted from the *Consideration of Others Handbook* and AR 600-20, *Army Command Policy, Appendix E.*

Lesson Twenty-Three

Foley, MG Robert F., and Goudreau, Maj Denise A., "Consideration of Others" in Military Review VOL LXXVI, NO. 01 - JANUARY - FEBRUARY 1996

MODULE V

Lesson Twenty-Six

Hughes, R. L., Ginnett, R. C., & Curphy, G. J. (2002). "Guidelines for Effective Stress Management" in *Leadership: Enhancing the Lessons of Experience* (4th ed.). Boston: Irwin/McGraw-Hill. pp. 451-458.

Lesson Twenty-Nine

Hughes, R. L., Ginnett, R. C., & Curphy, G. J. (2002). "What is Leadership?" in *Leadership: Enhancing the Lessons of Experience* (4th ed.). Boston: Irwin/McGraw-Hill. pp. 6–16.

Hughes, R. L., Ginnett, R. C., & Curphy, G. J. (2002). "Looking at Leadership through Several Lenses" in *Leadership: Enhancing the Lessons of Experience* (4th ed.). Boston: Irwin/McGraw-Hill. pp. 22-26 (not including Highlight 2.1).

Hughes, R. L., Ginnett, R. C., & Curphy, G. J. (2002). "Action-Observation-Reflection Model" in *Leadership: Enhancing the Lessons of Experience* (4th ed.). Boston: Irwin/McGraw-Hill. pp. 48-51.

Lesson Thirty

Hughes, R. L., Ginnett, R. C., & Curphy, G. J. (2002). *Leadership: Enhancing the Lessons of Experience* (4th ed.). Boston: Irwin/McGraw-Hill. pp. 107-122.

Yukl, G. (2001). *Leadership in Organizations* (5th ed.). Upper Saddle River, New Jersey: Prentice Hall. pp. 159-165.

Hughes, R. L., Ginnett, R. C., & Curphy, G. J. (2002). *Instructor's Manual and Test Bank* to accompany *Leadership: Enhancing the Lessons of Experience* (4th ed.). Boston: Irwin/McGraw-Hill. pp. 176-178 (questions 16-23).

Lesson Thirty-One

Hughes, R. L., Ginnett, R. C., & Curphy, G. J. (2002). *Leadership: Enhancing the Lessons of Experience* (4th ed.). Boston: Irwin/McGraw-Hill. pp. 166-177 (to bottom of Highlight 7.2).

Lesson Thirty-Two

Hughes, R. L., Ginnett, R. C., & Curphy, G. J. *Leadership: Enhancing the Lessons of Experience* (4th ed.). Boston: Irwin/McGraw-Hill, 2002.

"Learning from Experience," pages 425–430 (Do not include the section on Communication on page 430.), "Reflection and Leadership Development," pages 55–58, and "Setting Goals," pages 467–469.

Lesson Thirty-Four

Kelley, R. E. (1988). *In Praise of Followers.* Harvard Business Review. 66(6), 142–148.

Lesson Thirty-Five

Hughes, R. L., Ginnett, R. C., & Curphy, G. J. *Leadership: Enhancing the Lessons of Experience* (4th ed.). Boston: Irwin/McGraw-Hill, 2002.

"The Emotional Approach to Organizational Change: Charismatic and Transformational Leadership," pages 399–405, and "What Are the Common Characteristics of Charismatic and Transformational Leadership?" pages 405–416.

Lesson Thirty-Six

Associates of the Department of Behavioral Sciences and Leadership, USMA. Military Leadership: PL300 Course Guide (3rd edition). West Point, NY: McGraw-Hill, 2001. Pages 150-151 and 170-172. ISBN: 0-07-252026-4

Hughes, R. L., Ginnett, R. C., & Curphy, G. J. (2002). *Leadership: Enhancing the Lessons of Experience* (4th ed.). Boston: Irwin/McGraw-Hill. Bottom of p. 288 to top of p. 290, bottom of p. 296 to bottom of p. 300, and bottom of p. 440 to bottom of p. 442.